INTRODUCTION TO THE

Hospitality Industry

INTRODUCTION TO THE

Hospitality Industry

TOM POWERS
University of Guelph
School of Hotel and Food Administration

Study Guide Prepared by Jo Marie Powers

WILEY

JOHN WILEY & SONS
New York   Chichester   Brisbane   Toronto   Singapore

Cover photograph by Larry Dale Gordon/The Image Bank

ISBN 0-471-62957-X

Printed in the United States of America

10 9 8 7 6 5 4 3 2 1

preface

A number of colleagues have pointed out to me over the years that in their particular institutions, the management chapters in my text *Introduction to Management in the Hospitality Industry* were not used in the introductory course. To meet the needs of these institutions, this abridged edition has been prepared.

Although several chapters have, therefore, been deleted for this brief version, there is still very nearly as much material as appeared in the first edition written in 1976. This is so because, to keep up with the fast changing hospitality industry, a great deal of new material has had to be added. There are new chapters on food service and tourism. Two new chapters, on technology and computers in lodging, and on the factors behind the segmentation of the hotel business and its changing service mix, have also been added. In addition, a new chapter dealing with franchising appears for the first time in this edition.

Nevertheless, the basic commitments of the text remain. The student still needs to be able to see hospitality as a single, interrelated industry. The emphasis on problem solving *tools* rather than answers and on understanding industry-wide *trends* rather than simple facts and figures remains central. This is not a "how to" book. The commitment in the first edition to the importance of field experience and personal observation still comes through loud and clear in Chapter 1 and, I hope, throughout the rest of the text. Finally and most fundamentally the student is challenged throughout to realize that in building a career in hospitality he or she is building a business and a way of life as well. For all that, however, there is much here that is new.

In the chapters on food service, the improved availability of information on consumer trends and preferences makes addition of those topics possible. The food service chapters have also been reorganized to accommodate new material on the consumer's view of service, nutrition and alcoholic beverages. New or expanded services make discussion of topics such as mobile units, popular priced operations outside fast food, and the growing impact of competition from commercial operations on institutional operations essential.

There are new chapters on lodging. The first of these deals with the growing importance of computers and technology in lodging, where well over half of front offices are computerized and the property management system is becoming the norm. We look ahead, too, to the increasing adoption of automation in the "smart hotel room." Chapter 9, which is also new, discusses the forces behind the expansion in the number of hotel rooms available and the segmentation of amenities and services. The role of management companies and real estate developers, and the interaction between the two, is also discussed there.

v

We have added new chapters on tourism, too, to recognize the importance of changing demand factors and travel motives, as well as the favorable and unfavorable impacts of tourism. There is new material on casinos in tourism as well as other smaller scale attractions like waterfront developments, shopping centers and even museums and zoos. The discussion of campgrounds is strengthened by a broader understanding of the motives of campers.

The new chapter on franchising discusses its economic significance and details the services provided by franchisors while assessing the franchise relationship and its advantages and disadvantages for both parties.

Throughout the text there is major attention to assessing the impact of North America's rapidly changing demographics and the accompanying changes in life styles. Very few factors are likely to be as important in hospitality in the next ten years. In the last chapter, we consider the outlook for the hospitality industry in the first half of the 1990's and the years ahead.

The dynamic and everchanging hospitality industry is a hard taskmaster for all of us who work in this business. But it is exciting and I can only hope that students will take some of the pleasure in reading this text which I found in writing it.

I am indebted to many people for help with this text and most of all to my wife, Jo Marie, who should really be listed as co-author of this edition. She wrote the entire workbook section and also prepared the instructor's manual and the question and quiz bank. Without her contribution, this edition would just not have been possible.

In regard to the research for the section on gaming I am indebted to Dean James Healy and Professor Richard Wisch at Fairleigh Dickenson University and Dean Francis X. Brown and Professor Richard Gill at Widener University for arranging the contacts without which that research could not have been accomplished. Professor Steven Rossenberg of Fairleigh Dickinson and James Kilby, Boyd Professor of Casino Management and Operations at the University of Nevada at Las Vegas read the section of the manuscript pertaining to casinos and gaming and made numerous helpful suggestions. Dean Jerome Vallen of the University of Nevada at Las Vegas was also most helpful in the research related to this section of the text. Dr. Kenneth Hornbach, Director of Research for the National Parks Service, suggested publications I should consult and made several of them available to me for the chapters on tourism. Finally, my colleague at Guelph, Professor Richard Haywood was generous in directing my attention to material related to fairs and festivals and, generally, in identifying appropriate information on tourism's impacts.

This text has also benefited from the many suggestions of colleagues who have used the text. In addition, this revision has been reviewed by 14 reviewers. The thoughtful comments of these HRI educators resulted in numerous improvements in the final manuscript and I am grateful for their interest. It is a pleasure to list them here.

Earl R. Arrowood, Bucks County Community College; V. Chandrasekar, University of Central Florida; H.A. Divine, Pennsylvania State University; Jill

Dybus, Oakton Community College; Evan Enowitz, Grossmont College; Stephenson W. Fletcher, University of Massachusetts; James B. Healy, Fairleigh Dickinson University; Lenka Hospodka, Widener College; Carol Kizer, Columbus Technical Institute; Joseph Van Kornfeld, University of Nevada; Cynthia Nelson, Cuyohoga Community College; Karen O'Brien, Hunter College; Teresa M. Schultz, University of Wisconsin, Stout; Andrew Schwartz, Sullivan County Community College.

In spite of all the help I have had, there still remain errors and deficiencies in this text for which, of course, the author must accept the responsibility.

Tom Powers
Moon River,
Ontario

contents

4   The Future of the Restaurant Business   87

5   Institutional Food Service   107

11   Destinations: Tourism Generators   261

12   Businesses Serving the Traveler   291

13   Franchise Systems in the Hospitality Industry   315

14 Views of the Future 337

The Hospitality Industry and You

———— THIS CHAPTER IS ABOUT ————

The career decisions you are involved in now and those that lie ahead of you.
Naturally, the discussion is set in the context of the hospitality industry. You will
find here as well a discussion of the relationship of field experience and
education; it should be of immediate value to you. To support your career
decision, you need to know what businesses make up the hospitality industry and
what the industry's employment outlook is. Finally, we will look beyond the job to
the life's work that a career decision entails.

Courtesy of The Plaza.

What is the Hospitality Industry?

When we think of the *hospitality industry*, we usually think of hotels and restaurants. But the term has a much broader meaning. According to the *Oxford English Dictionary*, hospitality means "the reception and entertainment of guests, visitors or strangers with liberality and good will." The word *hospitality* is derived from *hospice*, a medieval "house of rest" for travelers and pilgrims. A hospice was also an early form of what we now call a nursing home, and the word is clearly related to *hospital*.

Hospitality, then, includes hotels and restaurants. But it also refers to other kinds of institutions that offer shelter or food or both to people away from their homes. Moreover, these institutions have more than a common historical heritage. They also share the problems of providing food and shelter—problems that include erecting a building; providing heat, light, and power; cleaning and maintaining the premises; and preparing and serving food in a way that pleases the guests. Of course, we expect all of this to be done "with liberality and good will" when we stay in a hotel or dine in a restaurant, but we can rightfully expect the same treatment from the dietary department in a health-care facility or from a school lunch program.

Saga Food Service, a Marriott subsidiary, provides food service on the ferries that serve travelers commuting to Seattle through one of North America's most beautiful waterways, Puget Sound.

The hospitality professions are among the oldest of the humane professions, and they involve making a guest, client, or resident welcome and comfortable. But there is a more important reason that people interested in working in these industries should think of them collectively. Today, managers, supervisors, and skilled employees all find that opportunities for advancement often mean moving from one part of the hospitality industry to another. For example, a hospitality graduate may begin working with a restaurant company, complete the necessary training, and in a short time take a job in a motor hotel. The next job offer could come from a hospitality conglomerate, such as ARA Services. ARA provides food service operations not only in plant and office food services but also in such varied areas as recreation centers, college campuses, health-care facilities, airline food services, community nutrition centers, and gourmet restaurants. Another such conglomerate is Marriott, which some people think of as a hotel company (which it is) or a restaurant company (which it is). But Marriott is also one of the largest airline food service companies in the world and one of the largest institutional food service companies in the United States. Likewise, Holiday Inns, as everybody knows, is in the motor hotel business; but it is also one of the largest food service companies in the United States.

The point, of course, is that the hospitality industry is tied together as a clearly recognizable unit by more than just a common heritage and a commitment to "liberality and good will." Careers in the industry are such that your big break may come in a part of the industry entirely different from the one you expected. The hospitality industry is one of the few remaining places in our specialized world of work that calls for a broadly gauged generalist—and the student who understands

Marriott In-Flite Services, the world's largest and oldest independent airline caterer, serves over 100 U.S. and foreign carriers in 50 major cities. Today the company also caters for railroads and health-care institutions from flight kitchens.

Luxury food service is vital to the success of first-class resort hotels—a fact that underscores the importance of regarding hospitality (hotels and restaurants) as one industry. (Photo courtesy of Resorts International.)

this principle increases the opportunity for a rewarding career in one of the hospitality industries.

THE EMPLOYEE'S ROLE IN THE HOSPITALITY INDUSTRY

As a successful employee in the hospitality industry, you must have three general hospitality objectives:

1. *You must help make the guest welcome personally.*   This requires both a friendly manner on your part toward the guest and an atmosphere of "liberality and good will" among the people who work with you in serving the guests. That almost always means an organization in which workers get along well with one another.

2. *You must help make things work for the guest.*   Food has to be savory and hot or cold according to design—and on time. Beds must be made and rooms cleaned. A hospitality system requires a lot of work, and you must help see that it is done.

3. *You must help make sure the operation will continue providing service and making a profit.*   When we speak of "liberality and good will," we don't mean giving the whole place away! In a restaurant or hotel operated for profit, portion sizes are related to cost, and menu and room prices must be related to building and operating costs. This enables the establishment to recover the cost of its operation and to make enough additional income to pay back any money borrowed, as well as to provide a return to the owner who risked a good deal of money—and time—to build the establishment. (The situation is surprisingly similar to subsidized operations such as school lunch or health-care food services. Here the goal is not to make a profit but to achieve either a break-even or zero-profit operation, or a controlled but negative profit—that is, a loss covered by a subsidy from another source. The key lies in achieving a controlled profit, loss, or break-even operation.

Hospitality employees, then, must be able to get along well with the guests and other employees, achieve their work goals, and do this within a budget.

Why Study in a Hospitality Program?

One way to learn the hospitality business is actually to go to work in it and acquire the necessary skills. In earlier times of small operations in a slowly changing society, hospitality education was basically skill centered. The old crafts built on apprenticeships assumed that knowledge—and work—were unchanging. But for reasons that later chapters will make clear, this assumption no longer holds true. As Peter Drucker, a noted management consultant, pointed out, "Today the center [of our society's productivity] is the knowledge worker, the man or woman who applies to productive work ideas, concepts, and information."[1] In other words, *studying* is a necessary part of your preparation for a career.

Why do students choose to go into the hospitality industry? Their reasons fall into three categories: their experience, their interests, and their ambitions. Figure 1.1 lists the various reasons that students cite, in order of frequency. As you can see, many students become interested in hospitality because a job they once had proved particularly attractive. Others learn of the industry through family or friends working in the field.

One important consideration for many students is that they like and are interested in people. As we just saw, working well with people is a crucial part of the hospitality industry. Many students, too, find they have a natural interest in food, and some are attracted by the natural glamour of the hospitality industry.

The employment outlook (as we'll see later in this chapter) is excellent in most segments of the hospitality industry, and many people are attracted to a field in which they are reasonably sure they can secure employment. Others feel that in a job market with more opportunities than applicants, they will enjoy a good measure of independence.

Many young entrepreneurs have chosen catering as a low-investment field that offers opportunities to people with a flair for foods and careful service. Catering, perhaps the fastest-growing segment of food services, according to the National Restaurant Association,[2] is also a business in which students sometimes get involved while in school, through either a student organization or groups of students setting up a small catering operation.

In the lodging area, one enterprising young couple expanded in an ingenious way the services of a small country firm. Once they and their inn had been

EXPERIENCE
Personal work experience
Family background in the industry
Contact with other students and faculty in hospitality management programs

INTERESTS
Enjoy working with people
Enjoy working with food
Enjoy dining out, travel, variety

AMBITION
Opportunity for employment and advancement
Desire to operate own business
Desire to be independent

Figure 1.1   *The reasons that students select hospitality programs.*

[1] Peter F. Drucker, *The Age of Discontinuity* (New York: Harper & Row, 1968), p. 264.
[2] *NRA News*, February 1985, p. 17.

established in the community, they arranged to represent a large number of rental-unit owners in the area, offering marketing services to the owners and providing "front office" and housekeeping services for their guests in some 50 units, ranging from one-bedroom condominiums to larger condos and even houses.[3]

There are many other opportunities as well—for instance, people with chef's training may open their own business, especially if they feel they have the necessary background. In the health-care area, home-care organizations are expanding in response to the needs of our growing senior citizen population and offer a wide range of opportunities. This interest in the possibilities for independent operations reinforces the importance of education in preparation for a career in the hospitality industry.

Whether you're studying the hospitality industry because you found your past work experience in the business especially interesting or perhaps just because the continuing growth in the area makes the job prospects especially attractive, your educational background is important. Hospitality students tend to be highly motivated, lively people who take pride in their future in a career of service.

Planning a Career

WHY DO WE WORK?

We all have several motives for going to work. Of course, we work to live—to provide food, clothing, and shelter. Psychologists and sociologists tell us, however, that our work also provides a sense of who we are and binds us to the community in which we live. The ancient Greeks, who had slaves to do menial tasks, saw work as a curse. Their Hebrew contemporaries saw it as punishment. Early Christians, too, saw work for profit as offensive. But by the time of the Middle Ages, work began to be accepted as a vocation, that is, as a calling from God. Gradually, as working conditions improved and work became something that all social classes did, it became a necessary part of maturation and self-fulfillment in our society.

Today, workers at all levels demand more than just a job. Indeed, work has been defined as "an activity that produces something of value for other people."[4] This definition puts work into a social context. That is, it implies there is a social purpose for work as well as the crude purpose of survival. It is an important achievement in human history that the majority of Americans can define their own approach to a life of work as something more than mere survival.

Work contributes to self-esteem in two ways. First, by doing our work well, we prove our own competence to ourselves. Psychologists tell us that this is essential to a healthy life, as this information gives us a sense of control over both ourselves and

---

[3] *Lodging*, September 1984, pp. 68–71.
[4] *Work in America* (Cambridge, Mass.: MIT Press, n.d.), p. 3.

our environment. Second, by working we contribute to others—others come to depend on us. Human beings, as social animals, need this sense of participation. For these reasons, what happens at work becomes a large part of our sense of self-worth.

Education for such a significant part of life is clearly important. The next section explores career planning in regard to employment decisions that you must make while you are still in school. We also will discuss selecting your first employer when you leave school. If you've chosen the hospitality industry as your career, this section will help you map out your job plans. If you are still undecided, the section should help you think about this field in a more concrete way and provide some ideas on exploring a career through part-time employment.

It's hard to overstate the importance of career planning. Young people, particularly in high school, find that their career plans change constantly. By the time they've graduated from high school, however, their career plans have begun to take definite shape. But there still may be more changes. For example, people who start out studying for a career in the hotel business may find the opportunities they want in food service. Others will begin preparations for the restaurant industry only to find they prefer the hours offered in industrial food service. This kind of change in plans is easier to cope with if you have a plan that can guide you until your experience enables you to judge the "fit" between yourself and the available opportunities.

For older students and those beginning a second career, careful planning is important. Again, these plans may be based on past work experiences and/or on interests in and inclinations toward the hospitality industry. In any case, give at least as much time and attention to planning for decisions that affect your career as you expect to give to decisions you will be making for your employer. Remember that no matter who you work for, you're always in business for yourself, because it's *your* life.

Employment as an Important Part of Your Education

Profit in a business is treated in two different ways. Some is paid out to the owner or shareholders as dividends (returns on their investment). Some of the profit, however, is retained by the business to provide funds for future growth. This portion of profit that is not paid out is called *retained earnings*.

PROFITING FROM WORK EXPERIENCE

The most obvious profit we earn from work is the income paid to us by an employer. But in the early years of your career, there are other kinds of benefits that are at least as important as is income. The key to understanding this statement is the idea of a lifetime income. You'll obviously need income over your entire life

Employment offers benefits from both earning and learning.
(Courtesy of Stouffer's Restaurants, photo by Tom Barr.)

span, but giving up some income now may gain you income (and, we ought to note, enjoyment, a sense of satisfaction, and independence) just a few years later. There is, then, a *job benefit mix* made up of *both money and knowledge* to be gained from any job. Knowledge gained today can be traded with an employer for income tomorrow: a better salary for a better-qualified person. The decision to take a job that will add to your knowledge is thus a decision for retained earnings and for acquiring knowledge that you can use later.

Every job, therefore, has to be weighed according to its benefit mix, not just in terms of the dollar income it provides. A part-time job as a supermarket stock boy (well, it is a "food-related" job in a way) might seem attractive because it pays more than a bus boy's job does. But if you think about the learning portion of the benefit mix and your *total* income, including what you learn, your decision may—and probably should—be for the job that will add to your professional education.

There is another important point to consider about retained earnings and the benefit mix. Very often, the only part-time job in the industry available to students is an unskilled one. Many people find these jobs dull, and they often pay poorly. But if you think about these jobs in terms of their *total income*, you may change your perspective. The work of a bus boy or a dishwasher won't take you very long to learn. Still, you can improve your total profits from such a job by resolving to learn all you can about the operation. In this way you can build your retained earnings— that bank of skills and knowledge nobody can ever take away from you.

Learning Strategies for Work Experience

When you go to work, regardless of the position you take, you can learn a good deal through careful observation. Look first at how the operation is organized. More specifically, look at both its managerial organization and its physical organization.

Managerial Organization   Later we will consider some of the typical organizational forms of hotels and restaurants. Even now, however, you can begin to think about this problem. Who is the boss? Who reports to (or works directly for) him or her? Is the work divided into definite departments or sections? Is one person responsible for each department? To whom do the department staff members report? If you can answer these questions, you will have figured out the *formal organization* of the operation. Indeed, most large companies will have an organization chart that you can look at. If your employer doesn't have such a chart, ask him or her to explain the organization to you. You'll be surprised at how helpful to hospitality students most employers and supervisors are.

While you're thinking about organization, it is also important to notice the "informal organization" or the "social organization" of the group you are working with. Which of the workers are influential? Who seem to be the informal leaders, and why? Most work groups are made up of cliques with informal leaders. After you identify this informal structure, ask yourself how management deals with it. These observations will help you both in your studies and in sizing up the real world of work.

The Physical Plant   You can learn a great deal about a physical plant by making a simple drawing of your workplace, like the one shown in Figure 1.2. On this drawing, identify the main work areas and major pieces of equipment. Then begin to note on it where you see problems resulting from cross traffic or bottlenecks. For example, if you're working in the *back of the house*, you can chart the flow of products from the back door (receiver) to storage and from there to preparation. You should also trace the flow of dishes. Dirty dishes come to the dishroom window and go to the clean-supply area after washing. How are they transported to the cooler or to the pantry people for use in service? If you are working in the back of the house, you will be looking mostly at the flow of kitchen workers and dishes from the viewpoint of the kitchen, dishroom, or pantry. A similar flow analysis of guests and servers (and plates) can also be made from the *front of the house* (that is, the dining room).

A study of guest flow in a hotel lobby can be equally enlightening. Trace the flow of room guests, restaurant guests, banquet department guests, and service employees arriving through the lobby. Then note where you observe congestion.

These simple charting activities will give you some practical experience that will be useful for latter courses in layout and design and in food service operations and analysis.

Learning from the Back of the House

Things to look for in the back of the house include how *quality is ensured* in preparation, menu planning, recipes, cooking methods, supervision, and food holding. (How is lunch prepared in advance? How is it kept hot or cold? How long can food be held?) How are food costs controlled? For instance, are food portions standardized? Are they measured? How? How is access to storerooms controlled? These all are points you'll consider a great deal in later courses. But from the very beginning you can collect information that is invaluable to your studies and your career.

Learning from the Front of the House

If you are working as a bus boy, waitress, or a server on a cafeteria line, you can learn a great deal about the operation from observing the guests or clients. Who are the customers, and what do they value? Peter Drucker called these the two central questions in determining what a business is and what it should be doing.[5] Are the guests or clients satisfied? What in particular seems to please them?

Employees in the hospitality industry derive personal satisfaction from pleasing the guests. So be sure to find out whether your job will allow you this satisfaction. Would you change things? How?

Wherever you work and whatever you do, you can observe critically the management and guest or client relations of others. Ask yourself, "How would I have handled that problem,

[5] Peter F. Drucker, *Management: Tasks, Responsibilities, Practices* (New York: Harper & Row, 1974), pp. 80–86.

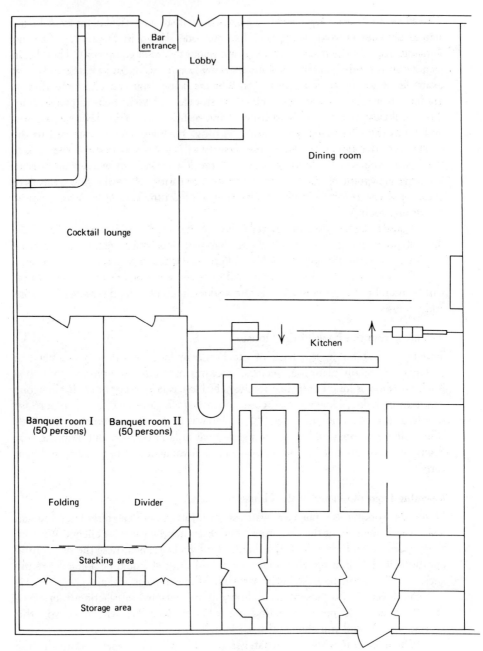

Figure 1.2   *A sample layout (not to scale).*

Atlanta's Peachtree Center offers a most dramatic and beautiful "front of the house." (Photo by Alexandre Georges.)

Dining and food service is an important part of any luxury hotel. The room pictured here is Appley's in the Sheraton Boston. (Photo courtesy of Fay's Photos.)

have handled that problem? Is this an effective way? In what other ways have I seen this problem handled?"

GETTING A JOB

Hospitality jobs comes from several sources. Your school most likely maintains a placement office. Many hospitality programs receive direct requests for part-time help. Some programs maintain a job bulletin board or file, and some even work with industry to provide internships. Of course, the "help wanted" pages of your newspaper often will offer leads, as may your local U.S. Employment Service office. Sometimes personal contacts established through your fellow students, your instructor, or your family or neighborhood will pay off. Or you may find it necessary to "pound the pavement," making personal applications in places where you would like to work.

Some employers may even arrange for hospitality students to rotate through more than one position and even to assume some supervisory responsibility.

Getting in the Door

It is not enough just to ask for a job. Careful attention to your appearance is important too. For an interview, this probably means a coat and tie for men, a conservative dress for women. Neatness and cleanliness are the absolute minimum. (Neatness and cleanliness are, after all, major aspects of the hospitality product.) When you apply for or have an interview for a job, if you can, find out who the manager is; then, if the operation is not a large one, ask for him or her by name. In a larger organization, however, you'll deal with a personnel manager. The same basic rules of appearance apply, regardless of the organization's size.

In addition find out something about the establishment at which you're applying for a job. (Read the company brochures or even visit the library to do a little research.) Try to think of one or two questions to ask about the company and/ or the job. This will show your interviewer that you are interested enough in the job to have done some homework. After your interview, you may want to write a thank-you letter to express again your appreciation and interest.

Don't be afraid to check up on the status of your application. Here's an old but worthwhile adage from personal selling: It takes three calls to make a sale. The number *three* isn't magic; but a certain persistence—letting an employer know you *are* interested—often will land you a job. Be sure to identify yourself as a hospitality student, because this tells an employer that you will be interested in your work.

Learning from a Job

Let's look at some ideas about learning on the job. One key is your attitude. If you are really interested and eager to learn, you will, in fact, learn a great deal more, because you will naturally extend yourself, ask questions, and observe what's going on around you.

Many hospitality managers report that they gained the most useful knowledge on the job *on their own time.* Let's suppose you're working as a dishwasher in the summer and your operation has a person assigned to meat cutting. You may be allowed to observe and then perhaps help out—as long as you do it on your own time. Your "profit" in such a situation is in the "retained earnings" of increased knowledge. Many job skills can be learned through observation and some unpaid practice: bartending (by a waitress or waiter), clerking on a front desk (by a bellman), and even some cooking (by a dishwasher or cook's helper). With this kind of experience behind you, it may be possible to win the skilled job part-time during the year or even for the following summer. One of the best student jobs, from a learning standpoint, is a relief job, either day-off relief or vacation relief. The training for this fill-in work can teach you a good deal about every skill in your operation. Then, if the need should arise, you will be able to pitch in when employees get stuck. For these reasons, one phrase that should never pass your lips is "that's not my job."

Other Ways of Profiting from a Job

In addition to income and knowledge, after-school part-time employment has other advantages. For example, your employer might have a career for you upon graduation. This is particularly likely if your employer happens to be a fairly large firm or if you want to remain close to the area of your schooling.

In addition, you may decide to take off a term or two from school to pursue a particular interest or just to clarify your longer-term job goals. This has the advantage of giving you more than "just a summer job" on your résumé, but be sure you don't let the work experience get in the way of acquiring the basic educational requirements for your career.

Wherever—and for however long—you work, remember that through your employment you may make contacts that will help you after graduation. People with whom you have worked may be able to tell you of interesting opportunities or recommend you for a job.

Don't underestimate a recommendation. Even if your summer employer doesn't have a career opportunity for you, a favorable recommendation can give your career a big boost when you graduate. In addition, many employers may have contacts they will make available to you—perhaps friends of theirs who can offer interesting opportunities. The lesson here is that the record you make on the job now can help shape your career later.

Employment at Graduation

Graduation probably seems a long way off right now, but you should already be considering strategies for finding a job when you finish your formal education. Clear goals formed now will direct your work experience plans and, to a lesser degree, the courses you take and the topics you emphasize within those courses. If you have not yet decided on a specific goal, then this question deserves prompt but careful consideration as you move through your education. You will have plenty of time.

The rest of this section offers a kind of "dry-run" postgraduation placement procedure. From this distance, you can view the process objectively. When you come closer to graduation, you may find the subject a tense one: People worry about placement as graduation nears, even if they're quite sure of finding a job.

THE STRATEGY OF JOB PLACEMENT

Most hospitality students have three concerns. First, many students are interested in such income issues as starting salary and the possibility of raises and bonuses.

Second, students are concerned with personal satisfaction. They wonder about opportunities for self-expression, creativity, initiative, and independence. Although few starting jobs offer a great deal of independence, some types of work (for example, employment with a franchising company) can lead quite rapidly to independent ownership. Students also want to know about the number of hours they'll be investing in their work. Many companies expect long hours, especially from junior employees. But other sectors, especially the institutional operations, make more modest demands (and generally offer more modest prospects for advancement).

Third, many students, particularly in health-care food service, want to achieve such professional goals as competence as a dietitian or a dietetic technician. Although professional goals in the commercial sector don't lead to formal certification, they are clearly associated with developing a top-flight reputation as an operator. These three sets of interests are obviously related, for example, most personal goals include the elements of income, satisfaction, and professional status. Our point is that although it may be too early to set definite goals, it is not too early to begin evaluating these elements. From the three concerns we've just discussed, the following are four elements for your consideration:

1. *Income.*   The place to begin your analysis is with the issue of survival. How much will you *require* to meet your financial needs? For example, your needs will be greater if you plan to support a family than if you need to support only yourself. If your income needs are modest, you may decide to forgo luxuries to take a lower-paying job that offers superior training. Thus, you would make an investment in retained earnings—the knowledge you hope someday to trade for more income, security, and job satisfaction.

2. *Professional Status.*   Whether your goal is professional certification (as a dietitian, for example) or a reputation as a top-flight hotelier or restaurateur, you should consider the job benefit mix. In this case, you may choose to accept a lower income (but, of course, one on which you can live and in line with what such jobs pay in your region). Although you shouldn't be indifferent to income, you'll want to focus principally on what the job can teach you.

3. *Evaluating an Employer.*   Students who make snap judgments about a company and act aggressively in an interview often offend potential employers, who, after all, see the interview as an occasion to evaluate the student crop. Nevertheless, in a quiet way, you should learn about the company's commitment to training. Does it have a training program? If not, how does it translate its entry jobs into learning experiences? Because training beyond the entry-level basics requires responsibility and access to promotion, you will want to know about the opportunities for advancement. Finally, you need to evaluate the company's operations. Are they quality operations? Can you be proud to work there? If the quality of food or service is consistently poor, can you help improve things? Or will you be misled into learning the wrong way to do things?

4. *Determining Potential Job Satisfaction.*   Some students study hospitality only to discover that their real love is food preparation. Such students may decide, late in their student careers, to seek a job that provides skill training in food preparation. Other students may decide they need a high income immediately (to pay off debts or to do some traveling, for example). These students may

decide to trade the skills they have acquired in their work experiences to gain a high income for a year or two as a waitress or waiter in a top-flight operation. Such a goal is highly personal but perfectly reasonable. The key is to form a goal and keep moving toward it.

The Outlook for the Hospitality Industry

We can expect a dramatic increase in the peak age groups that use hospitality services, and this growth will extend until the turn of the century. Accompanying this growth will be a general labor shortage caused by the smaller labor market for the hospitality industry: young people.

DEMAND FOR HOSPITALITY SERVICES

People under 35 years of age are starting their careers and often their families. Starting a family means large outlays for the purchase of a home, furniture, and appliances and the costs of having children. Thus, to roughly age 35, the combination of still relatively moderate income and heavy financial outlays limits new families' discretionary spending on such things as travel and dining out. But in middle age average incomes increase. People 35 to 44 years of age are those most inclined to travel, whereas people 45 to 54 years of age spend the most on food away from home. The middle years, then, ages 35 to 54, are the peak years for *spending* on hospitality services.

Figures 1.3 and 1.4 give a 50-year perspective on the number of U.S. consumers in these two middle-aged population groups. After a period of modest growth or even modest decline, since 1980 the number of middle-aged people has begun to increase rapidly. The 35 to 44-year-old group started first, and the 45 to 54-year-old group began to accelerate in 1985. These trends will continue to the year 2000, fueling the demand for services such as hotel rooms and meals away from home.

LABOR SUPPLY

Although people of all ages work in the hospitality industry, younger workers are a major source of both part-time and full-time workers. Figures 1.5 and 1.6 demonstrate why in the second half of the 1980s there have been serious labor shortages in some U.S. markets. Differing regional age distributions have softened the shortage in some markets. But in the Northeast, for instance, Friendly's (a chain that combines ice-cream specialties with family dining) reported an increase in 1985 in sales, but *no* increase in profit, and it attributed its poor relative performance to the labor shortage in its markets.[6]

[6] *Nation's Restaurant News*, October 21, 1985, p. 19.

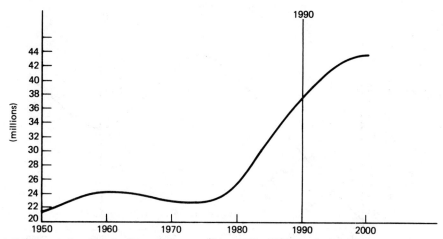

Figure 1.3   *People 35 to 44 years old, 1950–2000.* [Adapted from Peter K. Franchese, "Consumer Perspectives," *Proceedings: Chain Operators Exchange, 1985* (Chicago: International Foodservice Manufacturers Association, 1985).]

In Boston, Wendy's Restaurants were reportedly busing employees an hour or so from nearby towns where more teenagers were available, and paying them for their transportation time. Wendy's even went so far as to insert a brief employee recruiting message in its TV commercials in Boston.[7]

[7] *Nation's Restaurant News*, October 10, 1985, p. 3.

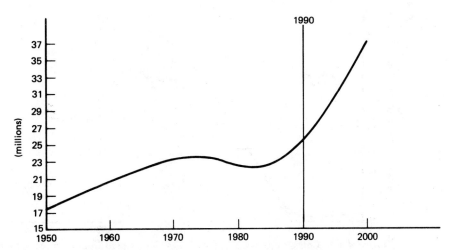

Figure 1.4   *People 45 to 54 years old, 1950–2000.* [Adapted from Peter K. Franchese, "Consumer Perspectives," *Proceedings: Chain Operators Exchange, 1985* (Chicago: International Foodservice Manufacturers Association, 1985).]

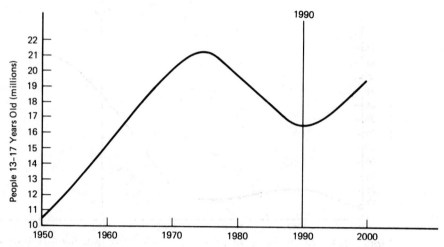

Figure 1.5   *Teenagers, 1950–2000.* [Adapted from Peter K. Franchese, "Consumer Perspectives," *Proceedings: Chain Operators Exchange, 1985* (Chicago: International Foodservice Manufacturers Association, 1985).]

As Figures 1.5 and 1.6 indicate, the shortage of teenagers will begin to ease around 1990, and not surprisingly, the shortage of college-age people will begin to moderate about five years later. It seems likely, however, that there will continue to be a serious shortage of entry-level workers throughout much of this decade. This means that getting a *first* job should be relatively easy. A closer look at population

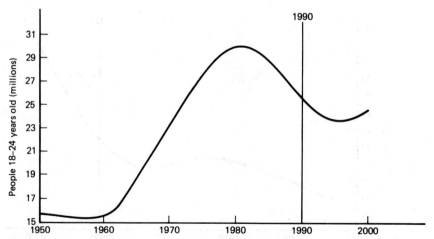

Figure 1.6   *College-age people, 1950–2000.* [Adapted from Peter K. Franchese, "Consumer Perspectives," *Proceedings: Chain Operators Exchange, 1985* (Chicago: International Foodservice Manufacturers Association, 1985).]

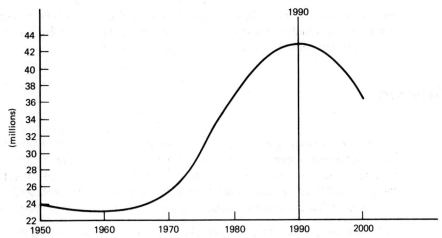

Figure 1.7 *People 25 to 34 years old, 1950–2000.* [Adapted from Peter K. Franchese, "Consumer Perspectives," *Proceedings: Chain Operators Exchange, 1985* (Chicago: International Foodservice Manufacturers Association, 1985).]

trends, however, underlines the importance of preparing for competition for higher-level jobs in the 1990s. Another way of looking at the growth of the middle-aged market is noting that this means that a lot of people in the U.S. work force are competing for middle-level jobs. Figure 1.7 reinforces that picture, showing the rapid and continuing buildup of people 25 to 34 years old, a buildup that began in the early 1970s and will extend into the early 1990s.

The first job may be easy to get, but as *Restaurant Institutions* observed: "Baby boomers—the largest and best educated generation in the U.S. history—crowd the next rung of the career ladder."[8]

Industry Conditions

Industry trends toward more competition, discussed in Chapters 3 and 7, mean that there will be more operations striving to serve the growing markets for hospitality services. Given an expansion in the industry into the 1990s in the face of a serious shortage of employee positions already, the outlook is for faster promotion opportunities in the hospitality industry than in many other areas of employment that are not expanding and that do not face the hospitality industry's current labor shortage.

Beyond the growth in traditional hospitality operations, another factor favoring people with hospitality industry education and experience is what might be called the "spread" of the industry. Convenience stores, for instance, and other retailers have begun to expand their food service operations. Because food service

[8] *Restaurant Institutions*, August 7, 1985, p. 62.

away from home is increasingly a necessity for families in which both spouses are employed, the number of nontraditional food service sites will probably continue to grow, expanding further the need for food service workers.

Summary

The hospitality industry includes hotels, restaurants, and other institutions that offer shelter and/or food to people away from home. An employee in the hospitality industry, therefore, must have the following three objectives: (1) making the guest welcome personally, (2) making things work for the guest, and (3) making sure that the operation will continue providing service and making a profit.

There are many reasons for studying in a hospitality program, among them being a good past experience working in the field, interests in the field, and ambitions in the field.

We also discussed why people work and how to get the most from a job, including weighing both retained earnings and the job benefit mix. We also pointed out that in the hospitality industry, you can learn a lot from the physical plant and from the front and the back of the house.

We then turned to ways to get a job—including preparing for an interview—and how to gain the most from whatever job you do find. We also talked about what you should consider in regard to a more permanent job: income, professional status, your employer, potential job satisfaction, and accepting an interm, less-skilled job.

Finally, we began our book-long discussion of the outlook for the hospitality industry, which we found to be bright.

The Restaurant Business

_____ THIS CHAPTER IS ABOUT _____

The restaurant business. To understand the opportunities restaurants offer you, you need to know what the major segments of the industry are and how big they are relative to one another. It is helpful, too, to understand the widely differing operating styles found in *full-service* restaurants and *specialty* restaurants. Dividing food service into an eating market and a dining market is a useful way of understanding what people want when they decide which restaurant to visit. Finally, to be knowledgeable about the business, you need to become familiar with the key operating ratios for restaurants and to know how they are used.

chapter

2

Courtesy of the Greater New Orleans Tourist and Convention Commission.

The Varied Field of Food Service

Commercial firms make up by far the largest sector of the food service industry. According to the National Restaurant Association (NRA), about 69 percent of the food purchased away from home is sold in restaurants, cafeterias, and taverns. Hotel, motel, and motor-inn restaurants account for another 5.6 percent. Sales in restaurants located in other retail establishments, such as department and drugstores, account for over 3 percent of the market for food consumed away from home. Contractors and caterers (who serve food under contract in settings such as industrial plants and office buildings, health-care facilities, and schools and colleges) generate 6.2 percent of food sales, and 2.6 percent of sales are made through vending machines. These estimates are summarized in Table 2.1.

The market for food away from home includes 97 percent of Americans, up from 85 percent in 1960. On the average, food service customers eat out three to four times a week. In 1970, Americans spent about 27 percent of their food expenditures away from home, and by 1985 that proportion has risen to just over 30 percent. Not surprisingly, this is a growth industry.[1] In the first half of the 1980s, food service sales increased 1.3 percent faster than did the U.S. economy as a whole, and their continued growth seems likely.

The Restaurant Business

One problem in describing the restaurant business is that it changes so fast that today's description may well be outdated tomorrow. Moreover, restaurants have so many forms that it is almost impossible to devise a model to fit all of them. Nevertheless, to describe the field even generally, we need some basic terminology.

[1] John J. Rohs, *The Restaurant Industry* (New York: Wertheim and Co., April 1985), pp. 8–12.

Table 2.1   *Commercial and institutional food service sales, 1984*

Restaurants, cafeterias, and fast-food bars and taverns	111,437,097	68.3%
Food service in hotels, motels, and motor hotels	9,164,681	5.6
Food sales in retail stores	5,394,529	3.3
Vending and nonstore retailers	4,256,258	2.6
Contractors and caterers	10,147,530	6.2
Recreation and sports	1,905,961	1.2
Institutions operating own food service	20,861,063	12.8
	163,167,118	100.0

Source: NRA News, June–July 1986.

Two obvious (and descriptive) terms are the *full-service restaurant* and the *specialty restaurant*.

THE FULL-SERVICE RESTAURANTS

The term *full service* refers to the *style of service* in the dining room, the *menu*, and the *style of preparation*. A traditional full-service restaurant offers a wide variety of menu choices, and most full-service restaurants prepare most of their food "from scratch" (that is, from fresh or raw ingredients). Waitresses and waiters serve the food. Some chains operate full-service restaurants, but most such restaurants are "independents." These are single operations, privately owned and not affiliated with any other food service organization.

There are really three kinds of full-service restaurants: first, the independent luxury restaurants specializing in haute cuisine[2] and, second, such lower-priced operations as neighborhood restaurants with simple and inexpensive fare, usually prepared "from scratch" and served by waitresses. These operations are sometimes called mom-and-pop restaurants, because they are often family concerns in which one spouse supervises the cooking while the other looks after the front of the house. Mom-and-pop restaurants are increasingly threatened by franchised and chain fast-food and coffee shops and budget steak house operations, which offer competitive prices in more modern surroundings.

The third kind of full-service restaurant grew up during the 1930s and 1940s. These restaurants are usually from three to five times the size of the first two, and they use semiskilled cooks working under close supervision in a recipe kitchen, in which the cooks follow recipes exactly, weighing and measuring each ingredient. The recipes and the supervision largely replace the skills of the chef. The meals are moderately priced.

For convenience, we will refer to the classic, "from scratch" full-service restaurants as *haute cuisine restaurants*. Haute cuisine restaurants remain popular, but they are usually found only in heavily populated areas that can supply enough customers who can afford the relatively high prices—as much as \$50 to \$100 or more per meal, including wines. Haute cuisine restaurants must charge these high prices to recover their costs and earn enough profit to pay their highly skilled employees and repay the owners for their efforts and capital risks. Because of their high food standards, haute cuisine operations tend to be quite small. At the other end of the scale is the *neighborhood restaurant*, denoting the mom-and-pop firm that offers a full-service menu at decidedly lower prices.

Many, though by no means all, full-service restaurants are currently experiencing financial difficulties because they are labor intensive, which means that they require a large number of employee hours per guest served. As the proprietors of the neighborhood establishments reach retirement age, their operations often

---

[2] Loosely translated, the term means "elegant dining," or food prepared in the manner of the classic French (or European) chefs.

close, because no one wants to work the long hours it takes to keep them profitable. Similarly, companies, such as Stouffer's and Marriott Hot Shoppes, that run moderately priced, full-service restaurants—our third category—have found these operations unprofitable and are either closing them or converting them into other styles of operation. But surprisingly, though often beset by high costs and labor problems, luxury restaurants can remain profitable if they can maintain the quality of their food and service. Indeed, in 1984 the full-service restaurants' share of total food service sales actually expanded for the first time in several years, growing from nearly 27 percent to just over 29 percent.[3]

THE SPECIALTY RESTAURANTS

A wide variety of restaurants can be called *specialty restaurants*, and here, too, it is difficult to establish neat categories. All of the specialty operations tend to simplify their production processes, and most of them use at least some self-service. The result is a drastic reduction in the labor in both the front and the back of the house, as Table 2.2 shows. Because specialty restaurants require less labor, they can pass on their savings to the guests in the form of lower prices. Furthermore, these operations, even with their lower prices, generally earn profits substantially higher than those in other operations. Although not all specialty restaurants are affiliated with chains or franchise groups, most of them are. A few exceptions will be discussed later in this chapter. Specialty restaurants may *look* different from one another. But to a surprising degree, they all are modeled on one pattern, dictated by the fast-food concept.

Fast Food

Fast food is the largest single type of specialty restaurant, and probably the fastest growing in terms of both sales and numbers of units. *Restaurants' Institutions*

[3] *Restaurants & Institutions*, March 15, 1985, p. 136.

Table 2.2   *Productivity in food service establishments*

FOOD SERVICE TYPE	DIRECT LABOR HOURS PER 100 GUESTS
Luxury restaurants	72.3
Family restaurants[a]	20.7
Cafeterias	18.3
Fast food[a]	10.5

Source: Agricultural Research Service.
[a] Specialty restaurant.

magazine estimated that in 1986 there were 140,700 fast-food units in operation, employing 1,960,000 food service workers.[4] The most popular menu item is still the hamburger. Table 2.3 shows the relative popularity of the major fast-food formats in 1984, as reflected in the 100 largest food service companies in the United States.

Automation is the key to the modern fast-food restaurant. When we think of automation, a factory, a lot of machinery, and repetitive tasks usually come to mind. But as Peter Drucker pointed out, "Automation is not 'technical' in character. Like every technology, it is primarily a system of concepts, and its technical aspects are results rather than causes."[5] Fast-food restaurants are not automated in the sense of depending on new, automatic machinery. Some new variations of the traditional food service equipment are found in these operations, but it is really the customer who has been automated!

The *automating concept* in the fast-food operation means fewer menu choices, less customer service, and different customer behavior. Through self-service, the customer replaces the entire front of the house staff, even to the point of cleaning up. There may be some choice in regard to cleaning up, but absolutely no choice in regard to self-service. Moreover, because fast-food operations offer a simple menu, very specialized, highly efficient kitchens can be built around this limited food choice.

The fast-food operation is, in many ways, more like a manufacturing enterprise than the traditional restaurant is:

[4] *Restaurants & Institutions*, January 8, 1986, p. 133.
[5] Peter Drucker, *The Practice of Management* (New York: Harper & Row, 1954), p. 19.

Table 2.3 *Relative popularity of fast-food categories in 1984, top 100 chains*

FAST-FOOD CATEGORY	NUMBER OF CHAINS	NUMBER OF UNITS	SALES (MILLIONS OF $)	
Hamburger	18	19,516	$18,290	61.2%
Chicken	11	8,089	3,891	13.0
Ice cream	7	8,996	2,228	7.4
Mexican	5	2,659	1,262	4.2
Roast beef	2	1,862	1,232	4.1
Seafood	3	1,890	885	3.1
Pizza	2	2,523	853	2.8
Donuts	3	2,609	802	2.6
Limited menu	5	1,335	448	1.5
Bakery	3	99	23	.1
			29,885	100.0

Source: Data from Technomic Consultants, *Dynamics of the Chain Restaurant Market* (Chicago: International Foodservice Manufacturers Association, 1985).

McDonald's has created a highly sophisticated piece of service technology by applying the manufacturing mode of managerial thought to a labor-intensive service situation. If a machine is a piece of equipment with the capability of producing a predictably standardized, customer-satisfying output while minimizing the operation discretion of its attendant, that is what a McDonald's outlet is. It produces, with the help of totally unskilled machine tenders, a fairly sophisticated, reliable product at great speed and low cost.

McDonald's represents the industrialization of service—applying, through management, the same systematic modes of analysis, design, organization, and control that are commonplace in manufacturing. These more than anything account for its success.[6]

New Fast-Food Products   Another way of contrasting fast-food operations with the more traditional restaurant is to observe how they introduce a new product. In a traditional operation, a new item can be introduced on the menu quite easily, because of the flexibility of a traditional kitchen. If the item succeeds, it will be continued; if not, it can easily be dropped. But introducing a new product in fast food is more complicated, because the fast-food restaurant itself is a highly specialized kind of machine. The process begins in the product development lab, a relatively new unit for the restaurant industry. Wendy's, for instance, reportedly had no people working in that area in 1979 but by early 1984 had a staff of 42.[7] The next stage is trying out the product in a few markets, where the product's appeal is tested and its compatibility with the production process is gauged. If the product passes these early tests, it will be tested in wider and wider markets until all the wrinkles have been ironed out. Finally, it will be adopted systemwide.

Nation's Restaurant News (NRN) traced the introduction of breakfast items at McDonald's. The Egg McMuffin was introduced in 1973, hot cakes in 1974, and scrambled eggs and sausage in 1975. During the test period, McDonald's determined the specific operating procedures and equipment required for each new product. Once this equipment was perfected, the company's chief supplier prepared a standard adaptation kit for the entire system.

Packaging was another technical problem that McDonald's encountered. Paper packaging, which was tried first, did not hold heat efficiently. "This hurt our breakfast image," a McDonald's spokesperson explained to NRN, "because it meant slow service. People coming into our restaurant were expecting our normal fast service, which we just couldn't provide if we had to make each item only as it was ordered."[8] Consequently, McDonald's designed a new insulated package that, for up to 10 minutes, retains product quality in a warming bin.

Once its new products—and the system to match them—were perfected, McDonald's launched a major advertising campaign to support the "rollout," or the

[6] Theodore Levitt, "Management and the Post Industrial State," *The Public Interest*, Summer 1976, p. 89.

[7] *Wall Street Journal*, January 1, 1984, p. 21.

[8] *Nation's Restaurant News*, August 4, 1975, p. 77.

systemwide introduction of its new product, using television, radio, and the other media.

Likewise, in 1984, when Taco Bell decided to introduce "Pizzaz Pizza," it followed the same general pattern: product development, test marketing, and then a rollout supported by a 12-week broadcast and print advertising campaign. An equipment package costing $10,000 to $15,000 per store had to be in place in each unit to support the rollout. In one franchise group participating in the market test, store sales rose by 15 percent.[9]

The physical limits of the existing equipment became clear in the case of Arby's. The company wanted to develop a 1/3-lb burger to broaden its product line so as to offset the limited market penetration of its signature product, roast beef. Although this new product was well accepted by consumers, *Nation's Restaurant News* reported that "roll out is not likely to occur in the near future because most of Arby's system remains unequipped for grilling or broiling."[10]

The problems that can develop in a *systemwide* introduction of a product are illustrated in the rollout of a new catfish dinner by Church's Fried Chicken. In April 1985, the company spent $5 million to introduce the new product, but then operational problems cropped up. Plans were made to increase the portion size from 1 to 1.75 oz so that the product would cook better, be less subject to breakage, and help speed service. Church's proposed to spend an additional $1 million to introduce the change but then had to stop the test for a period because the manufacturers were unable to procure the new portions of fish or guarantee their delivery.[11] The product did improve sales, but the purchasing and production problems had to be worked out on the spot.

The logistics of a systemwide distribution of key ingredients is not simple. When Wendy's introduced baked potatoes—a product ordered 600,000 times *daily* in 1985—the potato market was disrupted, with prices rising significantly.[12] And when McDonald's rolled out Chicken McNuggets, it had to arrange to have a total of 5 million pounds of chicken delivered each week to its 6,200 restaurants across the United States. In a final example, a decision by Burger King to put three strips of bacon on a cheeseburger increased the national demand for bacon so much that it had a noticeable effect on the national commodity market.[13]

Despite all these problems and complications, it is generally recognized that new products serve the following marketing purposes.

1. *They broaden the restaurant's appeal.*   That is, if two people in a party of three want hamburgers, but one wants chicken or fish, all of the party will be

---

[9] *Restaurant Institutions*, June 26, 1985, p. 70.

[10] *Nation's Restaurant News*, August 12, 1985, p. F18.

[11] *Nation's Restaurant News*, August 19, 1985, p. 100.

[12] Michael Culp, "Wendy's International Company Report," *Prudential Bache Securities*, March 8, 1985, pp. 8–9.

[13] *Wall Street Journal*, January 5, 1984, p. 21.

satisfied with, for instance, McDonald's menu. Or, as another example, Wendy's used new products—salad bars and baked potatoes—to attract more women to its restaurants.

2. *New products match changing consumer tastes.*   For instance, salad bars and "lite" menu items fit in with the current interest in health food.

3. *When salads and desserts are added, they enable the unit to offer a full meal, which helps it compete better with the fuller-menu family restaurants.*   The full meal, in turn, helps build higher average sales per guest.

4. *Some new products help spread business throughout the day, such as items that attract guests for snacks or a meal period such as breakfast.*

5. *Some products are added "defensively."*   For example, several chicken restaurants are reported to have added chicken-nugget products largely because they were losing customers to McDonald's, which, with its introduction of Chicken McNuggets, became the second-largest "chicken restaurant chain" in the world.

The point is that when a fast-food operation introduces a new product, it spends much more time studying it than a full-service restaurant would, and its reasons for doing so usually extend well beyond a mere increase in variety. In short, when a full-service restaurant introduces a new menu item, it is a minor change— just one item among several. But when a fast-food restaurant makes such a decision, the item introduced is seen as a "new product" that requires adjustments in both its production procedures and its marketing strategies.

It is fashionable in some circles to look down on fast-food operations, either because they don't seem to be "real restaurants" or because their food supposedly lacks nutritional value. But the customers have clearly voted with their feet. Moreover, a study conducted by one fast-food chain indicated that a customer who orders a specialty hamburger sandwich, french fries, and a milkshake receives approximately one-third of the recommended dietary allowance (RDA), or about the same nutritional value found in the typical school lunch.

As we'll see in the next chapter, such a meal *does* have more salt and fat than would be sensible if that meal were eaten every day, but the facts just don't warrant disdain of fast food on nutritional grounds.

The management of fast-food operation is more demanding than it appears. The preparation of the products has to be planned so that the food will be available almost the minute it is ordered (this is *fast* food, don't forget). In fact, most products must be thrown out if they are held for more than 10 or 20 minutes. To minimize waste, therefore, management must devise a sales-forecasting system based on operating experience, often keyed to 10-minute time segments throughout the operating day.

It is important to realize that a single fast-food unit of a chain or franchise system is itself a part of a complex "machine" (*system* is technically the more accurate word) that produces a standard, reliable product in every such unit. The achievement of these systems, then, is not measured just by the output of a single unit but also by the overall effect on a national (or regional) market of a standard product and service. The reputation of a system is valuable to all the franchisees, and in this sense, the *product* that McDonald's has developed is not just a hamburger but the entire McDonald's franchise as well. Therefore, to preserve the value of the franchise for all, each franchisee must meet the same high standards.

The Outlook for Fast Food The baby-boom generation fueled the explosion of fast food in the 1960s and 1970s, but the recession of the early 1980s hurt all restaurants, and it took until 1984 to regain the customer counts of 1978.[14] The number of restaurant units, however, continued to grow. During the first half of the 1980s, as Charles Lynch, former president of Saga, has pointed out, the increase in the number of restaurant units was five times the rate of the population growth,[15] with the lion's share of the growth going to fast food.

Furthermore, the growing number of young people in the 1960s and 1970s supported the development of fast food. But these same people in the 1970s and 1980s are now 25 to 34 years old, a group that eats out frequently and is relatively prosperous. Their growing number, therefore, has led to the upscaling of fast food to larger portions and more sophisticated decor, marked by the rapid growth of chains such as Wendy's and, more recently, "gourmet" hamburger chains such as Fuddrucker's. Some analysts feel, however, that fast food—with its 40 percent of restaurant sales—may have passed its time of fastest growth. John Rohs, for instance, a security analyst with Wertheim and Company who follows trends in the hospitality industry, expects fast food's proportionate share of restaurant sales may begin to decline.[16]

George Rice, the leading authority on eating-out trends in the United States, indicates that in early 1986, a significant proportion of consumers decided to eat dinner, which he calls a crucial competitive battleground, less often at fast-food restaurants.[17] Lunch is still an established well-served, and highly competitive market in which fast-food restaurants must fight with other kinds of restaurants for its market share. And fast food's outlook for continuing growth in breakfast sales as a whole is also bright.

Even though the growth rate of fast food will probably eventually slow, this does not mean that employment opportunities will shrink. Indeed, with so many units in operation, even a low growth rate—in percentage—still means a large total number of units. Note, too, that somes kinds of restaurants, such as Mexican and Asian, are likely to grow faster than is the entire segment. Furthermore,

[14] George D. Rice, "Foodservice Perspective & Implications," *Proceedings of the 12th Annual Chain Operators Exchange*, Miami, February 17–20, 1985.
[15] Charles Lynch, "Leadership in the Toughest Environment Ever," *Proceedings of the 13th Annual Chain Operators Exchange*, Las Vegas, February 23, 1986.
[16] Rohs, *The Restaurant Industry*, p. 12.
[17] George D. Rice, "Year in Review and a Look Ahead at the Opportunity for '86," *Proceedings of the 13th Annual Chain Operators Exchange*.

because of the shortage of qualified personnel and the high turnover, there will continue to be many opportunities for employment in the fast-food industry.

Other Specialty Restaurants

Although other specialty restaurants may not *look* like fast-food operations, their operating system is similar. Their "back of the house" production system has been simplified by a specialized menu that reduces skill levels, thus holding down wage costs and speeding service. Specialty restaurants might therefore be called "moderately fast food," for although the guests in these operations are prepared to wait a bit longer for food, they will not have to wait *much* longer. We will discuss three examples of specialty restaurants: family restaurants, budget steak houses, and pizza parlors.

Family Restaurants   Family restaurants, sometimes referred to as coffee shops, depart quite a bit from the fast-food format in that they offer waiter or waitress service, as well as self-service, in the form of salad bars, breakfast bars, and dessert bars. Specialty restaurants usually offer breakfast, lunch, and dinner. Another similarity to full-service restaurants is the extensive menu variety they appear to offer.

This resemblance to full service can, however, be deceiving. First, the staff is limited to one or more short-order cooks. Almost everything is prepared to order, sometimes from scratch (as with the sandwich and breakfast items that give the menu much of its variety) and sometimes from frozen prepared foods that are reconstituted to order. The production process therefore is really almost as simple as the fast-food process.

Furthermore, the service the customers receive is anything but elaborate. Place settings usually consist of paper place mats and a minimum of china and silver. Most meals consist only of the main course and perhaps a dessert. This reduction in courses also simplifies service. *Nation's Restaurant News* surveys show, for instance, that in 1985, four out of ten sales dollars came from platters, salads, sandwiches, and dinners. Breakfast sales accounted for another third of sales.[18] Take together, nearly three-quarters of the family restaurants' volume came from these main meal items. Given their relatively straightforward operating format, the cost of training new service employees remains minimal. And the flexible menu permits such restaurants to drop menu choices when their food costs advance too rapidly and to substitute less costly items.

The guests who visit a family restaurant want to be waited on, and in choosing a family restaurant, they are opting for an informal, simple, relatively inexpensive style of service. These operations generally offer a pleasant, modern restaurant located near dense pedestrian or vehicular traffic and convenient to shoppers and suburban family diners. But in menus and decor, family restaurants face competition not only from budget steak and pizza restaurants but also from upscaled fast-

---

[18] *Nation's Restaurant News*, August 19, 1985, p. F6.

food restaurants. Fast food's share of the breakfast market has been growing largely "at the expense of independently owned coffee shops while chain owned family restaurants barely held their own."[19] In fact, in the United States, McDonald's alone accounts for one-quarter of all breakfasts eaten away from home. Even so, although Americans tend to eat dinner out *less* often in fast-food and upscaled restaurants, according to George Rice, many ate out more often in mid-scale operations such as family restaurants.[20]

Budget Steak Houses   Before 1974, budget steak houses grew rapidly. However, they relied on one main product, steak, and when the price of beef began to soar, they felt serious cost pressures. Moreover, they relied principally on the evening meal for most of their sales. Finally, their main target market in the 1970s was the blue-collar family. During the recession of the early 1980s, therefore, many of these operations began to evolve to other formats, recognizing that the blue-collar workforce was not growing as fast as was white-collar employment. The budget steak houses' vulnerability to blue-collar unemployment in a recession became painfully apparent. Their experience offers an interesting example of a common food service strategy much in use in the late 1970s and early 1980s, that of repositioning, or changing the operating format and image in the customer's mind.

One of the largest chains, Bonanza, developed an upgrading concept called Freshtastick's, which featured decor upgrading and all-you-can-eat food bars offering salads, cheeses, breads, fresh vegetables, fruits, and desserts. Operations that used the new format also switched to a higher grade of beef. The new concept helped improve the company's luncheon volume, attracted new customers, and increased unit volume. Family steak houses have continued to diversity their menus by adding chicken and fish entrees, sandwiches, and elaborate salad bars. In an effort to widen their market, some have also added breakfast bars, thus expanding into another mealtime. Today's budget steak house has thus broadened its concept and so offers an interesting example of the way in which the competitive restaurant industry responds to changing customer preferences. In 1970 the budget steak house was a major growth concept. By the mid-1970s this concept was in trouble, and in the 1980s the "budget steaker" has largely become something else, offering a wider menu and upscaled decor.

Pizza Restaurants   Pizza restaurants, like budget steak houses, once depended almost exclusively on a single item. But in recent years, pizza restaurants have extended their product line so as to appeal to more customers. For instance, in 1984, Pizza Hut rolled out "Priazzo," a two-crusted Italian pie stuffed with a variety of foods such as pepperoni, cheese, and tomato sauce or a quichelike mixture of spinach, ham, and cheese. The product was targeted to customers who had not typically been tempted by more traditional pizza products.[21] Earlier, deep-dish

[19] *Nation's Restaurant News*, February 18, 1985, p. 1.
[20] Rice, "Year in Review."
[21] *Restaurant Business*, August 10, 1985, p. 145.

"Chicago style" pizzas had added menu variety, and then personal pan pizzas were added to speed service and as a competitively priced product for the lunch market. Domino's Pizza has even been reported to be testing a breakfast product called "Domino's Bake Ups," which are a kind of breakfast pie, made from pizza dough with fruit, ham and cheese, bacon and tomato, or western omelet toppings.[22] The major development in the pizza segment, however, has been the surge in home delivery and in drive-through service, which require new systems for making pizza faster.[23] But despite all their menu and service expansion, they are still principally pizza restaurants. The cost of their food product itself and their operations are relatively low. Furthermore, pizza's continuing popularity with consumers ensures its remaining in the front ranks of growth concepts. Another noteworthy aspect of the pizza business is that it is a stronghold for independents.

There are, of course, numerous other specialty restaurants, featuring, for instance, chicken, seafood, ice cream, Mexican food, and Asian food. They generally fit the pattern already described: limited menus, highly efficient productivity based on an "automated customer," and a product characterized by a relatively low food cost. Figure 2.1 summarizes schematically our discussion to this point. It rates various types of operations on a scale from left to right according to whether they are full service (at the far left) or specialty restaurants (at the far right). In turn, their typical price range is measured from lowest to highest on the scale at left.

The Dining Market and the Eating Market

One of the twentieth century's most innovative restauranteurs, Joe Baum, summed up the challenge of food service:

> *A restaurant takes a basic drive—the simplest act of eating—and transforms it into a civilized ritual; a ritual involving hospitality and imagination and satisfaction and graciousness and warmth.*[24]

Restaurants serve both our social and our biological needs. In order to try to see the restaurant business from both of these perspectives, we will divide restaurants into those serving predominantly our social needs—the *dining market*—and those serving our biological needs—the *eating market*. Of course, nearly all meals eaten in public have a social dimension, just as the most formal state dinner has its biological aspect. The main purpose, however, is usually clear.

The specialty restaurants we have been discussing are more or less part of the eating market. Although many of them seem to emphasize decor and service, they

---

[22] *Restaurants & Institutions*, November 13, 1985, p. 115.
[23] *Nation's Restaurant News*, August 2, 1985, p. F22.
[24] *Restaurants & Institutions*, February 5, 1986, p. 16.

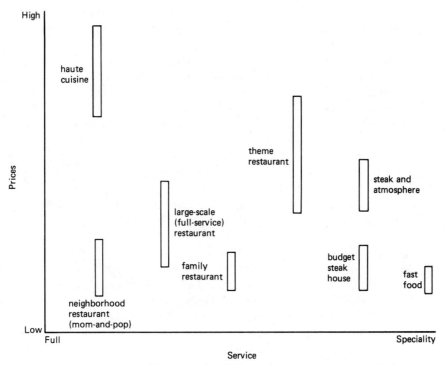

Figure 2.1   *The range of restaurants compared on the basis of service type and relative price.*

really concentrate on economy and speed. The dining market, serving our social and recreational needs, emphasizes the service ritual, food excellence, and often entertainment.

DINING WELL

From research undertaken by the National Restaurant Association, we have some clues why people dine away from home: to escape from boredom, to socialize, to avoid drudgery, to be waited on, to have foods different from those served at home, and, finally, because it is convenient.[25]

Because dining (as opposed to eating) is predominantly a social event, service rituals are important. The role of the server is, therefore, ideally much more than a mechanical one. The server in a good restaurant is expected to anticipate the guests' needs and to be attentive, but not disruptive. At lunch, but to a lesser degree at dinner, guests value promptness and efficiency. At dinner, the service

[25] *NRA News*, January 1986, p. 39.

needs to be both timely (no long waits) and well timed ("when I'm ready"). The servers are expected to be friendly, as signified by a warm smile, and to be accurate.

In the expensive restaurants serving the dining market, those that fall short on significant measures of service are, therefore, likely to lose customers quickly. The backgrounds of such customers are, again, important. The older consumer who dines in a fine restaurant is well educated, has a higher-than-average income, and is accustomed to dining out and to traveling.

The importance of service was illustrated in a Gallup survey which indicated that service strongly influences whether guests will return and whether they will recommend the restaurant to others. "It's incredible how much diners will put up with if they are treated properly. Mediocre food, too much noise, cramped tables all appear to be accepted as long as people are greeted with a welcoming smile and are made to feel that the management cares about them."[26] In the dining market, sometimes food is the primary consideration—and sometimes service is.

Haute Cuisine Restaurants

Most full-service haute cuisine establishments are small, independent operations, some seating fewer than 100 guests. Despite their modest capacities, these restaurants succeed because of their excellent quality. Many are staffed by European chefs who have brought with them a craft tradition that dates back to the Middle Ages and, incidentally, to a time when wage costs were relatively lower and labor was less expensive. Many haute cuisine operations, however, provide excellent food prepared by American staffs who are often less formally trained.

Excellence is the absolute prerequisite in these operations, because the prices they must charge are high. An operator may do everything possible to make the restaurant efficient, but the guests still expect careful, personal service: food prepared to order by highly skilled chefs and served by expert waiters or waitresses. Because this service is, quite literally, manual labor, only marginal improvements in productivity are possible. For example, waiters can move only so much faster before they will reach the limits of human performance. Thus, only moderate savings are possible through improved efficiency, which makes an escalation in prices inevitable. (It is an axiom of economics that as prices rise, consumers become more discriminating.) Thus the clientele of the haute cuisine restaurant expects, demands, and is willing to pay for excellence.

These distinguished operations generally require a "critical mass" of three different kinds. First, because of the high prices they must charge, most are located in or near major population centers that have a sufficiently large proportion of people with adequate income to ensure a satisfactory sales volume. Second, haute cuisine restaurants require chefs and service personnel with highly polished skills. It is, of course, difficult to find such workers anywhere, but they are most likely to be found in big cities. Third, and most important, successful haute cuisine restaurants require a special devotion from their operating personnel, especially their owners.

---

[26] *NRA News*, March 1986, p. 14.

Table 2.4 *Nine leading dinner house chains*

CHAIN	SPECIALTY
Red Lobster	Seafood
Chi Chi's	Mexican food
Bennigans	Full menu
TGI Fridays	Full menu
El Torito	Mexican food
Stuart Anderson's	Steak
Steak and Ale	Steak and seafood
Ground Round	American food
Brown Derby	American food

Source: Nation's Restaurant News.

The hours tend to be long, and the owners, although amply compensated, often devote their lives to their work.

Casual Dinner Houses

The variety of forms of the so-called casual dinner house is suggested by *Nation's Restaurant News's* list of nine leading dinner house chains (see Table 2.4). These operations appear to be restaurants who have taken to heart the advice of William Rice, the food editor of the *Washington Post* and a restaurant consultant:

> *The single minded visions of the restaurant as temple of gastronomy is too narrow today. The restaurant is becoming an urban recreation center. Customers want crowds, noise and distraction. Cooking should be free form. Dining should be fun. Informality is the rule. Uniform is out. Menu language is casual. Creature comforts are few but the energy level is high. No longer in this country is "restaurant" a French word. Today's restaurants are being designed to* accommodate *customers.*[27]

Casual dinner houses are changing with the times as their customers age. Several are "expanding their menus, dropping prices, bolstering their marketing program and adding more staff to reduce serving time." Those who survive the changing market will be "those chains that shift their image from 'fern bars' packed with young singles bumping their heads on hanging kayaks to restaurants serving families whose major draws are convenience and extensive, low cost menus."[28] One problem with these operations is that "everyone who opens up a neighborhood

[27] *Nation's Restaurant News*, November 4, 1985, p. 14.
[28] *Nation's Restaurant News*, November 11, 1985, p. 1.

At the heart of a well executed "theme restaurant" is a menu that delivers the promise of the concept to the guest in an interesting and authentic way. (Courtesy W. R. Grace and Company.)

bar makes it look like Friday's. The casual restaurant used to be unique and that was what attracted people to them in the 70's."[29]

Theme Restaurants

The haute cuisine restaurants and casual dinner houses we have been discussing are clearly full-service operations. *Theme restaurants*, on the other hand, are almost invariably specialty restaurants serving a limited menu. Some are chain restaurants; many are independents. They rely on creating, through decor and setting, an atmosphere that will entertain. Diners who flock to these operations seek a "total experience," not just a meal, and they are apparently willing to accept a smaller menu selection to get it. *Newsweek* comments on this diner's eye view:

> *Most theme restaurants succeed by lavishing attention on the decor. The food often sounds clever on the menu—but usually the fare is unimaginative and bland, although restaurant-goers don't seem to mind. . . . "The food is not the best in the world but there are so many rooms here I guess it stops you from getting bored," said a businessman after lunching at New York's Auto Pub, which is divided into sections like the Pit Stop, Lover's Lane, and The Drive-In Movie.*[30]

[29] *Nation's Restaurant News*, November 11, 1985, p. 151.
[30] *Newsweek*, February 3, 1975, p. 58.

Theme restaurants offer an atmosphere that will entertain. Shown above are Baby Doe's Matchless Mine, a hilltop restaurant in Monterey Park, California, and Crawdaddy's Restaurant, on the Tampa Bay Waterfront in Florida. Both represent concepts operated in a numbere of locations by Specialty Restaurants Corp., which also operates the 94th Aero Squadron restaurants and other themed operations. (Photos courtesy of Specialty Restaurant Corp.)

Theme restaurants create an atmosphere that will entertain. (Photo courtesy of Auto Pub Restaurant.)

Car themes are used in many of the popular fifties-concept operations, as suggested by some of their names: Caddy's, Studebaker, Cadillac Jacks, Chevy's, Packards, and T Bird. Other fifties themers use music as a unifying idea: Juke Box Saturday Night, Hard Rock Cafe, and the Philadelphia Bandstand. Ed Debevics, which operates on the West Coast and in Chicago, is built around a fictional 1950s character of that name, whose bowling trophies are hung on the wall. Its staff are trained to maintain the fiction that Ed Debevic is a real person who has just temporarily stepped out.

Another popular motif is the rejuvenated American diner. These new diners offer lower prices than do the dinner houses, but their atmosphere is more stylish than that of family restaurants. The combination has worked to produce a sales volume of over $2 million a year per unit. Many of the new diners are small chains or independents bent on becoming chains.[31] The older, established diners operate with low profit margins. They are usually 24-hour operations that are managed mainly by family members. Diners typically offer extensive menus and scratch preparation, as well as good location, familiarity, and low prices.

Most theme restaurants try to establish charming atmospheres—old mills, early American (often authentic) history, palatial elegance reminiscent of earlier European times—something that catches the guests' interest without being out-

[31] *Nation's Restaurant News*, January 27, 1986, p. 1.

Restaurant with an ethnic specialty offer a sense of adventure along with food that is out of the ordinary. (Courtesy W. R. Grace and Company.)

landish. Nautical and railroad themes are particularly popular. A number of abandoned railroad stations have, in fact, been converted into restaurants, and one theme restaurant is actually on board a moving train. The Star Clipper operates on the Cedar Valley Railroad, taking a 56-mile round trip out of Cedar Rapids, Iowa, at 12 miles per hour. It departs at 7:30 P.M. and returns at 10 P.M., and charges $35 for the trip and dinner. The Star Clipper is booked months in advance, and the owner is reportedly establishing another, similar operation.[32]

Theme restaurants seem to be limited only by their owners' imaginations. And themes rise and fall in popularity. In the 1960s and 1970s, Polynesian was an "in" theme; currently, it is the 1950s and diners. It will be interesting to see what the future brings. One company, McFadden Ventures, has developed a new building design that places all the equipment at the back of the building and uses hollow floors and ceilings to accommodate changes in wiring or plumbing. This design allows quick concept makeovers. Indeed, one of this company's units has used four concepts in only eight years—from "Elan" to "Cowboys" to "Confetti" to "Rialto."[33]

Theme restaurants are designed for the middle-class mass market. They typically offer a few popular dishes. The significance of a limited selection was

[32] *Nation's Restaurant News*, September 30, 1985, p. 86.
[33] *Nation's Restaurant News*, November 4, 1985, p. 13.

Benihana of Tokyo offers adventure by recreating the atmosphere of a Japanese country inn. All foods are cooked at a "hibachi table" in front of the guest, providing entertainment while the meal is being prepared. (Photo courtesy of Benihana of Tokyo.)

dramatized by a study of leading U.S. restaurants, in which restaurants offering more than 20 entrees on the menu spent 29 percent of their sales dollars on payroll. Those offering between 8 and 20 entrees spent 28 percent of sales on payroll, and operations with fewer than 8 entrees reported spending only 24 percent of sales on payroll. In a business in which net profit commonly runs below 5 percent, this difference is substantial.[34]

Ethnic Restaurants

The increasingly well traveled and sophisticated consumer seeks not only a meal but also a mini-adventure, or at least "a different experience" in both the atmosphere and the more distinctive foods in ethnic restaurants. Most ethnic restaurants are independents, frequently run by people whose families come from the ethnic region of the restaurant. Chi Chi's, for instance, is a chain of Mexican dinner houses.

[34] *Hospitality*, July 1976, pp. 14–17.

Many ethnic foods offer the consumer, besides "different" foods and an exotic ambience, a health appeal—less fat and less cholesterol. And because of the lower food costs of most ethnic restaurants, they can also offer very competitive prices. Ethnic restaurants have also entered the eating market as well the dining market. For example, Mexican restaurants have been among the fastest-growing fast-food segments in recent years.

SIGNIFICANT ENTRIES IN THE EATING MARKET

The most significant of the eating market's "refueling stops" is the fast-food operation we've already considered. Close behind are the other lower-price specialty units such as family and pizza restaurants. But not all units in the eating market are specialty restaurants.

Cafeterias

In cafeterias, customers choose their food from visual inspection as well as from a menu board. Cafeteria service is also used in many budget steak houses and other operations, but the distinctive features of the cafeteria, in additon to self-service, is menu variety. Because of the space requirements of an extensive kitchen and the cafeteria line, cafeterias require a larger building than do most other food service concepts, and so they are often located in suburban areas where land costs are lower than in a city's central business district.

The price/value perception is a key selling point for cafeterias. A family of four can spend almost the same amount at a fast-food restaurant as they would at a cafeteria, but cafeterias have a much wider variety of food to choose from, and with a "home style" appeal. Most cafeterias average about $4 per customer, not much higher than fast food.

As with so many other segments, cafeterias are moving toward more "lite" selections—baked and broiled fish and chicken and less beef. Cafeterias also appeal to older consumers, and the growth in that population group (which will be discussed in more detail in Chapter 5), together with cafeterias' superior price/value perception, makes them a segment to watch during the "middle aging" of America, as this value-conscious group becomes the population's largest segment.[35]

Country Cooking

"Country" chains such as Po Folks, Cracker Barrel, and Southern Cooker have a somewhat more limited menu than do cafeterias, but they offer more service. With the average check ranging from $3.50 to $4.50, as well as generous portions of food, these operations appeal to value-conscious, price-sensitive customers.[36] Using corny jokes, a lot of "down home" spelling on the menu, and a country decor, these operations offer some of the entertainment value of the more-upscale theme restaurants.

[35] *Nation's Restaurant News*, August 12, 1985, p. F52.
[36] Rohs, *The Restaurant Industry*, p. 32.

Fuddruckers, an early leader in the gourmet hamburger segment, merchandises a sense of plenty with its self-service condiments and trimmings bar. Because the meat is ground on the premises in the butcher shop (shown in the background), customers are convinced that they are receiving fresh, all-beef burgers. (Photo courtesy of Fuddruckers, Inc.)

"Gourmet" Hamburgers

The "gourmet" hamburger restaurant offers large portions, a price range of $5 to $6, and the fast service associated with fast-food or family restaurants. Some units are entirely self-service, whereas others offer table service. These operations, unlike fast-food restaurants, do serve alcoholic beverages. Their decor is generally either more upscale, like that of dinner houses, or "trendy," using art deco to give a stylish look. Such hamburger restaurants show solid growth prospects because of their good price/value relationship as well as their competitiveness with the more expensive casual dinner houses and the less distinctive family restaurants.[37] After 1990, however, population trends may work against them, as the population group they serve begins to shrink.

Takeout and Delivery

According to the National Restaurant Association, over than 85 percent of Americans use take-out food services. Two-thirds of food service consumers buy take-out food at least three times a month, and half of them do so at least weekly.

[37] This discussion also draws in part on Rohs, *The Restaurant Industry.*

In a busy society, convenience has become an important buying motive. The principal customers are singles; families with children, particularly those with working mothers; and people 18 to 34 years old.[38]

Fast-food operators provide 58 percent of take-out sales, and family restaurants provide 7 percent, according to a Gallup survey.[39] Throughout the 1980s, take-out food service has grown substantially faster than has the food industry as a whole; indeed, CREST reports that 39.5 percent of all restaurant traffic is for take-out food.[40] Takeout serves the at-home and the on-the-go markets. Forty-six percent of take-out food is consumed at home, and of the rest, 21 percent is consumed in the car and 15 percent at work, with 18 percent eaten in "other" places.[41]

Surprisingly, haute cuisine is a growth area for takeout as well. New York City's Quilted Giraffe, for instance, which sports a $115 average luncheon check, offers take-out service, with an average take-out sale of $15. In fact, its take-out volume is so good that a commissary is planned to supply three different Quilted Giraffe take-out units in New York. In Boston, the Creative Gourmet offers cold items to go for lunch, as does Mr. B's in New Orleans.[42] Takeout offers several advantages to operators of all kinds. Most obviously, it offers add-on sales in a new service format, but it also attracts customers who, if satisfied, are likely to return for a sit-down meal, and it generally enhances the restaurant's image. Because take-out food increases the restaurant's volume, it also reduces its food and payroll costs.[43]

Delivery   The delivery of prepared food is in its infancy with pizza, the only food product that is commonly delivered to the home. The delivery of food products, including pizza, is also a business different from that of the regular restaurants from which most deliveries are made. In fact, Pizza Hut is setting up independent units devoted to delivery, so as to avoid overcrowding its parking lots which are essential to its on-premise business. Domino's, the largest pizza deliverer, relies almost exclusively on delivery and generally does not even offer seating in its stores. The cost structure for the delivery business includes both the labor for the delivery and the transportation costs. These added costs lower margins and support the notion that delivery is a different business.

The delivery of fast food is still in the experimental stage. Two students at Indiana University are among the field's pioneers. Based on an in-depth study of student needs, which indicated a demand for the delivery of Mexican food,

---

[38] *NRA News*, December 1985, p. 14.

[39] *Nation's Restaurant News*, March 10, 1986, p. 143.

[40] Rohs, *The Restaurant Industry*, p. 30.

[41] George D. Rice, "Retargeting Consumers—Segmentation on Attitudes and Behavior," *Proceedings of the 11th Annual Chain Operators Exchange* (Chicago, International Foodservice Manufacturers Association, 1984), p. 7.

[42] *Nation's Restaurant News*, November 11, 1986, p. 10.

[43] *Nation's Restaurant News*, November 11, 1986, p. 10.

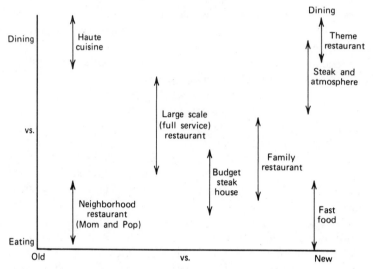

Figure 2.2   *The range of restaurants compared according to relative novelty and role in the eating or dining markets.*

hamburgers, pizza, and submarine sandwiches, they began a delivery service which eventually served Taco Bell and McDonald's, increasing those companies' unit volumes by 20 percent.[44]

Home delivery is also growing in the gourmet market. One Chicago company offers "mobile maitre d's who give customers verbal and written heating instructions" for the gourmet foods they deliver. Another Chicago operator advertises entrees such as bass poached in white wine and pears ($10.95) or chicken vesuvio ($8.95).[45] In addition to delivering to the home, many fast-food services are constructing mobile units that will take the food where the business is—to college compuses, seasonal resorts, construction sites, and military bases.[46] Other companies are experimenting with delivery units, some of them equipped for cooking and others just for holding hot food.

Figure 2.2 contrasts the older forms of restaurant operations with the newer ones (from left to right). It also shows the relative position of restaurant types with regard to the eating and the dining markets. Remember, though, that all public

[44] *Wall Street Journal,* December 7, 1984, p. 27.

[45] *Nation's Restaurant News,* November 4, 1985, p. 10.

[46] *Nation's Restaurant News,* September 23, 1985, p. 13.

Morrison's Cafeterias aim to expand their share of the eating market with "Home Cooking to Go" take-out centers, which feature both a pickup counter and a drive-through. (Photo courtesy of Morrison Incorporated.)

dining is partly a social activity and that even the most formal, highly social dinner fulfills the biological function of feeding people.

Restaurants As a Part of a Larger Business

Thus far, this chapter has examined freestanding restaurants—separate and distinct operations. A substantial part of the food service industry is, however, made up of operations that are the service arms of larger organizations. These operations are often hard to classify, because the broader goals of the large organization may impinge on the food service operation. Thus, the restaurants in hotels, as we will learn in Chapter 6, often open earlier and close later than their volume of food service sales would justify. They do this as a convenience to hotel guests and as a means of inducing people to choose this particular place for a night's stay. Similarly, Chapter 5, which discusses institutional food service, will demonstrate the importance of the special diet to health-care food service, quite apart from its cost effectiveness. In this chapter, however, we will briefly examine restaurants in retailing establishments such as department stores, drugstores, truck stops, theaters, sports complexes, and convention centers. It is interesting to see how trends in these eating establishments match those in the restaurant business elsewhere.

RESTAURANTS IN RETAILING

Restaurants in department stores and drugstores were originally built as store services: A shopper who had to leave the store for lunch might resume shopping in some other store. The restaurants, therefore, helped keep the shoppers in the store and often helped attract them there in the first place. Increasingly, in-store restaurants are becoming in themselves worthwhile businesses that often generate higher profit margins than do the store's other retail sales. In fact, if properly merchandised, the stores can *bring* shoppers into the store, not just *keep* them in.

Demonstrating that in-store restaurants have become big business, Walgreen's food service operations recently topped $125 million. And the giant Federated Department Store chain, according to *Nation's Restaurant News*, now rates its food service division as one of its five major business areas, and that division operates some 300 restaurants. A number of retailers have also opened restaurants outside their stores. Walgreen's operates a chain of freestanding restaurants called Wags; Federated has its own fast-food chain; and Carson Pirie Scott (a Chicago department store with a large food service operation) operates the restaurants at O'Hare Airport.

The economics of restaurant operations that gave rise to the specialty restaurant are now at work in retailing. Retailer-housed restaurants are being pressed to adopt specialty restaurant (especially fast food) service patterns to hold costs in line and to meet the guests' demand for speed.

Restaurant operations in truck stops generally feature a family restaurant or coffee shop style of operation that offers travelers a break in their journey—a chance to eat and to sit for a few minutes in a comfortable atmosphere. In addition, these operations usually provide special sections for truckers who need superquick service.

The truck stop restaurant is almost always part of a larger service package, which includes gas and diesel fuel, truck repair facilities, gift and sundry shops, and often a motel. Originally intended as an ancillary service, truck stop restaurants now do about a tenth of the dollar volume of all truck stop business.

Although we will discuss vending in more detail later, we note here the growing role of vending in the restaurant picture. In office buildings, factories, and other work settings, vending machines offer menus sometimes as extensive as those of a family restaurant. In some areas, in fact, they actually are replacing restaurant facilities. In a vending operation, one or two on-site employees together with workers at a remote commissary can replace an entire crew of food service employees.

Food service in retail stores has increasingly adopted a fast-food format. (Photo courtesy of Walgreen's Corp.)

Operating Ratios

Elsewhere in your hospitality curriculum you will undoubtedly study the subject of control. As a part of your introduction to the hospitality field, this section will therefore only briefly define some key food service control terms.

The truck stop restaurant is generally a part of a larger roadside service center.
(Photo courtesy of Truck Stops of America.)

Today's truck stop restaurant has a coffee shop style of operation, with a cheerful and comfortable interior. (Photo courtesy of Truck Stops of America.)

COST OF SALES

The *cost of sales* refers to the cost of a product *used* by the guest in the process of operations. The principal product costs include

> **Food costs**   The cost of food prepared for and consumed by guests.)
>
> **Beverage or bar costs**   The cost of alcoholic beverages and other ingredients, such as juices, carbonated water, or fruit, used to make drinks for guests.

Note that these (and all other) costs are customarily stated as a percentage of sales. For example, if the food cost is $25,000 and the food sales are $75,000, then the food cost percent will be $25,000 ÷ $75,000, or 33.3 percent. Although dollar costs are essential to the accounting system, the percentage of the cost (that is, its size relative to sales level) is more significant to managers, because the percentages for one month (or for some other period) can readily be compared with those of the other months, with a budget, and with industry averages.

CONTROLLABLE EXPENSES

Controllable expenses are costs that may be expected to vary to some degree and over which operating management can exercise some direct control.

Payroll Costs   Payroll costs are the wages and salaries paid to employees.

Employee Benefits   Employee benefits include social security taxes; such social insurance as workers' compensation, pension payments, and hospitalization; and other benefit expenses such as those for education and sports activities.

Direct Operating Expenses   Direct operating expenses usually vary, reflecting the volume of sales. The principal direct operating expenses include those for uniforms, laundry, linen, china, glass and silver, guest and cleaning supplies, and menus.

Other Operating Expenses   Most other operating expenses are fixed (some basic minimum amount of money essential to staying in business). But they can and sometimes do vary. One group, sometimes called *mixed costs*, includes a base minimum charge or an irreducible minimum cost, to which are then added costs according to usage, such as the costs for utilities, administration, and repairs and maintenance. Other costs in this group result from policy decisions by management regarding such activities as advertising and sales promotion, music, and entertainment. They need not vary with sales volume, but they do vary with the management's decisions.

CAPITAL COSTS

Capital costs are mainly determined when the operation is established. They include rent, insurance, depreciation interest, and taxes.

By categorizing cost information in this way, we focus attention on the operation's key variables. The cost percentages also reflect the efficiency of various segments of an operation. Food costs reflect management pricing and the kitchen crew's efficiency. Labor costs reflect efficiency in employee scheduling and the adequacy of sales volume in proportion to the operation's needs. They can be improved by either reducing employee hours or increasing sales.

This discussion brings us to yet another pair of terms: *covers* and *check averages*. The number of covers refers to the number of guests. (*Guest count* is the alternative term.) The *check average* is what it sounds like—the total sales for a period divided by the number of parties (that is, the number of checks). Because parties (a group of guests seated together) vary in size, the check average is usually quoted as the average sale per guest. This figure is found by dividing the total dollar sales by the number of guests served during the period and is sometimes referred to as the *average cover*.

Clearly, there are two ways to increase total sales: to increase the number of covers served by bringing in more guests or to increase the check averages by selling more to the guests who do come. In comparing check averages, it is important to note whether the figure represents food only or both food and beverages. The best way to collect and report these data is to show separately a food-only and a beverage check average and then to lump the two in a combined check average.

SALES

Food	$ 534,000	74.6%
Beverage	182,000	25.4
Total sales	$ 716,000	100.0%

COST OF SALES

Food	$ 230,700	43.2%
Beverage	52,000	28.6
Total cost of sales	$ 282,700	39.5%

CONTROLLABLE EXPENSES

Payroll	$ 185,400	25.9%
Employee benefits	20,800	2.9
Direct operating expenses	38,700	5.4
Music and entertainment	4,300	.6
Advertising and promotion	11,400	1.6
Utilities	16,500	2.3
Administrative and general	28,700	4.0
Repairs and maintenance	10,000	1.4
Total controllable expenses	$ 315,800	44.1%
INCOME BEFORE CAPITAL COSTS	$ 117,500	16.4%

CAPITA COSTS

Rent, property taxes, and insurance	$ 42,900	6.0%
Interest and depreciation	40,000	5.6
Total capital costs	$ 82,900	11.6%
NET PROFIT BEFORE INCOME TAXES	$ 34,600	4.8%

Number of covers served	74,918
Food check average	$ 7.128
Beverage check average	$ 2.429
Total check average	$ 9.557

Figure 2.3   *Statement of income and expenses, Suburban Restaurant (year ending December 31, 19XX).*

Figure 2.3 shows an example of a restaurant statement of income and expenses (also called an operating statement or a profit-and-loss statement). This statement shows the relationship of the costs we just discussed and also how the check averages are computed.

As a final way to compare and contrast differing restaurants, Table 2.5 presents selected *average operating ratios* of the typical operations of the kinds of restaurants we have been describing in this chapter. The similarities and distinctions among the types are not accidental but reflect some major differences in profit potential. The family restaurants and fast-food chains have a somewhat lower *prime cost* (products and labor cost), and that limited advantage passes right down to pretax profit. Although food costs are higher for suburban restaurants than for the

Table 2.5   *Comparison of U.S. restaurant operating statistics, 1980*[a]

	HAMBURGER CHAIN	FAMILY RESTAURANTS	SUBURBAN TABLE SERVICE RESTAURANTS
Food cost	35.5	35.1	41.0
Beverage cost[b]			
Disposable cost	4.1	3.1	29.0
Product cost[c]	39.6	38.2	39.0
Payroll and related[d]	26.4	29.5	30.4
Prime cost[e]	66.0	67.7	69.4
Other operating costs	15.6	16.1	18.0
Occupancy and capital costs	12.5	12.0	10.0
Pretax profit	5.9	4.2	4.4

[a] Data reflect estimates based on *Nation's Restaurant News*, August 15, 1981; and *Restaurant Industry Operations Report '81*, prepared by the National Restaurant Association and Laventhol and Horwath.

[b] Beverage cost as a percentage of beverage sales.

[c] Total food and beverage cost as a percentage of total food and beverage sales.

[d] Includes employee benefits.

[e] Total of product cost and labor cost.

other two groups, their overall *product costs* are roughly comparable, because of the lower percentage product cost for liquor. On the other hand, the extremely high food cost for budget steak operations has forced those operations to experiment with more diversified menus.

Payroll costs are, not surprisingly, highest in the most labor intensive operations—the family restaurant and the suburban restaurant—both of which offer table service. On the other hand, the higher disposable costs for the two quick-service operations has, in a way, "purchased" lower wage costs by eliminating labor. Disposables also have the effect of reducing the space required for dishwashing and thus reducing investment and the capital cost of depreciation.

Summary

We began our discussion of the restaurant business by differentiating the various types of restaurants. First are the full-service restaurants, the full service referring to the style of service, the menu, and the style of preparation. Such restaurants run from haute cuisine restaurants, at the top end, to neighborhood or mom-and-pop restaurants, at the bottom end. Second are specialty restaurants, ranging from fast-food operations to family restaurants to budget steak houses to pizza restaurants. We also described how a large fast-food chain introduces a new menu item, as compared with how an independent restaurant does this.

We then distinguished the dining market from the eating market. The dining market serves mainly our social needs, and the eating market serves mainly our biological needs, although of course, the two do overlap.

Next we talked about restaurants as part of a larger business, such as restaurants in department stores, drugstores, and truck stops that are meant both to attract customers and to keep them.

Last, we touched on the subject of restaurants' operating ratios, or their income versus their expenses. These expenses are cost of sales (food and beverage costs), controllable expenses (payroll costs, employee benefits, direct operating expenses, and other operating expenses), and, finally, capital or fixed costs.

Issues Facing Food Service

———————— THIS CHAPTER IS ABOUT ————————

Who makes up the restaurant business, both operators and consumers. The first part of the chapter looks at how restaurants are organized as chains, independents, or franchisees. The characteristics of these key players are analyzed in depth. Our focus then shifts to the industry's consumers, and we determine which age groups, sizes of families, and people at particular income levels make the best consumers. We will examine consumers' anxieties about health and nutrition and the consumer movement's concern about issues such as junk food, nutritional labeling, truth in menu, and alcohol. Finally, we will consider the issue of convenience, which is related to the life-styles of individual consumers, and we will review current industry responses to this concern.

Courtesy of W. R. Grace.

Organizational Form: Chain, Independent, or Franchise?

Even though we sometimes hear that the day of the independent is past and the chains will soon gobble up the entire food service market, nothing could be further from the truth. Chains do have enormous advantages in some markets, but in others they have disadvantages. It is useful, therefore, to examine the competitive advantages of both the independents and the chains and franchisees. In our discussion, we will treat franchised restaurants much like chains. If there are important differences, we will point them out.

THE CHAIN SPECIALTY RESTAURANTS

Chains have six strengths: (1) brand recognition or preference, (2) site selection expertise, (3) access to capital, (4) purchasing economies, (5) centrally administered control and information systems, and (6) personnel program development. All of these strengths represent *economies of scale:* the savings come, in one way or another, from the spreading of a centralized activity over a large number of units so that each absorbs only a small portion of the cost but all have the benefit of specialized expertise or buying power when they need it.

Brand Recognition

More young children in America recognize Santa Claus than any other public figure. Ronald McDonald comes second! Because McDonald's and its franchisees spend well over a half-billion dollars (in 1985, $686 million) on their advertising budgets, it's no wonder more children recognize Ronald than, say, Mickey Mouse, Donald Duck, or the Easter Bunny. As one writer put it, "McDonald's has taken the hamburger to the American public and created a generic item—the Big Mac. The company has done for the hamburger what Coke did for cola, Avon for cosmetics, and Kodak for film." The reasons for this success are threefold: simplicity of message, enormous spending, and the additive effect.

The *message* of modern advertising is affected by the form in which it is offered: 10-, 30-, or 60-second television commercials, for instance. Even in the printed media, the message must be kept simple, because an advertisement in a newspaper or magazine has to compete with other ads and news or feature stories for the consumer's casual attention. The message of the specialty restaurant resembles its menu: It boils down to a simple statement or a catch phrase. In fact, marketing people generally try to design a "tag line" that summarizes the benefits they want an advertising campaign to tell the consumer. Not long ago, Wendy's Restaurants used the slogan, "Ain't no reason to go anyplace else." Although this slogan set off a letter-writing campaign complaining about the grammar, Wendy's officials judged it effective in "breaking through the clutter." Classic tag lines of the past are still memorable:

One of the big advantages of a major franchise is a well-known brand name. (Photo courtesy of McDonald's Corp.)

"We do it all for you."

"You deserve a break today."

"Finger lickin' good."

Moreover, the *level of spending* for chain specialty restaurant advertising is higher. Chains spend more on advertising because their efficient, routinized operating procedures yield profits generous enough to make such expensive advertising feasible.

The *additive effect* of belonging to a chain or franchise group permits units to pool the budgets of many stores. Thus, the total advertising budget available enables them to use the expensive medium of television—and not just in a local market but in regional and national markets as well.

A site convenient to local auto traffic and with adequate parking is essential to success in fast foods. (Photo courtesy of McDonald's Corp.)

Of course, all this advertising will be effective only if the consumers get exactly what they expect. Therefore, some of the chains' most effective controls are aimed at ensuring the consistency of quality and service. The customer does know exactly what to expect in each McDonald's, and in an increasingly mobile society, that is important. For people on the go as tourists, shoppers, or businesspersons, what is more natural than to stop at a familiar sign? If that experience is pleasant, it will reinforce the desire to return to that sign in the local market or wherever else it appears.

Site Selection Expertise

The success of most specialty restaurants is also enhanced by a location near the heart of major traffic patterns. The technique for analyzing location potential requires a special kind of knowledge, and the chains alone can afford real estate departments that possess that expertise.

Access to Capital

Most bankers and other money lenders have traditionally treated restaurants as risky businesses. So an independent operator who wants to open a restaurant (or even remodel or expand an existing operation) may find it difficult to borrow the needed capital. But the bankers' willingness to lend increases with the size of the company: if one unit should falter, the banker knows that the franchise will want to protect its credit record. To do so, it can divert funds from successful operations to "carry" one in trouble until the problems can be worked out. Thus, the banks not only make capital available to units of larger companies, but they also lower the interest rates on these loans, sometimes substantially.

Purchasing Economies

Chains can centralize their purchasing either by buying centrally in their own commissary or by negotiating centrally with suppliers who then deliver the products, made according to rigid specifications, from their own warehouses and processing plants. Chains obviously purchase in great quantity, and they can use this bargaining leverage to negotiate the best possible prices and terms. Chains can also afford their own research and development departments for testing products and new equipment.

Control and Information Systems

Economies of scale is the important concept here. Chains can spend large sums on developing accounting procedures and procedures for collecting market information. They can devise costly computer programs and purchase or lease expensive computer equipment, again spreading the cost over a large number of operations. Moreover, in most chains, an expert staff dispatched from central headquarters reviews the units' efficiency. Unit managers may not always enjoy these inspections, but they make them stay on their toes.

Personnel Program Development

Some restaurant chains have established sophisticated training programs for hourly employees, using audiovisual techniques such as films, tapes, and slide shows to demonstrate the proper ways of performing food service operations. These standardized procedures in turn lower the cost of training and improve its effectiveness. This economy is especially important in semiskilled and unskilled jobs, which traditionally experience high turnover rates and, therefore, waste considerable training time.

Performance of the Top 100 Restaurant Companies

The advantages of the chains have helped the largest of them to increase their share of the food service market. The 100 largest restaurant companies, which operate 179 separate chains, were tracked by Technomic Consultants in an annual study, from which the data in this section are taken.[1] These companies operated 70,984 units in the United States and had total sales of $47,588 billion. As Figure 3.1 shows, the 100 largest companies' share of the food service dollar sales

---

[1] Technomic Consultants, *Dynamics of the Chain Restaurant Market 1985* (Chicago: International Foodservice Manufacturers Association, 1985).

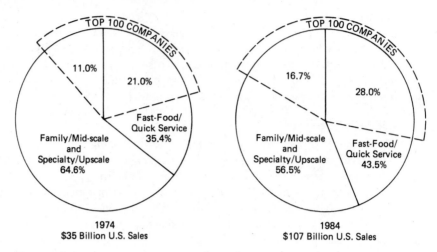

Figure 3.1   *Top 100 companies' share of sales volume of U.S. separate eating places by type of operation.* (International Foodservice Manufacturing Association.)

increased by nearly 50 percent in the past decade, from a 31 percent share in 1974 to nearly a 45 percent share in 1984. The 100 largest companies also owned 30 percent of all the units in operation. The larger share of the dollar sales, compared with the proportion of units in operation, reflects these chains' substantially higher-than-average unit sales.

Table 3.1 shows the growth in sales, adjusted for inflation, for the top 100 restaurant companies and for all other U.S. restaurants. From 1974 to 1979, the growth rate for the smaller chains and the independents was at least within hailing distance of that of the larger chains. During the recession from 1970 to 1983, however, the top 100's staying power was clear, as shown in the increase in sales of 36.3 percent, whereas sales for all other restaurants declined by nearly 2 percent. From 1983 to 1984, the large chains grew nearly five times as fast as did the smaller chains and independents. In the same period, the smaller companies and the independents grew by only 27 percent, but the top 100 more than doubled.

OPERATING ADVANTAGES OF THE INDEPENDENT

Although chains undeniably have advantages in the competitive battle for the consumer's dollar, the independents also enjoy advantages that ensure them a continuing place in the market, a different place from that of the chains, perhaps, but a significant place nevertheless.

We can follow the same method we used for the chain specialty restaurants to analyze the strengths of the independents. Just as the advantages of the large organization relate to economies of scale, the independent's operating advantages

Table 3.1   *Growth in sales: Top 100 companies and smaller chains and independents*

	GROWTH RATE, PERCENT	
PERIOD	TOP 100 COMPANIES	SMALLER CHAINS AND INDEPENDENTS
1974–1979	44.0	26.6
1979–1983	36.3	– 1.9
1983–1984	10.8	2.4
1974–1984	117.8	27.2

Source: Data from Technomic Consultants, *Dynamics of the Chain Restaurant Market, 1985* (Chicago: International Foodservice Manufacturers Association, 1985); *Statistical Abstract of the United States,* 198 (Washington, D.C.: U.S. Government Printing Office, 1985).

share their attributes as well. The independent's flexibility, the motivation of its owner, and the owner's closeness to the operation all affect its success.

Although the following analysis does not deal directly with the issue, we should note that economies of scale also are important to the independent restaurant. The small operation—the mom-and-pop restaurant—finds itself increasingly pressed by rising costs. We cannot specify a minimum volume requirement for success, but the *Restaurant Industry Operating Report '85* showed that urban and suburban restaurants had median sales of about $4,445 per seat. Rural restaurants, on the other hand, had median sales of only $2,365, suggesting that they have a more cyclical sales pattern, with off-day and off-season operations at a very low level of volume. Simpler operations can undoubtedly make a profit with substantially lower sales, but the problem of fixing the minimum economic size is a real one.

Brand Recognition

Ronald McDonald may be a popular figure, but he is not a real person. The successful restaurant proprietor, however, is real. In fact, successful restauranteurs often become well known, become involved in community affairs, and establish strong ties of friendship with many of their customers. This local celebrity can be especially effective "standing on the door," greeting guests by name as they arrive, moving through the dining room, recognizing friends or acquaintances, dealing graciously with complaints, and expressing gratitude for praise. "Thanks and come back again" has an especially pleasant ring when it comes from the boss—the owner whose status in the town isn't subject to corporate whim or sudden transfer.

Although the chain may have advantages among transients, the operator *of a high-quality operation* enjoys an almost-unique advantage in the local market. Moreover, word-of-mouth advertising may spread his or her reputation to an even larger area. The key to recognition for the independent is more than just personality; it is, first and foremost, quality. To build a reputation, the operation must be *different* from others and noticeably *better* than the run of the mill restaurant. This is hard to achieve with a "hamburger and chicken" menu. Hamburgers and chicken can be good, but not so distinctively *better* as to make a difference.

Site Selection

The chain operation continually faces the problem of selecting the right site as it seeks new locations for expansion. The established operator, however, gives location less attention. True, over the long term, an independent operator must adjust to changing urban patterns and real estate values, perhaps by moving. Not long ago, the finest independent restaurants were located in the city's center, whereas fast-food operations chose the suburbs. But now in the large cities and even in some medium-sized cities, the downtown area has begun to decay, and reports of crime and violence make these areas unattractive, particularly for the evening meal. When a center city location has not decayed, rising land values sometimes escalate rentals to the point that full-service restaurants often can no longer afford them. In the past few years, fast food restaurants—with their high seating density and higher operating margin on a high volume—have moved into the big-city downtown market, whereas the independent has joined the fast-food operator out in the suburbs, near the new shopping centers and office complexes and adjacent to the affluent residential areas. When contemplating such a move, a local operator can supplement his or her own knowledge of the area by hiring a consulting firm to conduct a location study. It's an expensive service but valuable if it is needed.

Access to Capital

In most cases, the chain will have the most ready access to capital. Nevertheless, the successful operator can often establish contacts with local financial institutions and investors.

Purchasing Economies

Once again, the chain enjoys substantial advantages in its purchasing economies. But the independent's problem may differ somewhat from the chain's. Because of the importance of quality in the independent operation, the price advantages in centralized purchasing may not be as important as is an ability to find top-quality products consistently. Thus, long-standing personal friendships with local purveyors can be an advantage for the independent.

Control and Information Systems

Because of its simple menu, the chain specialty restaurant can take advantage of the sort of information on marketing and sales patterns produced by computerized routines. This practice is, in fact, essential to companies operating many units in a national market. But the complex menu of the single, independent, full-service restaurant lends itself to the operator's subjective interpretations, impressions, and "hunches" about the changing preferences of the guests. Moreover, the independent operator can easily analyze some simple data (such as menu popularity counts) without paying for programming or computer time.

Improved control systems have recently become available to the independent with the advent of electronic cash registers (ECR) and point-of-sales (POS) register systems controlled by a minicomputer. A fairly wide variety of hardware and programming options has enabled the independent to obtain daily reports detailing sales as well as payroll and product costs.[2]

Cost-control procedures may be more stringent in the chain operation, but if an owner keeps an eye on everything from preparation to portion sizes to the garbage can (the amount of food left on a plate is often a good clue to the overportioning), very effective cost control can be achieved even when an ECR/POS system to fit the operator's needs is not available or when the cost of such a system seems prohibitive. By using the uniform system of accounts and professional advice available from restaurant accounting specialists, independents can readily develop control systems adequate to their needs.

This description of the independent operator suggests what has become a food service axiom: Anyone who cannot operate successfully without the corporate brass looking over his or her shoulder will probably be out of business as an independent in less than a year.

Personnel

The independent proprietor can and usually does develop close personal ties with the employees, a practice that can help reduce turnover. But even though "old hand" employees can act as trainers, the cost of training new workers tends to be higher for the independent, because of the complex operation and because he or she lacks the economies of a centralized training program.

Although advancement incentives are not as abundant in independent operations as in the chains, many successful independents hire young people, train them over a period of several years to become effective supervisors, and then help them move on to a larger operation. Often, too, the independent finds employees whose life goals are satisfied by their positions as chef, host or hostess, or head bartender. These employees often receive bonus plans similar to those offered by the chains.

The Independent's Extra: Flexibility

One strength that the independent boasts is the flexibility inherent in having only one boss or a small partnership. Fast decision making permits the independent to adapt to changing market conditions. And because there is no need to maintain a

[2] For a fuller discussion of the subject, see Thomas F. and Jo Marie Powers, *Food Service Operations: Planning and Control* (New York: Wiley, 1983), especially chap. 3.

Fast-food restaurants do offer fast service, but increasingly they are also providing a relaxing, pleasant place to eat. (Photo courtesy of McDonald's Corp.)

standard chain image, an independent is free to develop menus that take advantage of local tastes. Finally, there are many "one of a kind" niches in the marketplace, special situations that don't repeat themselves often enough to make them interesting to chains. Yet these situations may be ideally suited to the strengths of independents. Can you see a chain mass-marketing delicate meals featuring freshly gathered wild mushrooms in the way that a fancy little independent operation in Reading, Pennsylvania, does?

Between Independent and Chain

Between the independent and the chain lie at least two other possibilities. First, some independent operations are so successful that they open additional units, but without becoming so large as to lose the "hands-on" management of the owner-operator. *Nation's Restaurant News* refers to these as *independent group operators.*

FRANCHISES

Franchisees operate under the name and with the concept of a franchising organization but own their own businesses and have greater freedom of action than do managers of chain-owned units. The franchisees' proportion of restaurant sales has doubled since 1974 and currently accounts for over 40 percent of all restaurant sales.

Table 3.2 *Eating place^a size, 1977 and 1982*

	Percentage of Units		Percentage of Sales	
	1977	1982	1977	1982
Under $500,000	77.4%	62.5%	40.7%	25.8%
$1,000,000–$999,999	5.5	9.1	14.8	14.5
$5,000,000–$4,999,999	5.1	9.4	16.4	22.4
$10,000,000–$49,999,999	2.4	4.2	5.8	8.0
$50,000,000 and over	8.2	12.5	18.7	24.4

Source: Bureau of the Census, National Restaurant Association.

^a Includes restaurants, lunchrooms, and fast food.

RESTAURANT SIZE

Independents own half of all restaurants and will certainly continue to occupy a large share of the market. Furthermore, the majority of independent restaurants are operated by two or more members of the same family, which gives them some advantages in flexibility of scheduling and costs.[3] Nonetheless, the smaller units' sales have declined, as shown in Table 3.2. (Because the 1982 dollar was worth only about 65 cents in 1977 dollars, the table is somewhat distorted by inflation.) Units with sales of less than half a million dollars accounted for only a quarter of the market, down from 40 percent in 1977. For the same period, units with over a million dollars in sales (only 28.4 percent of all units) accounted for three-quarters of the market.

The Consumers

Consumers' needs and preferences shift quickly in our society. Indeed, they—and these changes—are as important to food service companies as competition from other companies is. Consequently, before a company can decide on its position and how it must change, it must determine the needs of its consumers. In this section we will look at the forces shaping consumer demand today, at just who the consumers are, and then at what their concerns are.

CONSUMER PROFILES

Table 3.3 shows us spending patterns by age group: The *proportion* of food dollars spent by younger consumers is higher than average, but the *absolute dollar amount*

[3] *NRA News,* August 1985, p. 28.

Table 3.3 *Weekly away-from-home expenditures by age group, 1982–1983*

	AMOUNT	PROPORTION
Under 25	$15.34	47.4%
25–34	21.03	38.8
35–44	25.26	35.4
45–54	25.70	34.5
55–64	20.31	34.1
65 and over	10.37	27.4
All Households	$19.60	35.6%

Source: U.S. Bureau of Labor Statistics; National Restaurant Association.

spent rises with age up to the age of 55. This says that younger consumers are very good customers, indeed, that although their number will be declining, they will remain an active and significant group in terms of consumer demand. Older consumers, however, are *even better* customers in terms of total dollars spent.

Table 3.4 views consumer behavior from a different perspective, that of income. It indicates that as incomes rise, the amount of money spent on food away from home increases in both absolute amount and proportion. That is certainly encouraging news in the light of current income trends. Unfortunately, compiling and publishing government statistics requires a lot of time, and so the most recent figures available are for 1983. The trends represented in these figures, however, have been relatively stable over the past 10 years. A U.S. Department of Commerce Bureau of Economic Analysis study predicts that in 1990, income per capita will rise by 17.6 percent in "real," inflation-adjusted dollars over that in 1983, an annual increase of 2.3 percent. And by the year 2000, another 14 percent increase

Table 3.4 *Weekly away-from-home food expenditures by household, by income level, 1982–1983*

HOUSEHOLD INCOME	AMOUNT	PROPORTION
Less than $5,000	$ 8.92	34.9%
$ 5,000—$9,999	9.26	26.1
$10,000–14,999	13.50	29.1
$15,000–19,999	17.73	33.5
$20,000–29,999	23.17	35.3
$30,000–39,999	28.56	38.0
$40,000–and over	40.65	42.7

Source: Bureau of Labor Statistics; National Restaurant Association.

Table 3.5 *Weekly away-from-home food expenditures by household size, 1982–1983*

HOUSEHOLD SIZE	HOUSEHOLD EXPENDITURES	PER-PERSON EXPENDITURES	PROPORTION
One	$14.14	$14.14	50.3%
Two	20.20	10.10	37.6
Three	19.53	6.51	31.4
Four	27.31	6.83	33.4
Five	24.58	4.92	28.0
Six or more	21.14	3.25[a]	22.8

Source: Bureau of Labor Statistics; National Restaurant Association.

[a] Estimate assuming average household of 6.5 persons in this category.

is expected.[4] The 1983 per-capita income was approximately $13,900. Thus, according to these projections, by 1990 this will have risen to roughly $16,400 and by 2000 to $18,800 (in inflation-adjusted, 1983 dollars).

Table 3.5 shows the impact of family size on eating out. Singles—a group that has been growing in recent years—are clearly excellent customers, and so it is hardly surprising that the industry has spent so much effort wooing them. Two-person households are nearly as good customers. On the other hand, families with five and six members spend less than average, both in total dollars and as a proportion of their income.

Families in which both spouses work are prime restaurant customers, for two reasons. First, they have a higher household income. Second, and just as important, they have a greater need to eat out because they have less time to prepare meals at home. Female-headed households, however, are generally not as good customers because of their significantly lower income, but when, as in most cases, the single parent is employed, they have the same or even greater time pressures as those of two-income families.

CONSUMER CONCERNS

The baby-boom generation is generally affluent, well educated, and discriminating and wants an active, pleasurable, and *long* life. Not surprisingly, therefore, they are concerned about their health, nutrition, and fitness. Consumerists and government officials have probably also heightened consumer interest in several areas, including truth in dining, sanitation, food ingredients, and labeling. Because of the time pressures of our fast-paced life-style, convenience is a prime consumer concern as well. We will next examine each of these consumer interests and concerns.

[4] *NRA News,* September 1985, pp. 36–37.

Heightened consumer concerns about nutrition and fried food are giving impetus to operations like El Pollo Loco (in Spanish, "the crazy chicken") that broil rather than fry their chicken. (Photo courtesy of El Pollo Loco.)

Health

Although nutrition and diet are very much on the consumer's mind, they are a part of a larger concern regarding overall health and fitness. Drive down a residential street in the early morning or late afternoon and count the joggers, if you doubt it. This interest in health, in turn, has affected restaurants beyond their menus. For example, in 1984, over 40 percent of consumers polled for a *Restaurants & Institutions* study of consumer preferences complained about smoking in restaurants, and the study suggested that smoking sections are likely to become a standard design feature. The biggest impact of health concerns for us, however, is on menus.

Nutrition

Statistics cited by the *Wall Street Journal* suggest that everyone is at least conscious of diet, and so the proportion of nondieters who use diet products is surprisingly high: 83 percent of those who drink light beer are nondieters; 65 percent for light margarine; 61 percent for diet soft drinks; and 59 percent for sugar substitutes.[5] Clearly, "weight consciousness" is more prevalent than dieting. Restrictive dieters, in fact, account for only 20 percent of consumers. Research in 1984[6] and 1985[7] shows a fairly stable set of consumer preferences with regard to food. How these consumer attitudes are categorized into market segments is shown in Table 3.6.

"Health food" leads the list in popularity for those who eat out, according to a two-year study by CREST. (CREST is the acronym for Consumer Reports in Eating Out Share Trends, a series of market research studies based on diaries that consumers keep for the researchers.) In fact, 4 out of 10 consumers have changed their eating habits because of nutrition concerns, thereby reducing their intake of sugar, fats, cholesterol, and caffeine and consequently choosing more frequently fruits, juices, and salads. Table 3.7 shows the 10 menu items that were selected most often from 1982 to 1984.[8]

In addition to a concern with fats, consumers have become interested in the fiber content of various foods, as fiber has been shown to reduce cholesterol levels and the incidence of heart disease.[9] It is also thought to lower the risk of cancer of the bowel and colon. Fiber includes all those components of foods that are not broken down in the digestive tract and absorbed into the bloodstream. The desirable levels of fiber intake—25 to 50 grams per day—is as much as two and a half times most people's current levels of consumption. Common servings of fruits, vegetables, and whole grain breads and cereals contain about 2 to 4 grams of dietary fiber.

Dietary Schizophrenia

Despite their avowed concerns, however, consumers are not necessarily consistent in their responses to health, fitness, and nutrition consciousness. For instance, Steve's Ice Cream, specializing in ultrarich, high-butterfat ice cream, was asked to put an outlet in a major fitness center! When it expressed surprise, it was told that "people want to reward themselves for all that work."[10] And when companies developed low-salt soups to respond to people's widely expressed concerns about sodium in their diet, they were surprised when the product didn't sell well.

[5] *Wall Street Journal,* December 11, 1985, p. 3.

[6] George D. Rice, "Retargeting Consumers—Segmentation on Attitudes and Behavior," *Proceedings of the 11th Annual Chain Operators Exchange* (Chicago, International Foodservice Manufacturers Association, 1984).

[7] Harry Bolger, "The Conscious Consumer—Eating Right and Eating Light," *Proceedings of the 12th Annual Chain Operators Exchange* (Chicago, International Foodservice Manufacturers Association, 1985).

[8] *NRA News,* September 1985, p. 43.

[9] *Restaurant & Institutions,* May 29, 1985, p. 76.

[10] *Restaurant Business,* May 20, 1985, p. 135.

Table 3.6 *Major food service segments by nutritional attitude*

SEGMENT	DESCRIPTION	PERCENTAGE OF CONSUMERS	INCOME LEVEL	TYPICAL OCCUPATION OF HUSBAND	EDUCATION	OCCUPATION OF WIFE	NUMBER OF HOUSEHOLDERS
Nutritionally fit	Most concerned with nutrition and health; less concerned with taste, convenience, or calories	30%	$25,000 and over	White collar	Well educated	Working wife	21 million
Conventional	Rates taste more important in selecting food than nutrition, convenience, or calories.	26%	$15,000 and over	Blue collar	Less educated	Homemaker wife	17 million
Busy urbanite, convenience cook	Hates to cook; rates convenience as the most important item in selecting food items	24%	$25,000 and over	White collar	Well educated	Working wife	14 million
Restrictive dieter	Conventional tastes, grown	20%	$25,000 and under	Blue collar; retired	Less educated	Homemaker wife	13 million

Source: George D. Rice, *Proceedings of the 11th Annual Chain Operator's Exchange* (Chicago: International Foodservice Manufacturers Association, 1984); Harry Bolger, *Proceedings of the 12th Annual Chain Operator's Exchange* (Chicago: International Foodservice Manufacturers Association, 1985).

Table 3.7 *Fastest growing menu items, 1982–1984*

ITEM	GROWTH RATE
Decaffeinated coffee	57%
Fruit	48
Breakfast sandwiches	39
Diet cola	39
Mexican food items	36
Main dish salads	31
Rice	29
Pizza	21%
French toast	17
Cheeseburgers	17

Source: CREST *Household Report; NRA News,* September 1984, pp. 43–44.

Apparently people aren't as prepared to give up the taste of salt as they are to talk about it.[11]

Industry Response

But menus have been changing to respond to consumers' nutritional concerns. In 1985, Mrs. Warner's became the first major fast-food chain to introduce baked, as opposed to fried, chicken.[12] Fish restaurants, too, are changing their methods of preparation. Long John Silver's, famous for its fried fish, is introducing broiled and baked dinners which Warren Rosenthol, the company's chairman, called "the wave of the future."[13] The company has also reformulated its fish breading to make it lighter and less greasy.[14] From the other end of the price spectrum, *Restaurants & Institutions* reported that Ben's Steak House in Tampa, Florida, one of the country's best-known steakhouses and famous for its charbroiled steak, now offers an all-vegetable plate on its dinner menu.[15]

Industry is playing both sides of the "dietary schizophrenia." Bakeries and snack chains, that is, doughnut and ice-cream specialty shops, are growing rapidly at the same time many of the health-conscious restaurants have experienced problems. As other examples, Grandy's fast-food chicken chain tested pan-fried

[11] *Wall Street Journal,* February 3, 1985, p. 19.
[12] *Restaurant & Institutions,* September 18, 1985, p. 184.
[13] *Nation's Restaurant News,* October 28, 1985, p. 2.
[14] *Restaurant & Institutions,* May 15, 1985, p. 38.
[15] *Restaurant & Institutions,* June 12, 1985, p. 190.

chickens but won't add them to its regular menu because "consumer demand is insufficient." Hardee's recently shifted from cooking its hamburgers on broilers— associated with a lower fat content—to grills because "consumer research tells us thickness and juiciness are what people want in a burger."[16] Thus, it seems that consumers are concerned about nutrition and health but want to reward themselves from time to time or have the best of both worlds; a salad with lots of rich dressing; a feeling of virtue *and* a full stomach. The industry, quite naturally, is responding to both sides of the consumer's personality.

Consumerism

Many of the concerns of individual consumers, such as health, fitness, and nutrition, are shared by lots of consumers. And some of these concerns have been selected by organized interest groups as important to consumer education, to raise the consumer's consciousness: this is *consumerism.* Dr. Robert Blomstrom former director of Michigan State University's School of Hotel, Restaurant, and Institutional Management pointed out that although some industry leaders regard the consumer movement as a fad, many others "believe that it is here to stay and that, if unheeded, it may lead to consequences which the hospitality industry will not be happy to accept." Blomstrom observed that American consumerism has been around since the mid-nineteenth century, and he defined it as follows:

> *Consumerism is, first of all, a social movement. It is a movement by which society, through representative groups and individuals, seeks social change. Consumerism has as its specific objective to achieve a balance of power between buyers and sellers. It is an effort to equalize the rights of buyers with the rights of sellers.[17]*

In view of its increasing size and visibility, the hospitality industry has begun to attract the attention of consumer groups. A sampling of hospitality issues typically raised by consumers may lead to a better understanding of how consumerism can affect the food service field. Our discussion will include complaints about junk food, labeling and truth in dining, problems related to sanitation, and the question of food additives.

JUNK FOOD AND A HECTIC PACE

One of the principal indictments by consumerists against food service (and especially against fast food and vending) is that it concentrates on nutritionless "junk food." Although fast food does pose some nutritional problems, the junk-food

---

[16] *Nation's Restaurant News*, May 6, 1985, p. 1.
[17] Robert L. Blomstrom, "The Hospitality Industry and the Consumer Movement," *The Institute Journal*, April 1973, p. 9.

charge is just not true. Regarding mechanical vendors, the charge may comment more tellingly on American food habits than on the nutritional adequacy of the food itself.

A study by the Warf Institute, commissioned by McDonald's, indicates that a typical meal at McDonald's—a hamburger, french fries, and a milkshake—provides nearly one-third of the recommended dietary allowance (RDA), or the equivalent of what a Type A school lunch provides, with, however, a deficiency in vitamins A and C. (The deficiency in these two vitamins can be remedied somewhat if the customer switches from a hamburger to a Big Mac, which contains the necessary lettuce and tomato slices.)

The continuing call for mandatory nutritional labeling, however, may, if it is accepted, actually help the industry's image in this area, as the information about the realities of nutritional value becomes more widely understood. Some voluntary nutritional labeling has already appeared. But nutritional labeling cannot solve all our problems; moreover, many of the fast-food critics just don't seem to like the look of the restaurants or the taste of the food. These criticisms are perhaps typified by the remarks of Dr. Leonard Bachman, Pennsylvania's secretary of health, quoted by *Nation's Restaurant News*. After charging that "fast foods with their abundance of useless calories and sugar" (the junk-food charge) are a part of the problem of Americans' poor diet, Bachman continued,

> *Meals should be taken in a leisurely way, with personal interaction . . . [people who opt for fast foods are being] dehumanized—they are becoming more like automobiles driving up to a gas station and being refilled. . . . The ubiquitous multimillion dollar advertising campaigns, particularly the millions spent on television advertising, has greatly influenced the public in the direction of fast foods.*[18]

Two problems here go beyond the junk-food issue. Critics such as Bachman believe they know what is good for people (which, in a medical sense, they may), and they resent the fact that people choose to disregard their expert advice. Bachman's main criticism, however, is really of Americans' poor eating habits, notably "the quick pace inherent in our society."

Whatever else is true, the duty of the American restaurant industry in a market economy is to serve consumers, not to reform them. But it is difficult for hospitality to deal with this kind of criticism, in which the industry becomes a scapegoat for the annoyance that some feel at a simple economic reality: the food service within the reach of most pocketbooks uses food service systems that are not (and cannot be) labor intensive.

The second problem that Bachman raises is the effect of advertising on consumer behavior. His remarks here reflect an old and complex debate in the general field of marketing. From our earlier explanation of the procedure for introducing a new product, perhaps you remember that restaurants are interested in

[18] *Nation's Restaurant News*, November 10, 1974, p. 4.

only offering what the guests want, not in forcing something on them. For example, notice that the decor and atmosphere in specialty restaurants have been growing warmer and friendlier to meet earlier criticisms of coldness and austerity. And salad bars were added because that is what consumers wanted. That is, the weight of consumer opinion is usually felt in the marketplace. Change in business institutions does, of course, come more slowly than consumerists would like, but particularly in competitive industries such as food service, change does come when it is clear the consumer wants it.

The junk-food criticism will not just go away, however. Studies conducted at Pennsylvania State University and elsewhere suggest that many guests do not follow the Big Mac–fries–milkshake meal profile referred to earlier. For instance, to save money or suit their tastes, many customers replace the milkshake with a soft drink, and the result is *distinctly less* than one-third the RDA.

Michael F. Jacobsen, executive director of the Center for Science in the Public Interest (CSPI), has asked some hard questions of the industry. Why not, he says, replace beef fat, palm oil, and other saturated fats used as frying agents in fast food? He points to the fact that a Whopper with cheese, a milkshake, and fries have 2 oz of fat, and Chicken McNuggets and Filet of Fish—supposedly "lite" foods—contain twice as much fat as a hamburger does. Jacobsen points to another fast-food menu problem, sodium. A Kentucky Fried Chicken dinner can easily account for 1500 mg of sodium, and three pieces of fish plus fries at Long John Silvers provide 2000 mg. These amounts of fat and sodium are at or above the daily limits recommended by the National Academy of Sciences for a 10-year-old.[19] And because fast food is often targeted to young people, it is significant that one fast-food meal can provide a full day's sensible use of a potentially hazardous food ingredient. Under the circumstances, then, we shouldn't be surprised if the call for labeling is answered in the near future. Fast food isn't just empty calories, but as a steady diet, it can pose some nutritional problems, depending on the choices consumers make.

NUTRITIONAL LABELING

A false advertising charge has been filed against McDonald's, claiming as "false and misleading" the company's claim that "only tender, juicy chunks of breast and thigh meat" are used in Chicken McNuggets, that McNuggets also contain chicken skin, sodium phosphate, and beef fat (as a frying agent). McDonald's replied that the proportion of skin in McNuggets is lower than on a chicken bought in a grocery store, but that doesn't answer the question of sodium phosphate and beef fat.

In regard to the nutritional labeling of fast food, the National Restaurant Association (NRA) has contended that the costs of such a move would outweigh any real benefit. The U.S. Department of Agriculture has ruled out labeling, largely because of the enormous cost of enforcing it.[20] The city of San Francisco did

---

[19] *Nation's Restaurant News,* January 27, 1986, p. F7.
[20] *Nation's Restaurant News,* January 20, 1986, p. 1.

pass a nutritional labeling act, however, and to avoid such statewide bills in California and Texas, several fast-food chains have reached "voluntary" product-labeling agreements with the attorneys general in those states.[21]

TRUTH IN MENU

The increasing use of convenience foods, frozen prepared foods, and foods prepared in remote commissaries has created an issue closely related to the nutritional labeling issue. The food service industry, in fact, has long advocated honest dealings with the consumers, but individual operators have frequently strayed from full candor.[22] Included in one's "right to know," consumer groups insist, is a right to know where and how restaurant food was prepared. Laws requiring menus to state who prepared the food and when, where, and how it was prepared have already been proposed.

The use of frozen food is certainly widespread. *Restaurants & Institutions* indicated that 90 percent of all operations use frozen food. Twenty percent of Denny's menu is purchased frozen, and Bonanza buys virtually all its entrees frozen.[23] Many operators feel it is their special method of preparation rather than the food's state before cooking that imparts quality. Most operators would like to think that "fresh" means prepared to order, whether or not the raw products are frozen and that "natural" means unadulterated and not necessarily anything more. But the fact is that frozen products, because of "field-side" or "on-board" freezing, are often of higher quality—that is, possessing more of the characteristics of the fresh—than does a "fresh" product that has worked its way through the channels of distribution, deteriorating gradually in unfrozen storage. For example, several fast-food companies purchasing Icelandic cod deal with packers who have on-board processing capabilities. Similarly, large frozen vegetable processors have equipment that follows the harvesters, processing the vegetables and freezing them immediately after they are picked. The term *fresh frozen*, then, is not really a contradiction in terms.

It is, of course, possible to cook top-quality food in one place, freeze or chill it, transport it, reconstitute it, and serve a tasty, attractive product in another place. The problem is not the technology but a culture that changes more slowly than does its own technical capacities. Someday, commissaries and other centralized production systems may make genuine haute cuisine available to the *mass market* at prices that that market can afford. Before this happens, food service-marketing techniques will be needed to complement (that is, to fulfill) the technology that already exists. Finally, when such a feat becomes possible, a consumer willing to accept gourmet food reconstituted from the chilled or frozen state will have to be waiting for it—and that is a marketing problem.

[21] *Nation's Restaurant News,* September 1, 1986, p. 1.
[22] John J. Bilan, "Taking Another Look at Accuracy in Menus," *Cornell Hotel and Restaurant Administration Quarterly,* November 1979, p. 8.
[23] *Restaurants & Institutions,* October 2, 1985, p. 106.

In the meantime, if the industry resists truth in menu because of the disruptions it clearly will cause, it might study the experience of grocery chains and retailers, who have learned not only to accept reasonable consumer demands but also to incorporate them in their marketing programs and to turn compliance to their advantage as well.

Some segments of the restaurant business have already become *service-intensive* retail establishments that give the final processing to products prepared elsewhere. The first person to show guests an advantage in choosing to accept remotely prepared food will have made an important marketing breakthrough. In the meantime, there are some signs that consumers are gradually beginning to accept remotely prepared food

Peter Drucker has called consumerism "the shame of marketing." Consumerism, he feels, reflects business's almost exclusive emphasis on selling (which begins with our product and how to sell it) instead of marketing, which begins with consumer preferences and moves towards supplying products that meet those needs.

> *Consumerism is also the opportunity of marketing. It will force business to become market focused in their actions as well as their pronouncements. Developing a positive response to consumerist sentiment is probably more effective than resentment and resistance. There is truth in the old adage, "If you can't fight 'em, join 'em."*[24]

SANITATION

As with so many consumer issues, sanitation involves government regulations—in this case, as embodied in public-health officers and inspectors. With the increasing use of off-premise prepared foods, the incidence of food poisoning in public accommodations has been rising steeply. The kinds of sanitary precautions associated with traditional food service operations are inadequate for food service systems that prepare food, freeze or chill it, and then transport it elsewhere. First, the risks of thawing and spoilage are high. Second, the food is handled by more people. Some operators resist the increased emphasis on sanitation, but most have accepted—many enthusiastically—the need to upgrade sanitation practices and to establish and enforce high sanitation standards. Although the National Restaurant Association has resisted legislation demanding the testing of food service managers' and food handlers' knowledge of sanitation as impractical and too costly, the association's affiliate, the National Institute for the Foodservice Industry (NIFI), has pioneered in the development of sanitation educational materials and programs. It is quite clear that for the most part, the industry and those calling for the highest standards of sanitation are, in principle, in the same camp.

[24] Peter F. Drucker, *Management: Tasks, Responsibilities, Practices* (New York: Harper & Row, 1974), p. 64.

ADDITIVES

The practice of adding preservatives, coloring agents, and flavor enhancers to food is as old as salt, paprika, and cloves. Recently, however, the practice has spread and intensified. There is no real consensus on the desirability of using additives extensively. Some food scientists insist on the advantages of additives, whereas some nutritionists and consumerists adamantly oppose nearly all use of additives.

Solutions to the additive issue emerge case by case and generally involve balancing the benefits against the risks. When the benefit of preserving food against spoilage (as with the calcium propionate in bread) is matched by little if any risk to health, the use of additives is accepted by nearly everyone. On the other hand, when the effect is purely cosmetic and some health danger appears to be present (as with the coloring in some presweetened breakfast foods), the consumerist's ire will continue, and with increasing effect.

One food preservation practice that has been condemned is using sulfiting agents. These are used commonly to freshen raw vegetables and fruits on salad bars and also are used in many processed foods, including dried potatoes, canned vegetables, dried fruits, corn syrup, sugar, some starches, soft drinks, and instant tea.[25] The National Restaurant Association recommended that restaurants stop using sulfites, and many operators have complied. The reason for the prohibition is that the ingestion of sulfites is hazardous to some asthmatics and has even contributed to several deaths. Unfortunately, sulfites are still used by some food manufacturers, but operators can limit the problem by avoiding the use of "vegetable fresheners" and "potato whiteners."[26]

Many additives, however, are perfectly harmless natural substances, such as the carotin used to give margarine its yellow color. On the other hand, the nitrites used to preserve ham, bacon, and other smoked meats, although they have a cosmetic effect (without them the meat would be gray) and reduce the risk of botulism, are also carcinogens; that is, they have been shown to cause cancer. It isn't as if we have to choose between botulism and cancer; neither event is very likely. But we do have to weigh the risk against the benefit.

Probably the best response to these questions as well as to other issues related to consumerism is simply to be well informed, open, and responsive rather than resentful. The guests who raise consumerist issues are not cranks. Rather, they are a part of one of the great mass movements of the twentieth century, and they tend to be intelligent and well educated. Their concern is not likely to vanish.

ALCOHOL AND DINING

The many fatal accidents attributed to driving under the influence of alcohol has handed to the hospitality industry a wide-ranging set of problems. On the one

[25] *Restaurants & Institutions*, December 5, 1984, p. 30.
[26] *Restaurants & Institutions*, January 23, 1985, p. 252.

At the end of a day's work, restaurants offer a place for relaxation—but there is a growing conservatism in North Americans' concerns with overindulgence. (Courtesy the National Restaurant Association.)

hand, in many jurisdictions, restaurants and bars that sell drinks to people who are later involved in accidents are now being held legally responsible for damages. The result has been, among other things, a great rise in liability insurance rates. Laws have been proposed—and in many jurisdictions passed—making illegal the "happy hours" and other advertised price reductions on the sale of drinks. In addition, in a less strictly legal sense, operators have been concerned about the image of their operations and the industry in general.

The industry's response has generally been swift and positive. One idea is "designated driver" programs. For instance, at Maggie's Lounges, part of a chain based in Maryland, one customer in a party signs a "Declaration of Non-Inebriation." The designated driver is identified with a large button and receives $5.00 worth of "Maggie's Money" good at the time of his or her next visit—when somebody else takes a turn as the designated driver.[27] Some operations also give the designated driver all the soft drinks he or she wants, at no charge. Alcoholic awareness training—teaching bartenders and servers how to tell when people have had too much to drink and how to deal with them—is also becoming more common. Studebaker's waitresses, for instance, receive 18 hours of alcohol awareness training during their first year on the job.

CONVENIENCE

We have spoken of consumer concerns, some represented by consumerist professionals and others just by consumer choices in the market. Another of these consumer choices is not related to health and fitness; some might even argue it pulls in the other direction because it reflects the hectic pace of life in much of North America. This is the concern for convenience, reflecting what has been called the "poverty of time." With the majority of families finding it necessary to have both spouses working—and with all the tasks and duties of the home remaining to be done—we live in a prosperous but unusually harried time.

As with consumers' interest in health and fitness, the industry has responded with products and services that fit the time pressures of our hurried life-styles. In shopping centers, "food courts" bring together a number of different kinds of units to facilitate "grazing," a pattern of "grabbing a bite on the run," eating on impulse: perhaps a gyro from one shop, french fries from another, a cookie from a third, and a cup of "gourmet coffee" to top it off. Grazing, too, is related to a desire to eat less and to choose only those foods that please the individual. Later we will discuss other responses to consumers' needs to save time: 24-hour convenience stores, drive-throughs, and conveniently located take-out units; in short, fast food faster.

Summary

We first considered the organizational forms of restaurants—chain, independent, and franchise. Chain specialty restaurants have six strengths: (1) brand recognition or preference, (2) site selection expertise, (3) access to capital, (4) purchasing economies, (5) centrally administered control and information systems, and (6) personal program development.

[27] *Restaurants & Institutions,* August 8, 1985, p. 19.

We also analyzed independent restaurants using the same six factors and pointed out the independent restaurants' advantages of flexibility, the owner's motivation, and the owner's closeness to the operation.

Franchised restaurants fall somewhere between the chains and the independents, having greater freedom of action than the chains do but also having access to expertise and capital that the independents do not.

Next we discussed consumers, from the perspective of age, income, and size of household. We then turned to the consumers' concerns, particularly health and nutrition and their impact on restaurants' menus. But even though restaurants have responded to consumers' demands by changing their menu items as well as their methods of cooking, the restaurants have often found consumers' convictions and desires to be contradictory. Such a contradiction may be, for example, a low-calorie dinner topped off by a rich dessert.

Finally, we looked at consumerism, or consumers' concerns translated into organized interest groups. The most widely discussed such concerns are junk food, nutritional labeling, truth in menu, sanitation, additives, and alcohol. We examined the arguments of both the consumerists and the restaurant industry and the actions of each. We ended with another consumer concern, convenience, which has become an issue in our busy lives, and we talked about how the as become an issue in our busy lives, and we talked about how the industry has responded.

The Future of the Restaurant Business

———————————— THIS CHAPTER IS ABOUT ————————————

The future of the restaurant business. The equipment and facilities in use in the industry such as scaled-down and mobile units make a good starting point. Another important factor is energy cost, which affects guests' transportation as well as food processing, disposables, and factors in the restaurant's immediate environment such as air conditioning.

Competition both within the industry and from other goods and services is shaping tomorrow's restaurants and the opportunities they offer. We will look at competitive activities such as advertising and promotion, new-product development, the expansion of "day parts" and services, as well as price and location. Looking at competitors that are, in a way, outside the industry, we will examine C stores, supermarkets, and the home itself.

The chapter ends with a brief look at the employment outlook and the growing labor shortage.

Courtesy of W. R. Grace.

The Restaurant Industry: A View of Where We're Going

The restaurant industry of today is much like the restaurant industry of 15 years ago. All the elements present now were present then; only the proportion of those elements has changed. In the next 10 or 15 years a similar kind of evolution will probably have taken place. To the question, "What will the restaurant industry be like tomorrow?" the answer is, "Like it is today—only more so."

Figure 4.1 presents a frame of reference for considering the major elements of the restaurant industry. The chart can help you visualize today's restaurant industry and how it is likely to look tomorrow. (This chart refers only to restaurants and does not attempt to address the many other elements of the food service industry, such as in-plant feeding, college feeding, or government food service. These elements will be considered later.)

In Figure 4.1, the vertical axis rates restaurants on a scale from low to high in terms of complexity of delivery, the haute cuisine restaurant having the most complex delivery system. A restaurant with a complex delivery system is characterized by high-quality food, a variety of menu choices, high prices, and a high-

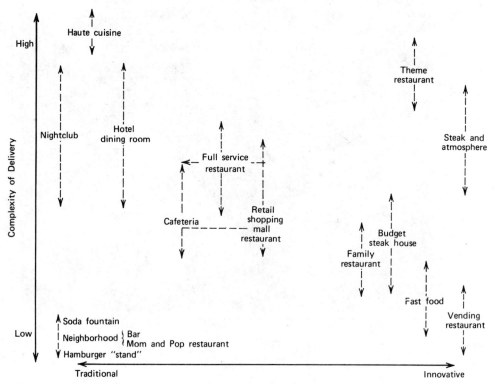

Figure 4.1   *A restaurant typology.*

status ambience. On the other hand, a fast-food restaurant (although the quality of the product may be excellent as far as it goes) offers relatively simple, inexpensive fare. It is no reflection on McDonald's to say that a hamburger can be only so good. The prices in these restaurants tend to be lower, and (in the sense that one would not take the boss out to dinner there) their status association is relatively low.

On the horizontal axis, we move along a scale from the traditional establishments at the left to the innovative operations at the right. There are three general kinds of vertical groupings in the figure, suggesting that there are three different "time-dimensioned" kinds of establishments represented at most price levels. First, we see the traditional restaurant, imported from Europe or in operation in this country for many, many years. Second, in the middle of the chart we find a grouping of restaurants representing typically American systems that grew up in the 1930s and 1940s and generally hit their peak in the 1950s. These tend to be more service intensive and to use a complex system of delivery. Finally, at the right we see a group of restaurants that have come on the scene mostly since the early 1960s, although earlier prototypes probably existed.

The restaurants classified in Figure 4.1 as relatively more traditional are in the decline stage of the product's life cycle. Their number, in short, is diminishing. Between 1970 and 1985, fast-food sales increased about seven and a half times, whereas all sales of food consumed away from home increased five times. Thus, fast-food sales are growing roughly half again as fast as are all restaurant sales.

Traditional table service restaurants are labor intensive, and as long as services are maintained, it is difficult to make great improvements in productivity. There is an absolute limit, for instance, to how fast this waitress can move.

Clearly, the growth potential in the restaurant industry lies with those operations that are less labor intensive and hence can offer guests reasonably priced meals.

Traditional restaurants will not disappear. At the upper end of the complexity of delivery scale we see that a strong demand remains for haute cuisine establishments. Moreover, there will always be the special niche in the marketplace that only the independents can fill, and this is likely to become more significant as the middle aging of North America raises the demand for innovation and variety. Increasingly, however, growth is in the mass-market specialty restaurants of the type clustered at the right of Figure 4.1. Thus, the restaurant industry of the next 10 years will contain all of the same elements it does today, but the *proportionate sizes* of the three groups will change.

We probably should note here that this is a view of what the industry will look like from the outside. Inside the industry and its operations, however, we will not find the continuity we did between the 1970's and the early 1980's. The changing ages and incomes of the population and the resulting changes in consumer tastes are likely to accelerate growth in some areas and delay it in others. Equally significant is the growth in competition both inside and outside the restaurant business. Finally, a growing labor shortage is bound to affect services and prices. We will begin our examination with a look at the "nuts and bolts," equipment and technology.

The Food Service Equipment of the Future—Or, What Now, Mr. Spock?

In 1975, a researcher looked into the future of food service, and this is what he saw:

> *The restaurant of 1986 will be automated. One individual will be capable of running a 10,000-meal-a-day commissary. Computer controlled, automated equipment will run the food processing operation from storeroom to cleanup as well as take care of inventory control and the reordering process. In addition, the computer will handle all records, write all necessary business reports (including the annual report), forecast requirements, and perform all cost accounting duties.*
>
> *Customers will dine in a computer-manipulated environment of aromatic and visual stimuli. They will stand before lighted menus picturing various entrees and punch out selections at order stations. Within 2½ minutes, they will be served the meal via conveyor belt running with the wall and stopping at the proper table. Dish busing commences upon the customer arising from the seat. Dirty dishes move onto a conveyor belt within an adjacent wall. The dishwashing process is completely automated. A 200-seat restaurant will require four employees and a manager.[1]*

[1] *Institutions/Volume Feeding*, October 1975, p. 47.

If technology can put an astronaut on the moon, it can surely bus tables. But it's not what is technically possible that counts; it's what makes economic sense. In the foreseeable future, even in the face of steeply rising wages, the 10,000-meal-a-day commissaries that come into use will require a good many more people than one, because it will make economic sense. Although a computer-operated food production, storage, and cleanup system is theoretically possible, it would be like using a computer just to add up a grocery bill. Less expensive methods are available.

The impatience with impersonal behavior patterns expressed by customers in vending restaurants suggests that the time when lines form "to punch out selections at order stations" may be pretty far off. Here again, the problem is cost effectiveness and guest acceptance rather than technological capabilities. In fact, the Food Institute reported, "An international burger chain has commissioned Hughes International to supply a six armed robot that takes orders, cooks the food, serves it, takes the money, clears tables and sweeps the floor for $100,000."[2] But the big problems are not essentially technical; they are economic and human. First, if this six-armed fellow replaced three full-time workers, it would take five years for the savings to pay for the investment—if the repair bills were not too high. Moreover, how will people feel about giving their order to something out of a science fiction film, taking their food from it, and having it clean up after them? As a novelty, it sounds interesting, but for a steady diet, people may need quite a lot of time to get used to it, much less like it.

The revolution in information processing has had an important impact on food service record keeping, and computerized report preparation has been a fact of life for some time. But as with the management information environment in other industries, the computer hasn't displaced people as much as it has increased management's ability to control costs and regulate quality. The available evidence suggests that the same will be true in food service.

Surprisingly enough, amid all this talk of technology and computers, there are few varieties of *new* equipment designed for use in the individual food service operation. The only "revolutionary" invention is the microwave oven, and even it has been around for some 30 years. What *is* revolutionary, though, is the increasing acceptance of the microwave oven after so many years of availability. The delay in acceptance suggests that it takes technical innovations a long time to be accepted and used. Another recent equipment innovation that is likely to affect fast food is the clamshell grill which was initially tested by McDonald's in 1984. This grill, which is fired to cook on *both* sides, cuts cooking time by up to 60 percent. This speeds service to hurried consumers, particularly in drive-through operations in which time is especially important. McDonald's is also using a radio headset that connects the order taker with the cook and manager, thus speeding services.[3]

Other food service innovations can currently be found in food preprocessing and the development of centralized food service systems, electronic cash registers

[2] *Restaurants & Institutions,* June 12, 1985, p. 70.
[3] *Nation's Restaurant News,* December 2, 1985, p. 32.

Decor designed to meet special customer interests helps make eating out a pleasant experience. The merry-go-round motif in this McDonald's dining room is aimed at young customers. (Photo courtesy of McDonald's Corp.)

(ECRs), and point-of-sales (POS) systems. The ECR/POS revolution is making possible much closer attention to daily, and even shift by shift, detail in regard to both food and labor cost. Centralized systems employ central production and/or storage units linked by transportation networks. In these systems, delivery trucks are dispatched and routed by computers to minimize transportation costs. The "system" links a group of service-intensive retail outlets (call them restaurants).

Although centralized production facilities (call them commissaries) have not been uniformly successful, the evidence suggests that such systems have failed because of one of three problems: (1) management was unable to change from traditional restaurant thinking to the "factory thinking" that commissaries require in operation; (2) management did not think through how the *entire company* (units and central office as well as commissary) had to change to adapt to a new system of operation; or (3) a successful commissary became unsuccessful when the company outgrew it.

Mr. Spock and Captain Kirk may well interrupt their trek to come to dinner. But the restaurant they'd choose in 2000 will *look* a good deal like the restaurant of today. If there is a "revolution," it will be the invisible revolution resulting from the way the already existing elements in the system are rearranged.

Mobile fast-food units are an equipment innovation that broadens the market for fast food by providing greater location convenience for consumers. (Photo courtesy of Burger King Corp.)

SCALED-DOWN AND MOBILE UNITS

A good example of the kind of "creeping revolution" that food service has been experiencing for the last 30 years can be found in the development of new kinds of units. Cost pressures as well as consumer demands for more convenience are encouraging the construction of scaled-down units in locations that wouldn't have been considered earlier. For example, a smaller unit being tested by Pizza Hut features a limited menu designed for fast service which is backed up by a new conveyorized oven that reduces cooking time.[4] Moreover, mobile units are being used not only to deliver food but also to operate from temporary sites where there is a short-term demand. A mobile unit costing $70,000 is reportedly often able to make essentially the same number of sales as can a regular unit costing over $900,000 to build, with obvious advantages in the return on investment.[5] The technology of smaller units is not as colorful as flashing order panels and six-armed robots, but it is more firmly grounded in consumers' needs and preferences and in economic reality.

[4] *Nation's Restaurant News*, August 12, 1985, p. 1.
[5] *Nation's Restaurant News*, February 10, 1985, p. 80.

Energy Cost and Food Service

Energy costs accounted for 10 percent of the operating costs of food service in 1985, up from 8.4 percent in 1982 and 7.8 percent in 1980.[6] Approximately 76 percent of U.S. energy comes from petroleum and natural gas. We can expect these scarce and expensive fuels to have a major impact on at least three aspects of the food service industry: transportation systems, food processing, and the use of what the industry calls *disposables*.

ENERGY AND THE TRANSPORTATION SYSTEM

At least until the internal combustion engine gives way to some other device, gasoline-powered cars will carry guests to their restaurants, hotels, and resorts. But even though auto transportation is expensive, barring a catastrophe, energy supplies seem reasonably secure. Costs will surely fluctuate, but the explosion in gasoline prices is probably behind us.

ENERGY AND FOOD PROCESSING

Freezing foods entails chilling the product to well below freezing and then holding it and the environment around it at that temperature. Thus, fresh or canned products save energy costs, an advantage that may overcome the labor costs and quality considerations that have, up until now, given frozen products some advantages.

Frozen prepared products have traditionally been used in restaurants to reduce labor costs. Freezing, however, is energy intensive: it requires energy first to reduce temperature and then, during reconstitution, to return the product to serving temperature. Moreover, freezing has drawbacks relating to product quality. The formation of ice crystals, a part of freezing, damages tissue, which changes the consistency of some products and, upon reconstitution, results in the loss of flavor-filled juices.

Chilled foods, however, were found to taste better than did frozen products, in tests conducted by the U.S. Army's Nattick Laboratories. In recent years, shelf life of chilled foods has been extended up to one or two weeks, depending upon the product, by rapidly chilling cooked or pasteurized food and holding it at temperatures ranging from 1 to 3°C, slightly lower than normal refrigerated storage. These chilled food will be available only to operations large enough to do their own central production and maintain their own refrigerated storage. It is unlikely that chilled rather than frozen prepared foods will be available from conventional suppliers in the foreseeable future. Nevertheless, the laborsaving advantage usually

[6] Julie G. Woodman, *The IFMA Encyclopedia of the Foodservice Industry*, 5th ed. (Chicago: International Foodservice Manufacturers Association, 1985), p. 13.

associated with frozen foods is now available to large institutions, and even to innovative operators in smaller units, in a form that is also less wasteful of energy.

One fact seems likely to remain true: The increase in the cost of labor, as well as its magnitude relative to energy cost, makes it likely that timesaving processing steps such as freezing will continue to be used as long as they result in significant labor savings, even though they consume energy. Labor is likely to remain the more important cost for the foreseeable future.

ENERGY AND DISPOSABLES

Because many disposable plastic products derive from petroleum, the cost advantages associated with discarding these products after use is related to the cost of petroleum. Because disposables have commonly been used even when petroleum prices have been higher than they are currently, the role of disposables appears secure at any foreseeable price level.

ENERGY AND THE GENERAL HOSPITALITY ENVIRONMENT

The almost-universal use of air conditioning in American food service imposes a heavy tax on guests in the form of energy costs passed on in the food prices. It seems unlikely, however, that energy prices could rise to a point that guests would tolerate the elimination of air conditioning. Newly constructed units, moreover, generally incorporate energy savings into all facets of their design.

Competition

Earlier we said that the restaurant industry of the future will look much like today's industry—from the outside. That is, the same kinds of operations will be offered to consumers, although there will be gradual changes in the market share of the various types of units. The competitive forces at work, however, suggest that developments *inside* the industry will be quite different in the 1980s and 1990s from what they were in the 1960s and 1970s. During the earlier 20-year period, increases in the consumption of food away from home were driven by the increasing number of working women and dramatically rising incomes. Expanding "new" kinds of restaurants—fast-food and family restaurants—took advantage of this market growth.

Of equal importance, the competition available to meet the growth of new restaurants was outmoded. Fast food drove many a mom-and-pop operation out of business, just as numerous traditional full-service operations were driven to the wall by specialty and family restaurants. The "new" offered numerous advantages, including self-service; menus that limited variety, and hence the skills and the payroll cost required; lower prices related both to the latter advantages and to high volume; a more modern look; careful location planning; and vastly more sophisticated marketing. Thus, the new restaurants advanced strongly and largely unchallenged into a market that was waiting for them. From time to time, there was talk of market saturation, and each downtown in the economy produced a shakeout, eliminating the weak, loosely planned, or poorly marketed operations. Nevertheless, in the 25 years from 1960 to 1984, the number of fast-food units grew from approximately 16,000, with roughly 6 percent of restaurant sales, to about 137,200 units, with an estimated 45 percent of restaurant sales.[7]

The conditions of market expansion and obsolete competition that marked the 1960s and 1970s no longer obtain, however. In the 1980s, more women have come into the work force, but the *rate of growth* in female employment has slowed significantly and will continue to do so. Working women have become a stabilizing, rather than a dynamic, force in food service demand. The trend is toward two-income families, not so-called yuppies (young, urban professionals), but families who need two incomes to keep ahead of inflation and maintain their now relatively more expensive standard of living. It thus seems that both the slower growth of personal income and the greater competition for consumers' dollars will put the brakes on restaurant expansion.

COMPETITION WITHIN THE FOOD SERVICE INDUSTRY

Competition within the food service industry has several parts: advertising and promotion, development of new products, expansion of day parts, and expansion of service, price, and location.

Advertising and Promotion

In 1985, restaurants spent over a billion dollars for television advertising alone. Indeed, McDonald's, the second largest advertiser in the United States (after Procter & Gamble), spent $686 million on marketing of all kinds.[8]

In competitive times, special promotions are particularly important to the overall marketing program. Operations may offer coupons that reduce the price of items sold, offer premium merchandise (such as special glassware) at bargain prices, or offer consumers opportunities to compete in games. According to CREST's *Family Report*, in 1977 only 6.5 percent of visits to restaurants involved this kind of promotion, but by 1984 that proportion had risen to 11.3 percent.

---

[7] The numbers used here for 1960 and 1985 are from different sources and hence subject to possible variation in definition. In fact, what was counted as "fast food" in 1960 and in 1980 probably included different kinds of establishments. Precision, of course, is not absolutely essential when the change is so dramatic. The 1960 estimate is from Urban B. Ozanne and Shelby D. Hunt, *Economic Effects of Franchising* (Washington, D.C.: U.S. Government Printing Office, 1971); and the 1985 figure is from *Restaurants & Institutions*, January 8, 1986.

[8] *Restaurants & Institutions*, July 23, 1986, p. 202.

Franchise units follow a common advertising theme developed by the franchisor and bring a national campaign into local media. (Courtesy of Country Kitchen International, Inc.)

Development of New Products

New products are used competitively in a number of ways. First, they are used to expand a restaurant's customer base, to draw in more customers. Sometimes a company introduces new products defensively or offensively because competitors have begun to gain market share. For example, Wendy's efforts to attract more women to its restaurants are a good example of new products' being used to expand a customer base. In 1979, Wendy's new product was the salad bar, and Wendy's was the first among the major chains to introduce it. In 1983 Wendy's upgraded its salad bar, and also in 1983 it introduced its baked potato line. Both products, salads and baked potatoes, had the desired effect of expanding Wendy's market share among women.

Chicken nuggets are a good example of a defensive product introduction; that is, a number of chicken restaurant chains felt they had to jump on the nugget bandwagon because they were losing customers to McDonald's new McNuggets. Indeed, McDonald's was becoming one of the largest chicken chains in North America, and so the chicken restaurants needed to defend their market share.

Burger King launched a counteroffensive in 1985 against the growing appeal of gourmet burgers when it reformulated its Whopper. Burger King raised the Whopper's meat content by 17 percent, from 3.6 to 4.2 oz, and changed the bun size so as to alter the bun-to-meat ratio as well as the appearance of the product. McDonald's responded by introducing the McDLT. McDonald's was successful in maintaining its market share, and by early 1986, Burger King had begun to lose share despite its efforts.[9]

Expansion of Day Parts

Serving more *day parts*, or meal occasions, means getting more productivity out of the operation's capital investment (land, building, equipment, and furnishings) by remaining open longer and thus raising sales volume. This tactic is reflected in the increased number of chains offering breakfast and/or moving toward 24-hour operations. Additional operating hours, however, also means an expanded payroll.

When volume can be improved during existing operating hours, not only can capital costs be spread over a larger volume, but in many cases current operating costs need not be increased by very much. The popularity of McDonald's McNuggets as a snack food brings in guests for a snack in off-meal hours, when the operation probably has idle staff. Similarly, most units are open for dinner, but many make only moderate sales. Thus, efforts to find entrees that will "reposition" the unit in the consumer's mind *as a dinner-occasion restaurant* will certainly continue.

Expansion of Service

The greater use of takeout and delivery is an important service expansion. The significance of this can best be seen in the statistic that in 1985 the number of meals and snacks eaten *inside* restaurants did not rise but that those eaten off premises were what accounted for the industry's growth.[10] As we noted earlier, the lion's share of takeout and delivery goes to fast food, but this service expansion is also enjoying success in the finer restaurants and family restaurants.

Price

Restaurant prices used to increase in the range of 8 to 10 percent but are now rising from 3 to 4 percent.[11] The days of easily passing on higher costs to the consumer are past, and instead, careful management at the unit level is necessary.

Location

The best restaurant sites are often already occupied. Thus, to obtain new locations, firms have resorted to purchasing all or part of regional chains so as to secure their

---

[9] *Nation's Restaurant News*, March 10, 1986, p. 143.

[10] George D. Rice, "Foodservice Industry Review and Forecast," *Proceedings of the 13th Annual Chain Operators Exchange* (Chicago: International Foodservice Manufacturers Association, 1986).

[11] Michael Culp, "What's Hot in Fast Foods?" *Barron's*, April 23, 1985.

Sidewalk Cafes—originally a European tradition—are a growing success in North America, where they have captured the casual mood of many of today's diners. (New York State Commerce Dept.)

locations for conversion. Another strategy has been to expand into what had once not been considered viable fast-food locations. For example, we are now seeing franchised fast-food units on college campuses and military bases, at toll-road service plazas, in downtown office buildings, and even in museums. Wendy's is testing operations in K Marts and has begun to expand from a successful test in Days Inns economy motels. And McDonald's has gone to great pains to customize its downtown office building locations and overcome landlords' objections to fast food.

Downsizing is also a way of expanding, as is seen in McDonald's snack units, as well as mobile units—one more way of bringing the business to the customers so as to acquire and keep market share. Downsizing and mobile units are really a part of a location strategy.

The practice of co-locating—locating two noncompetitive businesses on the same site—is spreading, too. For instance, Dairy Queen and Mr. Donut have agreed to exploit sites jointly. Similarly, Winchell's Donuts has developed a ministore to be located inside existing ARCO gas stations, and Dunkin Donuts also has taken a similar tack with gas stations.[12]

[12] *Nation's Restaurant News*, January 27, 1986, p. 72.

Limited food service in convenience stores eats into fast-food's market share.
(Photo courtesy of 7-Eleven.)

COMPETITION FROM RELATED BUSINESSES

Both convenience stores and full-line grocery stores have become serious competitors with fast-food restaurants.

Convenience Stores

In 1972, convenience stores—"C stores" for short—had 1.5 percent of fast-food sales but by 1985 accounted for 9.7 percent[13] and occupied 48,110 locations.[14] Although the traditional C store customer has been thought of as an 18- to 24-year-old male, a recent study by the National Association of Convenience Stores revealed that 44 percent of C store customers are female and two-thirds of them are white-collar workers or homemakers. Clearly, the stereotypes that suggested that C

[13] *NRA News*, March 1986, p. 21.
[14] *Restaurants & Institutions*, January 8, 1986, p. 179.

Grocery store deli departments are working hard to get a share of the food service market. (Photo courtesy of Piggly Wiggly.)

stores competed only in a small part of the fast-food market must be reexamined. Accordingly, the food service managers of Southland's 7-Eleven chain, the nation's largest C store operator, has called fast-food 7-Eleven's "greatest area of opportunity." Indeed, in 1984 7-Eleven had fast-food sales of $900 million. In addition to fountain beverages, hot dogs, deli sandwiches, nachos, and microwave products, many C stores are now offering sandwiches that are made on the premises for greater eye appeal and freshness.[15] In fact, *Restaurant & Institutions* reported that in 1986 food service in C stores increased 50 percent over that in 1984.

Supermarkets

Supermarkets have been adding salad bars, delicatessens, and bakeries which are competing directly with food service.[16] In addition, 25 percent of supermarkets with salad bars also make available eating areas.[17]

Grocery stores are also offering ready-to-eat take-out foods which are sold by the pound at prices well below what a restaurant must charge. In Denver, one grocery chain has replaced meat cutters with chefs, and a New Jersey chain has hired a leading restaurant consultant to redesign its stores and assist in training its

[15] *Nation's Restaurant News*, October , 1985, p. 1.
[16] *Restaurant Business*, August 10, 1985, p. 209.
[17] *Nation's Restaurant News*, May 13, 1985, p. 56.

staff. Stores offer items such as oven-ready stuffed pork chops, stuffed flank steak, and stuffed poultry. One dimension of the challenge is suggested by *Nation's Restaurant News:* "As frozen, store bought pizza becomes a stronger competitor to the pizza chains with improvements in quality and the trend toward convenience, pricing could become the critical factor in the future struggles for shares between the chains and the super markets."[18]

The Home As a Competitor

A study conducted by Purdue University's Department of Restaurant, Hotel and Institutional Management concluded that it is actually less expensive to eat fast food than it is to eat at home if meal preparation and cleanup time is given a realistic value.[19] The danger is, however, that the consumer may not choose to eat out even if it is a bargain. The growth of in-home "entertainment centers," particularly in the affluent households whose occupants make such ideal potential restaurant customers, raises the question of whether more people may choose to stay home to enjoy themselves. In addition, nearly half of all American homes have microwave ovens, and this makes the grocery freezer a dangerous competitor. Accordingly, food manufacturers have developed special luxury products, and many, such as Lean Cuisine and Le Menu, appeal to consumers' diet consciousness. Indeed, given the speed with which consumers can prepare frozen foods in a microwave and the time saved in eating quickly at home and moving to the next room for entertainment, eating at home may come to be seen as the most serious competitor of all of food service.

Figure 4.2 shows that the prices of food prepared and eaten away from home have been growing since 1980 at a somewhat more rapid rate than have the prices of food prepared away from but eaten at home. Thus, restaurants may have to compete not only with one another but also with food consumed at home, if these trends continue. This could be an especially difficult problem in an economic downturn: When consumers were asked how they stretched their budgets, over half (51 percent) said they ate out less often, and 54 percent said they entertained more at home. Not eating out—in an era of convenient eating in—is one of the easiest ways to cut back on spending. And the already-growing number of restaurants offering takeout and home delivery suggests that the industry is already seeking to meet the renewed competitive threat of eating at home.

Other consumer "life-style" competitors are skipped meals and the brown bag. The brown bag—a lunch brought from home—is probably principally an economy measure, and it might not be profitable to meet that particular price competition. On the other hand, consumers skip an average of two meals per week. No breakfast accounts for 65 percent of skipped meals, joined by no lunch, for 30 percent.[20]

Nutritionists tell us that skipping breakfast is actually not good for us. It can

---

[18] *Nation's Restaurant News*, August 12, 1985, p. F24.
[19] *Nation's Restaurant News*, August 19, 1985, p. 21.
[20] John J. Rohs, *The Restaurant Industry* (New York: Wertheim & Co., 1985), p. 9.

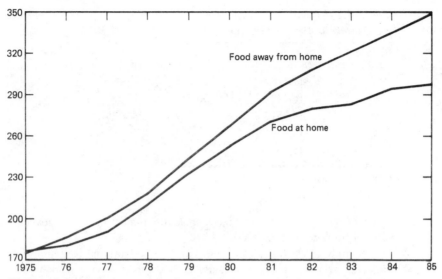

Figure 4.2 *Relative price levels, 1975–1985 (1967 = 100), of food at home and food away from home.* (Adapted from USDA/Prudential Bache.)

result in a weight gain because of insulin fluctuation and because of a tendency to have a high-calorie snack later or to overeat at lunch. Skipping breakfast also impairs performance, both physical and mental. And having just coffee and no breakfast has an even worse effect. The practice of skipped meals, then, might be thought of as a *marketing opportunity*. For example, individual restaurants or an industry group could use a public-service format to urge people to have a nutritious meal so as to improve their chances of losing weight and to feel better and work better.

Employment Trends

The changing age of America's population fits the good news–bad news pattern. The good news is the market opportunity arising from the higher average income as the baby boomers move into their peak earning years. The "baby bust," however, means shortages of restaurant labor, which are already being experienced in some areas and are likely to get worse for the next few years. There are roughly 3.5 million people working in fast-food operations, and nearly three-fourths of them are between 16 and 20 years of age.[21] Table 4.1 shows the dramatic change in the number of young workers between 1975 and 2000. The number of young people

[21] *Wall Street Journal*, May 28, 1985, p. 33.

Table 4.1   *Population changes for*
young workers, 1975–2000 (in millions)

YEAR	14–17	18–24
1975	17,128	28,005
1980	16,140	30,357
1985	14,731	28,739
1990	12,950	25,794
2000	15,382	24,601

Source: U.S. Bureau of the Census.

under 17 will be lowest in 1990, whereas the number of those between 18 and 24 will not hit bottom until 2000.

A study by Arthur D. Little & Co. for the National Restaurant Association projected a labor shortfall of nearly 200,000 food service workers by 1990 and approximately 1 million by 2000, assuming normal industry growth. The report pointed out that other industries employing large numbers of young workers such as retailers, service stations, hospitals, and banks would also be experiencing a labor shortage. An NRA report based on the Little study advised aggressive recruiting, upgrading pay and working conditions, and seeking out new labor sources. Increased labor productivity could be obtained, the study suggested, by using new technology such as automated or high-speed equipment and by improving management practices by streamlining menus, improving scheduling efficiency, and cross-training employees. It seems likely, too, that the labor shortage will encourage self-service.[22]

The population shifts that are leading to a labor shortage are only one reason for the greater number of opportunities. The aging baby boomers are already raising the demand for variety and innovation in restaurants. Many existing fine dining establishments are finding it necessary to adapt to today's more casual tastes, and new restaurants are being started by young entrepreneurs, particularly those with culinary training or experience.[23]

The most successful new chef owners generally have several years of experience, but many younger people with less formal culinary training are also finding success. The main criteria appear to be a good marketing sense, that is, knowing how to create a restaurant to satisfy a particular group of consumers, and a solid grasp of operating fundamentals.

[22] *Food Service and the Labor Shortage* (Washington, D.C.: National Restaurant Association, n.d.).
[23] *Nation's Restaurant News*, May 20, 1985, p. 231.

Summary

We began the chapter with an overview of the restaurant industry of the future and found that it will be like that of today, only more so. We then narrowed our view to the food service equipment of the future. Despite some technological advances, however, it is the customers who have refused to accept many of the automated devices. Microwave ovens are an exception, however, and are now widely used throughout the industry and in people's homes. In addition, such new concepts as scaled-down and mobile food service units have been used successfully.

Energy costs and food service was our next topic, especially energy costs in regard to transportation (that is, the mode of transportation that guests use to come to restaurants), food processing (such as the advantages of frozen versus chilled foods), disposables (such as throwaway plastic containers), and the general hospitality environment (for example, air conditioning).

We then examined the issue of competition, first how changes in outside forces—such as more women working and the slower growth of income—have affected the food industry. Second, we looked at competition within the industry itself, particularly advertising and promotion, the development of new products (such as salad bars and chicken nuggets), the expansion of day parts or meal occasions (the rise of snacks) and service (takeout and delivery), price, location (the chains' move to such places as campuses and military bases), and competition with supermarkets and the home itself.

Finally, we looked at employment trends and found that the food industry as a whole offers abundant opportunities.

Institutional Food Service

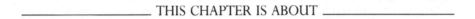

THIS CHAPTER IS ABOUT

The institutional food service market and the significant opportunities it offers you. We will analyze the four largest institutional segments: business and industry, college and university, health care, and school and community. Later in the chapter we will consider two specialized segments; military and in-flight food service. Some institutions operate their own food service; others use contract food service companies. We will look at both possibilities and consider the merits of each.

Institutional food service in all its segments uses a variety of preparation and delivery systems. We will consider conventional food systems, ready foods, and convenience systems as well as vending. Our discussion of institutional food service ends with a quick look at the future of institutional food service.

Courtesy of Warner-Lambert.

Comparing Institutional and Commercial Food Service

Dividing food service into commercial and institutional segments is somewhat artificial and misleading, as some of the same firms that profit from providing institutions with food services also operate in other areas of the hospitality industry. ARA Services, for instance, operates hotels in national parks, and Marriott, one of the largest contract food service companies, is also a major hotel and fast-food company.

There is, however, a difference between restaurant and institutional food service. Institutional food service was once a "captive market," in contrast with restaurants, where guests have a choice of facilities and menus. This distinction still exists, but its force has been greatly reduced. Companies such as Saga and Stouffer's have found that a marketing approach that begins with guest preferences and the assumption that patients, inmates, soldiers, and students are, in fact, *guests* wins more friends than the old "eat it and like it" institutional attitude. The institutional guests *does* have a choice in the long run. College students who don't like the food withdraw from board plans; patients who have a choice of hospitals often choose the institution with superior food service; and even inmates find ways to assert their food preferences. In an age of consumerism, moreover, even guests

A marketing orientation that offers the guests the services they want is important to today's institutional market. (Photo courtesy of Saga Corp.)

who can't "vote with their feet" and go someplace else, don't hesitate to complain. Therefore, competition among the various food service contractors is often decided on the basis of marketing techniques and management skills.

Even though many companies provide both restaurant and institutional food service and use similar marketing and managerial techniques in both areas, the major difference between the two markets is that the food service in institutions is a small part of a large operation with a larger purpose of overriding importance— health care, education, or manufacturing, for instance. In the restaurant, the challenge is to please the guest. In the institution it is necessary to meet the needs of both the guests and the client (that is, the institution itself).

The distinction between client and guest is important. The client is the institution and its managers and policymakers. These are the people who award the contract or, when the institution operates its own food service, hire and fire the food service manager. Pleasing the guest (that is, the individual diner, patient, student, resident, or inmate) is important, but the client must be pleased as well.

A commercial restaurant makes a profit by pleasing its guests. There may be a substantial difference in an institutional setting between the needs and wants of the guest and those of the client. In school food service, for instance, the client's (that is, the school's) goals are providing not only adequate nutrition but also nutrition education, by showing the students what a nutritionally balanced meal is like.

If the institution's food service is operated by a contract company, the contract must be arranged so as to provide the contract company with a profit (even if that requires a subsidy from the client). If an institution operates its own food service program, a profit is often *not* sought, but some stated budget target *will* need to be met.

These examples show how institutional feeding can differ from a restaurant operated for profit. They should also suggest that it is no easier to operate an institutional food service at a profit. Even though that profit may derive from a subsidy from the client, the operating company must still reach a budgetary target. In fact, "making your costs"—that is, achieving a target cost ratio—can be more difficult in an institution with a low budget than turning a profit in a commercial restaurant is.

The two segments also have different operating problems. For example, the number of meals and portion sizes are much easier to predict in institutional operations. Because of this greater predictability, institutional food service operations often operate in a less hurried atmosphere than that in restaurants, in which customer volume and menu popularity often fluctuate. And whereas employees tend to work long hours in commercial food service, the working hours in institutional food service are usually shorter, or at least more predictable.

On the other hand, although a guest may visit a restaurant frequently, few of them eat as regularly in their favorite restaurant as do the guests in institutional operations. Thus, varying the menu for a guest who must eat in the same place for weeks, months, or even years at a time can be a demanding task.

Table 5.1   *The institutional food service market, 1986*

	SIZE OF TOTAL MARKET (MILLIONS OF DOLLARS)	DEGREE OF PENETRATION BY CONTRACT COMPANIES
Business and Industry	$5,908	64%
Colleges and Universities	5,036	34
Hospitals and Nursing Homes	11,794	11
Primary and Secondary Schools	3,671	24
Total	$26,409	29%

Source: NRA News, December 1985.

Contract Companies and Institutional Operations

An important division within institutional food service is that between contract food service companies (hereafter,*contract companies*) and institutional organizations that operate their own food service (hereafter, *institutional operations*). The huge institutional market is still dominated by institutional operators, but the contract companies' share has been increasing. Table 5.1 shows that contract companies now provide nearly one-third of institutional food services. Health care is the area in which contract companies have the smallest share, but it has been increasing; from only 8 percent of the health-care market in 1981, compared with 11 percent in 1986. Contract companies have had even more success with public schools. The two areas in which the contract companies have expanded the least are colleges and universities and business and industry, because the contract companies are already established there. Contract companies manage just over one-third of college and university food services and two-thirds of business and industry.

Institutional Food Service Operations

There are four major divisions in institutional food service: business and industry, college and university, health care, and school and community. Two different ways of viewing the relative size of these divisions are summarized in Table 5.2. In the first column are the actual dollar sales as estimated by the National Restaurant Association (NRA). Because institutional sales are often subsidized, however, *Restaurant and Institutions* magazine believes that they can best be compared if their sales are estimated at their commercial value. The magazine therefore used purchases as a base to reach an estimate that is comparable to commercial restaurant sales, and these figures are the second set presented in Table 5.2. According to the

Table 5.2   *Institutional sales: Actual and commercial value, 1986*

	INSTITUTIONAL SALES	PERCENTAGE OF INSTITUTIONAL MARKET	COMMERCIAL VALUE OF INSTITUTIONAL SALES	PERCENTAGE OF INSTITUTIONAL MARKET
Business and Industry	$5,908	22.3%	$10,489	25.5
Colleges and Universities	5,034	19.1	6,164	15.0
Hospitals and Nursing Homes	11,794	44.7	11,438	27.8
Primary and Secondary Schools	3,671	13.9	13,043	31.7
	$26,409	100.0%	$41,134	100.0%

Source: NRA News; Restaurants and Institutions.

NRA method, institutions account for about 14 percent of food consumed away from home, but according to the magazine's method, the institution's commercial equivalent volume makes up nearly a quarter (23.9 percent) of the total food service market.

BUSINESS AND INDUSTRY FOOD SERVICE

Business and industry food service provides food for the convenience of both the guest (the worker) and the client (the employer). The client wants inexpensive food with enough variety and quality to satisfy the workers, as the client knows that food can directly affect the employees' morale. Quick service is also important, because the time for coffee breaks and lunch is limited.

The underlying forces that drive the food service's business and industry market are the size of the work force and the level of employment. The size of the work force affects the long-term outlook. When it was growing, the work force was a strong positive force, during the years when the baby boomers were leaving school and entering employment. Now that that surge is over, however, the Bureau of Labor Statistics estimates that the work force will increase at a modest 1.9 percent per year until 1995, and this slower growth will clearly affect business and industry sales.

Within the work force, the trend toward more office and other white-collar employment is determining where the food service business and industry volume will be. For example, some of the largest factory accounts will be reduced in size or even closed. On the other hand, the volume of food service in commercial and office buildings is growing at a significantly faster pace than it is in manufacturing plants.

Aside from prisons, mental hospitals, and other custodial institutions, no part of the institutional food service market is insulated from the rest of the food service business, and this is certainly true for the business and industry segment. As Joe Fassler, president of Greyhound management, put it, "Ten years ago your competitor was the other contract feeder. Today, other contract feeders are not our primary competitors. It is the commercial market."[1] One way that contract companies can meet the competition from commercial operations outside the institution is by developing their own version of popular restaurant strategies. Greyhound for instance, developed a fast-food operation called "Eatins' Easy," for its accounts. The new units generally include a range of products: burgers, fried chicken, fish, and hand-carved meat.

The advantages of this new format are startlingly similar to the advantage that fast food has in the commercial restaurant business.

The operation has an identity that helps secure patronage from an increasingly brand-conscious food service customer.

The facility is simpler to build than is a full-menu concept, and the investment required is only about half as much.

Operating costs are lower, too, because of the simpler menu and because customers are accustomed to serving themselves.

Fast food *is fast*—in-plant feeding at General Motors plants takes only 3 minutes, compared with 12 minutes under earlier formats.[2]

The merchandising of food service is receiving more attention, too. ARA, for instance, developed promotional programs of a number of menu selections that it has served for some time, but up until now without marketing planning and promotional support. These promotional programs include "Fresh Starts," a breakfast program with daily specials from around North America; "Kettle Classics," a variety of soups; and "Salad Garden."[3]

The purpose of employee food service operations changes with different employee levels. Many companies maintain executive dining rooms boasting fancy menus and elegant service. Such dining rooms are often used to entertain important business guests—customers, prospective employees, the press, and politicians. Executive dining room privileges can also be an important status symbol among managerial employees.

COLLEGE AND UNIVERSITY FOOD SERVICE

To understand college food service, one must understand the "board plan"; that is, students eating in residents halls may be required to contract for a minimum

---

[1] *Restaurant Business*, December 10, 1985, p. 189.
[2] *Nation's Restaurant News*, August 12, 1985, p. F56.
[3] *Restaurant Business*, November 1, 1985, p. 166.

number of meals over a term or semester. The food service corporation benefits from this arrangement in two ways. First, the absentee factor ensures that some students will miss some meals they contracted for, which permits the food service operation to price the total package below what all the meals would cost if every student ate every meal there. This makes the *package price* attractive, and because most college food service operations permit unlimited seconds, students can "load up" at those meals they do attend.

Second, and more important, the board plan provides a predictable volume of sales over a fairly long period—a term, a semester, or a year. At the start of that period, the operator can closely estimate what the sales volume will be. Because attendance ratios and the popularity of various menu items are fairly predictable, the operator can also estimate how much food to prepare for each meal.

Although some colleges offer only a full board plan (three meals a day, seven days a week while school is in session), flexible board plans have become more and more popular on many campuses, particularly those on which contract companies operate the food service. For example, some plans exclude breakfast, whereas others drop the weekend meals. There is now a wide variety of plans. Indeed, one food service company offers 91 different board plans on college campuses around the country.

With a flexible plan that invites students to contract for only the meals they expect to eat, the absentee rate goes down and the average price charged per meal

In college food services several different board plans may be available. Often, different styles of service—from fast food to formal dining—are offered to give a sense of variety. (Photo courtesy of Saga Corp.)

goes up, because of the lower absentee rates. Nevertheless, in plans that drop a significant number of meals, the *total price* of the meal contract also drops. In any case, both the full board plan and partial plans generally charge students on the basis of the average number of meals they consume.

Another approach that is gaining ground is for students to contract for some minimum dollar value of food service and to receive what is, in effect, a credit card with the amount they have paid credited to the card. As they use the card, the amount of each meal is electronically or manually deducted from the balance. Students receive the food purchased through their card at some discount from what competitive commercial operations charge, and so it is still a bargain. The contracts also give the operator a basis for projecting the demand for the school year for scheduling, purchasing, and general budgeting, and it also guarantees some minimum level of sales volume.

Flexible board plans represent one part of a marketing approach to college food service, an approach that adapts the services available to the guests' needs and preferences. In addition, with the arrrival of fast-food firms on a few large campuses, college food service operations have begun to develop their own formats to meet the demand for this kind of service. For example, the food service might feature Hawaiian luaus or outdoor steak fries, just to give their customers a sense of variety and change of pace. A contract company has to sell the client (the institution) so as to obtain or keep an account. But it must also sell the guests (the students) every day with quality and variety. Otherwise, the students will unsell the client and demand a change in food service.

One contact food service executive, C. J. Labante of ARA, summed up the goals of a college food service organization as follows:

> The business manager wants to maximize the dollars returned to the university (the difference between the charge to the student and the actual cost of operations). Food service on most campuses is income producing.[4] The student, on the other hand, wants to pay the minimum for food service. But he wants to receive a high quality program, food he enjoys.

> Students want to be served in a nice atmosphere. There is nothing worse than going into a stultified, aseptic atmosphere every day of the school year.

> Service management, I believe, is the art of trying to optimize the objectives of our clients and customers and, at the same time, to make sure we earn a reasonable bottom line profit.

College food service contracting companies stress the need for communication between the food service staff and the students. Many operators consult regularly with a student advisory group. All agree that, in addition to good food and tight

---

[4] The "income" produced for the institution by college food service is generally not a true net profit but, rather, a contribution to the interest cost and depreciation of the dormitory facility in which it is housed. Even in state schools, dormitories are usually constructed with money raised from sale of bonds, and the bondholders must be repaid in both principal and interest.

cost controls, a successful college food service operation must have "people skills"; that is, it must be able to deal effectively with the guests.

College enrollments should continue the decline that began in the early 1980s and is expected to last until the mid-1990s. Both contract companies and institutional operators will be affected by this trend, but the contract companies may be able to use it to their advantage through more vigorous marketing of their services to prospective client institutions. That is, as college enrollments drop and food service volumes drop right along with them, institutional budget targets will become harder to meet. The contractors will then have a competitive edge in seeking new accounts as the colleges seek the economies of scale that these companies offer.

HEALTH-CARE FOOD SERVICE

Health-care food service can be divided into three categories: large hospitals (over 300 beds), small to medium hospitals, and nursing homes. In all three of these settings, health-care professionals—dietitians, along with such paraprofessionals as dietary managers and dietetic technicians—play important roles.

The Dietetic Professional

"The dietitian," according to an authoritative study of the profession, "is a 'translator' of the science of nutrition into the skill of furnishing optimum nourishment. The word 'translator' is used in its familiar context of 'translating ideas into action.'"[5] The largest group within the profession—between 60 and 75 percent—is made up of clinical dietitians concerned principally with the problems of special diets and with educating patients who have health problems that require temporary or permanent diet changes. Another 15 to 25 percent of dietetic professionals are administrative dietitians concerned principally with the management of food service systems, for the most part in health care. (Dietitians also work in education and in non-health-care food services, and their commitment to community nutrition is growing rapidly as well.)

Dietitians who complete a bachelor's degree program and professional training (either in an internship program or in a coordinated undergraduate program that includes both academic classwork and professional experience) and who pass a registration examination are registered in the professional organization, the American Dietetic Association. Registered dietitians (R.D.s) are required by hospital accreditation standards and government regulations to supervise health-care food services either on a full-time basis or as consultants.

The dietary department in a large hospital is headed by either an administrative dietitian or a hospital food service manager. A nondietitian who is employed as the hospital food service manager is supported by a chief of nutrition services, who is a registered dietitian. Large hospitals generally employ a number of

[5] *The Profession of Dietetics: Report of the Study Commission on Dietetics* (Chicago: American Dietetic Association, 1972).

clinical dietitians who spend considerable time with patients and prepare special diets. Once a special diet has been written, the clinical dietitian translates it into production orders for the cooks and tray assemblers and then makes certain that these orders are followed. An important part of the dietitian's work is interpreting the diet to the patients, helping them understand the need for the diet, and preparing them to plan their own specialized diet.

In a smaller hospital, the food service manager is somewhat less likely to be a registered dietitian. In such cases, however, a consulting registered dietitian will provide professional guidance.

The Dietetic Technician

A somewhat newer face in health care is that of the dietetic technician, who has completed an appropriate associate degree program. Technicians occupy key roles in medium and large hospitals working under the direction of registered dietitians. Dietetic technicians screen and interview patients to determine their dietary needs or problems and, in large hospitals, often have supervisory responsibilities. In smaller hospitals, technicians may run dietary departments under the periodic supervision of consulting registered dietitians. One of the most common areas of employment for dietetic technicians is in extended-care facilities, such as nursing homes, where technicians serve as food service managers under the supervision of a consulting registered dietitian. Technicians must take a registration exam, and fully qualified technicians are registered by the American Dietetic Association. With increasing cost pressure in hospitals, there is pressure to reduce the number of registered dieticians, and so more and more work is being delegated to dietetic technicians.

The Dietary Manager

The dietary manager also has an important role in health-care food service. Dietary managers must have had a considerable amount of on-the-job experience and must also have completed a 90-hour course of instruction, covering subjects such as food service management, supervision, and basic nutrition. A separate organization, the Dietary Managers Association, provides for the education and certification of dietary managers who are not members of ADA.[6] Dietary managers are used principally in nursing homes. Some dietary managers have completed the dietetic technician's more extensive two-year course of instruction and may use either title.

Dietary Department Organization

The organization of the dietary department should be considered in the context of the overall health-care facility organization. Figure 5.1 depicts the organization of a medium-sized hospital. The work of the nursing division is, in general, self-explanatory. Other professional services include laboratories, X-ray services, and

---

[6] Ayres G. D. Carter and Ann L. Schrech, *The Role of the Dietary Manager: An Overview of the HIEFSS Role Delineation Study* (Hillside, Ill.: Hospital, Instition, and Educational Food Service Society, n.d.).

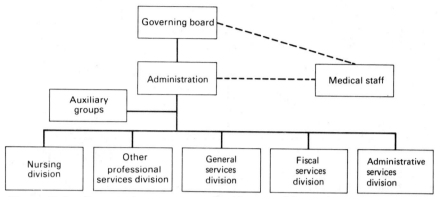

Figure 5.1 *Functional organization of medium-sized hospital.* (American Hospital Association.)

pharmacies. The dietary department is found in the general services division along with other support services, such as plant engineering and housekeeping. The fiscal services division includes functions such as accounting, receiving, and storage. Thus, in some hospitals, receiving and storage may be carried out for food service by another support unit. Administrative services include the personnel and purchasing functions. Here again, note that another division may assume these functions for the dietary department. This already-complex organization is further complicated by the medical and surgical staffs—the professionals on whose services the entire institution is centered.

Work in hospital food service is fast paced, and many employees find the medical atmosphere exciting. The organizational complexity and need for *nutrition care* (the provision of special therapeutic diets) as a separate concern makes a career in health-care food service one of the most complex and demanding of the food service careers.

The organization of the dietary department will vary in its assignment and reporting relationships according to the size and function of the hospital. The main functions appear in Figure 5.2.

The same kitchen usually prepares the food for all the employees, house diet patients, and visitors. Some hospitals maintain a separate diet kitchen; others allow the same crew to prepare the special diets following appropriate recipes. Patient food service personnel deliver the food to the floors and return dishes and other equipment to the kitchen after the meals. The cafeteria serves the staff, visitors, and in some cases, ambulatory patients. Some large hospitals offer internships and other educational programs for dietetic professionals just as they do for nursing and medical school graduates.

Nursing homes, extended-care facilities, and smaller hospitals perform these similar functions on a smaller scale. Thus, such an institution may employ only a consulting dietitian and may combine food production and patient food service. Or

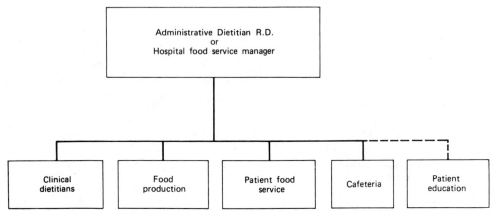

Figure 5.2   *Functional organization of the dietary department.*

the cafeterias in some nursing homes may be expanded to serve all ambulatory patients, often in traditional dining rooms.

Trends in Health-Care Food Service

In the past, health care was a "recession-proof" food service market with a strong growth potential. Although health care is still less sensitive to economic conditions than are many other food service segments, the government's standardization of fees under "Diagnosis Related Groups" (DRGs) brought its growth to a halt.[7] This is because the government previously paid Medicaid and Medicare bills on a cost-plus basis. But this led to a runaway inflation in medical costs, with the annual increase peaking in 1980 at 15.3 percent.[8] Once the government introduced standardized reimbursement, private health insurance plans began to follow in order to cap their own costs. In addition, the nursing home equivalent of the DRG, called the RUG (Resource Utilization Grouping), was introduced in 1986.[9]

A major effect of DRGs and RUGs has been to limit the number of days in hospitals or nursing homes for which Medicare or Medicaid will pay. This has reduced the length of the average health-care stay, the occupancy levels, and, thereby, the hospitals' revenue. In addition, DRG and RUG limit the other costs that will be reimbursed, further lowering revenue. Health care has consequently had to learn to live with less, which has had a dramatic impact on dietary departments. Because there are fewer patient meals to be served, the number of staff has often been reduced.

But on the other hand, the lower hospital occupancy levels have led to greater competition for patients, and the dietary department often play a key role in this

[7] *Restaurant & Institutions,* January 18, 1984, pp. 112–120.
[8] *Restaurants & Institutions,* January 23, 1985, pp. 140–144.
[9] *Restaurants & Institutions,* January 8, 1986, pp. 148–153.

competition, offering optional room service, upscale restaurant facilities on the premises, restaurant-style menus for patients, and even dessert carts. In addition, hospital dietary departments now offer to cater functions outside the hospital and encourage outsiders to come to eat in the hospital—all measures aimed at increasing the dietary department's contribution to the hospital's revenues.

Some hospitals are turning to centralized cook-chill systems because they offer substantial savings. And because these systems are also expensive to build, hospitals are selling cook-chill meals to other nearby institutions. The additional sales volume helps pay for the equipment and reduces the preparation facility's operation and capital costs.[10]

Entrepreneurial Opportunities   Because of the increasing number of elderly people in our population, more and more people require assistance in living at home. Indeed, this number has probably been increased by the institution of DRG/RUG measures, which force health-care institutions to move out people as quickly as possible. To meet the needs of these people living at home who cannot care for themselves, a number of home-care services have sprung up. Some offer simply housekeeping services, but others provide "sitter" service and limited nursing care. In addition, nutritional support companies offer nutritional care such as special diets. These home-assistance companies offer people with dietetic training an interesting opportunity to go into business for themselves with a minimum of investment.

SCHOOL AND COMMUNITY FOOD SERVICE

Over the past 35 years, the changes in our views of women and the family have had an enormous impact on food service in general. The best objective measure of the change in the role of women appears in the proportion of women employed outside the home or seeking such employment. This proportion is referred to as the *female labor-force participation rate*.

In 1900, about 20 out of every 100 women in the United States entered the work force, that is, were employed outside the home or were seeking employment. In 1920, after World War I, this number was only about 23 in 100 (actually, 22.7 percent), an overall change of less than 14 percent in the participation rate. From 1920 to 1940, the rate rose to just under 26 in 100, again, a change of just under 14 percent.

With World War II, the rate of change increased radically. The basis for estimating the 1940 rate and the 1947 rate changed slightly, as 1947 was the first year in which the rate was computed by current methods. Allowing for this difference, however, the rate rose from just over one-quarter (25.8 percent) of the women working in 1940 to nearly one-third in 1947 (31.8 percent), a rate of increase in that 7-year period of approximately 23 percent, compared with less than 14 percent for each of the two preceding 20-year periods.

[10] *Nation's Restaurant News*, February 11, 1986, p. F3-4.

In the 20 years between 1954 and 1974, the female participation rate jumped even higher, increasing from 34.6 percent to 45.6 percent. This was a *change* of 32 percent, or more than twice the rate of change experienced during the first two 20-year periods in this century. From 1970 to 1983, as Table 5.3 demonstrates, work-force participation increased dramatically for women in the age groups normally associated with raising children (ages 20 to 54), with the growth in the number of working women between the ages of 25 and 34 being particularly pronounced. Some combination of the growing social acceptance of working mothers and the effect of inflation and recession in reducing the rate of increase in family income probably accounts for these most recent developments.

We will consider these female labor-force participation rates in detail because of their enormous impact on the demand for food service. In 1900, only one in five women expected to work outside the home. Today, some two-thirds of women between the ages of 18 and 54 work or are seeking employment. And by 1995, that proportion will have increased to roughly 8 out of 10. The result, of course, is that many more women are midday food service customers. Moreover, the increase in family income provided by a second job allows more families to dine out in the evening. And a working wife, tired after a day's work, is quite likely to want to spend money for this purpose.

To see the impact of working mothers even more clearly, we should examine more closely the recent female labor-force trends. Table 5.3 shows that the change in women's labor-force participation has not been the same for all age groups, and these differences directly affect government-supported food service programs.

Labor-force participation by women under the age of 20 was not unusual in

Table 5.3   *Growth in female labor-force participation rates, projected and actual 1947–1995*

AGE GROUP	PARTICIPATION PERCENTAGES					RATE OF CHANGE	
	1947	1970	1980	1983	1995*	1947–1983	1980–1995
16–17	29.4%	34.9%	43.6%	39.9%	48.0%	35.7%	20.3%
18–19	52.2	53.5	61.9	60.7	68.9	16.3	13.5
20–24	44.8	57.7	68.9	69.9	82.0	56.0	17.3
25–34	31.9	45.0	65.5	69.0	81.7	116.3	18.4
35–44	36.3	51.1	65.5	68.7	82.8	89.2	20.5
45–54	32.7	54.4	59.9	61.9	69.5	89.3	12.3
55–64	24.3	43.0	41.3	41.5	42.5	70.8	2.4
65 and over	8.1	9.7	8.1	7.8	7.0	−13.16	−10.3
Total	31.8	43.3	51.5	52.9	60.3	89.6	14.0

Source: Bureau of Labor Statistics; *Statistical Abstract of the United States.*
[a] Bureau of Labor Statistics estimate.

1947. In fact, more than one-half the women 18 and 19 years old worked in the labor force in that year. At that time, as women married and bore children, they typically withdrew from the labor force. Recent years, however, have seen a shift from working women to working mothers.

As Table 5.3 shows, the increase in the participation rate for women in the child-bearing years was much greater than the increase in the rate for all women. As more and more mothers went to work, they increased the demand for different ways to provide meals away from home for their children.

Although the dramatic change in the number of women working outside the home has affected nearly every institution in our society, in institutional food service, its greatest impact has been on school food service and care for the elderly.

The National School Lunch Program (NSLP)

Early History   Historians have traced the earliest concern for feeding children outside the home to "private societies and associations interested in child welfare and education."[11] The first program of this kind seems to have started in 1790 in Germany. However, a national government first entered the field in Holland in 1900, with Switzerland following six years later.

In the United States, concern about hunger and nutritional deficiency deepened during the Depression of the 1930s. Ironically, the Depression was a time of agricultural surpluses. The earliest support for major, continuing federal involvement in school feeding arose, then, as part of the effort to use these agricultural surpluses constructively.

Concern for the nutrition of poor children, concern for the national interest, the need to stimulate demand for agricultural produce, and the need to accommodate young people too far from home to return there for lunch all helped build support for the school lunch program before World War II.

We have already noted that the women at work were, more and more, mothers. They thus had to make some provision to feed their children a midday meal, as they could not do it themselves. Thus, what was once a function of the family increasingly became an obligation undertaken by that familiar community organization, the school. Under these circumstances, it is not surprising that political support for the National School Lunch Program (NSLP) grew, and so did the size of the NSLP's financial appropriation.

Current Support   One reason for the rapid growth of the school lunch program in the 1960s and 1970s was the enormous growth in the school population that resulted from the baby boom. That reason no longer holds, however, and accordingly, government funding for school food service has been drastically curtailed and refocused. For instance, in 1985, only 9 percent of the federal contribution went to

[11] For an authoritative, extended treatment of the history of the NSLP, see Gordon W. Gunderson, *The National School Lunch Program: Background and Development* (Washington, D.C.: Food and Nutrition Service, U.S. Department of Agriculture, n.d.). Much of the following history of school lunch before 1970 is taken from Gunderson's excellent study.

Most experts agree that providing an attractive setting for school lunch programs has a favorable impact on participation rates. (Photo courtesy of American School Food Service Association.)

middle-class children, compared with three to four times that proportion in the late 1970s. Most of the cash assistance—$2.43 billion—is provided for free or reduced-price meals served to low-income children.[12] Even though this diminished federal support has changed the management of the school lunch program, it has served well the changing life-styles of the American family. Indeed, the question is how school food service will be paid for, not whether the country will have such a program.

The School Food Service Model

Even though the school lunch program has substantially changed in recent years, it remains an interesting model for transferring family functions to a segment of the hospitality industry. The question of public hospitality agencies' performing what were once family functions remains a lively one. Many are opposed to what they view as an unnatural, even antifamily, trend in our society. On the other hand,

[12] *Nation's Restaurant News*, December 9, 1985, p. F5.

Because working mothers can rarely take summers off, a special summer food service program has become an important service to families with working mothers. (Photo courtesy of U.S. Department of Agriculture, Food and Nutrition Services.)

with the high and growing number of women in the work force, it is generally agreed that *somebody* must provide the services no longer available in the home.

The first element in the model suggested by the school food service is that the program *meet several clearly defined social needs.* Although using up surplus commodities was an important early factor, the program appears to address more general social problems today. The program provides nutritious meals to needy children who might otherwise go hungry, and it helps make well-balanced meals available to all students.

USDA regulations require that school lunches conform to a basic pattern and provide one-third to one-half of a student's minimum daily nutritional requirements. The following four elements must be present in prescribed quantities.

1. *Body-building foods, such as meat, fish, eggs, and cheese, that provide protein and iron. (Bread and butter are served with these foods to supply carbohydrates and fat.)*

2. *Vegetables or fruits high in vitamin A.*

3. *Vegetables or fruits high in vitamin C.*

4. *Milk, to provide calcium as well as protein.*

The approved lunch offers more than a nutritionally sound meal. It has become part of the educational program itself, teaching students what foods are necessary to health and growth.

The second element in the NSLP model is that it pools subsidies. The federal subsidy usually requires matching state or local funds. Because the subsidies from the various levels of government are pooled, the result constitutes a "bargain." The student's lunch, even if he or she paid the full price, is less expensive than it would be if purchased anywhere else—even if it were brought from home.

The attractiveness of this bargain encourages participation; and participation ensures the third element of the model, a high volume. This high volume makes the meal program more efficient, and it results in further economies. In short, it improves the bargain.

The pattern of administration is the fourth and final element. There is general monitoring of the fairly broad guidelines at the national and state levels, but most operational decisions are made entirely at a local level. Technical advice is, of course, always available. Thus, the model encourages adaptation to local tastes and conditions.

The Response to Funding Changes If there were any realistic danger to the school food service program as a result of funding-level changes, the remarkable response of the school food service community to what was initially seen as a threat should certainly put anyone's fears to rest. That reaction, which is a tribute to the dedication, inventiveness, and resilience of school food service management, has had two related aspects: marketing and cost control. A consciousness of the "sovereign consumer," already present in many school lunch operations, has spread to a much broader audience among school lunch managers. With the higher costs passed on to the paying child, efforts to market the school food service competitively have been intensified. For example, to increase participation, youth advisory councils have been set up in some schools to provide customer feedback in much the same way as it is in colleges.[13] As a result, school lunchrooms have been remodeled to make them more attractive, and self-service bars have been introduced to provide a service that looks, and is, competitive with commercial food services. For example, an article on merchandising in the *School Food Service Journal* recommended that the school lunch program hold some kind of promotional event at least once every two weeks, to compete with fast-food operations. Moreover, school lunch personnel must begin to function as sales people: "In the school food *service* industry, you're inviting paying customers into your lunch room to eat your good products. . . . Nonprofit does not mean no profit or no business sense. You're a business."[14]

Even though the salaries of commercial operators and many other institutional employees are generally higher, the life-style advantages of employment in school food service shouldn't be overlooked in assessing career opportunities in this field.

[13] *School Food Service Journal*, September 1984, pp. 22–23.
[14] *School Food Service Journal*, June–July–August 1985, p. 26.

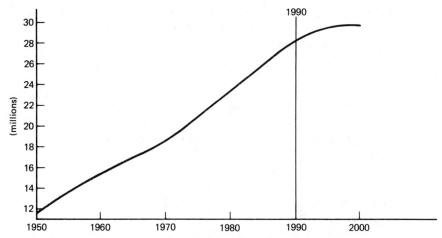

Figure 5.3   *People 65 to 84 years old, 1950–2000.* [Adapted from Peter K. Franchese, "Consumer Perspectives," *Proceedings: Chain Operators Exchange, 1985* (Chicago: International Foodservice Manufacturers Association, 1985).]

Some programs run year round, but most offer reasonable hours, time off at Christmas and spring break, as well as the possibility of summers entirely free for family or other pursuits.

FOOD SERVICE PROGRAMS FOR THE AGING

In our discussion of the school lunch program, we examined such basic causes as the national concern for adequate nutrition and an increase in the number of working mothers. A similar set of forces is at work in the creation of a food service program to serve aging Americans.

The first force is demographic—population trends relate to births, deaths, and average ages in the country. Few people realize how radical the demographic changes have been in recent years. As recently as 100 years ago, only a small proportion of the population survived past the age of 50; "old age" began in a person's thirties.[15] But by the beginning of this century, improved health care, better nutrition, better control of communicable diseases, and many other factors led to a radical increase in life expectancy. The strong influence of retirees in our society began, as Peter Drucker pointed out, when the babies born in the 1890s did not die in the 1940s, as they would have a generation earlier. We are, in fact, the first society in history in which a large proportion of our population has survived not just past 50 but well into their sixties, seventies, and eighties.

As Figure 5.3 illustrates, America's elderly population already is large, and the

[15] For an extended discussion of this issue and its more general social consequences, see Peter Drucker, *The Unseen Revolution* (New York: Harper & Row, 1976).

number of people over 65 will grow until the end of the century. (After the turn of the century, this population group will grow even faster, but that is beyond the scope of our discussion here.) The population group with the highest growth *rate* today, as illustrated in Figure 5.4, is the group of very senior citizens over 85 years of age.

In the commercial market, the greater number of retired people means a new leisure class. Those between age 65 and 75 are likely to be healthy, active, and— with improved pension and social security programs—relatively affluent. This group already has affected travel markets as well as other leisure services such as dining out.

In this chapter, however, we will focus on the relatively less prosperous elderly for whom institutional programs have been designed. People *over 75* are more likely to fall in this category, as they are more likely to be financially needy and to require assistance to survive. The rapid growth of this group is one reason for the increasing demand for institutional services for the elderly.

A second force at work is the change in the family. At the turn of the century, few women and even fewer married women went to work. And at that time, the few persons who did survive into old age lived with their grown children or other relatives. Today, however, working women and men have little energy left over to care for their aging parents and relatives. Therefore, different social arrangements are emerging to accommodate the increasing numbers of elderly people.

Some senior citizens can afford to enter retirement communities or other retirement centers that provide a host of services. But many elderly persons cannot afford these expensive arrangements. Although social security benefits give them some cash income to cover the costs of housing and clothing, an alarming propor-

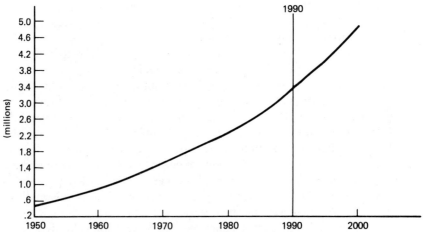

Figure 5.4   *People 85 + years old, 1950–2000.* [Adapted from Peter K. Franchese, "Consumer Perspectives," *Proceedings: Chain Operators Exchange, 1985* (Chicago: International Foodservice Manufacturers Association, 1985).]

tion of our senior citizens of modest means receive inadequate nutrition. In fact, over 15 percent of elderly Americans live below the poverty line.

One solution to the problem of caring for the elderly (a solution that our society seeems ready to accept because of the NSLP precedent) is an inexpensive food service administered under a program generally referred to as *congregate meals.* According to the Administration on Aging (AoA).

> *The national nutrition program for the elderly is designed to provide older Americans, particularly those with low income, with low cost, nutritionally sound meals. Emphasis is given to providing these meals in group settings. The nutritional projects provide at least one hot meal a day (meeting one third of the daily nutritional requirements) five days a week, to older citizens (60 +) and their spouses of any age.*

Although participants would be given an opportunity to pay for their meals, "no means test will be made and no one will be turned away on the basis of their inability to pay for a meal."

The congregate meals program offers older Americans not only sound nutrition but also a chance to continue their participation in community activities and to combine food and friendship. (Photo courtesy of U.S. Department of Health and Human Services, Administration on Aging.)

This legislation responds not only to the problems of low income among the elderly but to their other problems as well. To quote the AoA again:

> *Regulations promulgated by the Secretary of HEW provide that individuals eligible to receive meals are those persons age 60 or over who (1) cannot afford to eat adequately, (2) lack the skills and knowledge to select and prepare nourishing and well balanced meals, (3) have limited mobility which may impair their capacity to shop and cook for themselves, or (4) have feelings of rejection and loneliness which obliterate the incentive necessary to prepare and eat a meal alone.*

In facing the problems of the elderly, this food service program sets goals for itself that go beyond the obvious nutritional goals:

> *In addition to promoting better health among the older segment of the population through improved nutrition, the program can help reduce the isolation of the aged, offering older Americans an opportunity to continue to participate in community activities and to combine food and friendship.*

Social services for the elderly have also begun to emphasize *deinstitutionalization*. Early experiences in caring for our ballooning elderly population have taught us that it is both less expensive and more humane to help the elderly live in their own homes or apartments rather than in an institutional environment such as the county home for the aged. Food services provided by community or neighborhood organizations, which often administer other services as well, help maintain the elderly in their homes.

In fiscal year 1984, over 144 million congregate meals were served to nearly 3 million elderly, 56 percent of whom were in economic need. The cost to all parties (that is, government, participants, and other funding agencies) was over $574 million, and nearly 8000 sites were used for this service, most of them operating on a five-day week.[16]

Preparation and Delivery Systems

Most institutions use one of three preparation systems: conventional systems, ready food systems, and convenience food systems. *Conventional food service systems*, still the most common, prepare food "from scratch" in their own kitchens for every meal. Many institutions prefer these operations, because management has acquired the impression that "from scratch" food tastes better and is more readily accepted by consumers. In markets in which labor is plentiful, and especially in larger institutions in which the number of people served is large enough to justify the use

---

[16] *Fiscal Year 1984 National Summary of Program Performance* (Washington, D.C.: Administration on Aging, n.d.).

On a hospital's tray line, regular and special diet food are assembled for transportation to the patient's room. (Photo courtesy of Saga Corp.)

of a full kitchen crew, this traditional form of food service is still economically feasible.

In a *ready foods operation*, the institution's preparation employees work five days a week, eight hours a day, to prepare, plate, and then freeze or chill the food. A different crew reconstitutes and serves the food. This system is most frequently found today in large hospitals, but the use of central commissaries is also becoming common in school food service. The use of food chilled to 33° to 35° or 1° to 2° C instead of to the frozen state is becoming increasingly common in both hospitals and school food service.

Centralization of food preparation is increasingly common in school food service.
(Photo courtesy of U.S. Department of Agriculture, Food and Nutrition Service.)

Convenience food systems depend on foods provided by frozen food manufacturers. The institutions that adopt this system are usually small. The *portion cost* of the food is relatively expensive, but its use permits a food service when adequate kitchen facilities are not otherwise available. Moreover, the higher unit cost may be offset by the smaller food service payroll, because fewer and less-skilled employees are required for this system.

The most common institutional *delivery system* (the means of delivering prepared food to the guest) is the cafeteria. But some executive dining rooms offer waitress service, and patient food service has too many different equipment configurations and modifications to discuss here. In school food service, however, in which basically the same meal is served at many sites in a school district on any given day, more and more districts are moving to centralize food production in commissaries. The savings available from this strategy are impressive.

In Portland, Oregon recently, for instance, the annual savings from centralizing production for its 75 separate school lunch facilities was $600,000. Of this, $100,000 per year resulted from smaller food inventories, and an additional $500,000 came from lower labor costs. Not surprisingly, one factor in reducing the

Once food preparation is centralized, transportation becomes essential, so many school systems now operate their own transportation systems. (Photo courtesy of U.S. Department of Agriculture, Food and Nutrition Service.)

payroll was simplifying management in the school system. Through attrition, 68 kitchen managers at the school level were eliminated, replaced by a "lead assistant" in each satellite kitchen. The Portland school system also uses a quick chill system, and since it centralized its lunch preparation, the participation rate has risen, apparently as a result of the improved and standardized quality of its products.[17]

VENDING

Between 1975 and 1985, the dollar sales in vending nearly doubled, from $9.3 billion to $17.6 billion. Over three-quarters (76.4 percent), or $14 billion, of that represented either food or beverages (including candy and soft drinks). Table 5.4 shows the dollar sales of items sold through vending machines. After studying the table, you may wonder whether vending is really food service. Although three-quarters of vending volume directly competes with food service, roughly 65 percent of that volume comprises just hot and cold drinks. Still, the remaining balance is

[17] *School Food Service Journal*, June–July–August 1984, pp. 152–154.

Table 5.4   *1984 vended-product volume*

PRODUCT	PERCENTAGE OF TOTAL	DOLLAR VOLUME (MILLIONS)
Hot drinks	7.5%	1,240
Cold drinks	40.8	6,730
Packaged confections/snacks	16.3	2,680
Bulk vending (ball gum, nuts, etc.)	1.3	188
Milk	2.1	351
Ice cream	0.5	80
Pastries	1.9	320
Hot canned foods	0.9	149
Vended food service (sandwiches, salads, etc.)	5.3	880
Cigarettes	20.4	3,370
Cigars	2.8	458
All others	100.0%	$16,477

Source: "Census of the Industry," *Vending Times*, 1985.

$5 billion. Moreover, many people seem to be replacing one or more meals with several snacks, and so vending does compete, especially with fast food, in the snack market.

Table 5.5 compares vending sales in 1975 and in 1985. Although the dollar total for all vending is given at the bottom of the table, remember that dollar comparisons are distorted by inflation. For this reason, the detailed comparisons between product groups are in *units*. Even though some product categories have dropped somewhat, the heavy sellers, cold drinks and snacks, have risen substantially, as has vended food service in general. Because of these increases and the large drop in vended cigarettes, foods and beverages continue to be the major market for vending. Notice that vended food service (sandwiches, salads, and the like) has risen by 28 percent, and the following two case studies suggest the competitive impact of vending within the food service field.

An office building housing some 2500 employees was built in the heart of a large city. The designers refused to incorporate a restaurant, because kitchen facilities and storerooms would take up space destined for other uses. Dishrooms and the necessary plumbing and air ducts required for a kitchen would also have added to the cost of the building.

In addition, the building's management did not feel qualified to operate its own food service and had heard that leased restaurants often took up much of the building managers' time. Finally, management felt that a restaurant would also create traffic problems at the loading dock, with the numerous deliveries and garbage and trash removal.

Table 5.5   *Number of units sold through vending, 1975 and 1985*

ITEM	1975	1985
Hot drinks	4,563,000,000 units	4,820,000,000 units
Cold drinks	2,920,000,000	7,310,000,000
Packaged confections and snacks	6,760,000,000	7,600,000,000
Milk	1,105,000,000	89,000,000
Ice cream	304,000,000	230,000,000
Pastries	844,000,000	725,000,000
Hot canned food	265,000,000	233,000,000
Vending food service (sandwiches, salads, etc.)	790,000,000	1,015,000,000
Cigarette packs	4,510,000,000	2,530,000,000
Total dollar sales	$9,332,000,000	$17,548,800,000

Source: "Census of the Industry," *Vending Times*, 1986.

Although capital expense and operating complications argued against a restaurant, the designers wanted a food service available in the building as a convenience to the occupants. Consequently, they designed vending restaurants that would provide an ample menu selection, including not only sandwiches but also scrambled eggs, sausage, and pancakes for breakfast, and fried chicken, french fried potatoes, salisbury steak, and other traditional entrees for lunch and dinner. Although entrees such as these currently account for only 5 percent of food service vending sales, their presence constitutes an important service for the guest and, perhaps, a harbinger of future food service trends.

The food (including sandwiches, which make up some three-quarters of the vended food service sales) is prepared at the vendor's commissary. The food is delivered before the building's regular operating hours, to avoid congestion.

In another city, a professional building accommodating about 500 people opened a small table-service restaurant just off the lobby. The occupants of the building were unhappy with the quality of the operation, however, and the operator finally went out of business. Its eight employees were replaced by a vending restaurant that offered a variety of specialty sandwiches prepared in the vendor's commissary and heated for service in a microwave oven. The operation required one atttendant on duty from 8:00 A.M. to 4:30 P.M. on weekdays.

Guests are rarely enthusiastic about vending retaurants, but their impersonality can be reduced by "attended vending," which provides a specially trained hostess who makes change, gives refunds, and handles complaints. Still, vending remains primarily a mechanical, self-service process.

On the positive side, vending restaurants are convenient, can solve economic and operational problems for building and plant managers, and can increase food service variety. Most food service vending operations are found in public buildings, plants, factories, and offices, in which the clientele is too small to justify a full-fledged food service operation and too far from other restaurant facilities for the employees to reach them easily on their lunch hours.

The variety of products that vendors sell is growing and improving. Nearly one-half of the companies offering vended food services have their own commissaries, and their vending outlets usually are equipped with microwave ovens. In 1984, nearly 86 percent of vending food service companies operated microwave ovens in their accounts, and 305,000 of these units were in operation in conjunction with food service vending.

Most vending sales are in business and industry: over half (57 percent) in factories, 18 percent in office locations, and 8 percent in government, military, and other public locations. Colleges and universities accounted for 10 percent of sales, and grade and high schools accounted for 2 percent. Health care provided only 4 percent of vending sales.[18]

Vending has clearly become part of the "eating" market, as defined in Chapter 2, rather than the dining market. Vending companies have found that if they offer *manual vending* (that is, a cafeteria staffed by "real, live" people during part of the hours of service) acceptance of *all* of their products improves. One vendor speculated that this is true because the personal touch allows the guests to associate the vended food with the people who provide food services in the more traditional cafeterias.

Vending offers the hospitality industry a means of extending food service hours to meet the convenience of guests, and to provide acceptable service where it would be economically impossible to provide full manual food service. Sanitation in vending is important and can be troublesome. And the consumerist antivending reaction is likely to continue. Nevertheless, this component of food service, now serving $5 billion worth of food in direct competition with restaurant meals and more than $7 billion more in snacks and drinks, should not be ignored by either the food service student or the operator.

Who Operates an Institution's Food Service?

Now that we have discussed the clientele served by institutional food services, we can examine the arguments for and against the use of contract companies or institutional in-house food services. The principal arguments involve (1) economies of scale, (2) control of operations, and (3) management expertise.

---

[18] "Census of the Industry," *Vending Times*, July 1986, p. 50.

RESPONSIBILITY FOR INSTITUTIONAL OPERATIONS

Many institutions see no need to pay the overhead and profits of a contract company. Operating on the assumption that their own employees can manage as efficiently as a contract company can, these institutions choose to keep the overhead and profit they otherwise would have to pay to an outside company. These institutions obviously can exercise complete control over their operations; and to some extent they can limit the staff turnover traditionally associated with contract companies, who frequently promote or transfer their employees. "If we like a person," said one university official, "we might lose him to a contract company. In our own operation, if we treat him right we have a good chance of keeping him—of maintaining staff stability."

Institutional Operators

The magazine *Restaurant & Institutions* publishes a study of large organizations in food service called "The 400," which reports on the 400 largest hospitality operators in the United States. Each year, the 400 lists roughly 50 institutional operators in this group of largest organizations, including health-care institutions, state universities or university systems, and public agencies.

Contact Companies

Each year, 25 to 30 of the 400 largest U.S. food service organizations are contact companies, according to the annual *Restaurant & Institutions* 400. An important service that contact companies offer is centralized purchasing. ARA Food Service listed some typical savings that it achieved:

- A purveyor change made in central Texas that saved the company and its clients $104,000 a year.

- Negotiations with dairy suppliers in the same central Texas market that resulted in annual savings of $90,000.

- An audit of a supplier's books (impractical and too expensive for a smaller operation) that resulted in determining and recovering overbillings of $13,500.

- Consolidation of the purchases of several different accounts into one account that saved $30,000.

Because ARA negotiates on a national scale, for example, its coffee purchases and because the consolidated purchases for the firm annually run to 18 or 20 million pounds, ARA can ensure price stability for three to six months as well as minimum costs consistent with market conditions.

Contract companies also offer to their clients, at cost, extensive facilities planning services. These services include operational design (equipment), interior design, procurement, supervision of construction, and equipment installation. Specialized accounting and market planning services may also be offered to clients.

Many companies have developed specialized marketing techniques adapted to the needs of individual institutions. Thus, for instance, Ogden Food Services has developed a fast-food variation of their Nedick's hot dog, sandwich, and orange-drink operation to meet college students' preference for economy and speed.

Other Institutional Food Service Segments

Two other food service segments, military food service and in-flight and transportation food service, deserve mention here to round out the picture of the institutional market. Both offer career opportunities and often a chance to travel.

MILITARY FOOD SERVICE

Fourteen of the *Restaurant & Institutions* 400 are military food service groups. As listed in Table 5.6, these groups fall into four categories: military food service; post and base exchange food service organizations; military officers', noncommissioned

Table **5.6**   *U.S. military food service*

R/I "400" RANK	AGENCY	DOLLAR VOLUME[a] (MILLIONS)	NUMBER OF UNITS
23	U.S. Navy	$852.4	666
28	U.S. Army	676.6	1,089
37	U.S. Army Clubs and Recreation	518.9	1,116
46	Army and Air Force Exchange Service	428.2	2,773
49	U.S. Air Force Open Mess System	412.5	502
55	U.S. Air Force	323.7	639
79	U.S. Navy Officer and Enlisted Mess System	218.5	267
80	U.S. Marine Corps.	214.9	199
120	Navy Resale System	136.4	537
222	U.S. Coast Guard	59.6	388
247	U.S. Marine Corps Club System	51.0	163
285	U.S. Army Medical Dept.	45.0	51
369	U.S. Air Force Medical Service	32.6	82
387	U.S. Navy Medical Command	30.3	27

Source: Restaurants & Institutions, July 9, 1986.

[a] Estimated equivalent to commercial sales volume established by *Restaurants & Institutions*.

officers', and enlisted soldiers' clubs; and military health-care units. All four groups employ both civilians and military commissioned and noncommissioned personnel. For information on careers in this area, of course, you need go no farther than your local armed forces recruiter.

IN-FLIGHT FOOD SERVICE

Perhaps we should have called this section "Transportation Food Service" because Table 5.7 does include one railroad company, Amtrak, but the real center of gravity in this segment is the airlines. Seven airlines plus Amtrak are among 400 largest hospitality firms. A number of companies, such as Marriott, Dobbs House, and Gladieux, also have in-flight food service divisions, operating as contract caterers. The companies listed in the table, however, are much like institutional operators.

The airline food service business is fast paced and requires people who work well under pressure. The uncertain number of passengers on an outbound flight, sudden cancelations or additions to the airlines' schedule of flights, and the various equipment configurations used in different aircraft make in-flight food service a challenging field. And some carriers offer free or reduced-price travel as a fringe benefit.

The Future of Institutional Food Service

The forces working in the restaurant business discussed in Chapter 4 affect institutional food service as well. Trends in the restaurant sector can be expected to influence institutions, as fast food already has. Contract companies will continue to

Table 5.7   *In-flight and other transportation food service*

R & I 400 RANK	COMPANY	SALES[a] (MILLIONS OF DOLLARS)
65	Pan American World Airways	$258.2
66	Eastern Airlines	253.1
72	Delta Air Lines	230.0
98	Trans World Airlines	173.2
130	Northwest Orient Airlines	119.0
244	Republic	51.0
337	Amtrak	35.0

Source: Restaurants & Institutions.

[a] Commercial equivalent estimated by *Restaurant & Institutions.*

offer the greatest benefits to the smaller institutions, but most of the larger institutions likely will continue to feel that they can achieve adequate economies without outside help. Moreover, institutions of all sizes will continue to believe that institutional control of the food service operation can be facilitated by direct control.

The force of consumerism will be felt in those institutions in which food service systems account not for an occasional meal but for 25 percent or more of a guest's nutritional intake.

Summary

First in this chapter we compared institutional and commercial food services. Even though institutional food service is considered a "captive market," it is good business to please both the client (the institution) and the guests. We then differentiated institutional food services into contract companies and institutional operations and examined each.

Institutional food service has four major divisions: business and industry, college and university, health care, and school and community. In regard to business and industry, we discussed the introduction of fast-food and contract companies in factories and companies. We talked about the various ways that colleges and universities feed their students: the different kinds of board plans and the ways of attracting students to and keeping them in the plans. In the health-care food service, we described the dietetic professionals: clinical dietitians, dietetic technicians, and dietary managers. We then reviewed the dietetic department organization and the trends in the health-care food service—how dietetic departments are trying to help hospitals stay solvent. We next discussed school and community food service. First, we related the reasons for the establishment of a national school lunch program, including the increasing participation of women in the labor force and the concern for poor children. We described the school food service itself and the outlook for its future. Turning to food service programs for the aging, we found that the main reasons for their popularity are the greater number of elderly people in our society and the many living below the poverty level.

In our discussion of preparation systems, we described three: conventional food service systems, the most common, which prepare food from scratch; ready food operations, in which one crew prepares the food and another reconstitutes and serves it; and convenience food systems, which use foods provided by frozen food manufacturers.

We then examined vending systems: what they vend, how they are received, and how they will fare in the future.

Our next topic was the operation of institutional food services.

We also considered the arguments for and against contract companies and institutional in-house operations.

In closing, we outlined the other institutional food services: military food service and in-flight and transportation food service. We ended with a brief look at the future of institutional food services.

The Hotel and Motel Business

THIS CHAPTER IS ABOUT

Hotels and other kinds of lodging. We are concerned with the way changing travel patterns and consumer needs have shaped the lodging business to become what it is today. Fundamental *uses* of lodging are important and somewhat different for business travelers, conventioneers, and traveling families and tourists. Resort hotels, as destinations, serve still another purpose. Lodging can be thought of in terms of function and guest need but can also be categorized by location and service mix.

Lodging is fundamentally a community institution. In fact, sometimes hotels are built for the services they provide the community rather than to meet any immediate guest demand.

We will end the chapter by looking at franchise systems in lodging and what they offer both guest and operator.

6

Arthur Hailey's novel *Hotel*, written in the early 1960s, described a kind of hotel that even then was passing from the scene—a "grand old lady," an independently owned hotel staffed by old-timers who all seemed to have some personal bond with the aristocratic owner, Warren Trent. The wheeler dealer who finally displaced Trent was a none-too-thinly disguised portrait of an actual hotel tycoon who, in those days, made a practice of acquiring old properties and modernizing both their physical plants and their operating organizations. But if Hailey's novel addressed change in the hotel business, it covered only a small part of that change. Modernization now means much more than the mere sprucing up that Mr. O'Keefe, the hotel tycoon, planned for Hailey's St. Gregory Hotel.

Professional lodging has always followed the patterns of transportation of its time: caravansaries, inns along the Roman roads, post houses, and so forth. It has responded, too, to changes in destination patterns. Toward the end of the nineteenth century, North American hotels grew up to serve the rail traveler. Often, the hotel was physically connected to the railroad station. A few of these hotels still survive and some, such as Toronto's Royal York, remain thriving centers. Of the hotels built during the first half of this century, those not physically connected to the railroad station were usually convenient to it and to the major destinations in the downtown sections of cities. Indeed, there may be a revival of this pattern if there is also a revival of rail travel, with the high-speed rail corridors proposed for the 1990s.

The Evolution of Lodging

The two principal determinants of hotel location, transportation system and destination, changed in the great period of economic expansion that followed World War II. As a result, several waves of hotel and motel building have changed the face of American innkeeping.

THE MOTEL

Although a few "Mo Hotels," or motels, were to be found in the Southwest even in the late 1920s, and "tourist courts" began to appear in the 1930s, the big wave of motel building followed World War II.

The end of the war released a pent-up demand for automobiles. During the 1930s, depressed economic conditions prevented many people from buying a car; then during the war, automotive production concentrated on military needs. The explosive growth in auto travel that followed the end of the war brought people into the travel market, as both buyer and sellers.

The first motels were small, simple affairs, with commonly under 20 units (or guest rooms). These properties lacked the complex facilities of a hotel and were generally managed by resident owners with a few paid employees.

They were built at the edge of town, where land costs were substantially lower than those downtown. The single-story construction that typified motels until the late 1950s (and even the two-story pattern of later motor hotels) offered significant construction economies, compared with the downtown high-rise properties built on prime real estate. Capital costs represent the largest single cost in many lodging establishments, and so the lower land and building costs and the lower capital costs that resulted gave motels significant advantages. These savings could be, and generally were, passed on to the guests in the form of lower rates.

Probably more important, motels offered a location convenient to the highway. Because the typical guest traveled by car, he or she could drive downtown, returning to the accommodations in the evening. Meanwhile, inexperienced travelers, who had always been put off by the formality of hotels, with their dressy room clerks, bellhops who had to be tipped, and ornate lobbies, preferred the informal atmosphere of the motel, a "come as you are" atmosphere in terms of both dress and social preferences. In the motel they might be greeted by the owner working the front desk. Motel operators were proud of their informality. The personal touch they offered guests and the motel's convenience and lower prices were their stock in trade. Few motel operators had formal training, and many would gladly tell one and all that their lack of professional training was the very secret of their success.

THE MOTOR HOTEL

For a few years, it appeared that hotels (in general, the relatively large downtown properties) and motels (usually the small properties located at the edge of town) would battle for the new mobile tourist market. Unhappily for both the hotel and the mom-and-pop motel, the situation was not that simple.

In 1952, Kemmons Wilson, a Memphis home building and real estate developer, took his family on a vacation trip. He was depressed by the dearth of accommodations to meet his family's and the business traveler's needs. He returned to Memphis with a vision of a new kind of motel property that combined the advantage of a hotel's broad range of services with a motel's convenience to the auto traveler. That insight revolutionized the lodging industry.

Motels became larger and began to offer a wider range of services. Dining rooms or coffee shops, cocktail lounges, and meeting rooms appealed to the business traveler. Swimming pools became essential to the touring family. Room telephones, usually present in hotels but generally absent in motels, became the rule in motor hotels, thus requiring a switchboard and someone to operate it. Whereas hotels and motels once had offered coin-operated radios and television sets, free television and then free color television became the rule.

In 1953, the first Holiday Inn, with 100 rooms, opened. As of 1987, Holiday Inn operates approximately 317,500 rooms in 50 countries, and its format has been adopted by many other successful motor-hotel chains and franchise groups.

Although there were experiments with smaller inns having 50 to 75 rooms, most lodging companies determined that generally a 100-unit facility was the smallest that made economic sense. That size permitted full utilization of the

Hotels such as Western International's Bonaventure in Los Angeles marked a resurgence of the downtown hotel in the 1970s and 1980s. (Photo by Alexandre Georges.)

minimum operating staff and provided a sufficient sales size to amortize the investment in such supportive services as pools and restaurants.

THE AIRPORT MOTOR HOTEL

In the 1950s and 1960s, as air travel became more and more common, a new kind of property appeared, designed especially to accommodate air travelers. Even though these travelers arrive by air, they rent cars often enough to justify a lodging design similar to that of the motor hotel. Thus, the principal distinction of the airport property is its location. Airport motor hotels tend to emphasize their small- to medium-sized meeting-room capacities, because of the preponderance of business meetings at these properties.

THE DOWNTOWN HOTEL

Although the older downtown hotels faced new competition on the edge of town, new properties in the downtown market areas were fairly scarce because of changes in the transportation system and traveler destinations.

At about the same time that U.S. cities began their urban renewal, the interstate highway system began to penetrate the downtown areas. The downtown renewal area, with its new office and shopping complexes, often revived interest in hotel construction designed to serve these new destinations. Urban renewal, coupled with the limited-access interstate highways, opened up the city to the nation's highway travelers.

Downtown properties have many advantages. They are near the large office complexes and retail stores: by day they are near business destinations, and by night they are close to many of the large city's entertainment centers. This combination is particularly attractive to meetings and conventions, which often involve as much play as work. Although the downtown property generally depends less on the "off-the-road" travelers than do the motor hotels, their guests arrive often enough by automobile (and use rented cars often enough) to justify ample facilities for automobiles. These facilities commonly include a motor entrance, a waiting area often called the motor lobby, and on-premises parking accessible to a guest without any assistance from (and tips for) the hotel staff. In fact, many older downtown properties have been remodeled to include most of these facilities. Though on-premises parking has not always been feasible, reasonably convenient off-premises parking, with valet service to pick up and drive the car, is common. Thus, although not all downtown properties include the words motor hotel in their name, nearly all first-class downtown properties offer the services associated with them.

There are, of course, many other ways to classify hotels and motor hotels. J. B. Temple—for many years president of the food and lodging division of Holiday Inn and currently senior vice-president of Chatmar, Inc., a West Coast motor hotel company—suggested that we classify these properties by function and by location. The seven different location-oriented categories are the following:

Downtown *Central business district in a city of 50,000 or more.*

Midtown *Central city shopping or office area other than central business district in a city of 50,000 or more.*

Suburban *In a suburban or on the fringe of a city of 50,000 or more.*

Airport *On or contiguous to a commercial airport property.*

Small town *Anywhere in a town under 50,000.*

Roadside *On a federal, state, or local highway but not in any of the above locations.*

Resort *Virtually all motor hotels today have recreational, entertainment, or leisure attractions, but a "resort" is defined as one that is also a destination for travelers as opposed to an enroute overnight location.* [1]

In addition Temple offered three functional definitions:

Basic *A motor hotel mainly dependent on room business. It would have a smaller than average commercial area with only one dining room (fewer than 100 seats) and one lounge.*

Standard *A motor hotel dependent on a mix of rooms business, meetings, and food and*

---

[1] J. B. Temple, "Marketing for Motor Hotels," *Lodging,* June 1976, p. 26.

The Hotel Bonaventure's architect, John Portman, has become famous for developing fascinating interior play spaces in the centers of cities. (Photo by Alexandre Georges.)

beverage operations. It would have an average size commercial area, dining accommodations with more than 100 seats and meeting facilities for at least 100 people.

Complex A motor hotel with a large commercial area, multiple dining rooms, and accommodations for large meetings.[2]

The Uses of Lodgings

All lodgings have some functions in common: shelter for the night and food and drink either on the premises or nearby. Different travel purposes, however, create different guest needs.

[2] Temple, "Marketing for Motor Hotels," p. 26.

Grand hotels, such as Loew's Anatole Hotel in Dallas pictured here, provide a ceremonial setting that helps symbolize the importance of convention events. (Photo courtesy of Loew's Hotels.)

THE BUSINESS TRAVELER AND THE TRANSIENT PROPERTY

The backbone of most hotels' business is the business traveller. Each hotel's proportion of business travelers varies, of course, and also varies seasonally; for example, hotels usually have more tourists in the summer. This proportion also changes in the national market from year to year and according to a number of

Large function rooms, like this one, are necessary to serve the general sessions of large organizations. The Grand Ballroom at the Mayflower Hotel in Washington, D.C., offers a sumptuous setting for organizations to honor their top brass and impress their members. (Photo courtesy of the Mayflower Hotel.)

factors, including the business cycle. For example, in good times, there is more business travel, and during recessions, travel budgets are cut.

In a witty article in the *Cornell Hotel and Restaurant Administration Quarterly* entitled "How Architects Design Rooms Differently," a hotel architect, Morris Lapidus, emphasized practicality and comfort: "a no-nonsense room [has] some touch of luxury so that [a guest] feels that even though he's deprived of the pleasures of home, hearth, and fire he still has adequate working area where he can make his notes and get himself collected." Lapidus recommended giving the business guest convenience so that he can relax, and "enough psychological compensations to make up for his isolation."[3]

[3] Morris Lapidus, "How Architects Design Rooms Differently," *Cornell Hotel and Restaurant Administration Quarterly*, May 1974, p. 69.

The convention hotel must have supersuites "for the chiefs," as Lapidus put it, such as the one shown here, from New York's Waldorf Astoria. (Photo courtesy of Hilton Hotels.)

THE CONVENTION TRAVELER
AND THE CONVENTION HOTEL

Most convention hotels attract ordinary business travelers as well, and so these two markets are often linked in travel statistics. Lapidus provided an interesting and colorful description of the convention hotel and its function:

> *The convention hotel is a new form of American hybrid. All of us are familiar with the great American convention, where an organization or corporation gathers as many members as it can in one particular place and fills up a horrendous agenda with lectures, meetings, group discussions, film shows, workshops and lots of drinking. The main reason for all this endeavor is to conduct a forum for ideas, to keep members apprised of what the parent organization has been doing, and to get everybody's idea of where they are going and how they should get there. It is also a nifty tax write-off.*

> *The convention hotel should be a ceremonial hotel, so far as meeting areas are concerned. This is the place where the "tribe" honors the chiefs, hands out the awards to diligent*

Las Vegas's MGM Grand offers a wide variety of entertainments, including gambling, extensive sports facilities, a movie theatre, and several restaurants. (Photo courtesy of MGM Grand.)

warriors, and welcomes the initiates. The organization's brass must look and sound good on the platform at meetings and banquets. The warriors—and the warriors' wives when present—should be equally seated and treated. And the novitiates, for whom it is an honor just to be there, must have an opportunity to feel part of the inner circle.

The convention hotel must also have supersuites for the chiefs and many comfortable but similar rooms for the warriors. The novitiates may be housed more economically although this is seldom the case. They may share rooms and not be permitted to bring along their wives until they're full-fledged warriors.[4]

Lapidus also observed that the guest rooms at conventions are often social centers where friends or business associates come for a drink or an informal meeting. These rooms thus should be spacious and should separate the dressing area from the living

[4] Lapidus, "How Architects Design Rooms Differently," p. 69.

The MGM Grand offers opulent suites to "high rollers"—and to any others who are disposed to pay for luxury. (Photo courtesy of MGM Grand.)

quarters. The best arrangement, Lapidus declared, is to provide one double bed and a couch that can become a second double bed in larger rooms. Of course, there is a need for more modest single rooms for "warriors and novitiates," to use his analogy.

THE TOURIST MARKET

Many motor hotels, particularly those serving highway locations, accommodate traveling families in the tourist season. During this period, rooms can be rented to three or six people or more, at higher rates (and higher food and beverage sales). To serve this market, a room with two double beds and room for a rollaway is essential. (The same room can be rented as a single, and often at a lower rate, to business travelers during the rest of the year.) Because the traveling family is more price sensitive than is the expense-account business traveler, luxury in the room itself is distinctly secondary, and luxury in the overall plant (size of swimming pool, luxury food service facilities) is not usually emphasized in these properties.

Budget hotels generally have smaller commercial buildings. A Days Inn, pictured here, offers cut-rate gasoline as an "extra" economy service. (Photo courtesy of Days Inns.)

RESORT HOTELS

A transient property is where a guest arrives tired in the evening and leaves the next morning. A destination property, on the other hand, invites a guest to spend as much as a week or more and provides the extensive leisure facilities a vacationer expects. Accordingly, most resort guests are willing to pay higher rates for these services.

Some destination resorts offer a mix of activities suited to the sports enthusiast. The Homestead in Hot Springs, Virginia, for instance, offers in its advertising

> *horseback riding, woodland walking, trout fishing, mineral spa, swimming, three 18-hole championship golf courses, tennis, buckboard and surrey driving, skeet and trap shooting, ten pin and lawn bowling, loafing, and skiing.*

And the Greenbrier in White Sulphur Springs, West Virginia, describes itself as "a 6,500-acre estate secluded in the beautiful Alleghenies." In addition to sports, the Greenbrier, like most such "adult resorts," offers extensive meeting and convention facilities.

> *The new conference center includes ballrooms, auditoriums, theatre, exhibit hall and 25 meeting rooms fully equipped with the latest audio-visual equipment. Capable of serving groups of 10 to 1,100.*

A quite different kind of "adult destination" (where, as in the Homestead and the Greenbrier, children are always welcome) is found in Las Vegas, the number-one hotel city in terms of hotel sales. Las Vegas is famous for its gambling, but its resort hotels offer much more (including, sometimes, features for the children). For example, the Las Vegas Hilton advertises itself as the place

> *where the real superstars play in Las Vegas. Now the largest, most complete resort in the world. Incredible dining in eight unsurpassed restaurants, including the spectacular Japanese fantasyland, Benihana Village! Plus an 8½ acre outdoor recreation deck and even a unique "youth hotel" for the youngsters alone.*

These adult-centered resort hotels do, of course, welcome children, but other complexes are designed primarily with the family, and especially children, in mind. The most famous of these is Walt Disney World (WDW). Although the resorts we described include many other activities, we can properly say that at WDW, several hotels are integrated within a larger entertainment center. That center includes not only the theme park for which WDW is best known but also all varieties of water sports on a large lake, a sophisticated campground sporting its own entertainment centers, three golf courses, and the customary amenities and luxuries available at each hotel.

Lodging As a Community Institution

You may have seen the following card pasted up behind the counter in a shop:

> *This is a nonprofit business. We didn't plan it that way; it just happened!*

To a greater degree than in many other industries, that not-so-funny joke applies to hotels and motor hotels, except that the meager profits may not be all that unexpected. To see why, we need to shift our attention from the purposes of the individual guest to those of the community.

In many small towns, the hotel or motel is more or less a public institution. It is a gathering place for local leaders and provides hospitality for visitors to the city's principal businesses. Because of these community benefits, some small-town hotels have been built more or less as nonprofit operations, with both ownership and even capital lent without any real expectations of overwhelming profit. The benefits to the community—and to its principal institutions— are seen as sufficient to offset a lack of profit. Such resignation as this may not be the rule, but it is far from uncommon.

In practice, however, most hotel operators discover that an unprofitable hotel is also an unsuccessful hotel. Over the long haul, the need for operating subsidies, or the simple absence of sufficient financial return, makes the property lose its luster and then become downright unattractive. Eventually the owners grow reluctant to pay adequate executive salaries and to spend the funds necessary to maintain the physical plant. Gradually the plant decays, the organization grows demoralized, and the hotel closes its doors.

The community need for hotel services, however, often leads real estate developers to promote hotels as a part of real estate developments in large cities. A developer acquires the rights to a large tract of land and plans a complex of office buildings, department stores, and other retail establishments. The development may be situated downtown; it may work with urban redevelopment; or it may settle at the edge of the city as part of an office park or an industrial park consisting of offices, light manufacturing, or warehousing and distribution centers. Although the development's overt purpose is suggested by its title (urban redevelopment, office park, industrial park), one of the first buildings to go up will probably be a hotel or motor hotel. The developers hope, of course, that it will earn a profit, but they build it mainly because of its importance to the overall development.

The developer may not be particularly interested in entering the hotel field, but the development surely needs the hotel.[5] Visitors with business in the area need a place to stay. Headquarters units need space for sales meetings and other technical conferences. Those with offices or who are otherwise working in the area need a place to eat lunch, get a snack, meet for a drink, and perhaps entertain out-of-town guests at dinner at the end of the day.

Most development projects are preceded by a feasibility study of the project's economics. Two extracts from such feasibility studies, conducted in a medium-sized city (Middleton) in a basically rural area and a large metropolitan center (Bigton), suggest some of the developer's underlying motives. (Because these are confidential documents, the identity of the cities has been disguised.)

> [This is] one of a series of studies dealing with the proposed Middleton Square developments in the Washington Street Urban Renewal Project area in Middleton.
>
> The urban renewal area covers six city blocks between the existing downtown area and the shore of Lake Washington. The proposed Middleton Square development contemplates a comprehensive, integrated development of new office structures (one of which is already under construction), adequate automobile parking, a full range of retail facilities including a major full-line department store, and the 300-room hotel which is the subject of this analysis. All of these facilities are expected to upgrade and modernize Downtown Middleton.

In a study conducted in a Bigton hotel development under consideration, the following information came under the heading of "Impact and Location":

> A new, large, and spectacularly designed hotel in Downtown Bigton would have a significant impact on Bigton. Properly promoted, the proposed hotel would not only focus

---

[5] To this point, we have been concerned with various types of lodging establishments—hotels, motels, motor hotels, budget motels, and others. Accordingly, we have used the fullest, most specific designation we could. From this point on and in the next chapter, however, we will be concerned with transient lodging in general. To be brief, we will use the word *hotel* to describe the lodging establishment in general, although occasionally, we will revert to the fuller description for emphasis.

more attention on Bigton as one of the nation's great metropolitan centers, but the hotel would also substantially improve the inventory of transient lodging accommodations in the downtown area, and thereby strengthen that area's competitive position in the lodging market. If the hotel is as successful as predicted in this analysis, it will attract comparable competition to the downtown area—further reinforcing that area's position in the local lodging market.

The function of a hotel property, then, sometimes involves what economists call *externalities*—benefits external to the hotel itself, such as community development, the enhancement of property values in the area in general, and service to people who need food and lodging and would not visit the area without them. It's hardly surprising, then, that many new hotel properties have financial difficulties. This is particularly true for properties built during waves of real estate speculation such as those that occurred in the late 1920s, the early 1970s, and the mid-1980s. For sophisticated hotel operators, however, this situation creates real opportunities.

Franchise Systems

The word *franchise* comes from the language of political science and refers to a right bestowed by some authority. For example, when Kemmons Wilson created a successful operating format for a motor hotel, he began to *enfranchise* others with the right to use Holiday Inn's name. To do this, he adopted a practice similar to the *referral groups* already in existence and operated mainly by Quality Courts and Best Western Motels [6] (now Quality Inns and Best Western). At that time, as now, the franchiser provided the use of a name and some managerial and technical know-how. While we discuss franchising in general in a later chapter, we need to look here at its role in lodging.

A NATIONAL IDENTITY AND BRAND NAME

In a market of national travelers, the identity of the individual property has little meaning except to the local townspeople and its frequent visitors. On the other hand, "Hilton Inn," "Sheraton Inn," or "Holiday Inn" convey meaning to travelers from any part of the nation. To these travelers, the mere mention of these names suggests the kind, degree, and probable cost of the services available.

National franchising companies spend portions of their own budgets on advertising in appropriate regional markets and in the national market. Most

---

[6] There is an important technical difference between a *franchise system* (in which the franchising company grants a right) and a *referral system* (in which a property and its ownership become members). There is not a great deal of difference, however, in how they operate, though the referral group is sometimes characterized by greater owner autonomy. For our purpose, the word *system* will denote either kind of operation.

One of the major benefits that a franchise company offers is a nationally advertised brand name. (Photos courtesy of Sheraton Hotels and Days Inns.)

franchise systems also levy an advertising fee on each franchisee and pool these funds. Thus, the collective advertising fund makes it possible to purchase ads too expensive for an individual property. These include such media efforts as commercials on national radio and television and layouts in national magazines.

Franchise hotel-motel companies also print national directories showing the location of each of the system's properties. Perhaps the most important services that franchisers offer the guest—and therefore, the operator—are referral systems and quality assurance programs.

REFERRAL SYSTEMS

When a guest wants to make a reservation, he or she can call a single number and either have a reservation at a distant point confirmed immediately or obtain help in locating alternative accommodations. Once the guest begins a trip, accommodations for subsequent nights' stops are only as far away as the room telephone. Thus, once a hotel system has a guest's patronage for a single night, it is in a position to sell the guest all subsequent accommodations. Moreover, most referral or reservations systems are either computer based or use a WATS (Wide Area Telephone

System) line. WATS systems permit leasing of telephone lines, which drastically reduces the cost per call for high-volume use.

The first successful computerized reservations system was Holiday Inn's Holidex. Each inn has a terminal connected to a central computer by telephone wires. For each day of the year the local innkeeper "deposits" a certain number of rooms of each type available. The computer acts as a kind of "bank" or clearinghouse for all Holiday Inns. The computer sells all rooms "on deposit" for the day in question without consulting the inn in which the reservation is made. As each room is sold, the inn is notified of the guest's name, the type of room wanted, and other information (arrival time and so on). This information is then used to make up a reservation card for the arriving guest.

If the local innkeeper must increase or decrease the number of rooms available for a given day, or stop taking reservations entirely for that day, he or she sends a simple message through the inn's terminal to the central computer, which alters, as instructed, the number of rooms available. At the end of each month, the innkeeper receives a report of sales refused and can use this as a basis for planning sales strategies and front-desk procedures or for constructing additional rooms, if the demand is present.

Some chains rely solely on a WATS reservation system. Callers call an 800 number (at no charge to them) that reaches a central reservation office. Using leased WATS lines to reach the receiving property, that office then calls the property and secures a reservation, if possible, and confirms it for the guest. (Some WATS systems also use computers and "deposit" rooms in a way similar to the Holidex system, except that terminals are not present in all properties.) With either a WATS line or a computer-based system, an effort is made to accommodate the guest in a nearby property *in the system* if the guest's first preference is not available.

Many large systems use both a computer reservation system and WATS lines, and the largest systems supplement these with regional sales offices. Some smaller systems use teletype or telephones when the reservation volume does not warrant the high fixed cost of a computer or a WATS line.

INSPECTION SYSTEMS: QUALITY ASSURANCE

Almost all franchise and referral groups specify a minimum level of physical plant and service requirements before admitting a new operation to the system. These requirements generally include a restaurant, a swimming pool, certain types of furniture and fixtures, and such operating services as room service and a 24-hour front desk.

In addition to specifying operating standards, a system usually enforces the maintenance of these standards through regular inspections made by either the systems inspection department or an established member of the system. The detail and care devoted to quality assurance by the modern motor hotel system is based on chain or referral-group inspection systems.

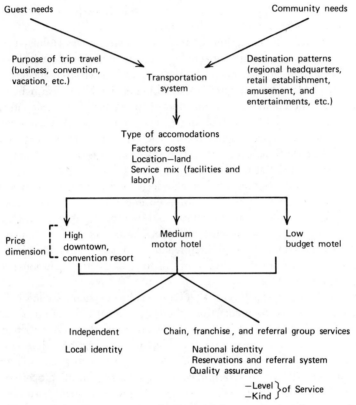

Figure 6.1   *Determinants of value and function in hotels, motor hotels, and motels.*

Determining Hotels' Value and Function

In this chapter, we described the evolution of the accommodations industry since the end of World War II, emphasizing the guest's needs and wishes and the community's needs as causes for this evolution. We must now organize these needs and this evolution into a clear pattern.

Figure 6.1 coordinates the demand for accommodations (at the top of the figure) with the guests' needs. These needs include the purpose of travel and the needs of the community, based on the community's destination patterns. The interaction between the accommodation needs of the individual and those of the community is shaped by the transportation system available in the community. Destinations become significant only if they can be reached.

Thus defined, purpose dictates accommodation type, and these types are further affected by the costs of making services available. These costs are determined principally by location and land value as well as by the *service mix*. The service mix refers to the relative elaborateness or simplicity of the facilities and the labor they require to render their services.

Because capital and operating costs, and hence rates, increase more rapidly than does the price level in general, new marketing strategies emphasize upgrading amenities.

Whether their rates are high, medium, or low, accommodations commonly participate in franchise and referral groups adhering to a common identity and providing the traveler with the convenience of a reservation system and the assurances of a certain level and kind of service. In many markets, however, independents with a strong local identity remain important.

Although the model of Figure 6.1 is neither precise nor predictive, it does help trace cause and effect as they interact to determine the functions and resulting service profiles of hotels, motor hotels, and motels.

Summary

We began this chapter by relating the history of lodging, leading up to the introduction of motels and then motor hotels and airport motor hotels. We also discussed downtown hotels.

We then outlined the uses of lodging by transient business travelers, convention travelers, and tourists and described the differences in the hotels targeted to them. We also looked at resort hotels and how they differ from other kinds of hotels.

Lodging as a community institution was our next topic. This included a discussion of why a community needs hotels and why they may be built, even though they may not make any money and, indeed, may even lose money.

We also again considered franchise systems and the advantages of having a national identity and a brand name. In our description of making reservations in a franchise system, we explained referral systems. We briefly discussed inspection systems as well.

Lastly, we summed up the chapter with a figure that showed how value and function are determined in the different kinds of hotels.

Hotel and Motel Operations

Hotel and motel operations. You need to understand what a hotel's major functional departments are and the work of each. The particular role of the food and beverage department in gaining patronage for the hotel is an important point, too. Of course, we will consider the "rooms side" of the house, reviewing the work of the front office. We will also consider support departments such as sales and marketing, engineering and accounting. Finally, we will look at the positions in each department in terms of the routes to advancement they offer.

Courtesy of Holiday Inns, Inc.

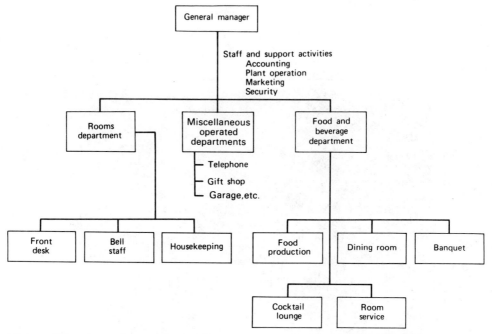

Figure 7.1 *Major functional areas found in hotels and motor hotels.*

Hotel properties[1] range from tiny to huge in size. Although large properties such as the Chicago Hilton or Bally's Grand in Las Vegas catch the public's imagination, the majority of properties built in recent years offer between 100 and 200 units. The examples in this chapter will assume a motor hotel in the 100- to 125-unit range.

Surprisingly enough, most properties perform basically the same functions, but the way in which they do them varies with the property size. When there are significant variations in routine practices in larger properties, we will note them. Our emphasis in this chapter, however, will be on the similarity found throughout the hotel business rather than on the variations.

Major Functional Departments

Figure 7.1 shows the basic functional areas of any hotel or motor hotel. This figure includes elements not found in some motels, however, as some motels lack food and beverage departments, and many do not have a gift shop or garage. Our

---

[1] Hereafter, in the interests of simplicity and economy, we generally will use the word *hotel* as a generic term to describe all kinds of transient lodging—hotels, motels, and motor hotels.

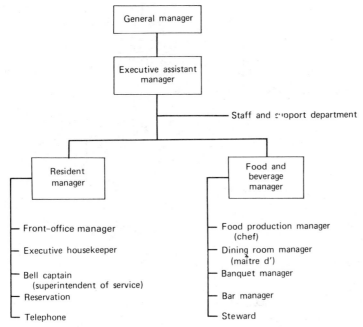

Figure 7.2 *Simplified organizational chart for large hotel.*

purpose, however, is not to draw a chart that represents all properties inclusively; that would be impossible. Rather, we have outlined the *major* activities usually present in *most* properties.

A large property may employ a general manager under whom an executive assistant manager assumes responsibility for day-to-day operations. Reporting to the "exec," very often, is a resident manager who supervises several departments on his or her side of the house, as Figure 7.2 shows, and a food and beverage manager.

On the other hand, in the 100-unit inn diagrammed in Figure 7.3, the general manager may be responsible—with an executive housekeeper and perhaps a front-office manager or chief clerk—for running the rooms and for supervising an assistant manager responsible for food and beverage. Thus, the executive staff may vary from two or three persons supported by a few department heads and key employees in a small property, to a large bureaucratic organization made of the many layers of authority necessary to operate a large complex property.

It is important to note that a smaller property may have *functional areas* (food production, bar, dining room, dish, pot, receiving, and cleanup, for instance, in the food and beverage area) but no true department heads. The restaurant in a small inn may be run by a restaurant manager who directly supervises all the employees with help from *lead employees* in each functional area on each shift. For instance, the hostesses for the day and evening shifts may provide leadership to the dining room during their shifts; a head cook on each shift does the same for the

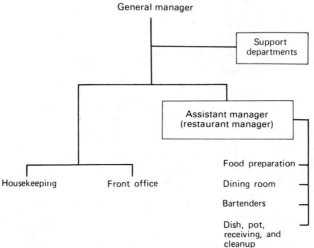

Figure 7.3   *Functional organizational chart for small motor hotel.*

kitchen. The manager may be responsible for hiring and discipline on both shifts, usually along with someone designated as an assistant when the manager is off duty. This arrangement is economical and convenient in small properties as long as the restaurant manager delegates enough responsibility to avoid becoming overcommitted.

THE ROOMS SIDE OF THE HOUSE

Room rental is a hotel's main business and its major source of profit. The day-to-day operations of the typical rooms department yield a *departmental income* (the revenue remaining after the direct operating costs of the department are taken out) of about 70 percent, compared with 15 to 20 percent for the food and beverage department. Thus, the people on the rooms side of the house are crucial to the operation's overall success.

THE FRONT OFFICE

More than any other group, the desk clerks represent the hotel to its guests. They greet the guests on their arrival and make them welcome (or not, depending on their manners). If something goes wrong, most guests will complain first to the front desk. And when the guests leave, the desk clerk checks them out. If anything has gone wrong, this will be a good time to catch it. ("I hope you enjoyed your stay, sir"—and then *listen* to the answer.) Although the duties of the desk overlap, they will differ with the work shift.

In the following discussion, a small inn serves as a model. The functions in a larger property may be broken down into specialties (reception desk, cashier, mail,

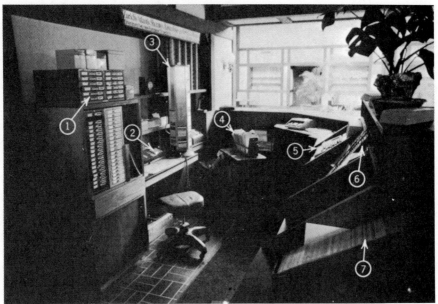

The territory of the front desk. The major elements found in most front offices are present here: (1) reservation files for future dates, (2) telephone switchboard, (3) telephone information rack, (4) house (tray) ledger, (5) front-office accounting machine, (6) room rack, and (7) reservations for today. Although the front desk looks different when it is computerized, its functions are essentially the same.

and key clerk) performed by different persons. Our purpose is to disclose the work and the functions. Your own observations will illustrate for you the variety of ways in which the work is organized. When a computerized front-office property management system (PMS) is used, fewer charges will be posted by hand if other charging departments are "on line" to the PMS, that is, interconnected so that charges automatically are picked up by the front-office computer.

The *morning clerk* works from 6:45 A.M. to 3:15 P.M. With a half-hour meal break, this is an eight-hour day. Because the evening crew comes in at 2:45 P.M. and the night auditor goes off duty at 7:15 A.M., all shifts overlap to ensure a smooth transition from one shift to the next. Some properties maintain a logbook in which information or events with which later shifts should be familiar are noted. The new shift's first task on coming on duty is to check the logbook to make sure they're fully briefed.

The morning shift's work is concentrated in the early hours (from around 7:30 A.M. until midmorning) on checking out guests. At the same time, of course, the employees on this shift answer the guests' questions and perform other routine tasks. But their main responsibility is checking out guests.

When a guest is ready to leave, the clerk verifies the final amount of the bill,

If a guest voices any complaints at checkout, the morning clerk should deal with them tactfully, so that the guest will return.

posts any recent charges, and assists the guest in settling with cash, check, or credit card, according to the house credit policy. This credit policy, which lays down guidelines for accepting checks and specifies the acceptable credit cards, is an important part of any clerk's training.

Although the technical aspects of the clerk's work are important, the courtesy a clerk accords a guest is at least as important. A departing guest must have an opportunity to register complaints if he or she has had problems. The morning clerk's work thus includes a special responsibility for ensuring that guests leave with the intention of returning to the hotel on their next visit to town.

As guests check out and their rooms become vacant, the clerk notifies housekeeping, or if the housekeeping department is on line to the PMS, it will automatically be notified. This permits housekeeping to make up the rooms promptly so that they will be ready when new guests check in later that day. As the rooms are made up, housekeeping notifies the desk so that early arrivals can be accommodated in rooms that are ready to rent. Alternatively, the room status can be changed to *ready to rent* at housekeeping's computer terminal later, when the room is made up.

Reservations[2] for the coming evening have accumulated in previous days, and many guests will come in during the morning. Where a manual reservation is in use,

---

[2] In large hotels, and particularly in convention and resort properties, the reservations office is a specialized area within the front office.

This room rack indicates that most of the rooms are vacant. Some of them are not yet ready to rent, and so the rack card shows them as "on Change."

sometime before noon the planning for evening begins with the *blocking* of vacant rooms on the room status board, often called the *room rack*. There are many different front-office systems. The simplest has a *rack card* for each room. (The color of the card denotes the room type—yellow for singles, blue for doubles, orange for suites, or some similar combination.) When guests are checked in, a portion of the form that the guest fills out, usually called the *registration card,* is inserted in the room rack, which shows that the room is occupied. When the guest checks out, the registration card is removed, and the rack card is inverted to indicate the room is *on change,* which means that it is being made up for the next guest. When housekeeping indicates that a room is ready, the card is turned again to indicated *ready to rent.*

Toward the middle of the morning, the clerk blocks the evening's reserved arrivals by placing a card in the room rack. On very busy days, reservations may be closed (which means that no reservations for that night will be accepted) before the beginning of the business day. On most days, however, the transient hotel gradually fills with reservations that come in during the day.

When a PMS is used, this procedure is much simpler. Although special-request rooms are individually blocked, most rooms are assigned automatically by the computer, taking account of whether rooms are on charge or ready to rent, according to information supplied continuously by checkouts and the housekeeping department. As you can see, the PMS makes front-office work much easier. In fact, a room rack is no longer necessary and is replaced by summary information made

ON CHANGE

————————————————————
————————————————————
————————————————————
————————————————————
————————————————————
————————————————————
————————————————————
————————————————————
————————————————————
————————————————————

HOLIDAY PRESS FORM 3-115   PRINTED IN U.S.A.

ROOM   1 Person $ ————
2 Persons $ ————   CONNECTS WITH ————
3 Persons $ ————
4 Persons $ ————   TYPE ————

The room status card gives the rate for the room and other important information. When inverted in the rack, it indicates that the room is "on change"—that is, not yet ready to rent. (Courtesy of Holiday Press.)

available in various reports that can be called up instantly on the computer's screen.

It is important that reservations be accepted only if a room will be available; therefore, a close watch must be maintained on checkouts, reservations, and early arrivals so as to avoid *overbooking*. Overbooking means accepting reservations for more rooms than the hotel has available. In the past, hotels deliberately over-booked to a certain extent, for several reasons. The most important was that many reservations turned out to be "no-shows"—the guest did not arrive as expected. Guests generally would not pay for a reservation even when they had "guaranteed"

The morning clerk "blocks" rooms for tonight's reservations.

it (that is, guaranteed payment even if they didn't arrive). A study by the American Hotel–Motel Association on the attitudes of actual no-shows indicated that these people (1) considered not showing up for a guaranteed reservation unfair but (2) claimed they had never done so!

With this kind of attitude, collecting from no-shows was not promising. Obviously, a hotel *cannot* afford to hold rooms empty, and so many operators carefully computed a "no-show percentage" and oversold their rooms by that amount. Regular reservations usually were held until 6:00 P.M. The percentage of no-shows at that time was generally quite high. Guaranteed reservations were to be held all night. Because some of these would not show anyway, a policy of conservative overselling was quite common. When a guest arrived with a guaranteed reservation that could not be honored, most hotels arranged other accommodations at their expense and paid the guest's transportation expenses to the other hotel.

The overbooking problem occasionally was worsened by some unforeseen event—for instance, a sudden change in weather that resulted in a cancellation of all flights out of town. Thus, guests who had expected to leave stayed over, and they generally could not be forced to leave. As a result, arriving guests found the reservations they had planned on were not available. Situations like this occurred infrequently, but they led to hard feelings and even some successful lawsuits. For this reason, in the late 1970s the practice of guaranteeing a reservation with a credit card became common. This practice, in effect, means that the room is paid for in advance. The guest will be charged for the room by the credit card company,

The room status board or room rack gives the clerk assigning a room to an arriving guest the information necessary to avoid putting the guest in a room that is already occupied or that hasn't yet been made up.

which will pay the hotel whether or not the guest appears. When a guest cancels a guaranteed reservation (before 6:00 P.M. on the night of the reservation), most reservation systems provide a *cancellation number*, which is given to the guest as proof that he or she actually did cancel. Some hotels that do not use cancellation numbers ask the clerk to give to the guest his or her first name.

The *afternoon clerk's* work is mainly checking in guests, most of whom arrive, in most transient houses, a little after 4:00 P.M. The afternoon clerk, therefore, takes over the reservation planning begun by the morning clerk and greets the guests as they arrive.

First impressions are crucial, and the desk clerk's warm welcome often sets the tone for the guest's entire stay. By remembering the names of repeat visitors, meeting special demands when possible (such as for a ground-floor room), and bearing in mind that the guest has probably had a hard, tiring day of work and travel, the desk clerk can convey the feeling that the guest is among friends at last. The clerk checks in the guest, and that process establishes the accounting and other records necessary for the stay. (At many hotels, an important part of checking in a guest is learning his or her expected date of departure. This information facilitates the reservation planning process just discussed.)

The *night auditor* is a desk clerk with special accounting responsibilities. When things quiet down (usually by 1:00 A.M.), the auditor posts those charges not posted by the earlier shifts, including (most especially) the room charge. He or she then audits the day's guest transactions and verifies the balance due the hotel from guests as of the close of the day's operations. The auditing process can be quite complicated, but simply stated, the auditor compares the balance owed to the hotel at the end of yesterday with today's balance. He or she verifies that the balance is the correct result of deducting all payments from yesterday's balance and adding all of today's charges. This process, summarized graphically in Figure 7.4, not only verifies today's closing balance of guest accounts owed to the hotel but also systematically reviews all transactions when an error in the balance is found. For this reason, the night auditor's job is important, requiring intelligence, training, and integrity.

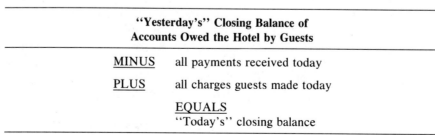

	"Yesterday's" Closing Balance of Accounts Owed the Hotel by Guests
<u>MINUS</u>	all payments received today
<u>PLUS</u>	all charges guests made today
	<u>EQUALS</u> "Today's" closing balance

Figure 7.4   *The night audit: A schematic view.*

Telephone

Because the system of accounting for hotels recognizes the telephone activity as a separate department for revenue purposes, one often hears about the *telephone department*. But only in the largest hotels is there a really separate organizational unit to match this designation, and in such hotels, it is headed by a chief operator. The telephone service in many properties is handled by a person who also serves as a second desk clerk. Many properties, particularly those of approximately 100 units with automatic phone systems, require the desk clerks to operate the switchboard as part of their regular duties.

Housekeeping

Housekeeping, that less-than-glamorous but essential department, is as much a production department of a hotel as the front desk and bell staff are service departments. It is clear that without clean rooms to rent, a hotel would have to close. For this reason, the management should always pay close attention to morale factors such as pay and worker recognition in the housekeeping department.

The housekeeping department is usually headed by an executive housekeeper. In a smaller property, a linen room assistant may double as an assistant housekeeper and inspector. In larger properties, the executive housekeeper will have at least one assistant and several supervisors, generally known as inspectors, who supervise maids in a designated area.

In some hotels, housemen take responsibility for cleaning the halls and heavy work such as moving furniture. There employees often form a separate subdepartment. Hotels with their own laundries often assign the supervision of that area to the housekeeping departments. Generally a working laundry supervisor or lead worker handles routine supervision under the executive housekeeper's general direction.

The Bell Staff

Many motor hotels do without a bell staff, because most of their guests prefer to "room" themselves. On the other hand, the bell staff plays an important role in the larger and more luxurious hotels. The process of rooming a guest includes more than just carrying luggage and showing a guest to a room. Rather, it begins when the clerk assigns a room. At this point the bellman takes charge, welcoming the guest in both word and manner and, on entering the room, demonstrating its operations and features. He or she shows the guest how to operate the air conditioning and turn on room and bath lights. The bellman will usually turn on the television and run through the channels and networks available. He may also indicate when the food service is open and provide other information the guest may need.

In luxury hotels, the *concierge* offers the guests important services. He or she is expert in giving directions to local attractions, securing tickets to shows, and recommending tours and other entertainment. The concierge knows about local transportation, tour schedules, and nearly any other information a tourist might want. In most hotels, the front desk and bell staff generally perform the functions of a concierge, but the smaller size of most bell staffs today has limited this service. Nevertheless, it is important to see that the guest (who is, after all, usually an outsider to the community) has some place in the hotel to turn for information. He or she is likely to need up-to-date information about airport limousine schedules; the hours of religious services and the locations of churches; and such entertainment possibilities as sporting events, movies, and the theater. Some hotels give employees special training in how to give directions and provide lists of local attractions.

FOOD AND BEVERAGE DEPARTMENT[3]

There's an old saying among hotel people that "if you can run the food, the hotel will run itself." Like more folklore, this exaggeration carries more than just a grain of truth. Perhaps a personal recollection will illustrate this point:

> *My first job as an innkeeper was in a hotel with a leased food and beverage department. That is, the owners had leased the food and beverage department to a food service management company to "keep the food problems out of our hair," as they put it. This is sometimes a disastrous "solution," and it certainly was in my case.*
>
> *A banquet held in the hotel was fouled up, and I, as the innkeeper, was apologizing to a prominent automobile dealer for the problems he and others had had. I concluded my explanation by commenting that unfortunately, because the restaurant was leased, there was not much I could do about it. His reply has always stayed with me.*
>
> *"Tom," he said, "suppose you came down and bought a car from me and a few weeks later had mechanical trouble. Suppose my service department couldn't fix the trouble, and you came to me to complain and I told you, 'It's beyond my control. My service department is leased.' Would you ever buy another car from me? Your food and beverage department is your service department."*
>
> *I was genuinely hard put to give any adequate answer to his question—because there wasn't any.*

Of course, the car dealer was right. Service in any part of the hotel is important. But nothing seems to enrage guests quite so much as slow breakfast service, cold soup, or tough steak.

Many hotels in recent years have emphasized the food and beverage department's role as a profit center, that is, a specifically identified, profitable part of the hotel's operation. The typical hotel food service department creates about half as much in dollar sales as does the rooms department but generally provides between 10 and 15 percent as much profit as that generated by the rooms department.

---

[3] The student may wish to review the section of Chapter 2 regarding restaurant operating ratios, as they are also used in the industry in discussing hotel food and beverage operations.

The services available at most hotels include a cocktail lounge whose hours of operation are designed as much to accommodate the guests as they are to make a profit on the bar itself. (Photo courtesy of Sheraton Hotels.)

Many old-time hotel keepers still regard the food and beverage department as a key marketing activity whose main purpose is to secure guest patronage for the hotel and only secondarily to generate profits. These operators don't throw money away. But they may price food and drink very reasonably and offer large portions or exceptionally good quality to attract patronage from the community. The reasoning is that this approach will attract guests to stay in their rooms.

On the other hand, more and more economy hotels—and even some that like to think of themselves as luxury hotels—are severely limiting their food and beverage operations. Typically, these hotels, often in the so-called all-suite category, offer a free continental breakfast, and some even offer a free cooked-to-order breakfast. In addition, rather than a cocktail lounge, some all-suite hotels offer a free cocktail hour. Some chains are also returning to leased food and beverage operations, usually with a separate franchised operation on the premises.

Restaurants

Many motor hotels offer coffee-shop service, a more or less formal dining room, and a cocktail lounge. The hotel restaurant's hours of operation are related to the guests' needs rather than just to food and beverage profits. For example, many

Food and beverage are, quite literally, the service department in a hotel or motel. (Photo courtesy of the New York Sheraton Hotel.)

hotels open at least one food room at 6:00 A.M. to serve those who have awakened early because they have come from another time zone, have an early plane to catch, or want to beat the morning traffic. The few guests who turn up before 7:30 in the morning hardly ever warrant the added payroll hours for cooks, waitresses, and the cashier. But if their schedules are accommodated, they are likely to return to the hotel and spend those rooms-department dollars that provide 70-percent profit margin.

Similarly, the dining room's sales volume falls off dramatically in most properties between 8:30 and 9:00 P.M., but many hotel dining rooms stay open to accommodate the few late-arriving guests. The bar, too, may serve only a few guests in the midafternoon or after 9:00 P.M., but again, the full service a guest expects must be available.

Although management personnel need not always be present at opening or closing time, some lead employee, such as the cashier or first cook, must accept responsibility for unlocking and locking food storage areas, turning lights and equipment on at opening and off at closing, setting up the cash register or closing it out, and so forth. Because of the large number of operating hours, one hostess is generally responsible for the day shift (from 7:00 A.M. to 3:00 P.M.), and a second is in charge of the evening shift (from 3:00 P.M. until closing). In smaller properties, one of these supervisors may be designated to act for management when the restaurant manager is not on duty.

Hotel menus, too, take on a special character related to the guests' needs. Breakfast and the evening meals are the most important to the transient hotel guest, who may not have arrived in time for lunch or may be away from the hotel for that meal. (Clearly, this statement does not apply to destination properties such as resorts). Once again, my own experience furnishes a good illustration of this point:

> *At breakfast, I always provided orange juice freshly squeezed in the dining room where the guests could see that it really was fresh. This was foolishly expensive from the restaurant's standpoint, but I received enough guest comment slips saying "I stay at this hotel because of the fresh orange juice" to convince me that we weren't really being extravagant.*
>
> *At the evening meal we offered, as a "Traveling Man's Special," one complete meal at a rock-bottom price featuring a low-cost appetizer, a wholesome but inexpensive entree, salad, and dessert. In a freestanding restaurant, this would make no sense because it would reduce the check average, taking sales away from more expensive items on the menu. But many travelers are cost conscious because they are paying their own expenses or, as with government employees (and professors!) they receive only limited reimbursement for their travel costs. A "bargain meal" thus attracts such customers to a hotel. Some guests told us they ate the inexpensive meal—but had a couple of cocktails before the meal and charged the whole amount on their expense accounts. The total cost was still within their company's travel allowance.*

Banquets

Some large properties offer a catering department (or banquet department) headed by a catering manager who books and sells banquets. Smaller properties include this activity among the restaurant manager's duties. Larger properties have special full- and part-time banquet service staffs. Smaller properties draw banquet service personnel from their regular crew and often supplement them with part-time employees.

Banquets are often profitable, but once again, in many properties the banquet menus and banquet rooms are meant principally to serve the rooms department. Thus, a meeting may occupy one conference room all day. Perhaps the hotel supplies a coffee break and a luncheon in another room. It probably charges the business people little, if anything, over what those meals and snacks would cost in the dining room. Moreover, it may not charge extra for the meeting facilities. If such a meeting accounts for 20 or 30 guest-room rentals—or even only 10 or 15—the logic we have mentioned before clearly applies. The 70-percent profit on room sales makes desirable this use of banquet space.

Food Production

In most properties, the person in charge of food production is called the *chef*. A chef is a person who has completed, either formally or informally, the training that qualifies him or her to be a master cook. The chef should also be a manager who can purchase food; hire, train, and discipline employees; and plan appetizing meals priced to yield a profit. All too often, however, the title of chef is bestowed on somebody who is, at best, a head cook. The cost of a *true* chef is, you see, beyond the means of most operations.

An increasingly common title in American food service is *food production manager*. Although these managers are almost invariably accomplished cooks, they

Modern hotels usually offer at least one informal dining room or coffee shop in which guests in informal attire will be comfortable. (Photo courtesy of Sheraton Hotels.)

emphasize kitchen management and rely on strict adherence to written recipes, rather than on their craft skills, to ensure quality. The type of management chosen by a property generally reflects the dollar volume of food sales. More sales may permit the expense of a chef or food production manager. Smaller properties may have to content themselves with a chief cook. In this case the restaurant manager generally supervises the kitchen quite closely.

With the greater availability of quality frozen prepared foods as well as the growing acceptance of limited menus, an approach to food service that requires limited culinary skills is becoming more and more common in hotels that don't try to reach the luxury standard.

Large convention properties may support a separate subdepartment, often made up of part-time workers who just prepare banquet food. Some properties even use a separate banquet kitchen.

Because of the hours of operation, a manager should clearly designate early and late supervision hours. This supervision may require a lead cook—or perhaps the restaurant manager or an assistant—to work as a supervisor.

The Exceptional Case   As a student of food service, you should be aware that in a few hotels—usually older and smaller ones—the food department actually generates more profit than the rooms department does. In these cases, the innkeeper or owner is an unusually talented foods person and devotes the greatest portion of time to the food department. In these properties, as in all the others, however, the success of the foods department invariably increases room sales.

Sanitation and Utility

Sanitation is so important that many food service programs offer entire courses on the subject. Our purpose here, then, is not to cover every aspect of sanitation but to note the work of restaurant employees in the area of cleanup and sanitation.

The category of employees we will discuss here include *dish, pot, receiving, and cleanup workers.* Receiving—checking incoming goods against the quality and quantity specified—is a responsible and skilled job in large hotels. The receiver reports directly to the hotel's accounting office. In smaller properties, however, receiving is combined with the work of some other station; the employees' skill levels in this area are minimal, and duties are limited to *counting* and *weighing* goods as they are received and *storing* them in the appropriate places. In these instances the receiver's job may be combined with that of the morning pot washer, for example. Breakfast often produces fewer pots to be washed than other meals do, and most food supplies are delivered between 7:00 and 11:00 A.M. In these cases, management inspects the incoming products. In larger properties, however, checking the quality of goods received is one of the receiver's most important jobs.

Dishwashers are important in at least three ways. First, a restaurant that runs out of clean dishes in the middle of a meal period would be a joke if the problem were not so serious. Second, the failure to wash dishes properly exposes the guest to food poisoning and the hotel to a serious loss of public confidence. Finally, dishwashing involves the control of a group of costs that, in most restaurants, loom as the largest expenses after food and labor: the breakage of china and glass, the disappearance of silver, and the cost of cleaning supplies.

Although breakage does occur in other areas (the waitresses and waiters account for the second largest breakage total, followed by the cooks), the dishroom is where the most dishes are handled and where breakage is the greatest. A careful dishroom crew can do a great deal to control and even reduce this large expense.

Although many other areas use cleaning supplies, probably the largest soap user is the dish machine. Too little soap results in poor sanitation. (In fact, mechanical soap-control devices generally control soap dispensing, but sloppy work and misuse of the automatic equipment can result in problems.) Too much soap or improper handling can result in significant and costly waste. Similarly, the improper use and cleaning of the dishwashing machine can lead to costly repairs. For example, draining the machine at the close of business without remembering to turn off the heat can burn out a portion of the dishwasher. Expensive repairs—and the problems of operating a restaurant without a dish machine while those repairs are being made—can be the result.

Breakage is not generally a problem in pot washing, but the restaurant's work depends as heavily on clean pots and pans as it does on clean dishes. Like dishwashers, pot washers also use significant amounts of costly soap. Pot washing, physically, may be the hardest job in the restaurant. It involves bending over a hot sink, breathing in the soap fumes, and strenuously scrubbing pots. In some large operations "pot machines," like dish machines, help with this work. But few smaller properties can afford this investment in equipment and space, and so pot washing there is done largely by manual labor.

The night cleanup crew is often composed of the closing dishwashers and pot washer, though a separate cleanup crew may be hired by larger properties. Cleanup is probably the most "unsung" work in the restaurant; and yet inadequate sanitation, at the very least, eventually results in a poor public image for the restaurant. Worse, a single outbreak of food poisoning can damage a property's reputation for years—to say nothing of the discomfort the guests suffer!

Many students find that the only summer jobs they can land are in the "sanitation and utility" areas. Unfortunately, students often view these jobs as a waste of time. In fact, many industry leaders brag that they "started in the dishroom." This boast is neither an accident nor a public-relations artifice. One of the keys to success in our field is encouraging unskilled workers to perform well in jobs that offer little intrinsic satisfaction. This encouragement starts with respect for the people who take these positions, a respect that often comes from having done the work yourself. (A little recognition and humane treatment can be awfully important to a job that others consider the "bottom rung.")

In some hotels, the supervisor of these functions is the steward, who may also be responsible for purchasing. In the typical property, however, the restaurant manager or, most often, his or her assistant is the supervisor in this area. This is another reason for mastering these jobs while a student. The assistant restaurant manager job in most hospitality operations—restaurants, hotels, and institutions— is most commonly assigned to people emerging from management training programs. Success in this job often launches a career, and a good working relationship with subordinates usually spells success in this entry-level job. Few things will help you toward that goal more than the ability to roll up your sleeves and help out when one of your crew gets "stuck."

STAFF AND SUPPORT DEPARTMENTS

Some departments or activities in the hotel offer no direct guest services. Instead, they maintain systems for the property as a whole, such as sales, marketing, and engineering. Some of these activities do, however, service the departments that deal directly with the guests: accounting and personnel immediately come to mind.

Sales and Marketing

Marketing means designing a hotel to suit the needs and tastes of potential guests— or shaping the operations of an existing property to its most likely guests. A second marketing function is encouraging the guests to choose your property by emphasizing all of those service activities that make the property pleasant and convenient.

Finally, marketing is promoting the activity among various potential guests and groups of guests. (This duty is often thought to be all there is to marketing, but it actually comes after the first two.)

Marketing is a general management function that involves all levels of the operation. One important day-to-day activity in this area is sales promotion. In large properties, a sales manager and one or more salespersons are responsible for finding sales leads and following up on them with personal sales calls and booking functions. Some properties define the sales department's work as the national convention market. Others identify local firms as the principal place to concentrate their efforts. Determination of just which market to approach is a crucial top management decision usually made by the general manager, the sales manager, and even the ownership. In chains, corporate policy may dictate these decisions, but most often the precise market for a particular property must be specifically designated by the local management. (Some properties—in particular, resort hotels—hire outside sales firms called *hotel representatives* to represent them in key markets.)

In smaller hotels, the innkeeper is responsible for managing sales. He or she will commonly make the sales calls personally and entertain people from potential sales accounts in the hotel. In some properties, the innkeeper is assisted in this work by a full- or part-time sales representative.

Because the work of the marketing department is essential, a major trade association, the Hotel Sales Marketing Association (HSMA), has developed to conduct educational and information programs for both sales personnel and general management. This organization, which publishes excellent materials on sales techniques of all kinds, has a student membership available, and many hospitality programs have student HSMA chapters.

Engineering

The engineering function is so important that many programs have one or more courses devoted to the disciplines that support it. Once again, we will simply describe briefly the work of this area. Large- and medium-sized hotels usually employ a chief engineer who supervises an engineering staff. Together, they are responsible for operating the hotel's heating and air conditioning; for maintaining its refrigeration, lighting, and transportation (elevator) systems; and for overseeing all of the hotel's mechanical equipment. Breakdowns in these areas seriously inconvenience guests. And of course, utility costs have always been significant and in recent years have been increasing at an alarming rate.

In small properties, the engineer is often little more than a handyman who carries out routine maintenance and minor repairs. Outside service people supply the more specialized maintenance skills. In these properties, the innkeeper often supervises the engineering (or maintenance) function.

Accounting

Sometimes referred to as the *back office* in contrast with the front office (or front desk), accounting is charged with two quite different duties, accounts receivable and financial reporting and control. In large hotels, the accounting department may be headed by a comptroller and consist of several skilled clerical workers. Chains generally develop sophisticated corporate accounting departments that supervise work at the individual property. In a small property, on the other hand, the work is usually done by some combination of the innkeeper's secretary, a chief clerk, and an outside accountant.

When guests check out, they may pay their bills with cash, but they often charge this expense instead. The accounts receivable (bills owed by guests) in a hotel are divided into two parts. First, a *house ledger* (or tray ledger), kept at the front desk, is made up of bills owed by guests in the house. Charges by guests posted after they have left and charges by other persons, such as resaurant patrons not in the hotel, are kept in what is often called the *city ledger*. The name is derived from an earlier time when charging hotel bills was not common. Instead, guests paid cash when they checked out, and any charge not in the house ledger was a charge from some local customer, someone "in the city" rather than "in the house" who had a charge account at the hotel. Incidentally, the word *ledger* originally referred to a book on whose pages these records were kept. Today, records of charges are maintained on separate forms called *guest folios*. Increasingly, they are maintained "in memory" on a computer. The function, however, and even the terminology, are the same.

The other, less-routine, accounting function is preparing operating statements, conducting special cost studies, and overseeing the hotel's cost control systems. In small properties, much of this work is done by an outside accountant, whereas the larger properties often have their own full-time accounting staff headed by a comptroller or chief auditor.

Income and Expense Patterns and Control

THE UNIFORM SYSTEM OF ACCOUNTS

Hotel accounting is generally guided by the Uniform System of Accounts for Hotels, which identifies important profit centers in hotels as *revenue departments*. The uniform system first arranges the reporting of income and expense so that the relative efficiency of each major department can be measured by the *departmental income* (which was once called *department profit*). Table 7.1 shows a typical rooms-department schedule of income and expenses for a 120-room motor hotel, and Table 7.2 shows a food and beverage department schedule for such a property. The rooms-departmental income and the food and beverage departmental income figures help the innkeeper evaluate the performance of key department heads working in those areas.

To determine the property's overall efficiency, a manager deducts four categories of *undistributed operating expenses* from the total of the various departmental incomes. These costs—administrative and general expense, marketing and guest entertainment, property operation, and maintenance and energy costs—are judged

Table 7.1 *Rooms-department schedule of income and expenses*

	DOLLARS	PERCENT
Room sales	$2,555,110	100.0%
Departmental expenses		
Salaries and wages	355,160	13.9
Employee meals	10,220	0.4
Payroll taxes and employee benefits	76,653	3.0
Laundry and dry cleaning	38,327	1.5
China, glass, silver, and linen	25,551	1.0
Commission	38,316	1.5
Reservation expenses	17,886	0.7
Contract cleaning	7,665	0.3
Other expenses	76,647	3.0
Total rooms expenses	$ 646,425	25.3%
Rooms departmental income	$1,908,685	74.7%

to be costs that pertain to all departments in a way that cannot be perfectly assigned to any one department.

The amount remaining after deducting these four categories of expense from the total of departmental income is called *total income before fixed charges.* (Until recently this amount was called, somewhat more colorfully, *house profit.*) This figure is probably the best measure of the success not of the total property but of the general manager or innkeeper as well.

For this reason, many managers receive bonuses based on their performance as measured by this figure. It is fair to evaluate the manager without regard to the remaining costs, which can best be described as capital costs. Almost all of these costs—rent, property taxes, insurance, interest, and depreciation—are a direct function of the cost of the building and its furnishings and fixtures. The responsibility for these costs lies with the owners who made the decisions when the property was first built and furnished. These costs, therefore, lie beyond the control of the manager. Table 7.3, a typical statement of income and expense for a 120-room property, shows how all of these figures relate to net profit.

KEY OPERATING RATIOS AND TERMS

In Chapter 2 we introduced some ratios and food service terms, which are used in hotel food service as well. In addition, the hotel industry has other indicators of an operation's result:

Occupancy is generally indicated as a percentage.

$$\text{Occupancy percentage} = \frac{\text{Rooms sold}}{\text{Total rooms available}}$$

Table 7.2 *Food and beverage department schedule of income and expenses*

	DOLLARS	PERCENT
Food sales	$1,031,382	72.9%
Beverage sales	381,993	27.1
Total food and beverage sales	$1,413,375	100.0%
Cost of sales		
Food cost (after credit for employee meals)	$ 347,544	33.6%[a]
Beverage cost	81,046	21.4%[a]
Total food and beverage cost	428,590	30.3%
Gross margin	984,785	69.7%
Public-room rentals	25,440	1.8%
Other income	18,374	1.3
Gross margin and other income	$1,028,599	72.8%
Departmental expenses		
Salaries and wages	159,347	32.5%
Employee meals	21,201	1.5
Payroll taxes and employee benefits	101,763	7.2
Music and entertainment	40,988	2.9
Laundry and dry cleaning	12,720	0.9
Kitchen fuel	4,240	0.3
China, glass, silver, and linen	26,854	1.9
Contract cleaning	5,654	0.4
Licenses	2,826	0.2
All other expenses	70,669	5.0
Total food and beverage expenses	$ 746,262	52.8%
Food and beverage departmental income	$ 282,337	20.0%[a]

[a] The student should notice that these two cost percentages apply respectively to food sales and to beverage sales, whereas all other ratios are total sales.

Average rate is an indication of the front desk's success in selling both the least-expensive and the higher-priced rooms.

$$\text{Average rate} = \frac{\text{Dollar sales}}{\text{Number of rooms sold}}$$

The average rate is also a mix of the double-occupancy rooms sold (rooms with two or more guests). This is reflected by the ratio

$$\frac{\text{Number of guests per}}{\text{occupied room}} = \frac{\text{Number of guests}}{\text{Number of occupied rooms}}$$

Because housekeeping is the largest and most controllable labor cost in the rooms department, many hotels compute the average number of rooms *cleaned* in the following ratio:

Table 7.3 *Highway motor hotel statement of income and expense for year ending December 31, 19XX*

	DOLLARS	PERCENT
Revenues:		
Rooms	$2,555,110	60.2%
Food—including other income	1,031,382	24.3
Beverages	381,993	9.0
Telephone	101,865	2.4
Other operated departments	80,643	1.9
Rentals and other income	93,376	2.2
Total revenues	$4,244,369	100.0%
Departmental costs and expenses:		
Rooms	$ 646,425	15.2%
Food and beverages	1,131,038	26.6
Telephone	131,575	3.1
Other operated departments	55,177	1.3
Total costs and expenses	$1,964,215	46.2%
Total operated departments' income	$2,280,154	53.8%
Undistributed operating expenses:		
Administrative general	$ 415,948	9.8%
Marketing	195,241	4.6
Property operation and maintenance	241,929	5.7
Energy costs	199,485	4.7
Total undistributed expenses	$1,052,603	24.8%
Income before fixed charges	$1,227,551	29.0%
Property taxes and insurance:		
Property taxes and other municipal charges	$ 110,353	2.6%
Insurance on building and contents	21,222	0.5
Total property taxes and insurance	$ 131,575	3.1%
Income before other fixed charges	$1,095,976	25.9%
Capital costs:		
Depreciation and amortization	$ 331,060	7.8%
Interest	428,681	10.1
Total capital costs	$ 759,741	17.9%
Net income before income taxes	$ 336,235	6.4%

$$\frac{\text{Average rooms cleaned}}{\text{per maid day}} = \frac{\text{Number of rooms occupied}}{\text{Number of 8-hour maid shifts}}$$

All of these ratios are usually computed for the day, the month to date, and the year at year's end. Comparisons of these indicators with earlier operating results and with the budget provide important clues to an operation's problems or success.

CAPITAL STRUCTURE

We will discuss some of the financial dimensions of the hotel business further in Chapter 9. At this point, however, we need to describe briefly the capital costs found on the hotel's income statement because they are a significant part of a hotel's cost structure. *Capital costs* include rent, depreciation, and interest. A related cost, property taxes, can be included here because these taxes are dependent on the value of the land and the building.

Depreciation is a bookkeeping entry that reflects the assumption that the original cost of the hotel building, furniture, and fixtures should be gradually written off over their useful life. Interest, of course, is the charge paid to the lenders for the use of their funds.

The hotel industry is *capital intensive*. That is, it uses a large part of its revenue to pay for capital costs, including real estate taxes. Hotel development is attractive to some investors because it is highly *leveraged*. Leverage, as a financial term, refers to the fact that a small amount of an investor's capital can often call forth much larger amounts of money lent by banks or insurance companies on a mortgage. A fixed amount of interest is paid for this capital, and so if the hotel is profitable, the investor's earning power will be greatly magnified. But the investor's modest initial investment need not be increased. Earnings go up, but interest does not. Nor does investment—hence the word *leverage*.

Leverage, as developers have discovered repeatedly, can be a two-way device. Operating profits boom in good times and cover fixed-interest payments many times over. When times turn bad or the effects of overbuilding begin to be felt, revenues fall, but interest rates (and required repayments on the principal of the loan) do not. The result can be a wave of bankruptcies.

Entry Ports and Careers

An old adage says that there are three routes to advancement in the hotel industry: sales and marketing, accounting, and food and beverage. According to this adage, sales and marketing is the best route to the top in good times, but accounting, with its mastery of cost control, is the surest route in bad times. These three routes do seem to lead to advancement, but they are by no means the only places to start.

FRONT OFFICE

Many people begin their careers in the lodging industry in the front office, the nerve center of the hotel and the place where its most important sales take place. Obviously, the front office is an important area, and front-office techniques can be mastered fairly quickly. Many people find front-office work, with its constant change and frequent contact with guests, the most rewarding of careers. Moreover, improved pay scales in this area in recent years have upgraded the long-term attractiveness of this work, as has the increasingly sophisticated use of the computer in the front office. Another advantage of working in this area is a more-or-less fixed work schedule, though the afternoon shift's hours (from 3:00 P.M. to 11:00 P.M.) and those of the night auditor (from 11:00 P.M. to 7:00 A.M.) are viewed by many as drawbacks to those specific jobs.

ACCOUNTING

Today accounting has become a specialized field, and successful training in this area can be so time-consuming that one can hardly expect to master the other areas of the operation. But it does offer interesting and prestigious work for those who like to work with numbers. Moreover, the hours in this area tend to be reasonably regular, and the pay is usually good.

SALES AND MARKETING

The key to the success of any property is sales. Thus, it is not surprising that many successful hotel operators have a sales background. On the other hand, salespeople often find that a grounding in front-office procedure and in food and beverage operations (with special emphasis, respectively, on reservations procedure and banquet operations) leads to success in sales. Successful sales personnel are much in demand, and a career in sales offers interesting and financially rewarding work.

FOOD AND BEVERAGE

Food and beverage is one of the most demanding areas of the hotel operation, and it is an area in which Murphy's law most often applies: "If anything can go wrong, it will!" Success calls for the ability to deal effectively with two separate groups of skilled employees—cooks and serving personnel. Along with mastering both product cost-control techniques (for both food and alcoholic beverages) *and* employee-scheduling techniques, the food and beverage manager must also work in sanitation and housekeeping and be able to compose menus. He or she must complete all these duties against at least three unyielding deadlines a day: breakfast, lunch, and dinner.

We should note that there are a number of hotels, particularly in the economy market, that are deemphasizing food service. This is true even for some upscale, all-suite properties. This trend, however, is found in only a minority of properties, and we will argue in a later chapter that food service is still the key to a hotel's competitive strategy.

Summary

The first topic we discussed in this chapter was the major functional areas of a hotel and who runs them. Although big hotels have true departments and department managers, smaller hotels would designate these as areas, supervised by lead employees.

We next examined the rooms side of the hotel. The front office is particularly important, as it is the guests' first real contact with the hotel. The front office generally has a morning clerk, an afternoon clerk, and a night auditor, all with both different and overlapping duties. All help in making reservations, either through a computerized property management system (PMS) or by hand. Other rooms-side departments are the telephone department, the housekeeping department, and the bell staff.

The food and beverage department is very important to the hotel, as it may determine whether guests return to the hotel (or come in the first place). We described the kinds of restaurants that various kinds of hotels offer, banquet facilities (if any), food production, and sanitation and utility.

We next looked at hotels' staff and support departments: sales and marketing, engineering, and accounting. The accounting department is sometimes referred to as the back office. We explained the hotel departments' various expenses and income, operating ratios and terms, and, finally, capital costs.

We finished the chapter with a look at the best routes to advancement in the hotel industry—front office, sales and marketing, accounting, and food and beverage— and the advantages and disadvantages of each.

Automating Operations and Services in Hotels

─────── ──────── THIS CHAPTER IS ABOUT ───────────────

How technology is used in the hotel business to improve the efficiency of operations and the services to guests. We will look first at the fundamental elements of a computer system. As more and more departments are brought "on line," both accounting and many guest services are becoming automated. Computers and property management systems are becoming so fundamental to hotel operations that a basic understanding of them is essential. The future seems likely to hold more innovations in the development of the "smart hotel room." Finally, communications techniques such as videoconferencing represent a new competitor for hotels and yet a technology that hotels are increasingly making available to hold guests' business.

Courtesy of NCR.

Computers: The Heart of Lodging Technology

The key to most automation in hotel operations and services is the computer. Computers come in various sizes and have various names, but they all, from *microprocessors* to *mainframes*, work in essentially the same way. For those who have had a computer course, this section will be a review. But for those who are not as familiar with computers, we have italicized important technical terms the first time they appear. These terms appear in a glossary at the end of the chapter.

One word that we will often use in regard to computers is *systems*, as referring to the interactive whole.[1] A computer, for instance, is just a box or chip unless something is input to it. Furthermore, nobody will know what the "box" is doing unless it has output devices. Thus, we can speak of a *computer system* as containing *input devices*, a *central processing unit* (CPU), and *output devices*. A computer system is shown diagrammatically in Table 8.1. At a hotel's front desk, the keyboard is generally the input device used. The central processing unit (CPU) is the heart of the computer. Most hotels have *cathode ray tube* (CRT) *screens* and printers as output devices.

The CPU[2] has three elements, the *control unit*, the *arithmetic/logic unit*, and *memory*. The control unit interprets instructions from computer programs, directs the CPU's other parts, and controls the input and output devices. Some find it useful to think of the control unit as the computer's brain.

The *arithmetic/logic unit* performs calculations (that is, adding, subtracting, multiplying, and dividing) and logcial operations such as comparing one set of numbers with another.

The computer's *memory* holds instructions in the form of computer programs and data that have been input, such as charges and payments to a guest's bill. In addition, while the computer is working, its memory holds the results of work in progress, and when a calculation is completed, it holds the information that has been processed and the answer. In some cases, data may be stored outside the computer in what are called *external memory devices*. An example is the special programs used to perform the night audit, which are often held on a night auditor's *disk* except when in use.

The computer operates by converting all information to *binary numbers*, which are quite different from the number system we are used to. The binary number system is based on just two numbers, 0 and 1, and has been compared to an on-off switch or a true-false test. Each character (letters or numbers) is stored electronically as some combination of eight zeros or ones. A single binary number is

---

[1] For a further discussion of applications of the systems concept to thinking about hospitality management, see Thomas F. Powers, "A Systems Perspective for Hospitality Management," *Cornell Hotel and Restaurant Administration Quarterly*, May 1978, pp. 70-76.

[2] The description of the CPU is adapted from Jerome S. Burstein, *Computers and Information System* (New York: Holt, Rinehart and Winston, 1986) chap. 5, esp. pp. 131-135.

Table 8.1   *Fundamentals of a computer system*
The elements found in any computer are fundamentally the same. They are the means for (1) supplying data to the computer, (2) processing the data, and then (3) making the results available in a usable form. The main units are described below.

INPUT	PROCESSING	OUTPUT

Keyboard

Central Processing Unit (CPU)

Printer

CRT Screen

The most common input device is the keyboard, where both instructions and data are typed into the computer.

The CPU is made up of three units:
- The *control unit* runs programs and oversees the computer's functioning.
- The *arithmetic/logic unit* performs all calculations.
- The computer's *memory* stores programs and data.

Printers make copies of reports or guest bills when a permanent record is requested.

CRT screens are used by clerks and other computer operators to check the status of records and reports while the computer is operating and to monitor input data as they are entering it.

called a *bit*, and a *byte* is a string of bits (usually eight bits per byte) that the computer processes as a unit.

The size of a computer is often expressed in terms of the information it can hold in memory, usually stated in thousands (abbreviated K) of bytes. Thus, a 256K computer's memory holds 256,000 bytes of information. The computer converts programs as well as the data input into binary numbers, stores and manipulates them as necessary, and then transforms the resulting information into "human-readable," as opposed to "machine-readable," form.

The computer speeds huge volumes of information for managers at all levels of the hospitality organization. (Photo by Elyse Rieder.)

Interfaces

Many hotels' accounting and operating systems are *interfaced* (electronically interconnected) to the computer (see Table 8.2). In this way, for example, housekeeping can be informed instantaneously, via its terminal screen (or printer), of guest checkouts. Or if the telephone system is interfaced to the computer, when rooms are made up, the maid (or inspector) can dial an appropriate code on any phone, thus informing the front desk that a room is ready to rent. When the hotel's call-accounting system is interfaced, long distance calls are automatically posted on the guest's folio. (Remember that in this system, the guest folio is not a piece of paper but a set of electronic impulses stored at an appropriate address in the computer's memory and printed out as hard copy only when needed.)

Another common interface is with the food and beverage point-of-sale (POS) terminals. If a guest charges a check to his or her room, it will be entered at the POS end, and the charge will be instantaneously posted to the guest's ledger in the computer.

Table 8.2   *Common interfaces in hotel computer systems*

Chain Headquarters

Telephone System
- Housekeeping inputs room status by phone.
- Phone control (on/off) is at checkout and check in.
- Guest's name is displayed for operator when guest dials from room phone. Guest's name can also be displayed in outlets.

Point-of-Sale (POS) Terminal
- Posts food and beverage charges directly to guest's folio.
- Posts group's charges too master folio.
- Posts other charges (gift shop, in-house movies).
- Verifies credit.

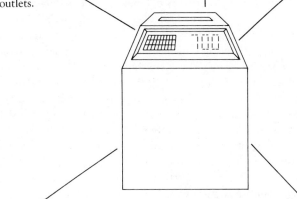

Call Accounting
- Posts long distance call charges directly from phone company to guest's folio.

Energy Management Systems
- Controls air conditioning.
- Shuts off lights at checkout.
- Regulates peak usage levels.

Payroll
- Time clock registers start and stop of work hours.
- Computer prepares actual payroll and checks.
- Computer "modeling" of labor utilization includes
    Labor-use reports.
    Labor-use analyses.
    Labor forecasts.

Payroll interfacing allows the computer to register the start and stop times for each worker. Using these data, the computer prepares the payroll checks, labor-use reports, labor-use analyses, and labor forecasts.

Terminals are said to be *smart* or *dumb*. For instance, there may be two or more terminals at the front office, one of which (a "smart" terminal) contains the computer itself. The other terminal is connected to the computer, uses the computer to make all calculations, and has no computational power of its own—it is a "dumb" terminal. On the other hand, the dining room may contain a "smart" terminal with enough computation power to total guests' bills, keep track of cash received, and produce a number of food and beverage reports. At the heart of this "smart" POS as well as of call-accounting systems, energy control units, and other "smart" terminals is a *microprocessor*, a tiny, single-purpose computer in the form of a single silicon chip, smaller than your fingertip.

The hotel's computer may also be interconnected with the company's main computer in a remote head office. This interconnection may be permanent and continuous, in which case the property's computer is said to be *on line* to the head office. Very often, however, the head ofice uses periodic (usually daily) *polling* to monitor the unit's activity. In polling, the head office's computer in effect "calls up" the property's computer using long distance lines and, in computerese, asks for the appropriate reports and data. These are transmitted almost instantaneously in *machine-readable* form via the phone line to the head office's computer. Polling is usually done late at night when phone rates are at their lowest.

In some cases, the *data* generated by the property will be further analyzed at the head office. The resulting report can then be *downloaded*, that is, transferred in machine-readable form from the central unit to the property, in what is essentially the reverse of polling. With polling, usually unprocessed or partially processed data are carried to the central office. With downloading, finished reports or other communications are sent to the individual properties.

Computers come in several sizes. Most hotel computers are *microcomputers*, the type of computer most commonly known as a personal computer (PC). *Minicomputers* are faster and have more memory than a microcomputer does. A larger or more complex hotel might use a minicomputer, or the head office's computer in a small hotel chain might be a minicomputer. The largest computers are known as *mainframes*. In the hotel business, mainframes are used in the head office to compile operational reports and manage functions like companywide accounting, payroll, and accounts payable. National reservations systems also rely on mainframe computers.

HARDWARE AND SOFTWARE

Most of what we have been discussing relates to *hardware*, the actual physical equipment in a computer system. Equally important is the *software* or computer programs. Many computer programs used in hotels are *canned programs*, that is, standard software packages that have been designed for special purposes such as front-office accounting. Some units develop their own software which is more expensive but may give greater flexibility to meet special needs.

Common Uses of Technology in Hotels

Most of the uses of technology that we will examine are computer or micro-processor based. Some of them improve the hotel's efficiency and cost effectiveness by doing jobs better, faster, and with fewer errors. Some, such as *videoconferencing*, offer what amount to new services. Others directly affect guests by giving them greater security or convenience. The frequency of use of some major applications of technology is shown in Figure 8.1.

TECHNOLOGY AND OPERATIONS

The main technological improvement for hotels is the computerized property management system. Other technological innovations are call accounting, security, and word processing.

Property Management Systems (PMS)

A property management system (PMS) has been defined by Professor Alan J. Parker of Florida International University's School of Hospitality Management as a number of individual programs that, together, manage the front- and back-office

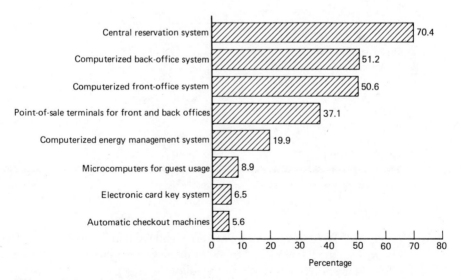

Figure 8.1 *Technological characteristics of property automation.* (U.S. Lodging Industry 1986. Laventhol & Horwath.)

Table 8.3 *Property management systems*

Front-Office Functions

CORE FEATURES	OPTIONAL FEATURES
Guest Accounting and Service	Guest history
• Check in and checkout	Travel agent accounting
• Folio accounting	Budgeting statistics
• Telephone information	Word processing
Operations	
• Guest reservations	
• Night audit	
• Group registration and folio accounting	
• Housekeeping: Room status	

Back-Office Functions

CORE FEATURES	OPTIONAL FEATURES
Accounts payable	Inventory
Payroll	Purchasing
General ledger	Budgeting
	Forecasting
	Purchasing

Other Service Functions

Sales and marketing analysis
Package and meal plans
Function-Room Scheduling
Banquet and catering sales
Word processing
Promotional mailings
Maintenance scheduling
Forecasting
Graphics: Menus

Source: Adapted from Douglas Engel and Joseph Marko, "Property Management Systems," *Lodging*, February 1986, pp. 17–20.

systems.[3] (The functions of the PMS are highlighted in Table 8.3.) The PMS may also include the hardware and the software needed to automate the front and back office. Many hotels use a PMS for the following reasons:

1. To improve operational efficiency by eliminating repetitive tasks and by having information current and readily available.

[3] *Lodging*, October 1984, p. 63.

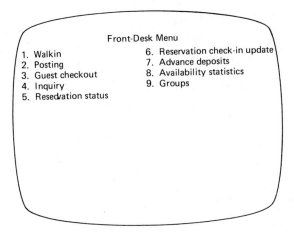

Front-Desk Menu

1. Walkin
2. Posting
3. Guest checkout
4. Inquiry
5. Resedvation status

6. Reservation check-in update
7. Advance deposits
8. Availability statistics
9. Groups

Figure 8.2 *Menu.*

2. To improve guest service through accurate, faster dissemination of information and new opportunities to keep track of guests' likes and dislikes.

3. To improve internal operational controls by adding a level of standardization that is difficult to establish and maintain in a manual system.

4. To save money by improving efficiency, reducing payroll, and eliminating outside service bureau costs.

However, the actual operating savings in properties of fewer than 300 rooms will probably by eaten up by additional computer-related expenses such as specialized maintenance and supplies.[4] But greater convenience for guests is increasingly a competitive necessity when over half the competition offers that convenience.

A PMS is *menu driven*. In many systems, the *menu*, or list of possible courses of action, is shown on the CRT screen, as in Figure 8.2. In other systems, the menu doesn't come on the screen. The options are there, but the clerk is expected to know what they are and how to deploy them.

The starting point for a clerk is probably a menu of options such as that shown in Figure 8.2. For a walk-in guest (one without a reservation), the clerk presses "1." The screen will then change to the "guest walk-in menu" (technically, the "guest walk-in routine"), such as that shown in Figure 8.3. Note that this menu is displayed at the bottom of the screen. This is because from this point on, the clerk will be working with a guest record that will be displayed in the space above the menu. The clerk continues the process of registering a walk-in guest by pressing "1" for "Guest information" plus "Enter." At this point the screen presents the guest-information form for registration, as shown in Figure 8.4. Note that a *submenu* (subroutine) *prompt* tells the clerk that he or she is now in the process of filling in the details.

[4] *Lodging,* February 1986, p. 17.

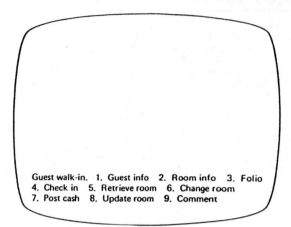

Guest walk-in.   1. Guest info   2. Room info   3. Folio
4. Check in   5. Retrieve room   6. Change room
7. Post cash   8. Update room   9. Comment

Figure 8.3   *Guest walk-in menu.*

The process moves along, prompted by the options at the bottom of the screen. The computer displays for the clerk the different types of rooms and rates available, assigns a room number when given a room type, and creates a folio for the guest, all on instructions from the clerk. A similar set of operational routines is available to check in a guest with a reservation, to post charges, to check out a guest, to update a guest's records, and so forth.

The system also provides reports that give an overview of the operation's status at any particular time. For instance, the computer may report on the reservation

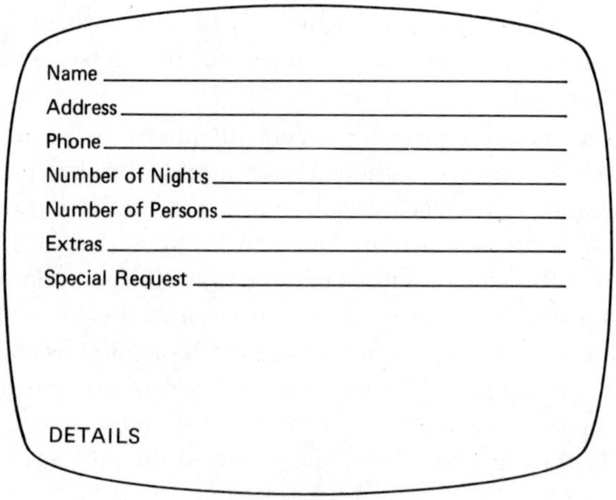

Name _____
Address _____
Phone _____
Number of Nights _____
Number of Persons _____
Extras _____
Special Request _____

DETAILS

Figure 8.4   *Guest information format.*

status for today or any future day, on reservations not yet arrived, on the number of rooms occupied, on change or ready to rent, and so forth.

Call Accounting

For many years, hotels relied on charges called back by the long distance operators after a guest completed a long distance call. Now in most hotels, the voice callback has been replaced by at least a teleprinter. As the call charges are printed out, the teleprinter paper is torn off and used as a voucher to post long distance calls. If the callback system is interfaced with the PMS, the calls will automatically be posted to the guest folio almost as soon as the call is completed. This saves the clerks' time and ensures that all charges will be posted and will be posted before the guest departs.

Security

Most hotels still use conventional metal keys, but a small growing number, are using a variety of electronic "one-time" key systems that offer added security. The problem with conventional keys is that guests often lose their keys, and thieves find it easy to steal or buy them.

Electronic key systems replace the mechnical lock and key with a plastic device. The plastic key is encoded with a unique number for each guest registered in the hotel. A microcomputer at the front desk encodes the key and has literally millions of combinations available for each guest room.[5] The computer system provides a printout of all the keys issued and indicates who issued each key. In the event of a theft, this makes it possible to determine who might have had access to a room. Maids' keys, pass keys, maintenance keys, and so on also are encoded by the microcomputer.

Each guest room's lock is controlled by a microchip. In some systems, the chips are connected to a main power source and interfaced with the front office's microcomputer that issues the keys. Others operate on long-life batteries, and when a new key is issued, the room's microchip is reset to the new combination. Both systems enable the room's microchip to record the most recent entries—up to 14 in one system—by the type of key (guest, maid, passkey and the like). In most systems the individual keys can be used again after they are reprogrammed but present no threat if lost or discarded aftr the guest has checked out.

Word Processing

Jon Williams, the AH&MA's manager of computer services, points out that word processing ties together two technologies, the typewriter and the computer. Material is typed into a microcomputer (in some cases, word processing uses the memory of a larger, propertywide computer), and the operator can read what is typed on the screen. If changes need to be made, the appropriate material is recalled to the

---

[5] *Lodging*, October 1984, pp. 41–42.

screen, and any insertions or deletions are made. Most word processors provide automatic page numbering, page formatting, and a spelling check.[6] Word processing is useful for all correspondence but is especially helpful for direct mail. A form letter appears as individually typed, and in fact, certain words, sentences, or paragraphs can be inserted. Using a feature called a *mail merge*, the word processor can prepare personalized, individually typed letters for each name on a mailing list that has been separately input to it. Word processing not only improves the quality and quantity of output but also reduces labor requirements.

Glossary of Computers in Lodging

Arithmetic/logic unit. The part of the computer that performs calculations (adding, subtracting, multiplying, and dividing) and logical operations such as comparing one number with another.

Binary numbers. The number system used in computers. In the binary number system there are only two digits, zero and one, which in the computer represent the presence or absence of an electrical impulse. They have been compared to an on–off switch.

Bit. A single binary number, a zero or a one.

Byte. Eight bits, the unit generally used by the computer.

Canned programs. Prepared software, standardized programs.

Cathode ray tube (CRT). A video monitor used as an output device in computer systems.

Central processing unit (CPU). The computer's processing component, made up of the control unit, the arithmetic logic unit, and the computer's memory. The CPU can be thought of as the "guts" of the computer.

Computer system. The interactive whole that makes up the computer: the input device or devices, central processing unit, and output devices.

Control unit. The part of the CPU that controls input, processing, and output. It can be thought of as the computer's brain.

CPU. See Central processing unit.

CRT. See Cathode ray tube.

Data. Raw or unprocessed facts, like a record of sales transactions.

Disk Storage. An external storage unit.

[6] *Lodging,* March 1985, p. 77.

Downloading. The dissemination of processed information by a central computer. Some hotel chains "download" to their units instructions or management reports processed in the central office.

Dumb terminal. A terminal that displays transactions but that has no computing or storage capacity.

External memory device. An auxillary storage that supplements the computer's memory capacity.

Hard copy. Computer records printed out on paper (as opposed to being displayed in the CRT).

Hardware. The physical components of a computer system, as opposed to its **software** or program elements.

Information. Data that have been processed so that they are useful and have meaning, as in a cashier's shift report, a daily operations report, or other management report.

Input devices. Generally, any data-entry device. The most common input devices in hotels are keyboards. POS terminals may also be thought of as input devices.

Interface. The point at which two components in a system interact, or the act of interaction between components. Commonly used to denote the interaction of two elements in a computer system.

Machine readable. Data or information in a form that can be read (only) by the computer, such as information coded in binary numbers.

Mainframe. A large computer such as is used in central reservations systems.

Memory. The computer's capacity to store data and information as electronic impulses.

Menu, menu driven. Computer software that is often composed as a series of subroutines that can be used by the operator. The operator chooses a subroutine from a "menu" of options. The system then displays the appropriate form for action, along with a prompt indicating a further menu of choices for action.

Microcomputer. A small computer such as a personal computer.

Microprocessor (microchip). A single silicon chip that contains the computer's control and arithmetic/logic unit.

Minicomputer. An intermediate-sized computer, between a microcomputer and a mainframe.

On line. Directly connected to or interacting with the computer.

Output devices. Devices that translate machine-readable information into a form that people can read. In hotels, the CRT and printer are the most common devices.

Personal computer (PC). A microcomputer designed to be used by individuals in the home or in business. Many front-desk systems use PCs.

PC. See *Personal computer.*

PMS. See *Property management system.*

POS. Point of sale (cash register).

Polling. The process by which one computer orders another, according to a predetermined pattern, to transfer data and information to the polling computer.

Property management systems (PMS). A combination of programs that automate the front and back offices. PMS may also indicate front- and back-office hardware.

Smart terminals. Terminals that can be programmed and have computational capacity.

Software. Computer programs.

Subroutine prompt. Display of a menu presenting subroutine options within any given routine.

System. A set of interrelated elements, an interactive whole.

Word processor. Computer systems that can be used to input, edit, and print text material such as letters and reports.

VIDEOCONFERENCING

Videoconferencing is based on another space age technology that uses computers and microprocessors. Videoconferencing allows companies and other groups to bring people together on the screen. As it has developed thus far, groups find that the necessary preparation and entertainment format somewhat restrict its uses. It is hardly conducive to an informal chat but is used for such events as new product introductions, large sales meetings, and other motivational meetings that lend themselves to the prepared format required by electronic media. Thus far, the impact of videoconferencing has not greatly affected the hotel business. That is, a video conference generally hasn't canceled out conventions that might have gone to a hotel. It is probably being used today in place of—or, commonly, in addition to—printed media and direct mail.

The main elements of the videoconferencing system are an *originating site*, an *earth station*, a *communications satellite*, and a special receiving disk at the *receiving site*. The program is transmitted from the originating site or sites to a *satellite-*

transmitting antenna called an *uplink*. The satellite transmit the signal to one or more receiving sites.[7]

Many hotel companies have equipped their properties for videoconferencing because it generates food and beverage and conference-room revenues and even some guest-room sales. HI-NET Communications linked 1500 U.S. properties in 1986, offering the ability to show a video conference both in the meeting rooms and in every guest room in the property.(HI-NET also offers closed-circuit television programs, including pay-per-view movies.[8])

Glossary of Videoconferencing Technology

Downlink. The electronic equipment in an earth station that receives satellite signals.

Earth station. Sending and receiving communication equipment that interacts with a satellite and with locations that are transmitting or receiving video signals.

Originating site. Place at which the television signal is produced for transmission to a satellite.

Receiving site. Place at which signals are viewed on television, such as hotel meeting rooms.

Satellite. An electronic device in space that sends and receives signals.

Satellite-Transmitting Antenna. The earth station's sending device, sometimes called an *uplink*.

Slow-scan television. A telecommunication system using ordinary telephone lines to transmit images. Two-way voice transmission generally accompanies slow-scan TV on a separate phone line.

Uplink. The satellite-transmitting antenna of an earth station.

Videoconferencing. An electronic system that transmits television images, generally via satellite, from one or more originating sites to one or more receiving sites.

At least one expert observer of the hotel business, Daniel R. Lee, feels that videoconferencing will, in the long run, compete with lodging, particularly in the small-meeting market. Lee estimated that roughly half of the demand for lodging is based on the need for communication between people at distant points and that

[7] *Lodging*, October 1984, pp. 37–38.
[8] *Hotel and Motel Management*, June 1986, pp. 36–37.

half of that, or 25 percent of lodging demand, does not require intimacy, such as one-on-one meetings. It is this "nonintimate" communication that Lee sees as competing with the market for lodging. Lee also noted that communication devices such as electronic chalkboards and microprocessor receivers and transceivers improve telecommunications as a meeting medium. The simplest video-supported communication is slow-scan television. Pictures or images are digitalized and transmitted through a normal telephone line. No satellite hookup is required for this kind of communication. "The process," Lee stated, "is much like a slide show with a new still image shown to the audience every 5 to 20 seconds. Two way voice communication is accomplished through a separate telephone line."[9]

The vigorous response of lodging companies to this competitive challenge suggests that they will play a major role in videoconferencing as it emerges. As Lee pointed out, however, the revenue sources—food and beverage and conference-room rental—that videoconferencing will tap are much less profitable than is the guest-room revenue related to small meetings, and so even if the room revenue lost is largely replaced by videoconferencing revenue, the impact on profits will still be negative.

Lee noted that research indicates that people do prefer person-to-person meetings to the more impersonal videoconference but that these reports do not take costs into account. "In fact," he asserted, "much of the shift toward teleconferencing will not be voluntary. Once it is widely available and the cost savings become known, businesses and other major travel users may mandate its use by their employees."[10]

Any negative impact from videoconferencing and the related communications technology is likely to be felt only gradually. It may slow down the increase in demand for lodging, but by Lee's estimate, its effect is likely to "amount to only some 10 to 15 percent of today's total lodging demand," with that effect spread over the next 10 to 20 years.[11]

ENERGY MANAGEMENT[12]

As much as 10 percent of the hospitality industry's costs are either directly or indirectly for energy for such things as lighting, air conditioning, and heating. Because energy costs are escalating, there has been much attention in recent years devoted to developing equipment to control them. As with so much other technology in the hospitality industry, the computer and microprocessor are central to

[9] Daniel R. Lee, *Lodging* (New York: Drexel Burnham Lambert, 1984), p. 107.

[10] Lee, *Lodging*, p. 10.

[11] Lee, *Lodging*, p. 10.

[12] For a fuller discussion of this topic, see Frank D. Borsenik, *The Management of Maintenance Systems and Energy in the Hospitality Industry*, 2nd ed. (New York: Wiley, 1987).

this effort. To understand the hotels' energy management control systems, we must begin with how a hotel's energy charges are computed by the power company.

Demand

Demand charges are based on the peak load—that is, the maximum demand for power—that the property requires during the billing period. In some operations, equipment may be turned on when an employee comes to work. Let's suppose that the morning cook comes in at 5:30 A.M. to open the restaurant at 6:00 A.M. This is a convenient time to turn on the air conditioning for the day. So the first thing the cook does is to flip the switches turning on the air conditioning and then to turn on the kitchen exhaust fans and the stoves and ovens. All that equipment running at once creates a very heavy demand, and so a very simple way to minimize this would be to give the cook a timed schedule for turning on the equipment. Of course, automated equipment can also be used to turn on the equipment.

Peak-load control systems can be set to turn off equipment such as the air conditioning during the day when the hotel's total electricity use approaches the upper demand level set by management. Usually, equipment is turned off according to a predetermined set of priorities and then only for periods of 15 to 20 minutes.[13]

Usage

The electric bill is based not only on the peak demand but also on the total electric use. Programmable thermometers can be used in some parts of the hotel to avoid wasting power. For instance, if a meeting room is to be used for a luncheon at noon, the thermostat may be set to turn the air conditioning on at 10:30 A.M. and off at 1:45 P.M.

The temperature inside a building mainly depends on the outside temperature. Thus, thermostats may be set to turn up the air conditioning at 9:00 A.M. as it warms up outside and then to turn it down at 5:00 P.M. as the temperature drops. With "optimized start" and "optimized stop" equipment, instead of relying on a regular time-of-day setting, thermometers sense the actual outside temperature. For example, if it warms up later than 9:00 A.M. on a summer day because it is cloudy, the increase in air conditioning can be delayed.

Control Systems

Computers and microprocessors record and analyze energy use and actually control the equipment requiring energy. An energy management program is based on the hotel's actual use of energy. A remote sensing system can be linked to a PC programmed to summarize energy use and operating patterns and to provide detailed reports. The equipment may be controlled by a central computer to which

[13] Robert E. Aulbach, *Energy Management* (East Lansing, Mich.: American Hotel and Motel Association Educational Institute, 1984), p. 143.

all of it is connected. Alternatively, equipment may be wired to individual micro-processors that provide sensing and logic in order to control the units under different operating conditions. When separate microprocessors are used to control equipment settings, they can be tied together for monitoring purposes.[14]

THE SMART GUEST ROOM

To this point, we have been looking at how technology can improve a hotel's operating system. There is also technology that can be used in individual guest rooms. Some applications of this technology are already in use while others have not yet come down enough in price to be widely used.

We have, for instance, discussed electronic locks and keys. There also are systems available that dispense with keys altogether, using thumbprints or a scan of the retinas of the guest's eyes. It is also possible to have the lights turn on as the guest enters the room (and to monitor rooms that are supposed to be empty), by using ultrahigh frequency or infrared monitors. In addition, individual guest room safes, using an individually reprogrammable chip that is set to a number designated by the guest, are in use in some hotels. There also is a device that permits the guest to view a person knocking at the guest-room door through the room's closed-circuit television screen. An increasingly popular service is a well-stocked refrigerator in a guest's room offering cocktails, beer, wine, and snacks. When the guest removes an item, the appropriate charge is automatically registered at the front desk. If the system is interfaced with PMS, as the guest removes the item from the refrigerator, the charge is automatically posted to the guest's room.

A fairly new service but one likely to spread rapidly is the video guest checkout. There are few things as annoying to guests as having to stand in a long line to pay their bill on departure, especially if they have a plane to catch. But an in-room video checkout permits guests, by using a touch pad on the room TV, to call up their bill for inspection. If all of the charges are accepted, the guests can then direct that the bill be charged to whatever credit card they used to check in. The video checkout will be available by the end of 1988 in all properties in one chain (Marriott), and it seems clear that the competition will have little choice but to follow suit as quickly as possible.

Greater personal convenience, greater personal security, and a feeling of being able to control one's immediate environment all add up to both greater convenience and the "fantasy factor" of the guest's experience, which we will discuss in the next chapter.

[14] Aulbach, *Energy Management*, p. 144.

Summary

We first gave a brief sketch of computers: the various kinds and their principal parts and functions. Then we focused on how computers are interfaced to hotels' accounting and operating systems.

The chapter next began a discussion of the new technologies that are used in hotels, including property management systems (PMS) and how they are used in making reservations and registering guests' long distance calls. Electronic key systems are another new technology that help ensure guests' security. Word processing facilitates the hotel's correspondence. Finally, videoconferencing enables people to "meet," via computer, and although it could reduce the use of hotels, it has not done so yet. Rather, many hotels are offering videoconferencing facilities.

We also examined energy management: demand, usage, and control systems. Ending the chapter was a description of a "smart" computerized guest room, some of whose features are now in use.

Forces Shaping the Hotel Business

_____ THIS CHAPTER IS ABOUT _____

The economics of the hotel business and how it shapes the opportunities lodging offers you. Hotels, we will see, are capital-intensive, cyclical, and highly competitive businesses. Understanding these forces helps explain how the variety of hotel "products" on the market today have come about.

Management companies operate hotels built by investors. The interest of investors and developers has multiplied opportunities for management companies and, at the same time, made the hotel industry even more competitive, encouraging the creation of many new types of lodging.

Competitive tactics are all important in lodging. To gain a better understanding of competition in lodging, we review services and amenities provided, such as restaurants, concierge service, superfloors, fitness facilities, as well as guest room amenities.

The chapter closes with a brief look at the future of the lodging business.

Courtesy of John Portman and Associates, photo by Jaime Ardiles-Arce.

The Economics of the Hotel Business

To understand the hotel business, we will begin with its economic dimensions. The hotel business is cyclical. First, the demand for hotel rooms rises and falls with the business cycle. Generally, the demand for hotel rooms changes direction three to six months after the economy does, as reflected in the gross national product.[1] This is not surprising, as both business and pleasure travel are easy expenditures to eliminate when the economy is not good and to restore when it improves. In any local market, the hotel business is likely to have its own cycle, related to the supply of hotel rooms rather than the demand for them. But the cycle generally starts with the demand for rooms, potential or actual. Let us illustrate this with an example.

AN EXAMPLE OF THE HOTEL BUSINESS CYCLE

"Oldtown," a quiet city of 100,000, has been a stable community with a balanced economy for many years. Not long ago, during a period of general economic expansion, a large national company built a large factory complex in Oldtown. The ripple effect from this spread to the suppliers for the factory complex as well as a number of other companies who, when they heard about the factory complex, learned what an attractive site Oldtown was. Employment soared: some people were transferred to Oldtown, and others moved there seeking jobs.

Our story now shifts to Major Hotels' corporate offices where in a meeting with the vice-presidents of operations and real estate the vice-president for development suggests that Major ought to look into building a hotel in Oldtown. There is immediate agreement to do a preliminary study. Three months later the preliminary study shows encouraging results, and so a consulting firm is hired to do a formal feasibility study; an architect is hired to do preliminary design work; and informal conversations with Major's bankers begin. Six more months pass. The results of the consultant's feasibility study confirm Major's preliminary study; the preliminary design is a beauty, and everybody agrees this could be a great hotel; the bankers, having looked at the studies and the design, decide to process quickly Major's loan application. (They have had a surge in deposits and need to get that money into interest-earning loans.) Best of all, the ideal location has been found, and negotiations to acquire a site are going well.

At a meeting of Major's executive committee, a formal proposal to go ahead is presented. The discussion touches briefly on the competition, but everyone quickly agrees that Oldtown's existing hotels are tired and will be no match for the proposed property. When somebody asks, "Is anybody else going in there?" the answer is, "A few people have been nosing around, but there's nothing firm as far as we can tell." Everyone agrees that it is time to purchase the site and sign a design

---

[1] John J. Rohs, *CFA Lodging Industry Update* (New York: Wertheim & Co., 1986), p. 13.

contract with the architect. Because this is a meeting, everybody's commitment is on the public record.

The same series of events is taking place at Magnificent Hotels, LowCost Lodges, Supersuites, and a couple of other companies. But because each company keeps things fairly quiet until everything is settled, there are only vague rumors that others are also interested in Oldtown.

Finally, 18 months after the first vice-presidential meeting at Major, the company announces that a 300-room hotel will be built in Oldtown, and the ground breaking is set two weeks hence. The story is front-page news. Over the next six months, similar announcements from Magnificent, LowCost, and Supersuites make the front page, too.

At Major, these other companies' announcements make quite a stir. At a meeting of the executive committee, they all shake their heads and agree that those other companies are crazy; they have no sense at all in overbuilding like this. One very junior vice-president who is sitting in raises the possibility that Major should abandon the project, but he is quickly shouted down. Thousands of dollars have already been spent on feasibility studies and architectural work; a site has been purchased; and contracts have been signed for construction. "Besides," says the financial vice-president, "what would our banks say if we pulled out now? Do you think we'd get another loan commitment as easily next time?" Because *everybody* has agreed to the project publicly, for any to admit that he or she was wrong would also be publicly embarrassing.

Eighteen months later, Major's beautiful new property opens, and the general manager hands the following situation report to the vice-president of operations:

> *Within four blocks of my office, there are a thousand rooms under construction. Every place my sales staff goes, they trip over our competitors' people. Magnificent is slashing its convention rates for next year; LowCost has announced a salespersons' discount when its hotel opens next month; and Supersuites is offering free cocktail parties every evening.*
>
> *I think we will do all right after the first couple of years because our operation is going to be stronger and of better quality, but don't expect much for our first two or three years until we are established.*

There are no further announcements of lodging construction in Oldtown.

We have spent quite a bit of time looking at this cycle of events to illustrate the significance of factors such as the complexity of the decision to build a hotel, the lead time required, the preliminary expenditures, and the public corporate and individual commitment to the decision. This cycle shows that an increase in demand can set off a series of events that usually cannot be stopped even when it becomes clear that the market is or will be overbuilt.

In some markets, the demand keeps increasing, and in three to five years another round of building starts, this time fueled by all the old forces plus—for those who didn't get in the first time—a need to be represented in the growth market. In other markets, it takes years for the demand to catch up with the overbuilding.

Figure 9.1   *Hotel construction starts were high in 1985.* [Randall C. Zisler and Robert A. Feldman, *The Real Estate Report* (New York: Goldman Sachs, April 1986).]

Our example was of a local market, but this is usually part of a larger, national market. This cycle of hotel building usually ends, much to everybody's surprise, in overbuilding. Figure 9.1 shows the cycle of hotel construction between 1968 and 1985.

A CAPITAL-INTENSIVE BUSINESS

For the restaurant business, the biggest costs by far are food and payroll, followed by other direct operating expenses. Thus when sales fall precipitously, so do expenses. Hotels also have some large variable costs, most being in the food and beverage department. Lodging itself, however, is capital intensive; that is, it requires large investments of capital in fixed plant and equipment. And capital costs such as depreciation, interest, insurance, and property taxes are fixed costs. Thus, even if there are many vacancies at Major's new hotel, its capital costs will continue and must be met, or the mortgage lender will (generally) foreclose.

What may happen in this situation is complicated. The mortgage holder— let's say an insurance company—may foreclose, and then it will own a hotel that it doesn't know how to operate. If it acquires a lot of hotels in this way, which sometimes happens, it may hire a management company or even establish its own hotel-operating division. (In fact, in 1986 the Prudential Realty Group owned and operated 102 hotels with 35,000 rooms.) Most mortgage holders, however, just want to find another company to take over the mortgage. They are in the business of lending money at interest, and they want a "performing loan" (one that is making payments on time) on their books rather than a hotel full of guests looking for an owner to complain to if their eggs aren't cooked right.

The original developers probably were able to borrow 60 to 70 percent of the total cost of the property and arranged to meet the rest of the investment through their own resources or by attracting other equity (owners rather than lenders) investors. If the property's mortgage is foreclosed, the equity holders' stake (30 to 40 percent of the investment in this example) will be lost.

The property may be sold by the mortgage holder at a "distressed price," at, let's say, 65 percent of its original cost. The new owners will receive a significant operating advantage because their capital costs will be lower, reflecting the lower purchase price. Indeed, a recapitalized property with lower fixed costs can destabilize the market and, in bad times, set off a wave of financial crises in that market through rate reductions that can't be matched by the existing capital costs at other properties.

A COMPETITIVE BUSINESS

Room rates usually are fairly stable because most hotels do have a high fixed-cost structure. But the lodging business is much more competitive than is auto manufacturing or other such industries, and this makes a local or regional oversupply of rooms very serious. Older and outmoded properties may be "withdrawn from the market," that is, torn down or converted to another use, often sooner than expected.

A GROWTH BUSINESS?

Pannel Kerr Forster, in a report on trends in the hotel business, estimated that in 1985 there were 2.7 million rooms in the United States, with 400,000 more scheduled to be built by 1992.[2] That is about a 15 percent increase in the number of rooms, around 2 percent per year. A 2 percent growth rate certainly doesn't qualify lodging as a growth industry (10 or 20 percent might), and the number of rooms is not the best measure of growth. Rooms sold is a much better indicator and has been growing at roughly 1 percent a year since the end of World War II.[3]

---

[2] *Trends in the Hotel Industry, USA Edition 1985* (Houston: Pannel Kerr Forster, 1985).

[3] When I first made such a statement in 1974, in an article in *The Institute Journal* published by the American Hotel Motel Association Educational Institute, it caused considerable irritation in some quarters in the hotel business, presumably because "growth" was good, and so nongrowth must be bad. I am happy therefore, to note that I now have plenty of company among the experts. For instance, Daniel Lee, security analyst at Drexel Burnham Lambert, stated, "Although cyclical, the lodging business is not a 'growth' industry" (Daniel R. Lee, "A Forecast of Lodging Supply and Demand," *Cornell Hotel and Restaurant Administration Quarterly*, August 1984, p. 37); and Glenn Withian, managing editor of the *Cornell Quarterly*, stated, on the basis of Laventhol and Horwath data, "The number of hotel rooms occupied per day has remained relatively flat for more than three decades" (Glenn Withian, "Hotel Companies Aim for Multiple Markets," *Cornell Hotel and Restaurant Administration Quarterly*, November 1985, p. 51).

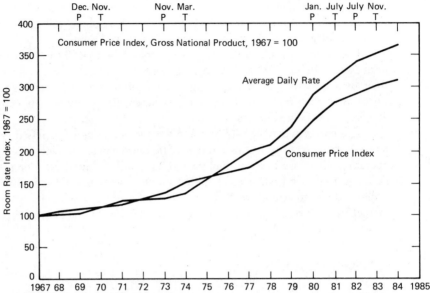

Figure 9.2   *Consumer price index versus average daily rate.* (Pannel Kerr Forster & Co., *Trend of Business—1986.*)

But many factors appear to be slowing the growth of lodging demand. First, travel patterns and consumer preferences have changed. With faster airplanes, businesspersons can fly into a city, do their business, and fly home on the same day. Shorter trips have become the rule. In addition, long distance telephoning is substituting more and more for face-to-face meetings, and videoconferencing could have a similar, though smaller, impact. In pleasure travel, campers and trailers, or even second homes, are often used instead of transient lodging.

The lodging industry's pricing practices have almost certainly contributed to these trends. Throughout the early 1970s, hotel prices increased at about the same rate as did other prices. From 1972 until quite recently, however, room rates increased substantially faster than did the costs of other goods and services, as illustrated in Figure 9.2. In 1984, room rates increased roughly five percentage points more than other prices did, and, in 1985, about three and a half points more.[4] As early as 1984, the president of Quality Courts charged that hotels were frightening guests away because of their "excessive product pricing and a decrease in the perceived price value relationship."[5]

Price increases have not been limited to room rates. According to Laventhol and Horwath analyst, Bjorn Hansen, "Hotels have been very aggressive in raising their (food) prices—and customers are starting to show resistance." Saul Leonard

[4] Rohs, *CFA Lodging Industry Update*, p. 9.
[5] *Nation's Restaurant News*, December 17, 1984, p. 93.

of the same firm observed, "If you're an egg eater, you've got to spend at least $15 to eat breakfast in a hotel. You can get breakfast at a nearby coffee shop for $1.29."[6] When the cost of both food *and* room are added together, the cost of hotel-based travel has soared even more than the escalation in just room rates suggests.

Considerations in the Hotel Investment Decision

Despite price resistance, overbuilding in some markets, and the cyclical nature of the business, new hotels continue to come on the market. This is because developers need hotels to open up new or redeveloped areas and because lenders are interested in granting mortgages to hotel builders and developers. There are at least three considerations in a hotel investment: financial, real estate, and operation.

FINANCIAL

The decision to build a hotel may be motivated by purely financial considerations related to interest rates, tax-law changes, or the desire to hedge against inflation. The 1981 tax law encouraged hotel development by allowing shorter tax lives for properties, thus enabling higher depreciation deductions. This was a great advantage to people and corporations with incomes in the highest tax brackets because the depreciation acted as a tax shield. The 1986 tax reform, however, reversed these advantages, resulting in a significant decline in new hotel construction.

Investors are also attracted to hotels because they are an inflation hedge. As one real estate investment and operating company explained in a brochure addressed to potential investors, "Hotels have the ability to respond almost instantly to changes and fluctuations in the economy and market. For instance, while office and retail properties are usually locked in to long-term leases—some lasting as long as 20 years—hotel rates can be changed virtually overnight."[7]

REAL ESTATE

Hotels also may be built because a community or development needs the property; that is, the hotel may be part of a larger project. The underlying value of the real estate and its appreciation may be a more important consideration to some investors than is the profitability of the hotel. For example, a number of foreign investors in North America have apparently been willing to invest money in hotel properties for their long-term appreciation and as a safe investment.

[6] *Nation's Restaurant News*, November 4, 1985, p. F3.
[7] "VMS Hotel Investments: A Unique Destination for the Individual Investor," n.d., p. 3.

OPERATION

The hotel's operation is often the first investment consideration that students name, but it may be a secondary consideration to some investors.

Risks and Rewards

Our discussion of the cyclical nature of the hotel business suggested that it can be risky for investors. On the other hand, "on an operating basis, hotels have historically outperformed all other types of property. Figures shown in a recent report state that hotel properties showed a compound annual return of nearly 22 per cent—higher than any other form of income producing property."[8] Thus, although there are risks, clearly there are also substantial rewards to investors to compensate for that risk.

Management Companies

Hotels are often built by people who have neither the skill nor the interest to operate them, and so to answer their needs, management companies have come into existence.

The first management company may have been the Cesar Ritz Group. Before the turn of the century, Ritz, with his famous chef, Escoffier, was "paid a retainer to appoint and oversee the managers of separately owned hotels. That arrangement allowed the hotel to advertise itself as a Ritz hotel."[9] The first U.S. "hotel management company" was the Treadway Hotel Company, which began operating small college inns in the 1920s.[10] During the 1930s, the American Hotel Corporation managed bankrupt hotels, but as late as 1970 there were only three or four management companies in operation in the United States. The period since then has been characterized by rapid hotel property development and several periods of "shakeout." Many hotel owners (and their mortgage holders) found themselves in financial difficulty. Under these circumstances the number of management companies grew rapidly, and in 1985 the president of one of the larger companies, Robert M. James, estimated that there were about 125 management companies, although only a few of them were national organizations. The arrangement between the management company and the hotel owner is called a *management contract* and has been defined as follows by Professor Eyster of the Cornell Hotel School.

A management contract is a written agreement between a hotel–motor inn owner and operator in which the owner employs the operator as an agent (employee) to assume full

---

8 "VMS Hotel Investments," p. 1.
9 Daniel R. Lee, *Lodging* (New York: Drexel Burham Lambert, 1984), p. 23.
10 Information in this section is taken from Robert M. James, "Management Companies," *Lodging*, June 1985, pp. 105, 128.

Some budget properties offer no food or pool, just a high-quality room and excellent housekeeping. These properties have targeted business travelers as their principal market. (Photo courtesy of Red Roof Inns.)

operational responsibility for the property and to manage the property in a professional manner. As an agent, the operator pays in the name of the owner, all property operating expenses from the cash flow generated from the operation; it retains its management fees, and remits the remaining cash flow, if any, to the owner. The owner provides the hotel–motor inn property to include land, building, furniture and fixtures, equipment, and working capital and assumes full legal and financial responsibility for the project.[11]

There are two kinds of management companies. First, most chain organizations such as Hilton, Holiday Inns, or Sheraton serve as management companies for the hotels under their franchises. Independent management companies, on the other hand, operate properties under several franchises. The independent companies offer the owners more control over daily operations and more flexibility in terms and in brand affiliation than do the chain companies.

Lodging Trends: Segmentation or Fragmentation?

Until quite recently the North American lodging industry was product oriented and relatively standardized.[12] In effect, the hotel business defined its customers' needs for them by offering a standardized product. The market a few years ago could

[11] James J. Eyster, *The Negotiation and Administration of Hotel Management Contracts*, quoted in Robert M. James, "Management Companies," *Lodging*, June 1985, p. 105.

[12] I am indebted to Mr. Ray Yelle, president of Commonwealth Holiday Inns of Canada, for his observations regarding the transition that is taking place in lodging competition.

Most budget properties offer a simpler variety of the same basic services that other motor hotels provide. (Photo courtesy of Days Inns.)

be represented by three major types. First were first-class properties—Hilton, Westin, and Marriott, for instance. A second major group was made up of companies serving business and tourist travelers with a very good standardized product such as Holiday Inns, Quality, and Ramada. The third group was lower-cost properties made up of older independent motels and, especially from 1975 onward, a growing group of properties built specifically for the rate-sensitive market, such as Days Inns. By the mid-1980s, however, the lodging market had changed dramatically, and products designed to suit the needs of specific travelers' market segments had emerged.

The emergence of properties aimed at specific market segments led some to speak of the fragmentation of the market. Part of this change was the reduction of services at one end of the market and the expansion of services at the other end. Luxury accommodations are the specialty of some hotel companies such as the Four Seasons. Other companies provide differentiated, upscale, service-intensive "executive floors" in mid-scale properties. Another interesting development is the introduction of the all-suite hotels, hotels that are less service intensive but that feature higher-quality guest rooms.

The budget motel room is basically similar to rooms in more expensive properties. (Photo courtesy of Days Inns.)

ECONOMY LODGING

In the early 1980s, Days Inns, Econolodge, and other established economy chains found themselves competing with Quality's Comfort Inns. And by the mid-1980s, the lower-priced, budget-oriented properties had become a major force in the market. Especially the entry of Holiday Corporation into the economy market, with Hampton Inns, meant that the large corporations with "deep pockets" (that is, with ready access to the funds to finance expansion) had arrived. The size of the economy segment in 1986 was suggested by a survey of economy chains which showed that the largest 50 chains of economy lodging were operating about 325,000 guest rooms, or nearly 15 percent of the market, in approximately 3300 locations.[13]

Economy properties offer "standard sized, fully furnished, modern rooms at rates 20 to 50 per cent below area average rates."[14] In conventional motor inns and hotels, the commercial building or its equivalent—lobby, restaurants, cocktail lounge, and meeting and banquet rooms—is a major part of the initial investment. But in the economy format, some or all of these facilities are eliminated. Hampton

[13] *Hotel Motel Management*, May 19, 1986, pp. 22–26.
[14] *Hotel Motel Management*, May 19, 1986, pp. 22–26.

Inns, Holiday Corporation's economy chain, generally contain 110 to 130 units and offer a lobby and breakfast area and a hospitality suite.[15] Some economy properties offer a limited food service or have a franchised restaurant on the premises, such as Wendy's or Arby's at Days Inns. Many economy properties are located near local restaurants, whereas others, such as La Quinta Motor Inns, provide a freestanding restaurant on the same site as the motel.

The plans for expansion in the economy market announced by corporations such as Holiday and Quality, as well as the already-established chains like Days Inns and Motel 6, have at least two limitations. The first is the cyclic nature of the business. Many industry observers feel the hotel business is already overbuilt in most markets, even in the economy segment. The second factor is the refranchising cycle.

Refranchise or Convert?

Franchises are usually granted for several years, commonly 25 or 30. At the end of the original franchise agreement, new terms will be negotiated if the franchise is to be renewed. By the early 1980s, a number of older mid-priced hotels were due for refranchising. Generally, the refranchising has meant huge investments for upgrading the hotel. Not only must the rooms be redecorated, but often the air-conditioning plant must be replaced. The lobby and food service units must also be refurbished, and other major capital improvements such as an indoor swimming pool may be required. Although such an investment may make sense in some locations and may be financially possible for *some* owners, others find that the upgrading required is not economically justified or feasible.

Obviously, the properties that do not upgrade and refranchise do not just "go away." Some simply become independents, many of which then compete in the economy market. An increasing number choose to "convert" to another company. For instance, Quality's economy chain, Comfort Inns, includes a number of reconversions from its own mid-scale Quality Inns and from other franchise groups. The existing inventory of older mid-scale properties is a competitive threat to the economy segment because it may make sense for more and more mid-scale properties to minimize their investments by refranchising to the standard of the economy market.

MID-SCALE PROPERTIES

Existing mid-scale properties are generally upgrading their facilities as new properties are built and older ones are refranchised. New players are also arriving in this market.

The Courtyard Concept

Probably the best-known and perhaps the most-copied new concept is "Courtyard by Marriott." This product was developed after extensive consumer research and

[15] *Hotel Motel Management*, June 30, 1986, p. 38.

Guest rooms at Courtyard by Marriott are designed with distinct functional areas for relaxing, working, sleeping, and dressing. King-sized beds are a feature in 70 percent of the rooms. (Photo courtesy of Marriott Corp.)

testing in the Atlanta area. Based on successful prototypes, Marriott proposed spending $3 billion to develop, by 1990, 300 courtyards with over 50,000 rooms. The courtyard concept in many ways resembles the economy market, in that the commercial building is scaled down dramatically to include a very small lobby and minimal food and beverage facilities. In turn, the scaled-down food and beverage operations require much lower payrolls. The restaurant menus are highly simplified and rely on convenience and preprepared foods. Finally, only limited meeting space is provided, generally only one or two small conference rooms.

Instead of capital investment in public space for food and beverage facilities— and expenditures for their operations—the courtyard property invests in unusually well appointed and large guest rooms and offers them at highly competitive rates. Most of the rooms contain king-sized beds, separate working and dressing areas, a sofa bed, in-room coffee service, a phone with a long cord, and remote-control television with cable and free movies. Rates range from $40 to $60. The property features a central landscaped courtyard with a swimming pool and a "socializing area." Northern locations have indoor swimming pools. Operating costs are minimized by clustering the courtyards in areas that can support more than one property, so as to achieve economies in management and marketing expenses.[16]

[16] *Hotel Motel Management*, February 3, 1986, p. 31.

The courtyard concept is clearly popular with other companies. Whether companies have deliberately copied Marriott or simply reached the same conclusions is not clear. Nevertheless, the announcements of new products that are similar to Marriott's courtyards have become so frequent that some in the trade describe them as "courtyard clones."

Older Properties

Some older mid-scale properties move to the economy category. Others, however, seek to position themselves in the mid-scale market, but without the extensive upgrading required in the typical refranchising. One new chain, Park Inns, was established with the avowed intent of serving mid-scale franchisees that are concerned about refranchising. Company officials forecast that by the end of the decade more than 700 U.S. hotels will have changed their corporate affiliation.[17]

With their full complement of food, beverage, and meeting facilities, these older properties will continue to offer physical plants that are competitive with those of the new and refranchised properties. And because many of these properties are 20 to 30 years old, they may have lower capital costs, reflecting their depreciated values. This could result in a considerable reduction in their break-even point, which means that they can offer significantly lower rates for roughly comparable facilities. The mid-priced category, which in 1985 represented roughly 70 percent of the market, is highly competitive. It is pressed from below by economy properties and from within by new entrants and older properties that may offer lower rates.

UPSCALE PROPERTIES

The upper end of the lodging market has been split into three types, *upscale, all-suite,* and *luxury*. Some companies, such as Hilton, Westin, and Sheraton, compete principally in the upscale market. (Note, however, that Hilton Inns and Sheraton Inns are often judged to compete in the mid-scale market. The *inn* designation generally denotes a franchised property operating in a smaller or suburban market.) The competition in this segment is with the mid-scale chains moving into the market and with the all-suite properties.

Mid-scale companies have invaded the upscale market: Holiday with the Crown Plaza Holiday Inn, Ramada with the Ramada Renaissance, and Quality with the Quality Royale. Another competitive tactic of the mid-scale operators aimed at gaining a share of the upscale market is that of "executive floors." An increasingly common approach—sometimes referred to as "a hotel within a hotel"—are rooms offering luxury features, more amenities, and expanded services such as free newspapers, overnight shoeshine service, and a complementary breakfast. But perhaps the greatest competition in the upscale market is from the all-suite properties.

[17] Company sources.

All-Suite Properties

Market research suggests that two-thirds of all business travelers are potentially all-suite customers; that is, they can afford all-suite rates. One-third of these people have tried an all-suite hotel, and two-thirds intend to try one.[18] Since their inception, all-suite hotels have outperformed the market in terms of occupancy, room rates, and profit. In fact, 35 to 40 percent of their gross revenue has been available to cover fixed charges, compared with only 25 percent from standard hotels.[19]

A conventional hotel room has 300 to 400 square feet, whereas a suite ranges from 500 to 800 square feet. This generally includes a separate dining room—which may be used as a work or lounging area—a bedroom, and a kitchenette. The suite appeals especially to business travelers who want a more spacious, homelike atmosphere as well as space for work and relaxation. On the weekends, the roominess is a special advantage for traveling families with children because both parents and children can have rooms of their own without additional cost.

The rates at all-suite hotels are generally competitive with those of comparable conventional properties. This is possible because their food and beverage service is quite limited. As with economy properties, the elimination or severe curtailment of investment in food and beverage facilities (capital costs) and operations (operating costs) makes the provision of larger and more luxurious guest rooms economically viable. Most all-suite units offer a complementary breakfast, and many offer cocktails at no charge in the late afternoon and early evening. This permits the property to schedule employees for only the hours required for this limited service and to offer the service in a predictable, economical format.

All-suite properties are less dependent on the off-the-road, drop-in traveler and consequently can afford an inexpensive location away from the expressway interchange favored by many hotel companies. In fact, the all-suite hotel company is commonly located near its corporate clients.

In some respects, the all-suite hotel label is misleading because there are suite properties at every level of the market, from Quality's Comfort Inns' all-suite properties to L'Ermitage at the very top of the luxury scale. Although some authorities suggest that all-suite units could take up 10 percent or more of the market by the early 1990s,[20] all-suite properties may eventually become the rule outside those areas with exceptionally high land costs and outside the strictly budget category.

The Long-Stay Market

One particular all-suite segment deserves specific mention, and that is the property designed for long-stay guests. The market leader in this area has been Residence Inns.

[18] Michael M. Dickens, president, Guest Quarters Inc., Address to the 8th Annual National Hospitality Industry Investment Conference, New York, June 9, 1986.
[19] Felig Jarvis, "All Suite Hotels," *Lodging*, June 1985, pp. 103, 121, 122.
[20] Rohs, *CFA Lodging Industry Update*, p. 16.

Residence Inns, a leader in the long-stay market, offers an all-suite property especially designed to meet the needs of guests who will be staying for more than a few days. The exterior courtyard view shown here resembles a low-rise condominium development. The guest facilities are designed for business entertaining. (Photos courtesy of Residence Inns.)

Residence Inns estimates that the extended-stay segment is 5 percent of the lodging market. Residence Inns' data also show that almost half (40 percent) of its guests are extended-stay guests, that is, those who stay 5 to 29 days. The next biggest group (30 percent) is long-stay guests, remaining 30 or more days, whereas only 30 percent stay a more conventional four or fewer days.[21] According to Residence Inns, a typical guest is between 25 and 44 years old and earns $35,000 or more per year. Three-quarters of its guests have professional, managerial, or administrative jobs, and the rest are in technical occupations (15 percent) or sales (13 percent). Eighty-five percent of Residence Inns' business comes from the 500 largest companies in the United States, and roughly half of its guests earn over $50,000 per year.[22] Thus, Residence Inns has chosen a highly profitable specialized market with clearly defined needs.

[21] Jack P. DeBoer, chairman and chief executive officer, Residence Inns, Address to 8th Annual National Hospitality Industry Investment Conference, New York, June 9, 1986.
[22] Company sources.

Luxury hotels offer not just comfort but also elegance in every appointment. Pictured here are a guest room and a mirrored bathroom from the Park Hyatt on Water Tower Square in Chicago. (Photos courtesy of Hyatt Hotels.)

LUXURY HOTELS

Another property type that has grown from being relatively rare to becoming quite common is the luxury hotel, as typified by the Four Seasons or Mandarin properties. These hotels—a tier above those labeled as upscale—are characterized by very comfortable, even opulent guest rooms, excellent food service, and highly skilled personal service.

The executive floors mentioned earlier in connection with the mid-scale market have their parallel in the luxury and superluxury markets in the "Towers" concept. Originally begun at the Waldorf Astoria Hotel in New York City, the Waldorf Towers were aimed at wealthy travelers, heads of corporations, and visiting diplomats and heads of state. The Hilton company found this segmentation strategy one worth developing further and did so, first in the Palmer House Towers in Chicago and then in several other properties. The idea has been adopted by other upscale hotels to maintain not only the profit but also the glamour and reputation that accrue to those who host the wealthy, famous, and successful.

OTHER SPECIALIZED SEGMENTS

Conference Centers

More money—$40 to $60 million—is spent each year on corporate education than in colleges and universities. This therefore is a very attractive market and one for which many hotels compete. Specialized conference centers have grown up to meet the particular needs of this market. Some of the centers are operated by large companies such as General Motors, IBM, or AT&T. Others, however, are built as separate businesses to compete for the conference business. Some meeting coordinators prefer these kinds of properties because of their special design and their ability to focus their whole attention on the conference. Many conference centers are operated by hotel companies. Marriott, for instance, operated 22 such properties in 1986 and was actively seeking more management contracts in this area.[23] The facilities provided at such centers usually include tennis, swimming, golf, and game rooms. Some centers also offer gyms, saunas, bowling, horseback riding, and libraries.[24]

Condominiums

Condominiums, or "condos" as they are often called, generally offer the features of an apartment building—multiroom apartments with full kitchens—sometimes combined with those of a hotel, such as on-premise food and beverage service. The units, however, are usually sold to individual owners, but the overall property is operated by a management company. Condos that service the vacation market are most commonly located in resort areas.

Two kinds of condo ownership are available. Some condos are sold outright, and their owners have the right to year-round occupancy. Another, increasingly common practice is to sell "time-shares," the right to occupy the condo permanently and as an owner for a limited and specific time, with others having that right for other time periods. The price of a time-share usually depends on the desirability of the particular time period, with less attractive time periods costing substantially less than peak periods do. On the other hand, some time-sharing arrangements require the owners to buy shares in high, middle, and off seasons. Thus, for instance, a time-share package might be offered for one week each in the months of July, October, January, and April. Time-share-swapping networks enable the owners to swap with one another a week they own in Miami for, say, the same week or even a different week in Aspen.

Condos are competitive with hotels in two ways. First, they represent a form of interindustry competition in the same way that a second home or a camper does. That is, the owner of a condo in a resort location is much less likely to be a hotel customer because his or her funds are already invested in a vacation property.

23 *Hotel Motel Management*, June 9, 1986, pp. 19–21.
24 David E. Arnold and Joan K. Spence, *The Executive Conference Center—A Statistical and Financial Profile* (Philadelphia: Laventhol & Horwath, 1982).

Besides being an alternative to a hotel for their owner, condos—both those sold outright and those marketed as time-shares—are often rented out by the management company when the owner does not want to use the property. On a day-to-day basis, this makes them very real competitors with the hotels in their market. Some condo properties, particularly those offering many services, are operated by hotel companies and are marketed as resorts. Indeed, some companies have sold significant portions of a resort as condos or have built a condo component into their plan for the development and financing of a new resort. In effect, the sale of condominiums has become an important source of financing for the owners of the resort.

Segmentation: For Guests or Developers?

Much of the development of new *product* segments—economy, all-suite, executive floors, superluxury—can be related to specific market segments. For example, economy segments are aimed at rate-conscious consumer groups such as retirees. (Days Inns reported that 11 percent of its rooms are occupied by seniors.) Residence Inns has a clearly targeted segment in mind, and its range of products, from executive floors to superluxury, is for the expense-account market.

Glenn Withian, managing editor of the *Cornell Hotel and Restaurant Administration Quarterly*, suggests that the consumer market is not the sole driving force behind segmentation, however; segmentation also meets the business needs of the hotel companies, their potential franchisees, and the developers. Segmentation first offers a strategy to hotel companies to maintain growth in a mature market. If, for instance, there are already a number of established Holiday Inns in a market, that city may still be ripe for a Hampton Inn or an Embassy Suite. This pleases both the potential franchisee looking for an investment opportunity and the franchisor.

> *Most hotel companies are largely service companies that sell a product—a specific kind of hotel—to developers. . . . Today, hotel companies are offering developers a range of hotels so the company can match the hotel product to the site. Having multiple brands or chains allows hotel companies to provide a product to meet developer needs.*[25]

Nevertheless, the interests of hotel companies, franchisees, and developers heighten the possibility that markets will be overbuilt. The cycle we discussed at the beginning of this chapter will be more pronounced then if the players limit their attention to just consumer demand.

---

[25] Glenn Withian, "Hotel Companies Aim for Multiple Markets," *Cornell Hotel and Restaurant Administration Quarterly*, November 1985, pp. 39–51. In the argument cited here, Withian is quoting industry analyst Daniel Lee.

SOLUTIONS TO OVERSUPPLY

One solution to an oversupply of rooms in a market is, as we said earlier, time and a continuing growth in demand. The other solution is to withdraw from the market or to convert the property to other uses. For instance, 13 hotels with about 5700 rooms were taken off the market in New York City between 1980 and 1985, either through conversion to another use such as apartments or because they were closed. It is estimated that 1.1 percent of hotel rooms are withdrawn each year.[26] Although the closing of a hotel is usually a sad day, especially for its owners, staff, and frequent guests, most properties do eventually reach a point that the continued investment to maintain and refurbish a property is not warranted. Indeed, in periods of oversupply, properties are more readily judged substandard because the newer and better properties are more likely to be filled first. And a number of industry observers have suggested that during the last half of the 1980s we might expect this.[27]

Competitive Tactics: Services and Amenities

In the competitive hotel marketplace, one of the means of differentiation is designing a hotel property to suit the needs of a particular market segment. In many cases such strategies involve changes in the mix of services and facilities from what was once the industry standard (see Figure 9.3). For example, some properties have curtailed their services, and others have expanded them, in what one analyst sees as a response to the "polarization" of consumers.[28] That is, the industry is trying to find appropriate price-value relationships for particular consumer segments. Indeed, segmentation—in facilities, services, and rates—marks a major shift in the lodging industry from an operational focus to a marketing focus.[29]

HOTEL FOOD SERVICE

One characteristic of many of the newer lodging formats is the reduction in food services.

Bed and Breakfast—Plus

The practice of giving away a continental breakfast is certainly not new but has been common in small motels for some years. But the advertised, standardized

---

[26] Lee, *Lodging*, p. 73.

[27] See, for instance, Rohs, CFA *Lodging Industry Update*, p. 8, or the remarks of several speakers at the 8th Annual National Hospitality Industry Conference. Hervey Feldman, president of Embassy Suites, referred to the mid-1980s as the worst crisis our industry has ever faced. Carl Mottek referred to the mid-1980s as the universal buyer's market, and James Pickett, president of Pickett Companies, called it a time of obsolescence, disruption, demolition, and conversion.

[28] Rohs, CFA *Lodging Industry Update*, p. 15.

[29] *1986 US Lodging Special Analysis* (Philadelphia: Laventhol & Horwath, 1986), p. 2.

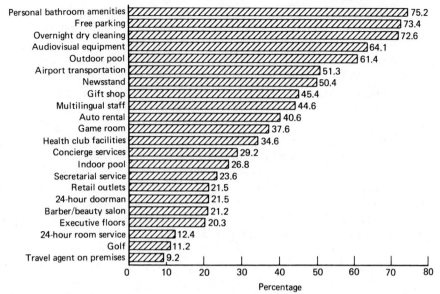

Figure 9.3 *Guest services.* (U.S. Lodging Industry 1986. Laventhol & Horwath.)

availability of a "free breakfast," that is, one covered by the price of the room, has a special appeal. In the economy market, for instance, a continental breakfast of juice, pastry, and coffee is generally all that is provided. In some all-suite properties, as well, a continental breakfast is the standard, but a number offer a full, cooked-to-order breakfast. All-suite properties also commonly provide a free cocktail party, typically from 5 to 7 P.M. Residence Inns have a grocery-shopping service available without cost to their guests, and some of their properties also have arranged for food service delivery from local restaurants.[30]

Many all-suite properties also provide a scaled-down, on-premise restaurant. But very few, if any, however, offer substantial meeting and banquet facilities. Some all-suite operators, such as the Hotel Luxeford operations, go to a great deal of trouble to arrange for their food service to be operated by a well-known, local restauranteur.[31] In the all-suite market, then, there is not as great a curtailment of food service as is found among most budget properties.

Quick-Service Delis and Leased Food Service

Fast-food operations such as Arby's and Wendy's are replacing "Daybreak" operations at Days Inns. In Toronto, Pat & Marios, a roadhouse chain, operates the restaurant in the high-rise airport Venture Inn, one of a chain of Canadian budget hotels. And delicatessens are also proving successful in some Radisson, Hyatt, and

[30] *Nation's Restaurant News*, April 1, 1985, p. 33.
[31] *Nation's Restaurant News*, March 10, 1986, p. 44.

Ramada properties.[32] Most Embassy Suites lease their food service units to other operators. All of these lease arrangements with fast-food and roadhouse chains have the advantage of giving the food service headaches to another specialist company. Some customers favoring a particular fast-food service may actually be drawn to the property by a fast-food brand name, and virtually all customers will know what to expect. The disadvantage is that the lodging operation loses a large measure of control over its "service department."

On-Site Franchised Restaurants

Probably the best-known practitioner of the on-site franchised restaurant is La Quinta Motor Inns. This economy motel chain offers a build-to-suit leased restaurant on the motel site. It has used this arrangement with several restaurant companies, including Denny's, Cracker Barrel, Bob Evans Farms, Waffle House, and Shoney's. According to *Nation's Restaurant News*, La Quinta is now also interested in fast-food chains such as McDonald's and Wendy's because they are serving breakfast—quickly. Generally, such a lease specifies the minimum number of hours of operation and allows the guests to charge their food to their room.

Conventional Hotel Restaurants

A single direction for hotels' food services is by no means clear. Some hotel operators are finding that they can't compete successfully with local top-quality food service restaurants in attracting local trade and so are building smaller restaurants and reducing the number of the food service outlets in the hotel from two or three to one.[33] Even some luxury hotels, according to Laventhol and Horwath's Bjorn Hansen, are opting for more casual outlets rather than formal dining rooms.[34]

On the other hand, Marriott chose to send several of its chefs to study in the south of France, and a number of other hotels have contracted with leading French and American chefs for consulting services.[35] Thus, these companies are, if anything, increasing their emphasis on fine food. Indeed, the president of Doubletree Inns stated, "Strong, community oriented restaurants and lounges add 7 to 8 points to our occupancy rates." In a similar vein, the president of Royce Hotels explained, "If you call secretaries in West Palm Beach and ask them where to stay, they probably say Royce because they eat in the restaurant and visit the lounge. Eighty percent of our business is generated through local referrals."[36]

Restaurants As a Competitive Strategy

Hotel restaurants do not generally make money after all the charges are considered. Bjorn Hansen of Laventhol and Horwath has estimated that after all the overhead

---

[32] *Nation's Restaurant News*, April 22, 1985, p. 3.
[33] *Nation's Restaurant News*, November 4, 1985, p. F5.
[34] *Nation's Restaurant News*, August 12, 1985, p. F58.
[35] *Nation's Restaurant News*, January 20, 1986, p. F3.
[36] *Nation's Restaurant News*, March 10, 1986, p. F29.

expenses, a hotel restaurant actually loses about 5 percent on sales.[37] Nonetheless, the food service in many markets secures local referrals, and the resulting higher occupancies more than offset its limited profits. When the lodging market becomes highly competitive, the chances are that the importance of a good-quality food and beverage operation will be "rediscovered" by more and more operations. On the other hand, it is quite clear that there is and, for the forseeable future will be, an important segment of the lodging industry that does not offer any significant food service.

OTHER SERVICES AND AMENITIES

A wide range of services, distinctive physical plant features, and products outside the food and beverage department are used by hotels to differentiate a property from its competitors.

The Concierge and Superfloors

Many hotels are adding a concierge to the lobby staff, and others are creating *superfloors*, that is, special areas such as executive floors or tower suites. These floors usually offer special lounges and other services. Although there are many variations, we will look at a specific example at one hotel company:

At CN Hotels' new Toronto property, L'Hotel, three classes of *service* are available: premiere, silver, and gold. The word *service* is emphasized because the basic product, the room and its furnishings, is virtually the same in all three classes. The silver and gold floors are a part of a strategy of meeting the particular service tastes and needs of upscale, frequent travelers.

Guests entering the hotel intending to go to the *premiere*—or "regular"— floors (about 65 percent of the hotel) register at the front desk and are shown to their room by a bellman. The concierge in the lobby provides them with standard services such as information, reservations, and tickets.

Guests entering the hotel intending to go to the *silver floors* register at the lobby concierge's desk using a special express registration procedure. Upon arriving at their floor, they are met by a host or hostess and shown to their room. (Their bags are sent up by the doorman.) The silver floor has a small but very comfortable lounge that offers the guests a complimentary continental breakfast, an honor bar (that is, guests may pour their own drinks and sign a chit for them) from 4 to 10 P.M. daily, and complimentary canapés served from 5 to 7 P.M. Other services include complimentary local phone calls, complimentary cable television with remote control, complimentary tea or coffee with their wake-up call, evening turn-down service, and an overnight shoeshine. Special personal amenities include hair dryers, plush bathrobes, extra-heavy towels, fresh fruit, and freshly cut flowers. Rooms on the silver floor cost about 25 percent more than those on the premiere floors do.

---

[37] Bjorn Hansen, "Hotel Food Service: Where's the Profit?" *Cornell Hotel and Restaurant Administration Quarterly*, August 1984, p. 96.

Guests on the gold floors are generally recognized by the doorman because they are repeat guests. They are sent directly to their floor, where they are met by the gold floor concierge and shown to their room after the very brief registration formalities are concluded in the gold lounge. In the center of the gold lounge, consisting of several rooms furnished in the style of a private club, is the office of the concierge and his or her staff. Prompt, personal service is emphasized in the lounge. The continental breakfast on the gold floor is deluxe, and all the amenities offered on the silver floor are provided here as well. In addition, each room is supplied with a small box of fine chocolates. The gold lounge offers an honor bar, secretarial services, and a "board room" for small meetings. The full dining-room menu is available from room service. Guests on both the silver and gold floors are offered complimentary limousine service to the center of downtown. Rates on the gold floor are about 45 percent higher than those on the premiere floors.

Service-differentiated floors are not an automatic success, and CN has had to invest in promoting the availability of these floors. The demand for the upscale floors had increased, however, by 30 percent a year and a half after they opened, and this increase gave promise of continuing.

Luxury hotels, such as the Four Seasons or Dallas's Turtle Creek, offer substantially the same services as those available on the gold floor, but to *all* their guests. On the other hand, many motor hotels and virtually all economy properties have completely eliminated the bell staff, on the theory that today most people prefer *not* to be bothered with a bellman. The level of service intensity, then, varies widely in the industry.

Fitness Facilities

According to the *Washington Post*, 2000 hotels—10 times as many as three years earlier—list some kind of health and fitness facility in their advertising.[38] Health-club memberships have been growing at a 20 percent rate; company fitness programs are becoming common; and more than half of all U.S. firms are expected to start programs within the next decade. Thus, all these people who have committed themselves to a fitness program quite naturally don't want to break their routine when they travel, and so it is not surprising that hotels and motels are adding fitness programs. Resort and convention hotels invest in more elaborate facilities, whereas economy and mid-scale properties offer more modest arrangements. The basic equipment required are exercise bikes, treadmills, rowing machines, weight-training equipment, and floor mats.[39] Fitness centers are expensive but easy to add, and easy for competitors to copy.

Amenities

Susan Chandler, a marketing and amenities consultant, suggested that once the basics the guest requires (which she defined as shampoo, soap, and a shower cap)

[38] *Lodging*, January 1985, p. 60.
[39] *Hotel and Motel Management*, June 1985, pp. 79–83.

Exercise centers—such as the one at the MacKinae Hotel—are among the growing group of amenities and services lodging is offering guests to get and keep their business. (Courtesy of MacKinae Hotel & Conference Center.)

have been provided, an important purpose of amenities is to exploit what she calls the *fantasy factor,* "responding to the person within the guest—whom he or she would wish to be . . . and bolstering their most cherished image of themselves." She emphasized that this fantasy factor can be activated by thoughtful service such as remembering the guest's name or providing VIP recognition somewhat in the manner of the gold and silver floors. Chandler also noted, however, that basic amenities can cost as little as 30 cents a day, up to $3.50 or more.[40]

According to a joint study by Procter & Gamble and the American Hotel and Motel Association (AHMA), the five most popular personal amenities that guests use are shampoo, larger bars of soap, toothpaste, hand and body lotion, and mouthwash.[41] Table 9.1 lists other items, and Table 9.2 gives a more comprehensive view of services and product usage.

ASSESSING SERVICES AND AMENITIES

As a competitive tactic, what stands out is the ease with which many of the services and amenities we have been discussing can be copied. The first hotel or motel in a city that put in a television set undoubtedly had an advantage, but not for long.

[40] *Lodging,* January 1986, pp. 25–28.
[41] *Lodging,* July–August 1986, pp. 26–29.

Table 9.1 *Popular guest-room amenities, in order of frequency of guest usage*

1 Shampoo	8 Shoeshine cloth
2 Larger bars of soap	9 Stationery
3 Toothpaste	10 Cologne or perfume
4 Hand and body lotion	11 Shower cap
5 Mouthwash	12 Sewing kit
6 Bath gel	13 Suntan lotion
7 Hair conditioner	

Source: Lodging Magazine.

And shampoo—once rarely seen in a hotel room—has now become commonplace. Indeed, in regard to personal-care amenities, it is becoming necessary to have them just to avoid damaging the property's reputation, but it is difficult to see them as offering any lasting competitive advantage. Similarly, exercise facilities are an easily duplicated service. But finding or training a good concierge is almost as difficult as providing memorable food service. Again, food service is very difficult to do well, and its very complexity ensures that it will not be easy to copy. Although some property types may be able to dispense with food service and rely on

Table 9.2 *Services and products used by guests*

SERVICE OR PRODUCT	PERCENT USING
Television	91
Personal care items	76
Restaurant/coffee shop	70
More than two towels	69
Wake-up call	59
In-room coffee maker	54
Cocktail lounge	29
Swimming pool	29
Pay TV	20
Exercise facilities	15
Check cashing	10
Room service	10

Source: Lodging Magazine.

restaurants in their neighborhood, it seems likely that they will have greater difficulty in differentiating themselves from their competitors. Soap, shampoo, or a weight room probably won't help either. As the ultimate differentiating service, food service's role seems secure.

The Outlook for the Lodging Business

Perhaps the easiest way to set the stage for our discussion of the outlook for the lodging business is with a personal recollection:

> *The first job I had in the hotel business was in my father's hotel, the Fargon, in the year I graduated from high school, 1949. The hotel advertised that every room had access to a bath—which was true, as there were two of them on each floor. Our least expensive room was a "plain court room," which rented for $1.40 per night. These were tiny rooms that looked out on a small air shaft. The plain outside room was not much larger, but it did have an outside window. It rented for $1.65. Both rooms had access to a bath—down the hall.*
>
> *Of course we also had rooms with a "connecting bath." As I recall, a single-with-bath rented for the princely sum of $2.50, and a double was somewhere above $3.00. The rooms were clean but small and had no radio and, of course, no TV.*
>
> *Lest anyone think poorly of my father's hotel, let me tell you that this was an AAA-approved hotel and that in his day, my father had a reputation as a leader in the industry. In fact, this book is dedicated to him out of respect for his achievements.*

UPGRADING

The fine little hotel in which I worked in high school couldn't even compete in today's market. The story of the hotel industry since that time is one of continuous upgrading: radios, televisions, swimming pools, larger rooms, bigger beds, plushier rooms. And that story line seems unlikely to change. The industry is highly competitive, and so improvements are quickly matched. Hotel guests have consistently opted for the improved property with the higher rates. Even though there is still a place at the lower end of the market for economy properties, it is interesting that the first Holiday Inns in the early 1950s were, in many ways, the economy chain of *their* day, and that gradually the upgrading process has moved them to what is called mid-scale today. Today's economy properties resemble closely the Holiday Inn rooms of a few years ago, and we are now seeing economy chains announce *their* move into the mid-scale market.[42]

---

[42] *Hotel and Motel Management*, June 1985, p. 5.

Summary

The chapter began by examining the economics of the hotel business in regard to both the business cycle and the local market. We illustrated the latter with an example of the hotel business cycle. We then moved on to a discussion of the hotel business as being capital intensive and competitive, and perhaps as being a growth business.

Our next topic was the considerations in a hotel investment decision: financial, real estate, and operation.

Management companies were described: how they came into being, what they do, and the differences between chain and independent operations.

We followed this with a discussion of segmentation and fragmentation in the lodging business. First, we divided hotel properties into economy, mid-scale, upscale, and luxury, as well as conference centers and condominiums, and described and differentiated each. Included in this section were discussions of the benefits and drawbacks of refranchising or converting, the courtyard concept, all-suite hotels, and the long-stay market. We then talked about whether this segmentation relates to developers and the consumers.

We described the competitive tactics that hotels are now using, especially in their services and amenities: food service, concierge service, superfloors, fitness facilities, and personal amenities. We identified a memorable food service as the most successful of these tactics, and the least easy to copy.

The chapter ended with a brief look at the future of the lodging business, pointing at the overall upgrading of hotel properties as the principal change.

Tourism: Front and Center

—————————— THIS CHAPTER IS ABOUT ——————————

Tourism and why it is so important both to the economy and to the hospitality industry. Travel is growing in North America and all over the world. This chapter will help you understand current travel trends as well as their economic impact.

The United States is an international tourist attraction whose popularity is often influenced by the value of the U.S. dollar. On the other hand, the economic effects of U.S. citizens traveling abroad are important and have an impact on the dollar's value, too. The role of tourism in the international economy is an important topic, because of its impact on the U.S. balance of payments and the U.S. economy.

Tourism, we will argue, is not an industry, but it is a vitally significant factor not only for hotels but for food service as well.

chapter

10

Courtesy of the Greater New Orleans Tourist and Convention Commission.

Tourism is the collection of productive businesses and governmental organizations that serve the traveler away from home. According to the U.S. Travel Data Center, these organizations include restaurants, hotels, motels, and resorts; all facets of transportation, including rental cars, travel agents, and gasoline service stations; national and state parks or recreation areas; and various private attractions. The industry also includes those organizations that support these firms' retail activities, including advertising companies, publications, transportation equipment manufacturers, and travel research and development agencies.

Tourism's importance to the hospitality industry is obvious. Some parts of the industry, such as hotels, derive almost all of their sales from travelers. Even food service attributes roughly 25 percent of its sales to travelers. And many leisure-oriented businesses with a major food service and hospitality component, such as theme parks, are also dependent on travelers.

In the economy as a whole, the importance of tourism and the hospitality industry is increasing each year. Indeed, as employment in "smokestack" industries—that is, manufacturing—falls, the service industries, especially those businesses serving travelers, must take up the slack, by providing new jobs. Tourism, then, is central not only to the health of the hospitality industry but also to the economy as a whole.

Travel and Tourism

Travel and tourism are as American as baseball, hot dogs, apple pie, and the interstate highway system. In fact, Americans take over a billion trips each year.[1] In 1985, over 41 million Americans took one or more trips.[2] Moreover, tourism is growing rapidly, fueled by more leisure time, rising family incomes, and more favorable demographic trends.

GROWING LEISURE

There are several reasons for the increase in leisure time. People at work now have more time off. Most companies' vacation policies have become more liberal. And the number of legal, paid holidays has increased, and significantly for tourism, more of these are timed so as to provide three-day weekends.

Although the typical workweek has stayed at 40 hours for many years, flex time and other flexible scheduling arrangements are giving more people more leisure time. In Europe, some manufacturing industries have even broken with the 40-hour workweek norm, and in Sweden, the average workweek is now 28.8

[1] *Economic Review of Travel in America* (Washington, D.C.: U.S. Travel Data Center, 1985), p. 6.
[2] *National Travel Survey—1985 Full Year Report* (Washington, D.C.: U.S. Travel Center, 1986), p. A-1.

hours.[3] In the United States as well, we may soon see pressure for shortening the workweek.

INCOME TRENDS

The two-income family has become a major factor in travel. Within the two-income family, however, there are two somewhat different groups. In some cases, the wife has chosen to work because she wishes to follow her professional or occupational interests. This is an upscale group commonly associated with "yuppies," though it is by no means limited to professional people, despite what the term *yuppy* (young *u*rban *p*rofessionals) implies. An alternative reason for wives to work, however, is to *maintain the family's income*, as in many households, the husband's income has not kept pace with inflation and the cost of maintaining a satisfactory standard of living. In others, layoffs have meant that the husbands are unemployed for a period, forcing the wives to go to work to maintain the family's income.

The latter group of two-income families shows the other side of the replacement of blue-collar jobs with service industry jobs: When workers find that they must replace a $15-an-hour manufacturing job with a $5-an-hour service job, the chances are good that their spouses will have to return to work to help maintain the family's income.

What is emerging is a group of prosperous, free-spending, two-income families, plus another group that must be more careful about spending its money. The latter, however, has chosen to sacrifice the convenience to the family of having the wife at home. Nonetheless, many of these families are able to maintain their income at or near the prosperous level they aspire to, meaning that they remain significant prospects for the travel and tourism business.

Almost all two-income families have time pressures, which means that many people may have to sacrifice leisure time for household and family maintenance chores. Therefore, when they do get away, time is at a premium, and they seek "quality time." Though sensitive to price/value comparisons, these travelers generally seek good value for their money rather than low-cost recreational experiences.

DEMOGRAPHICS

Our earlier discussion of the "middle-aging of America" suggested the impact of demographic changes on tourism. Middle age generally means higher income and a greater propensity to travel. Only 18 percent of Americans fall into the latter half of middle age, from 50 to 64, but the people in this age group dominate the luxury travel market.[4] These travelers are typically "empty nesters," whose children have left home. At the same time, they are at or near their peak earnings.

[3] Kenneth E. Hornback, "Social Trends and Leisure Behavior," paper delivered at the 1985 National Outdoor Recreation Trends Symposium, Myrtle Beach, S.C., February 24–27, 1985.

[4] Jeffrey P. Rosenfeld, "Demographics on Vacation," *American Demographics*, January 1986, p. 40.

In the United States outdoor recreation is the fourth most popular reason for travel. (Photo courtesy of the Recreational Vehicle Industry Association.)

Another significant demographic development for tourism is the increasing number of senior citizens. Although this group, made up largely of retirees, is generally not as prosperous as is the group we just discussed, they have much more leisure time. Authoritative estimates indicate that 27 percent of households headed by a person aged 65 or older have enough discretionary income to do some leisure traveling. Accordingly, elderly travelers often choose group travel at off-peak times and seasons and tend to be more price conscious. The travel industry has responded with numerous special price arrangements aimed at senior travelers.[5]

Travel Trends

The main reason in 1985 for traveling was to visit friends and relatives. Other pleasure travel ranked just behind that, and business and convention travel was in third place. Roughly two-thirds of all trips were vacation trips.[6] Table 10.1 summarizes the purposes of traveling.

A trip is defined as travel of 100 miles or more away from home, and Table

[5] Rosenfeld, "Demographics on Vacation."
[6] *National Travel Survey*, p. A5.

Table 10.1 *The purpose of travel*

PURPOSE OF TRIP	PERCENTAGE OF TRIPS	PERCENTAGE OF PERSON TRIPS
Visit friends or relatives	37	40
Other pleasure	32	35
Business or convention	24	17
Other	7	8
	100	100

Source: National Travel Survey—1985 Full Year Report (Washington, D.C.: U.S. Travel Data Center, 1986).

10.1 also shows the number of trips times the number of people taking them. For instance, two persons taking a trip together account for one trip but two "person trips." The discrepancy in Table 10.1 between the percentages of trips and of person trips probably arises from the fact that more people travel together on vacation and pleasure travel jaunts, whereas more people travel alone on business trips.

MODE OF TRAVEL

After automobiles, airlines are the second most common means of travel, and airline travel has increased in recent years. In 1985, for instance, air travel accounted for 20 percent of all travel, up from 17 percent in 1984. Bus travel accounted for only 2 percent, and train and "other" travel, an additional 1 percent each.[7]

PRICE SENSITIVITY

The trends in auto and air travel support the notion that travel is price sensitive. That is, as gas costs have risen, travel by car has fallen significantly. Moreover, according to studies by the Hertz Corporation, consumers are now buying smaller cars, keeping them longer, and driving them shorter distances.[8] This is hardly surprising. After the purchase of a house, the auto is usually a family's largest consumer expenditure. And as the cost of autos has risen in recent years along with operating costs, particularly gas, consumers have traded down. As recently as 1976, an intermediate-sized car was the average on the road, but that fell to a mid-sized car between 1977 and 1982. Then in 1982, the average moved down a notch further to a compact. Moreover, in 1972, the average age of cars on the road was 5.7

[7] *National Travel Survey*, p. A3.
[8] Hornback, "Social Trends and Leisure Behavior."

years, according to the Hertz study but had risen to 7.6 years by 1984. Thus even though cars remain far and away the most common form of transport, as they become more expensive to own and operate, consumers change their behavior accordingly.

Conversely, the deregulation of airlines has led to greater price competition and lower fares. And as the cost of air transport has fallen, the frequency of air travel has increased dramatically.

TRAVEL AND LODGING

According to the National Travel Data Center, roughly 40 percent of travel (in 1985, 40.9 percent of person trips, 42.8 percent of all trips) included overnight stays in hotels or motels. And the majority of hotel and motel users are pleasure-oriented travelers. In fact, 47 percent were traveling for pleasure such as sightseeing, entertainment, or outdoor recreation. Twenty percent of hotel and motel guests were visiting friends and relatives. The balance—or one-third of loding guests—were attending conventions or on business. But because pleasure travel tends to be concentrated in the summer months, it is still reasonable to say that the year-round backbone of most hotels' business is the one-third of travelers who are on business.

The business travel market is an upscale market, made up of more-affluent, better-educated persons likely to be employed in a white-collar job. Over half of business travelers, for instance, have completed college, compared with 22 percent of the adult population. Over two-thirds have white-collar jobs—double the national rate—and 42 percent have household incomes of $40,000 or more, three times the national average. Roughly one in five business travelers (22 percent) are frequent travelers, but these people account for 70 percent of all business trips taken in the United States.[9]

WOMEN AND TRAVEL

Women business travelers have also increased in importance to hotel operators. To explain this, in 1973, women accounted for only 18 percent of all managers, but by 1984, one in three managers were women. In the same period, the percentage of female lawyers rose from 6 to 16 percent. The growth in the number of female physicians was healthy but less dramatic, from 12 to 16 percent. And the number of women who decided to become their own bosses has shown the greatest growth rate, jumping 10 percent from 1980 to 1982, ten times the growth rate for men.[10] Clearly, the hospitality and tourism businesses' new emphasis on women travelers is a response to market trends.

[9] *National Travel Survey.*
[10] Suzanne D. Cook, "The Business of Travel," *American Demographics*, July 1985, p. 48. The travel statistics, however, are updated from the *National Travel Survey*, p. 26.

The Economic Significance of Tourism

In total business receipts, tourism has consistently ranked second or third among all businesses. Only grocery stores—and in some years, automobile dealers—have greater sales. Measuring the industry in terms of employment, tourism provides more jobs than does any other industry except the health services.[11]

Although tourism currently generates over $250 billion in receipts, that is only a superficial, first-order measurement of travel importance. You may recall the term *multiplier* from your economics courses. A multiplier measures the effect of initial spending together with the *chain of expenditures that result*. (For example, when a traveler spends a dollar in a hotel, some portion of it goes to employees, suppliers, and owners, who in turn respend it—and so it goes.) Although the precise computation of the *travel multiplier* need not concern us, some experts estimate that the final impact of tourism is three to three and one-half times greater than is that of the initial expenditures of the tourists themselves. Figure 10.1 illustrates how the multiplier works in practice.

TRAVEL INDUSTRY RECEIPTS

Travel industry receipts are growing faster than is the economy in general. In good years, tourism generally grows about as fast as does the economy as a whole, and sometimes faster. In recession years, however, tourism actually holds up better than does the rest of the economy. Hence, tourism is an important source of both growth and stability in the local, state, and national economies.

As Figure 10.2 illustrates, since 1984, travel industry sales have outpaced the general level of economic activity as measured by the gross national product (GNP). In fact, travel industry sales, adjusted for inflation, have increased at a compound rate of 3.4 percent, compared with GNP growth of 2.8 percent.[12]

TOURISM AND EMPLOYMENT

Approximately one in every twenty civilian employees is employed in an activity supported by travel expenditures. That is roughly 5 million persons. The impact of tourism on employment in areas closely related to tourism is depicted in Figure 10.3. Although only about one-quarter of food service employment can be traced to tourism, a much larger proportion of hotel and motel employment serves travelers away from home.

The U.S. Travel Data Center explained the significance of tourism to employment:

---

[11] Cook, "The Business of Travel."
[12] *Economic Review of Travel in America*, pp. 8–9.

THE TOURIST DOLLAR MULTIPLIER EFFECT

TOURIST SPENDING FOR	TOURIST INDUSTRY EXPENSES	SECONDARY BUSINESS BENEFICIARIES
Hotels	Wage, salaries, and tips	Employees
Restaurants	Payroll taxes	Government agencies
Entertainment and recreation	Food, beverages, and housekeeping supplies	Food industry
		Beverage industry
Clothing	Construction and maintenance	Custodial industry
Personal care	Advertising	Architectural firms
Retail	Utilities	Construction firm
Gifts and crafts	Insurance	Repair firm
Transportation	Interest and principal	Advertising firm
Tours	Legal and accounting	News media
Museums and historical	Transportation	Water, gas, and electric
	Taxes and licenses	Telephone companies
	Equipment and furniture	Insurance industry
		Bank and investors
		Legal and accounting firms
		Air, bus, auto, and gas
		Taxi companies
		Government companies
		Wholesale suppliers
		Health care

Figure 10.1 *The flow of the tourist dollar into the economy has a multiplier effect.*
[Michael Evans, *Tourism: Always a People Business* (Knoxville: University of Tennessee , 1984).]

> *The travel industry continually outperforms the overall economy in creating new jobs. Since 1958, the earliest year for which appropriate data are available, payroll jobs in travel-related businesses have increased 221 percent, more than two and one-half times as fast as the overall economy.*

> *The travel industry has contributed to job growth far in excess of its size. Just in the last decade travel industry employment has increased by nearly sixty percent, three times the growth rate for all U.S. industries. The 2.9 million new jobs provided by the industry since 1974 comprise eighteen percent of the national increase in employment.[13]*

The growth of tourism employment relative to total employment is summarized in Figure 10.4.

---

[13] *Economic Review of Travel in America*, p. 29.

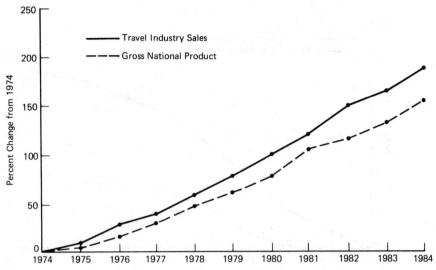

Figure 10.2   *Travel sales and GNP, 1974–1984.* (U.S. Travel Data Center.)

PUBLICITY AS AN ECONOMIC BENEFIT

Communities often spend large sums of money to advertise their virtues to visitors and investors. They establish economic development bureaus to bring employers to town and even offer tax rebates on low-cost financing. Tourism also offers a chance to achieve many of these same benefits. That is, a tourist attraction brings visitors to a city or area, and they can then judge for themselves the community's suitability as a place in which to live and work. The impact of a major tourist event is suggested by the experience of Vancouver, British Columbia, with Expo '86. The number of visitors to British Columbia in 1986 rose a whopping 80 percent over

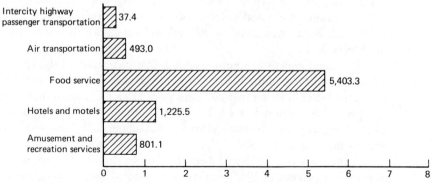

Figure 10.3   *Employment in industries serving tourists (in thousands).* (U.S. Travel Data Center.)

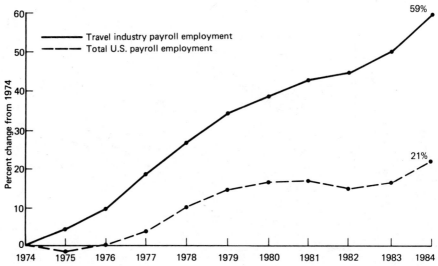

Figure 10.4   *Growth in travel industry employment and total U.S. employment.*
(U.S. Travel Data Center.)

that of the previous year! Because British Columbia abounds in natural beauty and splendor, probably many visitors considered relocating there, and many more may have decided to make at least a return visit.

The United States As an International Tourist Attraction

There are two measures that reflect the overall popularity of the United States as a travel destination. Table 10.2 shows the first of these, the total of all receipts from tourists. But because currency values are fluctuating, this total should be compared with a measure of physical volume such as tourist arrivals, which are shown in Table 10.3. Both tables show the receipts and arrivals for the entire world and for the Americas.

The rapid growth in tourist spending that characterized the late 1970s subsided in the first half of the 1980s. The United States' share of the world market has fluctuated between rather narrow limits: from 11 and 13 percent in terms of dollar receipts and between 6.5 and 8.3 percent in arrivals. The United States' market share in terms of both receipts and arrivals fell substantially between the late 1970s and the first half of the 1980s.

A comparison of Tables 10.2 and 10.3 shows that the United States' share of arrivals (6.5 percent in 1985) worldwide was significantly lower than its share of dollar receipts (11.4 percent in 1985), which suggests that international travel to the United States is more expensive for many travelers than is travel to other countries.

Table 10.2 *U.S. share of world and Americas region international tourism receipts, 1970–1985 (billions of dollars)*

YEAR	WORLD INTERNATIONAL TOURISM RECEIPTS	U.S. SHARE	AMERICAS REGION TOURISM RECEIPTS	U.S. SHARE	U.S. TOURISM RECEIPTS
1970	$17.9	12.8%	$4.8	47.8%	$2.3
1975	38.6	11.9	9.7	47.4	4.7
1980	95.3	10.5	20.9	50.7	10.6
1981	97.7	12.4	25.2	51.2	12.9
1982	94.6	13.1	22.9	54.1	12.4
1983	97.5	11.7	24.6	46.4	11.4
1984	100.8	11.3	25.7	44.3	11.3
1985	105.0	11.4	26.6	45.1	11.6

Source: U.S. Travel and Tourism Administration.

In both numbers and expenditures, the number of American visitors abroad has long exceeded the number of foreign arrivals and receipts in this country. In the 1950s and 1960s, the American economy was much stronger than that of most European countries. Thus, the dollar's purchasing power remained strong abroad, and foreign travel constituted a real bargain for Americans. Then the serious inflation in the United States during the late 1960s and the 1970s and the growing strength of the European economy reduced the dollar's purchasing power abroad and boosted the purchasing power of many foreign currencies in the United States.

Table 10.3 *U.S. share of world and Americas region international tourist arrivals, 1970–1985 (millions)*

YEAR	WORLD INTERNATIONAL TOURIST ARRIVALS	U.S. SHARE (PERCENTAGE)	AMERICAS REGION INTERNATIONAL ARRIVALS	U.S. SHARE (PERCENTAGE)	U.S. INTERNATIONAL TOURIST ARRIVALS
1970	158.7	7.8	35.7	34.7	12.4
1975	206.9	7.6	41.6	37.7	15.7
1980	279.0	8.0	56.1	40.1	22.5
1981	287.8	8.3	53.9	44.1	23.8
1982	287.5	7.6	51.4	42.7	21.9
1983	292.3	7.4	51.2	42.4	21.7
1984	312.3	6.7	52.4	39.7	20.8
1985	325.0	6.5	53.5	39.8	21.3

Source: U.S. Travel and Tourism Administration.

In 1982, after 20 years of increases, the number of overseas visitors to the United States and the level of visitor expenditures began to decline. This trend continued in 1983 and 1984 and was only moderately reversed in 1985 when the number of visitors rose by a half million and spending rose by $600 million. In the same period, U.S. travelers' expenditures abroad increased by 8 percent to nearly 15 percent.

Underlying these developments were the rising value of the U.S. dollar and unfavorable economic developments outside the United States. As the value of the U.S. dollar rose, travel to the United States once again became more expensive for visitors. Conversely, travel outside the United States once again became a bargain that Americans sought.

In 1985, 21.3 million foreign visitors spent $12 billion in the United States. In the same period, however, 28.9 million Americans spent $17.3 billion overseas. An additional amount—the difference between what Americans spent on foreign airlines and what visitors from overseas spent on American carriers—accounted for another $5 billion of unfavorable balance. The proportions of the continuing travel deficit are shown in Table 10.4 and Figure 10.5.

International travel has had the same effect on the United States' balance of payments (the difference between American spending abroad and American receipts from overseas) as exports (sales overseas) and imports (purchases from overseas) have. Because our balance of payments influences the strength of the U.S. dollar in world markets and in the domestic economy, both governmental and private agencies actively promote travel to the United States in a number of ways. For example, a federal agency, the United States Travel and Tourism Administration, was established specifically to attract travelers to this country. Tourism is now a major export industry in the United States.

As Figure 10.6 shows, more than one-half of our receipts from foreign visitors come from our Canadian and Mexican neighbors. Visitors from Japan, England, West Germany, and France make up another 14 percent of the market.

Whatever the economic and political ramifications of the travel gap may be,

Table 10.4   *United States travel deficit, 1970–1985 (millions of current dollars)*

1970	$2,487
1975	3,216
1980	1,354
1981	478
1982	2,081
1983	5,549
1984	8,597
1985	10,280

(U.S. Travel and Tourism Administration)

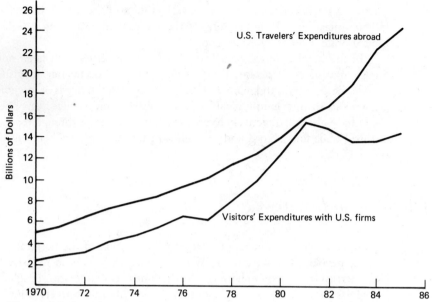

Figure 10.5   *The travel gap reopens.* (U.S. Travel and Tourism Administration.)

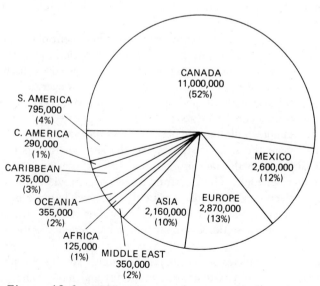

Figure 10.6   *1985 international tourist arrivals to the United States. Total arrivals: 21,280,000.* (U.S. Travel and Tourism Administration 1986 Annual Report.)

the fact is that overseas visitors—over 21 million of them in 1985 spending $12 billion—make up a huge market, clearly one that those serving travelers in the United States cannot afford to ignore.

In the hotel industry, some properties in large cities with large numbers of foreign tourists attribute one-third or more of their occupancy to visitors from outside the country. And many hotels, responding to the needs of foreign visitors, are anxious to hire multilingual managers, clerks, and service personnel. Some hotels have also begun actively to promote foreign business through representation at travel trade fairs abroad and through solicitation of foreign tour business from travel agents.

Is Tourism an Industry?

Let us pause here for a moment to review the concept of the hospitality industry that we developed in Chapter 1. We concluded that such an industry could be characterized by a common heritage, by the similarity of operating problems shared by the various components, and by the high mobility that workers enjoy.

Although we constantly use the term *hospitality industry*, there is no such thing as a corresponding tourism industry. This is because tourism is a highly varied, though often interrelated, bundle of economic activities. Although these economic activities often court the same customer, the services rendered, and the operational problems encountered, are different enough to limit the mobility of a trained employee from one activity to another. This is the principal difference between the hospitality industry and tourism.

It is true, of course, that some positions in one component of the hospitality industry cannot be transferred within the industry. A desk clerk, for instance, has skills peculiar to the hotel business, and a greenskeeper's knowledge is useful mainly in the club business. The heart of the hospitality industry, however, is food service, in which there is a great deal of intraindustry mobility for workers. But the field of tourism lacks this kind of common thread.

A few more examples will illustrate our point. An airline, a car rental agency, and a hotel may share the same customer, but the services they provide differ strikingly. The airline provides its transportation strictly from point to point on some predetermined schedule. The car rental agency also provides transportation and related support services, but it dictates neither a schedule nor a destination. Moreover, its customers travel alone or with companions of their own choosing. Hotels, in turn, provide a stationary shelter for some period specified by their guests.

Some operational problems of tourism and hospitality are superficially similar. For instance, the reservation systems used by hotels and motels and car rental companies are based on a model originally developed for the airlines. In actuality, though, operational problems within tourism vary widely. For instance, aircraft maintenance, automobile maintenance, and hotel maintenance obviously require different facilities, skills, and planning. It is unlikely that the same person could, for instance, service an airline radar system, an automobile generator and voltage regulator, and a hotel's plumbing and air conditioning.

Differences also appear in the structure of the firms. The airline and car rental fields are dominated by a few very large companies, but the hotel industry is a highly competitive field on which not even the successful motel chains can claim a corner.

Most importantly, as we said earlier, there is little ease of movement among the tourism segments. Tourism is not one career field but many. Thus, the car rental agent seeking work at an airline ticket counter would have to be retrained. A skilled waitress works in tourism and might have learned a great deal that would be useful as a stewardess, but we don't hear much about waitress experience as a qualification for employment as a stewardess.

The important point to see here is that although tourism may be a related set of economic activities, it is not an industry for which overall educational career preparation is possible.

Some hotel companies such as Westin and airline companies such as United now have the same owners. The president of Westin Hotels some years ago

One feature that ties together the hospitality industry is the importance of food service to every segment. This is just as true of theme parks, as Great Adventure's Yum Yum Palace, shown above, suggests. (Photo courtesy of Great Adventure.)

became president of the holding company that owns Westin and United Airlines, and so it is true that there is some interindustry mobility, but it is principally at very senior levels.

Hospitality managers should, of course, acquire a general understanding of tourism, as the two fields share many professional interests. Tourism also constitutes an important market for many hospitality firms. For example, the success of the airlines in selling to travelers will directly affect the occupancy rates of the hotel industry, and the hotel guest may well want the service of a rental car.

State, regional, and local travel promotion also is important to hospitality firms, and so such promotion deserves their support. In general, however, the relationships among the industries that serve the tourist, though complementary and interdependent, do not extend into interindustry career ladders.

Noneconomic Effects of Tourism

So far we have stressed the economic impact of tourism, for instance, its effect on the gross national product and employment. But tourism also has other impacts, both unfavorable and favorable.

CROWDING

A successful tourist attraction may, in effect, self-destruct from its own success. One of the major potential problems of tourism is crowding: so many people want to see the attraction that its own success destroys the attraction's charm.

For example, at successful theme parks, this problem is addressed by designing places where guests will be waiting in line as "staging areas" with interesting views and even live or mechanized entertainment to distract the visitors. Another theme park tactic is to have lots of cleanup help, so that paper, cigarettes, and other trash never accumulates, thus reducing or eliminating some of the evidence of crowding.

Another example is that in areas of scenic beauty such as popular national parks, trails often become more and more difficult as they progress. Indeed, most people turn around and return to the parking lot once the pavement ends. And even fewer continue once the unpaved trail actually becomes difficult to follow. In effect, reducing the amenities is a subtle form of exclusion, of which the ultimate example is the wilderness area, where entrance is only on foot or by horse. Difficulty of access can thus reduce crowding.

Along with crowding, tourism can result in noise, odors, and pollution. A special form of crowding is the traffic jam. Not surprisingly, people who live in a tourist attraction area may have mixed or hostile feelings about further development because of their concern for privacy, the environment, or just their ability to get safely to and from home on crowded highways.

Another possible impact of crowding is "crowding out." For example, a beach

Hersheypark offers an eighteenth-century German village commemorating the early settlers in the area surrounding Hershey, Pennsylvania. (Photo courtesy of Hersheypark.)

or other scenic area formerly used by local people may be bought and its use restricted to paying visitors. This has happened on several Caribbean islands and in some cases resulted in the local populace's becoming unfriendly or even hostile as they found their beaches becoming inaccessible to "natives." This led to sharp clashes between the local people and the visitors, an unfriendly environment, and then a drop in the number of visitors.

These potentially unfavorable developments related to tourism give rise to the notion of "carrying capacity," that is, that an area can accept only a certain number of visitors without being hampered as a desirable destination.

FAVORABLE NONECONOMIC EFFECTS

But not all noneconomic effects are necessarily unfavorable. Tourist success can often fuel local pride: Some tourist "events" such as festivals and fairs may be staged to celebrate some aspect of the local culture. Agricultural fairs, for instance, which draw thousands—and sometimes hundreds of thousands—of visitors, celebrate a

Concerts and other cultural events are important regional attractions in many areas of North America. Pictured here is the Art Park in Lewistown, New York. (New York State Commerce Department.)

region's agricultural heritage and its favored crops as well as provide for important educational activities such as 4H meetings and contests.

In other cases, a local tradition may be observed. In a Portuguese community, it may be a blessing of the fishing fleet; in an area where many of German descent live, it could be "Oktoberfest." In these cases, adults are reminded of their background, and the young see their heritage dramatized as visitors come to admire it. Indeed, much early travel was for the purpose of pilgrimage, and religion still plays an important part in travel in some areas.

Because of its important impact on the hospitality industry, tourism is significant to hospitality students. But even if this weren't your field of study, it would be important for you to know about it. This is because whatever problems tourism raises, its positive impacts not only economically but also culturally and socially make it an important phenomenon of contemporary mass society.

Summary

This chapter opened with a definition of tourism and the reasons that it is important to the hospitality industry. We then explained why people are traveling more: more leisure time, rising family incomes, and more middle-aged people who have the time and money to travel.

The main reason for traveling is pleasure, and then business. Although more people travel by car than by any other means, as cars have become more expensive to buy and to operate, people have been turning more and more to air travel, the second most popular mode of travel. In addition, most hotel and motel users are people traveling for pleasure, followed by those traveling on business. More women now are traveling, as well.

The economic significance of tourism is clear: Tourism ranks second or third in total business receipts. Moreover, about one in twenty people is employed in an activity supported by travel expenditures. Indeed, communities seeking potential employers may profitably use tourism as an attraction.

The United States is also an international tourist attraction, its popularity often based on the value of the U.S. dollar versus that of other currencies. Foreign visitors to this country are an important means of alleviating the U.S. balance-of-payments deficit.

We then discussed whether tourism is really an industry in the way that the hospitality business is. And finally, we closed the chapter by touching on the noneconomic effects of tourism, both unfavorable (such as crowding) and favorable (such as festivals, fairs, and the celebration of local traditions.)

Destinations: Tourism Generators

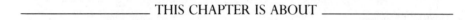

THIS CHAPTER IS ABOUT

Destinations and travelers' motivatons. Travel has changed dramatically; it is no longer aristocratic, and understanding its popular, democratic basis is important in understanding today's guest.

Some destinations such as theme parks are family oriented, and others such as casinos are aimed at adults. This chapter discusses the makeup of these attractions and the common hospitality elements in them. We also look at urban entertainment centers such as shopping centers, sports facilities, and zoos. We examine "temporary" attractions such as fairs and festivals and their impact on tourism, and we consider, too, natural environments. In all, we see attractions as "play environments" which are shaping America's leisure market and are a vital part of our way of life.

Each of these areas of activity relies heavily on hospitality industry operating components and offers significant career opportunities to HRI graduates.

Courtesy of American Airlines.

Motives and Destinations

If people had no place they wanted to go, tourism would be in trouble. In fact, people travel for many reasons, for instance, work and recreation. In this chapter we will be concerned almost exclusively with recreation, but even for this, the motives are varied because recreation is more than "just play." It is, in some ways, not just the opposite of work; it is its counterweight. Recreation relates to relaxation but also to stimulation, to gaining renewed energy, as well as to playing.

Perhaps the earliest motive for travel was religion and a renewal of commitment. Today's pilgrimage attractions include Lourdes in France and Fatima in Portugal and, in the New World, Guadeloupe in Mexico and Ste. Anne de Beaupré in Quebec.

Health interests have also long been a major travel motive. In ancient times, the Romans were drawn to springs thought to have health-giving properties, which became fashionable again in the eighteenth century. Hot springs in the United States, such as Hot Springs, Arkansas, and French Lick Springs, Indiana, are less popular today than they were a few generations ago. In regard to another kind of health interest, the Mayo Clinic attracts so many people that its home in Rochester, Minnesota, probably has more hotel rooms per resident than does any other city in the United States.

Scenic beauty, especially the mountains and the seashore, have long been a major attraction. Scenic beauty is often coupled with *health-building* activities— hiking, skiing, and swimming, for instance—so that both body and mind are refreshed by vistas and activities. Today's state and national park systems are the most extensive response to these touring motives.

Sporting events, from the first Olympics in 776 B.C. to the Kentucky Derby and the Superbowl, have attracted thousands of serious sports enthusiasts as well as untutored onlookers. Indeed, sports arenas have become such big business that some institutional food service companies have created special divisions just to manage sports food service.

In regard to history, art appreciation, and *culture* in general, every year the battlefields of yesterday throng with thousands of visitors on guided tours, and the Louvre is one of France's major cultural treasures, as is Chicago's Art Institute. Music and theater festivals all across Europe and North America are used more or less consciously by many cities to enhance the cultural life of the area—and to attract visitors' spending to strengthen the local economy.

Destinations can be divided into *primary or touring destinations* and *secondary or stopover destinations*.[1] Primary destinations have a wide market and draw travelers from a great distance. These kinds of destinations, such as Walt Disney World, attract visitors from the entire North American continent and all over the world. Because such a high proportion of their visitors are away from home, these primary magnets create a heavy lodging demand. Orlando, Florida, for instance, is like

---

[1] Robert Christie Mill and Alastair M. Morrison, *The Tourism System* (Englewood Cliffs, N.J.: Prentice-Hall, 1985), chap. 8.

Rochester, Minnesota, a city with a disproportionately high number of rooms per capita.

Secondary destinations draw people from nearby areas or induce people to stop "on their way by." Some secondary destinations may in fact have a *higher number of visitors* than primary destinations do. The Grand Canyon, for instance, attracts fewer than 3 million visitors a year, though they come from all over the world. In contrast, many regional theme parks draw that many visitors, and Atlantic City, which is mainly a regional casino gambling center, attracts well over 10 times that many. In general, we can say that a primary attraction requires more services per visitor, but this does not detract from the importance of successful secondary attractions. Indeed, even smaller secondary attractions make important contributions to their locale.

The balance of this chapter will be an examination of those destinations and attractions to which hospitality services are important enough that the attraction can usefully be thought of as part of the hospitality industry. Our main interest will be in the impact of these kinds of destinations on opportunities in the hospitality industry, their significance for hospitality managers, and the possible careers in such complexes.

Mass-Market Tourism

Until quite recently, travel was the privileged pastime of the wealthy. The poor might migrate—to move their homes from once place to another in order to live better or just to survive—buy only the affluent could afford travel for sightseeing, amusement, and business. That condition has not really changed; some affluence is still required for business and recreational travel. What *has* changed is the degree of affluence in our society. We have become what economists call the "affluent society."

When travel was reserved for the higher social classes, its model was the aristocracy. In hotels, for example, dress rules required a coat and tie in the dining room. But as travel came within the reach of the majority of Americans, the facilities serving travelers adapted and loosened their emphasis on class. Many of the new establishments have, in fact, become "mass" institutions.

A Walt Disney World training official summed up this change. Speaking of the attitude of some college-educated employees (when first hired) toward the guests that the employees considered "hicks," he said, "We point out to them that we, at Disney World, are *performers, not reformers*. We're here to help people have a good time, not to improve their manners or to change them in any other way." Thus, Disney World has virtually no dress code for guests. People come as they are. All comers are served and enjoy themselves as they see fit within the limits of reasonable decorum.

In Las Vegas casinos, mink-coated matrons play blackjack next to dungaree-clad cowboys. These are not "social clubs" that inquire who your father was or

The demand for alternatives to traditional lodgings has grown
rapidly in recent years. Campgrounds are now more flexible in
terms of operations and financing. (Photo courtesy of the National
Park Service.)

which side of the tracks you live on. The color of your money is the only concern.
Likewise, anybody with the money can buy a reserved seat in any of the country's
new superdome sports centers. What we see developing are new "play environments"—places, institutions, and even cities designed almost exclusively for play.

These essentially democratic institutions supply a comfortable place for travelers from all kinds of social backgrounds. Accordingly, as the popularity of these
facilities increases, we see a new, more egalitarian kind of lodging institution
beginning to flourish.

Planned Play Environments

Recreation is as old as society. But a society that can afford to play on the scale that
Americans do now *is* new. Some anthropologists and sociologists argue that "who
you are" was once determined by your work, what you did for a living, but that

At Walt Disney World and other theme parks, employees are "performers not reformers." A relaxed, come-as-you-are atmosphere is intended to support the guests' fun, and dress codes, such as those in the more traditional resorts, are the exception in the newer-style operations. (Photo courtesy of Walt Disney World.)

these questions of personal identity are now answered by *how we entertain ourselves*. In his book *Future Shock*, Alvin Toffler speaks of the emerging importance of "sub cults" whose life-styles are built around nonwork activities. For these people, work exists as a secondary matter, as only a means to an end.

Play environments, of course, are not newer than play itself. Fairs at which work (or trade) and play were mixed date back to the mid-1800s in the United States and to medieval times, or even earlier, in Europe. The first amusement park was Vauxhall Gardens in England, built in the 1600s, and the first U.S. amusement park, Coney Island, dates from 1895. What *is* new, however, is the sophistication that a television-educated public demands in its amusement centers today, and the scale on which these demands have been met since the first modern theme park opened at Disneyland some 25 years ago. Disneyland, in effect, showed the commercial world that there was a way to entice a television generation out of the house and into a clean carnival offering live fantasy and entertainment.

Artificial Environments

THEME PARKS

According to the *Wall Street Journal*, a number of traditional amusement parks have closed their doors because they "offered little more than thrill rides and cotton candy and these days Americans want much more than that."[2]

According to industry sources, the United States has about 35 major themed attractions and 550 other, more traditional amusement parks.[3] Theme parks, which account for only 6 percent of all amusement parks, receive over a quarter of the parks' receipts. These parks have clearly become an important part of both the national tourist market and the local entertainment market. The number of their visitors in 1985 was estimated at 230 million, the equivalent of roughly one visit for every person in the United States. In practice, though, about half the guests visit at least twice a year.

The *New York Times* described this new breed of park as follows:

> *Most new amusement parks are variations on the basic Disney conglomeration of colorful animal characters, reproductions of historical buildings, ingenious thrill rides, and quality stage shows, all in a lavishly landscaped, spotlessly clean outdoor setting suitable for a day long family excursion.*
>
> *Gone are the rickety ferris wheel, the sawdust midways, the bingo barkers and the girly reviews that gave so many parks questionable reputations in the pre-Disney days.[4]*

Themes

Just as restaurants are expected more and more to offer atmosphere as well as food, today's television-oriented traveler expects a park environment that stimulates and entertains in addition to offering rides and other amusements. One way to meet this demand is to build the park around one or more themes.

Canada's Wonderland follows themes such as "International Festival," "Medieval Faire," "Happyland of Hanna-Barbera," and the "Grande World Exposition of

---

[2] *Wall Street Journal*, August 2, 1972, p. 1.
[3] Personal communication with Ms. Pat Durickna, director of public relations, International Association of Amusement Parks and Attractions.
[4] *New York Times*, May 30, 1976, p. 20.

Audio-Animetronics are featured in the hippolike robots that are a part of the Adventureland cruise at Walt Disney World. (Photo courtesy of Walt Disney World.)

1890." Walt Disney World in Florida offers "Main Street, U.S.A.," "Adventureland," "Frontierland," "Fantasyland," and "Tomorrowland."

Some parks are built around one general theme. For instance, Busch Entertainment's "Old Country," located near historic Williamsburg, Virginia, uses a seventeenth-century European theme for the park as a whole and within that general theme offers eight areas themed to specific countries or regions: Banbury Cross (England), Aquitaine (France), Rhinefeld (Germany), Heatherdowns (Scotland), Hastings, New France, Oktoberfest, and San Marco (Italy).

Whatever the theme, parks offer rides, one of the most popular being water rides. In fact, Busch has developed a separate theme park, adjacent to its Busch Gardens in Tampa, built around water and water rides. Adventure Island, as it is called, offers 13 acres of tropically themed lagoons and beaches featuring water slides and diving platforms, water games, a wave pool, a cable drop, and a rope gym.

Although some parks cater to nostalgia (a romantic longing for the past), others recreate the past in a more realistic way. The "Towne of Smithville," in New Jersey, for instance, has restored a mid-1800s crossroads community. It offers a Civil War museum and a theater as well.

Morning on the Veldt. With the towers of Timbuktu an impressive backdrop, giraffes and zebras gather for an early feeding on Busch Gardens' 60-acre Serengeti Plain, where more than 400 exotic mammals roam freely. (Photo courtesy of Busch Gardens.)

Some parks take their themes from animal life. Busch Gardens in Florida offers "The Dark Continent," a 300-acre African themed park which includes the Serengeti Plain, home of one of the largest collections of African big game. It also serves as a breeding and survival center for many rare species. The animals roam freely on a veldtlike plain where visitors can see them by taking a monorail, steam locomotive, or skyride safari.

Busch has also developed a park, Sesame Place in Langhorne, Pennsylvania, near Philadelphia, that blends physical and play activities with science experiments and computer games. In one experiment, called star lightning, the visitor can make gases, enclosed in a glass ball, interact with electromagnetic fields to create lightning and rainbow colors. Another experiment uses a laser and turning mirrors controlled by the guest to create a hands-on experience of the effects of reflection. Sesame Place also offers one-week computer camps, school field trips, and college-accredited computer courses for teachers.

Like virtually all modern theme parks, Sesame features full-sized cartoon characters, including Ernie and Bert from Sesame Street. And Big Bird and Oscar are featured in a video show in which the audience participates. Like other parks, too, Sesame Place offers rides and theater-style entertainment.

At Marineland, the "Shark Dive Adventure" offers visitors who are certified scuba divers a chance to submerge only inches away from sharks and other denizens of the deep. (Photo courtesy of Marineland.)

The sea offers other enticing themes. Marineland, in California, besides shows related to its ocean theme, offers to anyone who can swim a swim-through aquarium known as "Baja Reef." For those who are certified scuba divers, there is available a trip in a special stainless steel cage into a 560,000-gallon tank filled with over 60 sharks.

An official of the Disney organization summed up the theme parks' approach to education this way: "Before you can educate, you must entertain." Theme parks do, indeed, constitute a rich educational medium.

Scale

Theme parks are different from the traditional amusement parks not only because they are based on a theme or several themes but also because of their huge operating scale. As in nearly everything else, Disney leads the way in plant scale. The entire Walt Disney World (WDW) in Florida comprises 27,400 acres and has a 60,000 maximum one-time guest capacity. The food operation at WDW has 70 food locations that seat 10,000. The total system has a maximum capacity of 23,330 meals *per hour*. The career significance of WDW and similar enterprises is

Sea World includes specialized education program formats for students from kindergarten through university age. Live bat starfish are the subject of study in this photo. (Photo courtesy of Sea World.)

suggested by the fact that WDW has become the largest private employer in the state of Florida, with up to 17,000 permanent employees.

REGIONAL THEME PARKS

Theme parks catering to a regional rather than a national market have been growing at a rapid pace in recent years. This development seems to be based on the increasing cost of transportation and the pressure of inflation on many family incomes. Regional parks are treated to a smaller geographic area than, for instance, Disney World is, and often have a narrower market.

For instance, Atlanta's Six Flags offers special parties for high school graduating classes and offers an annual Christian Music Festival featuring "top Christian talent" that might not be as popular in other regions of North America. In Pigeon Forge, Tennessee, near Knoxville, Dollywood recreates the Smoky Mountains of the late 1800s through crafts and country music as well as atmosphere, old-time "home-cooked" food, and rides. Country music is a regular part of the "Parton Back Porch Theatre," and during the National Mountain Music Festival in July, it

The forces of evil—dragons and dragonettes stir up the lagoon at Walt Disney's Epcot Center in Florida in an effort to disrupt the good guys whose mission is to paint the sky with rainbow colors. (Copyright © The Walt Disney Company, 1986.)

features Dolly Parton, for whom the park is named. A crafts theme is featured during a month-long National Crafts Festival in October. Regional parks such as Dollywood are clearly major sources of tourism: Dollywood attracted over 1 million visitors in its first year of operation.

Not surprisingly, regional parks have a significant commitment to food service. Knott's Berry Farm, for instance, in Buena Park, California, the nation's oldest themed park, has 35 eating places on its 150 acres and additional food service in the adjacent Knott's Market Place. Not far away, Marineland features a Burger Galley, International Cafe, Pacific Pizza, an Ice Cream Shoppe, Seaside Sandwich Shop, and Corby's Corner. Marineland also has outdoor catering locations that can handle company picnics and special groups of from 150 to 5,000.

Employment and Training Opportunities

The regionalization of theme parks is a favorable development for hospitality students because of the opportunities they offer for employment experience. Theme parks often operate year-round, but on a reduced scale from their summer peak. During the months when school is out and, too, when outside weather conditions favor park visitation, attendance soars. To meet these peaks, the crew expands each summer. To supervise this expanded crew, college-age people are chosen, usually from last year's crew, as supervisors, assistant managers, and unit managers. These positions are often quite well paid, but more significantly they offer a chance to assume responsible roles beyond those that most organizations offer to people of this age. Generally these opportunities are accompanied by training and management development programs.

As a personal note: I have graded more summer field-experience papers than I care to recall, and consistently the best opportunities and training experiences I have encountered have been in regional theme parks. A word of advice, then, is to take a close look at the regional theme parks in your area as a possible summer employer.

CASINOS AND GAMING

To move from the innocent amusement of theme parks to casinos and gaming may seem a giant step, but they have a good deal in common as tourism attractions. We will look briefly at two quite different markets: Las Vegas and Atlantic City, New Jersey.

Some might think that Las Vegas and Atlantic City are the only two centers of gambling in North America, but a moment's reflection on the variety of legal gambling activities around us quickly leads us to discard that notion. Gambling is fairly widespread in the United States, including casinos, card rooms (legal in 9 states), horse racing (37 states), lotteries (25 states), and off-track betting (22 states). In fact, only 4 states (Hawaii, Indiana, Mississippi, and Utah) outlaw gambling altogether. An additional 8 states permit only bingo games (Georgia, Kansas, North Carolina, South Carolina, Tennessee, Texas, Virginia, and Wisconsin). All 10 of Canada's provinces have legalized horse racing, and the provinces and 2 federal territories have lotteries and permit off-track betting.[5]

[5] *Marketing Bulletin*, Las Vegas Convention and Visitors Authority, December 15, 1985, p. 8.

The question of gambling does raise serious moral and social issues, but it is clear that the practice, in one form or another, is quite widespread. Efforts to legalize casinos in several jurisdictions in both the United States and Canada have failed repeatedly. Though fairly widespread in the Caribbean islands, casino gambling is limited to only two states in the United States. Gambling's profit potential for companies and the favorable economic impact for communities is so great, however, that we are likely to see continuing pressure to allow it in other mainland jurisdictions, such as Miami and New Orleans.

Las Vegas

The first settlement in Las Vegas can be traced back to 1829, but the town's formation dates from 1905 when it was a small desert railroad town. Casino gambling was legalized in 1931. Following World War II, Las Vegas grew more rapidly as large hotels were built, and by the 1950s Las Vegas had become an established tourist destination combining casinos, superstar entertainment, and lavish hotel accommodations. Today, a city of 500,000, Las Vegas has over 54,000 hotel and motel rooms, nearly 1 for every 10 inhabitants. The city's annual occupancy rate ranges from the high seventies to the low eighties, as compared with a nationwide 67 percent. In 1986 there were 4,500 rooms under construction in Las Vegas and 4,000 more proposed, according to the Las Vegas Convention and Visitors Authority.

But Las Vegas has a good deal more to offer than casinos. The city is also known for its incredible stage shows featuring such extravaganzas as the Bally's "Grand Jubilee." In addition, hotel room rates in Las Vegas are among the most affordable in the resort industry, and eating inexpensively is no problem. Many hotels sell breakfast for as little as 99 cents and offer a buffet-style dinner for less than $5.00. Las Vegas also sports 12 championship golf courses and 19 tennis and 7 racquetball facilities. Obviously, entertainment and sports facilities as well as lodging and food service bargains are used to attract visitors to play in the casinos.

But there are also national attractions around Las Vegas, which enhance the city as a destination. The famous Hoover Dam and Lake Mead, with its 500 miles of shoreline, are less than a half-hour away. Death Valley is a half-day's drive away, and the Grand Canyon is an easy day's drive from Las Vegas. Less well known attractions within an hour's drive include the Valley of Fire, Red Rock Canyon, and a clutch of ghost towns.

Las Vegas is thus a fully developed tourist mecca, served by 18 major airlines and 30 charter air companies. McCarron International Airport averages nearly 400 flights daily.

In addition to its recreational features, Las Vegas has a highly developed convention business, including a 1.1-million-square-foot convention center with another 1.3 million square feet available at major hotels in the area. A million conventioneers attend over 500 conventions held in the city annually, and another 13 to 14 million tourists pass through the city each year.

The fact is that there is not very much else in Las Vegas other than tourism,

The town that casinos built! *The top picture shows Las Vegas as an insignificant desert railroad town just after the turn of the century. Pictured below is the famous Las Vegas "strip" today.* (Photos courtesy of the Las Vegas Convention and Visitors Authority.)

the businesses that serve the tourist, and the businesses that serve *those* businesses and their employees. Las Vegas is the ultimate in destinations, the city that tourism built.

Of course, gambling is the mainstay of the Las Vegas economy; something over $2.5 billion is wagered each year in Las Vegas. Other traveler expenditures, however, are not inconsequential. Tourists spent an average of $88 per day in 1985; trade show delegates spent nearly $200 per day; and convention and meeting

Plush casinos like this are the drawing card that attracts nearly 12 million visitors each year to Las Vegas, from high rollers to nickel slot players. (Photo courtesy of Las Vegas Convention and Visitors Authority.)

delegates spent $150 per day—all in addition to the sums expended in gaming.[6] That amounts to well over $2.5 billion in nongambling expenditures per year.

In 1985, nearly 125,000 people were employed in the lodging, gaming, and recreation fields in Nevada. Of these, 77,000 were in Las Vegas, and another 32,000 worked in Reno, the other major gambling center in the state.[7] The spending of all these employers—along with the purchases of their employees— adds up to an enormous economic impact.

Atlantic City

Atlantic City has a lot to teach us about tourism, both good and bad. Atlantic City has always been a tourist city since its founding in the mid-1850s, and it was once the premier resort city on the East Coast of the United States, famous for its boardwalk and its resort hotels, catering principally to prosperous upper-middle-class Americans. But with the coming of automobiles, motels, lower-cost travel, and changing tastes in leisure, Atlantic City began to deteriorate. From 1960 to 1975, the city's population declined by 15,000, the number of visitors fell to 2,000,000, the number of hotel rooms decreased by 40 percent,[8] and Atlantic City became a case study in the difficulty of reviving a tourist center once it had gone downhill.

As one observer put it, Atlantic City was a tourist resort without any tourists.[9]

[6] *1985 Summary*, Las Vegas Convention and Visitors Authority.

[7] *Marketing Bulletin*, p. 7.

[8] *1985 Annual Report*, Atlantic City Casino Association, p. 6.

[9] Personal communication, David Gardner, executive vice-president, Atlantic City Casino Association. Mr. Gardner was employed as a city planner in Atlantic City during the 1960s.

From a peak tourist center for earlier generations, Atlantic city became virtually an abandoned hulk, rusting away at its moorings. Like many older, worn-out tourism centers, its plant was outmoded and in bad repair. Perhaps more serious, it no longer had any appeal in the market, and the revenue wasn't there to rebuild. Then in 1976, gambling was approved, and in 1978 the first casino hotel opened.

The city's turnaround has been remarkable. From 1978 with the opening of the first casino through 1985, $2.7 billion was spent on new facilities, and over 50,000 casino and noncasino jobs were created. In 1986, over 30 million people visited Atlantic City, making it the number-one tourist destination in the United States.

The casinos are required to reinvest 1.25 percent of their gaming revenues in the community and state—an estimated $1.6 billion in the first 25 years—through the state-run Casino Reinvestment Development Authority. Since casino gambling was approved, casino hotels have paid over $2.5 billion in taxes, regulatory fees, and required reinvestment.

Atlantic City is quite different from Las Vegas. Although there are two major cities within a day's drive of Las Vegas—Los Angeles and San Diego—Atlantic City has one-quarter of the U.S. population within a 300-mile range. New York City, Philadelphia, and Washington, D.C. all are within 150 miles. Over half of Atlantic City's visitors arrive by car, and another 45 percent arrive by bus. Because it lacks a modern, full-scale airport, less than 1 percent arrived by air in 1985.

Atlantic City's skyline is a study in contrasts. Its 11 new or renewed casino hotels are the latest word in casino glitter, but between them are open spaces where old buildings have been razed, and in many places hulks remain, boarded up. Outside the boardwalk's immediate vicinity, much of the city is still dilapidated slum housing, though that is rapidly being replaced with public housing for lower-income residents, private apartment developments aimed at the middle class, and, on the ocean front, expensive condominiums.

In contrast with Las Vegas's 54,000 hotel rooms, Atlantic City's 11 hotels now have only 11,000 rooms. In early 1987, there were, however, an additional 5,000 rooms under construction and 3,500 in the planning stages, including 3 new casino hotels. As you can see, by the early 1990s, the hotel inventory should be on the order of 20,000 rooms.

Atlantic City is in many ways still in the early stages of its turnaround, with a major takeoff likely to occur in the early 1990s. A rail line to Philadelphia to connect with the high-speed rail lines running from Washington to New York is expected to bring 2.2 million riders to Atlantic City annually. The process of developing Atlantic City's municipal airport, 10 miles away in Pomona, has begun with the refurbishing of its facilities.

In 1985, Atlantic City had 27 citywide conventions and trade shows which attracted 175,000 attendees, who spent over $115 million in the area. Although these are impressive figures by themselves, they are clearly smaller than Las Vegas's 1 million delegates. In fact, Atlantic City's present convention hall has less than half the exhibit space of Las Vegas's center, but a new convention center equal in size to the present one is planned for the early 1990s. A 1000-room, noncasino hotel will be incorporated into that center, which also is being built in conjunction with a new rail terminal.

As convention and exhibit space, as well as more hotel rooms, becomes available, along with greatly improved transportation facilities, the growth prospects for Atlantic City are bright indeed.

The economic impact of Atlantic City is also being felt outside this city of 40,000 people, in the 100,000-person Atlantic County, and in the wider South Jersey area. Atlantic City has led all other New Jersey labor markets in growth since 1980, according to the Governor's Economic Policy Council, and the New Jersey Department of Labor has identified Atlantic County as one of the fastest-growing areas in New Jersey.

Casino Markets and the Business of Casinos

The business of casinos, obviously, is gambling, at table games such as roulette, blackjack, and dice. In addition, a major and growing gambling pastime is the slot machines. From the casino's point of view, what matters in evaluating a customer is his or her volume of play, because the odds in every game clearly favor the house. Big winners are good news for the casino because of the publicity they bring. But in the long run, the casino wins.

Casino markets can be divided into four general groups: tourists, high rollers at the tables, high rollers at the slot machines, and the bus trade. Tourists are those who visit the city to take in the sights, see a show, and try their hand at "the action"—but with modest limits in mind as to how much they are prepared to wager and lose, usually up to $100 but often as much as $250 or $500.

The high roller, one casino executive told me, can be defined as a person who "plays with black chips," that is, hundred-dollar chips, and whose average wager is therefore $100. The high roller needs a minimum gambling budget of $2500 per visit. For them, gambling is the major attraction, but they thrive also on the personal attention given to them by the casino and hotel staff and the "comps"— complimentary or no-charge services and gifts—provided by the casino. Some high rollers wager more than the average and, a few, much more. In general, the level of "comps" is based on the volume of play—with some casinos prepared to provide free transportation, luxurious hotel suites, meals, and show tickets, for instance. For those who are heavy gamblers, the hotel may provide a limousine or even a helicopter to bring them from their home and return them—and keep on file such information as the hat, shoe, or suit size of the gambler's spouse; and the player's preference in food, wines, flowers, chocolate; and the like.

Some casinos rate high rollers in terms of the "buy in," that is, the amount of chips they buy, but an increasingly common measure is the player's theoretical loss. This is based on the estimated average wager and the average time spent at the table. What is of interest, here, is the dollar volume of play, *not* whether the player wins or loses during any particular trip. But again, over the long run, the casino always wins. The theoretical loss is based on the dollar volume of play times the casino's average winning margin at the game. Some casinos are prepared to provide in comps as much as 35 to 50 percent of a player's theoretical loss.

More modest but still significant is the high roller slot player. This person usually plays the dollar machine and has a $500 gambling budget per visit. Comps and special recognition are extended to these players, too, according to their level of play. Some casinos have begun to issue cards with an electronic identification embedded in them. These cards are inserted into the machine to record the player's level of play, and comps are issued based on the volume of play (not losses).

A final category could be called the "low roller," the bus trade. These are generally lower-income people, often retirees, and, surprisingly, often people on unemployment compensation. They, too, come for the gambling but usually have a budget of only between $35 and $70. They often are attracted by a bargain low price.

In Atlantic City, this bus trade provides the backbone of the year-round volume of business. In fact, on a typical day in Atlantic City, somewhere between 1000 and 1500 charter buses arrive laden with "day trippers," there for somewhere between 4 and 12 hours. These players, too, are attracted by relatively generous comps. A typical bus deal, costing $10 to $12 in early 1987, might have included round-trip bus transportation, a $5.00 meal discount coupon, and a $10 roll of quarters ("coin," as it's called in Atlantic City) to get them started.

Casino Staffing The casino gaming staff is made up of dealers (and croupiers), a floor person (once called the floor man) who supervises several dealers, and a pit boss. (In craps, a boxman assists the dealer, handling the bank.) In the pit—a group of similar games—the pit boss is assisted by a pit clerk who handles record keeping.

The pit boss is really a technician, expert from years of experience in the practice of the game. He or she generally supervises the play, approves "markes"— that is, approves the extension of credit (within house limits)—approves in-house food and beverage comps for known players, and generally provides personal attention to high rollers.

The floor person supervises between two and five dealers, depending on the game, and never more than four games. They are also responsible for closely watching repeat customers in order to estimate their average bet, a figure that is crucial to the casino's marketing intelligence.

Slot machine areas are staffed by change people working under a supervisor. Change people and supervisors also offer recognition and personal contact for frequent visitors and slot high rollers.

Comps above a certain dollar level are generally approved by the casino's senior management. Comp services for a "junket" group are approved by the casino's marketing staff. Junkets are similar to tours that might be sold by a travel agent except that the "sights" are generally the casino and its hotel environment, and there may be no charge for any of the services because of the expectation of casino play by the visitor. Junkets are put together by the casino or, more commonly, by junket brokers in distant cities.

Working in casinos is very difficult. It requires a quick mind and an ability to work with people who are under considerable pressure. Players sometimes become abusive and unreasonable, and staff are expected to avoid, whenever possible, a difficult scene and permanently alienating a player and his or her friends. Not surprisingly, the higher the roller is, the greater will be the patience that may be expected of the staff.

Dealers need to be alert to players' attempts at cheating, and they themselves are constantly scrutinized by supervisors and security personnel because of the temptation of dishonesty where so much cash is changing hands.

I would be uncomfortable if I did not close this section with a personal observation:

Gambling does raise serious moral and social questions for many, including me. Often gamblers exceed the limit of what they can afford, damaging their ability to care for their families. My observation, moreover, is that gambling creates an environment that often degrades people and raises money and material things to a higher level than they deserve. A real and somewhat scary question, though, is whether this emphasis on money and things and deemphasis on people are a result of gambling or whether gambling is a reflection of those traits at large in our society. Whatever are my views on the moral and social aspects of casinos and gambling, however, I don't feel that I can be a serious student of the hospitality industry and ignore such a large and growing business that is part of our industry and that appears to have so much appeal to our customers.

Urban Entertainment Centers

Urban entertainment centers vary widely. Some are designed on a smaller scale as a draw for local traffic and an enhancement to the local environment. Others are on a scale nearly as grand as those we considered in regard to theme parks, and there are many in between.

Sports stadiums have been with us since the time of Rome's Colosseum, but the latest variety of such centers is the covered "superdome," such as those in Houston and New Orleans. Describing the New Orleans superdome opening, the *New York Times* spoke of the 9.7-acre, 27-story facility as the "second in what promises to be a continental string of mammoth sports emporiums. Cities are now vying to build the largest, most expensive stadiums."[10] *The Economist* described the publicly owned domed stadium as essential to gaining the status of a big league city. "The tenant teams not only draw in the fans and help pay off the stadium bonds and overhead, they also create jobs and general business."[11]

These facilities host not only sports events but entertainers and rock concerts as well. They provide gathering places that entertain residents or visitors to a city.

[10] *New York Times*, August 4, 1977, p. 40.
[11] *The Economist*, June 16, 1984, p. 25.

Superdomes host not only sports events but entertainers and rock concerts as well. The New Orleans stadium, shown here, covers nearly 10 acres. (Photo courtesy of Louisiana Superdome.)

Typically, they reach out to an area around the city—and sometimes to the entire nation—drawing in the visitors and tourists.

A similar facility, the convention center, mixes business and pleasure. The visitors to a convention or trade show *are* on business. But many of these gatherings are more social than professional, and even the most business-oriented meetings are, in large part, devoted to having a good time.

Convention and trade show centers were once largely the preserve of great metropolitan centers such as New York with its Coliseum and Chicago with its McCormick Place. Increasingly, however, cities such as Seattle and New Orleans, large but of second rank in size, have developed urban entertainment centers as a means of challenging established travel patterns and increasing the travel business in *their* market.

In fact, the urban play (and business) centers now extend into cities of the third and fourth rank. Although medium-sized cities cannot bid in the national convention market for the large conventions, they often can attract smaller national meetings and regional conferences. For this reason, many cities successfully sell bond issues to build civic meeting centers that improve a community's ability to compete for its share of the travel market. That travel market, more and more city leaders are learning, means more sales for local businesses, increased employment, and more tax revenues.

Whether the results of these civic efforts always justify such an investment is open to question. In any case, though, somebody must operate these centers, and the skills involved (dealing with various traveling publics, providing food service, and managing housekeeping and building operations, to name only a few) clearly fall within the hospitality graduate's domain.

Increasingly, urban planners are including in their developments plazas designed to accommodate amusements, dining, and other leisure activities. The prototype of this kind of plaza is Rockefeller Center in the heart of New York City, with its ice-skating rinks in winter, and horse shows, karate demonstrations, and model airplane contests in milder seasons.

Of the more recently constructed plazas, according to the *Wall Street Journal*, the First National Plaza in front of the First Chicago Building is a model for plazas to come. A computer controls the fountain, so that visitors won't get splashed on windy days. From May to October the plaza features free noontime entertainment, late afternoon concerts, an outdoor cafe, and a popcorn stand that nets $10,000 a summer! It also has, year-round, a restaurant, a bar, a legitimate theater, and retail shops.

In the center of downtown Chicago, the First National Plaza offers summer dining and entertainment. (Photo courtesy of the First National Bank.)

City waterfront redevelopment projects, too, have become centers that attract visitors and enrich the lives of the local people. Often coupled with these are aquariums. Thirty American cities had aquariums under construction or in the planning stages in 1986, sparked by such successes as those in Baltimore and Monterey, California. Baltimore's National Aquarium, for instance, is credited with contributing some $90 million to the state's economy. At the Monterey Bay Aquarium, 2.4 million visitors helped restaurants at Fisherman's Wharf weather their winter sales slump. In addition, there have been so many visitors to the Monterey site that it set off a local hotel construction boom.[12]

Museums were once thought of as stuffy, but *The Economist* recently characterized the best-equipped science museums as "grown up playpens. Interaction is the key word. Visitors can take a weather-reporting class, watch a fish spawning cycle, experiment with sounds and colors or bone up on elementary mathematics of chance. There are also plenty of satellites, laser guns and deep sea diving bells."[13]

Another kind of "living museum," a zoo, can be a major tourism generator. For instance, each year roughly 5 million visitors come to the San Diego Zoo. The zoo also operates an 1800-acre wildlife preserve 30 miles north of San Diego. The zoo and preserve, like so many other tourist destinations, have a substantial educational mission. The preserve, for instance, is visited by 40,000 elementary and secondary schoolchildren each year. An important service provided to visitors, of course, is food service, and because the number of visitors to destinations such as aquariums and zoos—like so many other seasonal attractions—expands when school is out, these operations can offer summer experience opportunities to students, with a decent chance at getting into a supervisory position.

Shopping centers are usually thought of as catering principally to local shoppers. But even so, such centers can be more than a little ambitious. The new St. Louis Centre suggests the scale of a large, locally centered mall and the often close relationship of such centers to the hospitality industry. The centre was begun as an urban renewal project in 1972 and was completed 13 years later, in 1985, at a total cost of $17.5 million. Comprising a two-block stretch of downtown St. Louis, the centre serves about 10 million people each year, of whom nearly a million are out-of-towners. The centre has 16 fast-food restaurants and 4 sit-down restaurants, whose combined annual food service volume is $12.5 million. An all-suite hotel is also planned for the centre in conjunction with the expansion of the city's convention center.[14]

Finally, we will look briefly at a mega-shopping center in Western Canada built on the grandest scale yet undertaken. In the case of the West Edmonton Mall, the aim from the very first was to attract tourists as well as local residents to the center, as Edmonton, Alberta, a city of 560,000, could not support a mall of this scale by itself.

---

[12] *Wall Street Journal*, November 22, 1985, p. 27.
[13] *The Economist*, June 14, 1986, p. 82.
[14] Personal communication, Ms. Patsy Baldwin, assistant general manager, St. Louis Centre.

The scale quite literally boggles the mind. Consider its total indoor area of 5.2 million square feet, equivalent to 28 city blocks. The ceiling peaks at 16 stories with a mile-long, two-level main concourse, served by 15,000 employees. The interior plantings include $3 million worth of tropical plants—among which is a grove of 50-foot palm trees—and the 37 animal displays include Siberian tigers and a 300-pound grouper! The mall houses an amusement park and a water park with a 5-acre pool where you can surf on 6-foot waves, water-ski, ride the rapids, and get a suntan, even when the outside temperature is well below zero. The sights include an 80-foot-long Spanish galleon, an 18-hole miniature golf course, a 50,000-gallon aquarium, and four submarines (more than the Canadian navy has, in fact). The

A shopping center with a difference. *Canada's West Edmonton Mall is both a mall and a theme park. Among its attractions are four submarines.* (Photo courtesy of Triple 5 Corp.)

Canada's West Edmonton Mall boasts a 5-acre swimming pool with a 6-foot surf.
(Photo courtesy of Triple 5 Corp.)

33-foot-long computer-controlled subs will seat 24 people. Built by a family of Iranian immigrants, the Ghemezians, the mall is dedicated to the idea that shopping is more than just a utilitarian chore and can be an opportunity for fun. The mall has its own tourism promotion budget of $5 million (roughly equivalent to the budget of the province of Alberta)[15] and its own tour-packaging travel agency.

About 36 percent of the visitors to the mall are from Edmonton and its trading area. Another 18 percent are from Alberta outside the 60-mile trading area. The other 46 percent come from the rest of Canada and the United States. Half of these Canadian visitors and 75 percent of the Americans come specifically to visit the Edmonton Mall. U.S. visitors average a four-day stay. Visitors, interestingly enough, spend as much or more outside the mall as they do inside the mall.

On the average, 400,000 people visit the mall each week. Annually, the mall generates 6 million tourists (that is, people from outside Edmonton), of whom about a half-million come from the United States.[16] Naturally the mall has a major impact on hospitality industry firms in Edmonton and is itself a significant part of the local hospitality industry, with 10 restaurants, numerous fast-food operations, and a 360-room luxury hotel.

The Ghemezians have proposed even larger malls in Minnesota and outside either Buffalo, New York, or Toronto, Ontario. The *Minneapolis Star Tribune*

[15] *Wall Street Journal*, October 7, 1985, p. 1.
[16] Personal communication, Ms. Deane Eldredge, director of public affairs, Triple 5 Corporation.

estimated that if the proposed mall functions as projected, it will draw 6.5 million non-Minnesota visitors to the Minneapolis area and the mall, more than half a million more than Disney World's non-Florida draw. Some financial analysts have expressed skepticism about the long-term financial viability of malls this size, but if they do prove successful, we can expect to see more like them.

Temporary Attractions: Fairs and Festivals

Fairs date from the Middle Ages when they served as an important center for economic and cultural revival. Festivals also have their roots in early history and were originally religious events.

World's Fairs are year-long attractions, but even a local fair such as the agricultural fair in Duquoin, Illinois, which annually attracts a quarter of a million people to this town of 7000, can have a major impact on a city. Some fairs celebrate local industry, whereas others have cultural and historical roots, such as is the case with Mardi Gras in New Orleans. Tradition is not enough, however. A successful event must also have direction, purpose, and goals.[17] Indeed, a festival or fair is a quasi-business activity. Its success is measured by its ability to attract visitors, to cover its costs, and to maintain sufficient local support to keep it staffed, usually almost entirely with unpaid volunteers.

Events such as these affect the economy of the cities and regions that sponsor them. Local patrons spend from their family entertainment budget money that might have left the community. Visitors "spend in food, lodging, souvenirs, gasoline, public transportation and the like. In some cases the event itself makes purchases which add to the dollar stream of the community."[18]

The economic effects of fairs and festivals have a major impact on the community and especially on its hospitality industry. For this reason, hospitality industry managers are often prominent sponsors and backers of such events. We ought not lose sight of the fact, however, that, like so many other aspects of tourism, fairs and festivals also have important social and cultural benefits to their communities: They celebrate the local heritage and bring members from all parts of the community together to work as volunteers.

In some cases, a festival may even be used to help in the regeneration of a community. In New Haven, Connecticut, the Office of Housing and Neighborhood Development uses neighborhood festivals as a centerpiece in its Commercial Revitalization Program. Large or small, then, these kinds of events can be a vital part of the life of a community, city, or region.

---

[17] Marlene E. Boland, *"The Dynamics of Community Festivals,"* Master's thesis, School of Rural Planning and Development, University of Guelph, 1985, p. 52.
[18] Laurence S. Davidson and William A. Schaffer, "A Discussion of Methods Employed in Analyzing the Impact of Short-Term Entertainment Events," *Journal of Travel Research*, Winter 1980, p. 12.

The National Park System is a uniquely American innovation that has been copied the world over. (Photo courtesy of the National Park Service.)

Natural Environments

Not everything, by any means, that attracts tourism is man made. In the public sector, national and state parks, forests, and waters should interest hospitality students just as much. These uniquely American recreation areas have been copied the world over. As far as hospitality innovation goes, they are, in fact, relatively new. The first park created by Congress, Yosemite, was established toward the end of the Civil War, in 1864.[19] The National Park Service itself was not established until 1916.

From 1950 to 1965, the number of visits to national parks increased by nearly four times, from 33.3 to 121.3 million. In the next 15 years, this number more than doubled, rising to over 300 million in 1980.

Beginning in 1981, however, the number of visitors to national parks flattened out, and there was actually a modest decline from 1982 to 1983. Figure 11.1

---

[19] The first national park was Yellowstone, established in 1872. Yosemite was originally a California state park created by the U.S. Congress. It became a national park in 1890.

Scenic beauty—here the grandeur of the Grand Canyon—is a magnet for tourism, generating many hospitality industry jobs both inside and nearby national and state parks. (Richard Frear/National Park Service.)

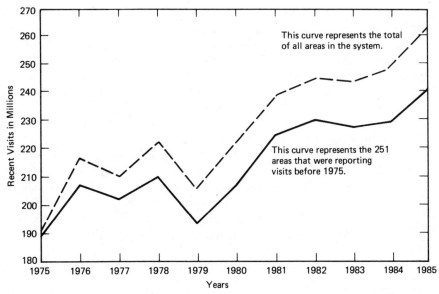

Figure 11.1 *Visits to all areas versus to pre-1975 areas, showing the effect of new areas and their initial high growth rate.* (National Parks Statistical Abstract.)

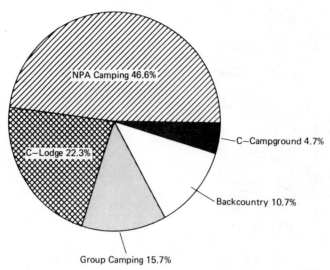

Figure 11.2   *National Park Service overnight stays in parks: 15,780,166.*
(National Parks Statistical Abstract.)

summarizes the 10-year visitation record and shows the impact of newly opened parks, which have accounted for much of the growth in the period.[20]

In 1985 there were 15.78 million overnight stays in national parks. As Figure 11.2 indicates, only about 3.5 million of these were in hotels.[21] Camping is the major accommodation for park visitors and outdoor enthusiasts, a subject that we will discuss in the next chapter. In addition to nearly 16 million overnight stays in national parks, there were an estimated 30 million visitors who spent the night in state parks and perhaps another 12 million in national forests.

The National Parks Service Act of 1916 established the National Park System with the clear intention of providing recreation and, at the same time, preserving the parks intact for the enjoyment of future generations. The increased crowding of existing facilities has led those interested in preservation as well as recreation— including the National Park Service itself—to propose drastic limitations on use of private automobiles within parks. The National Parks and Conservation Association (NPCA), a private group that supports a conservationist view of natural parks, has suggested that such accommodations as hotels, cabins, and campgrounds be restricted or even reduced within these parks. Similar proposals have been advanced for such high-intensity recreation activities as downhill skiing (with its requirements for ski lifts), snowmobiling, hunting (particularly in the eastern states), and seashore activities.

The NPCA does not argue that hospitality facilities and services should be

[20] *National Park Abstract, 1985*, p. 3.
[21] *National Park Abstract, 1985*, p. 32.

unavailable. Instead, it proposes that *staging areas* with lodgings and other services be established in nearby communities and that these staging areas be connected with parks by low-cost transportation. Proposals like this would reduce private auto use and help preserve the *natural beauty*, a park's principal attraction and reason for being. It might also create major new commercial recreation areas and opportunities for hospitality firms and graduates of hospitality programs. Moreover, given the leadership of the national parks in the field of recreation, this pattern might well extend to state parks and forests in future years if it is accepted by Congress and the people.

Summary

In this chapter we discussed recreation, its motives, and its destinations. After explaining why people travel, we divided their destinations into primary or touring, and secondary or stopover. Then we talked about planned play environments, such as national and regional theme parks, casinos (as exemplified by Las Vegas and Atlantic City), urban entertainment centers such as sports stadiums and mega–shopping centers, and, lastly, the natural environment, especially national parks.

Along the way, we pointed out the possible employment opportunities for both temporary jobs and permanent careers. Destination attractions are often big hospitality businesses in themselves and act as magnets that keep the flow of tourism not only going but also growing.

Businesses Serving the Traveler

_____ THIS CHAPTER IS ABOUT _____

Allied industries that—like hospitality—serve the tourist. It is important for you to understand the role and function of these *allied industries* in order to complete the picture of tourism as an economic and social force. First, we will concentrate our attention on passenger transportation and travel intermediaries—travel agents and tour operators or wholesalers.

Later in the chapter we turn to what some people see as competitors and others as part of the hospitality industry: camping and campgrounds. To consider camping properly, we will need to look not only at campgrounds but also at campers and the recreational vehicles (RVs) they use—and we will be concerned with career prospects in camping.

Finally, once again we will try to look into the future a bit, this time considering the prospects for tourism in the 1990s.

Passenger Transportation

In Chapter 10 we looked at travel trends as a part of tourism. Here, we'll briefly survey travel again, this time to gain a perspective on the travel business as an allied industry that works with hospitality firms in serving travelers. Tourist expenditures make up practically all of the sales of firms engaged in public intercity travel—*common carriers*, as they are called. Common carriers include the airlines, bus companies, and railroads.

In the past 10 years, the number of passenger miles of intercity travel has increased by just over 36 percent, as shown in Table 12.1, to over 1.3 trillion passenger miles. (One person traveling one mile equals one passenger mile, and four people traveling one mile equals four passenger miles.) Total travel by private vehicle has also increased, and travel by auto, truck, and RV (recreation vehicle) is still the dominant mode of travel. But private vehicles' *share* of travel has declined to just over three-quarters of passenger travel. Common carrier travel, however, has raised its share by 5.2 percentage points, a *share* increase of nearly a third.

The number of passsenger miles traveled by air has doubled, accounting for nearly all of the increase in common-carrier volume, as shown in Table 12.2. The picture that emerges is of the airlines' overwhelming and growing dominance of the public transport market. In 10 years, the airlines have increased their share of the market from 14 to 21 percent.

Channels of Distribution: Travel Agents

Those who manufacture consumer goods talk about the several "layers of business" between the manufacturer and the final customer. Some of these layers are wholesalers, manufacturer's representatives, and brokers. Typically, these intermediaries move the product from the manufacturer to the retailer, who then sells to the final

Table 12.1   *U.S. intercity transportation by common carriers and private vehicles (billions of passenger miles)*

VEHICLE	1975		1980		1985	
	MILES	PERCENT	MILES	PERCENT	MILES	PERCENT
Common carriers	166.2	17.3%	236.5	21.1%	300.4	23.5%
Autos, trucks, and recreational vehicles	793.2	82.7	881.1	78.9	1002.6	76.5
Total	959.4	100.0%	1117.6	100.0%	1309.0	100.0%

Source: U.S. Travel Data Center.

Personal service is very much a part of allied tourist businesses, just as it is in the hospitality industry. (Photo courtesy of Delta Airlines.)

user, the retail customer. Although most hospitality firms provide goods and services directly to the customer without any intermediaries, the travel agent represents an important exception.

A travel agent may be either of two kinds of intermediaries who bring travel customers and tourist firms together. In 1986 there were roughly 28,000 firms

Table 12.2   *U.S. intercity transportation by common carriers (billions of passenger miles)*

SECTOR	1975 MILES	1975 PERCENT	1980 MILES	1980 PERCENT	1985 MILES	1985 PERCENT
Air	136.9	82.4%	204.4	86.4%	274.7	89.7%
Bus	25.4	15.3	27.4	11.6	27.1	8.8
Rail	3.9	2.3	4.7	2.0	4.6	1.5
Total common carriers	166.2	100.0%	236.5	100.0%	306.4	100.0%

Source: U.S. Travel Data Center

This scene at Old Faithful Inn highlights the vital links between the travel industry and hospitality. Travel links, destination and traveler services are all needed to keep the wheel of tourisim turning. (Courtesy the Wyoming Travel Commission.)

specializing in arranging passenger transportation and accommodation. Of these, over 90 percent, some 25,500 firms, were travel retailers, that is, firms that sell directly to travelers and make individual travel arrangements for them. Another 9 percent were tour operators or wholesalers.

These firms schedule reservations with all of the firms that serve travelers—carriers, hotels, restaurants, and attractions such as those we discussed in the last chapter. Then they sell the services of these firms in return for a commission on those sales. Travel wholesalers often retail their own tours, but they also work with the retail travel agencies that sell the tour package to customers in their local markets.

Retail travel agencies book transportation for clients on all kinds of carriers. They also sell packaged tours and sometimes put together their own package tours, although this is not their primary business. Their commissions vary according to the services they provide.

Thirteen percent of all travelers consulted a travel agent in 1985, and 9 percent actually used an agent to make reservations.[1] Commissions on domestic air

[1] *National Travel Survey* (Washington, D.C.: U.S. Travel Data Center, 1986), p. 12.

Already an American institution, Walt Disney World's Cinderella Castle symbolizes North America's most famous theme park. (Photo courtesy of Walt Disney World.)

fares are about 10 percent, and those on international travel are roughly 11.5 percent. Hotel and cruise commissions range from 10 to 15 percent. In 1986, 67 percent of domestic and 80 percent of international air travel were booked through travel agents. Travel agents therefore play a major role in the hotel business, with 23 percent of domestic hotel reservations made through travel agents. The comparable statistic for foreign hotel accommodations is 79 percent, and a whopping 92 percent of cruise bookings are handled by travel agents.[2]

　　Hotels (especially resort hotels) often profit handsomely from associations with travel agencies. In return for the commissions they pay these agencies, the hotels have their properties represented in many local communities. The travel

[2] Personal communication, American Society of Travel Agencies.

wholesaler, too, can be important to hotels, because a listing in a wholesale package guarantees a listing with all of the wholesaler's retail affiliates.

Some hotels, however, avoid travel agent representation and the accompanying commissions if it produces, on balance, relatively little income.

Camping

Much of the park visitation discussed in the last chapter constitutes what is called *day use*: the family piles into the car and visits the park for a day of hiking, picnicking, fishing, and so forth and returns home in the evening. Nevertheless, a significant portion of the use is overnight, and most of that use involves camping.

The growth in the number of overnight stays in parks was dramatic through the mid-1970s. Since that time, however, the number of overnight stays in national parks has shown a modest decline, although that in state parks has continued to expand. The explanation for these trends probably lies in travel costs. Many national parks are located at a considerable distance from population centers and therefore involve considerable travel. There are more state parks, though they are generally smaller in area, and many are located near their state's population centers. It thus appears that many visitors have switched to parks nearer home as destinations, as has been the case with other destination categories. Another possible factor is the national parks' policy of discouraging the overuse of national parks by limiting in-park facilities.

Parks are campers' territory. As Table 12.3 shows, only a fifth of overnight stays in national parks were in concession hotels and motels. The state parks' proportion of overnighters who camped is even higher, probably about 90 percent. So even though there has been a switch in destinations, total park visitation *and* total camping continue to show healthy growth.

Table 12.3   *Overnight stays in national parks by type of accommodation*

YEAR	CONCESSION LODGING	CAMPGROUNDS	BACK COUNTRY, GROUPS, AND MISCELLANEOUS	TOTAL[a]
1950				4.5
1960				9.4
1970				16.2
1975				17.5
1980	3.2	9.1	3.6	15.9
1985	3.5	8.1	4.1	15.8

[a] *Source:* National Parks Statistical Abstracts.

Travel and tourism today are mass culture institutions on which many businesses, large and small, are dependent. (Photo by Alan Dorow.)

There are about 7000 campgrounds in the United States.[3] Although they range in size from very small to over 3000 sites, the average campground has about 150 sites and covers 50 to 60 acres. There is a trend toward longer operating seasons with somewhere between one-third and one-half of the campgrounds remaining open all year.

Campgrounds are increasing in size and are expanding the services they offer. The more profitable ones are often part of a chain or franchise group. Like other forms of the competitive lodging industry, campgrounds feel pressure to match the improvements of their competitors and so continually are upgrading their amenities. For instance, cable TV hookups and baby-sitting have become more popular, and there also are available more food services, sports instruction, guide services, and entertainment at campgrounds. Many campgrounds also offer some kind of shelter as well as the raw campsite, with about a quarter of the campgrounds renting trailers to campers. Other amenities such as hiking trails, stocked fish ponds, beach frontage, and marinas are likely to become more common as the trend toward competitive upgrading continues.

[3] Operating and facility data in this section are taken from Herbert E. Echelberger, "Nascent Trends in the Private Campground Industry," paper delivered to the 1983 National Outdoor Recreation Trends Symposium and *American Campground Industry 1984 Economic Analysis* (Burlington: U.S. Forest Service and the University of Vermont, n.d.).

PRIVATE CAMPGROUNDS

Private campgrounds participated in the growth in outdoor activity and park usage of the 1960s, and by 1972 there were more than 50 companies franchising or affiliating campgrounds. After the oil crises and recessions of the 1970s, only one major chain survived, Kampgrounds of America, or KOA. But even KOA declined in size from a peak 817 campgrounds in 1976 to approximately 675 in 1986.

In 1985, a small chain, Yogi Bear Jellystone Campgrounds owned by Leisure Systems Inc., began to expand, and by early 1987, Leisure Systems operated approximately 85 campgrounds in 33 states and 2 provinces. The company's plans were to double in size again in the next year. Interestingly, Leisure Systems campgrounds are intended as destination campgrounds. In fact, they refer to their operation as "camp resorts." Leisure Systems have an average size of 325 sites. Although there are a number of other small regional chain and franchise groups, there are no comprehensive data on them.

Larger campgrounds—and those that remain open year-round—have higher-than-average incomes and profits. The largest single source of income, accounting for roughly two-thirds of revenues, is campsite rental fees. Another quarter of income is derived from store sales and vending machines. The two largest items of expense in a campground, accounting for nearly half of its revenue, are salaries and wages and purchased goods and supplies. Utilities and capital costs are the next largest category of expenses, each accounting for about one-tenth of income. Other expenses include advertising, insurance, and property taxes.

CAMPERS

A series of studies conducted over several years by the Survey Research Center of the University of Michigan indicates the great popularity of camping among North Americans and sheds some light on consumer behavior in this area.[4] Most families are favorably disposed toward camping. Two-thirds of the heads of all households, in fact, agreed when asked if they thought camping was the best vacation a family could take. And when asked to choose between a vacation at a resort or at a state or national park, more people (47 percent) chose a camping trip than a resort vacation (only 41 percent). The principal reasons given were a love for the outdoors and a preference for a peaceful vacation away from the hustle and bustle of everyday life.

The family most likely to go camping is young, lives in the West, and has three or more children. Its relatively large size may be why it prefers camping, because of the higher cost of hotel stays and retaurant meals. Over half the respondents in the survey said that a recreational vehicle (RV) gave as much or

---

[4] The studies cited here appeared in the April, May, and June 1982 issues of *RV Dealer*. The validity of the demographic data, however, was reconfirmed as of late 1983 by the center. The results are also generally consistent with earlier studies published in 1980, suggesting a continuity of behavior over a considerable period of time.

Family camping is fast growing in popularity in North America. The A. C. Nielsen national research firm recently released data showing that more than 58 million adults camp out annually. This number is topped only by swimmers, bicyclers, and anglers as the most popular leisure activity. (Photo courtesy of KOA.)

Camping serves the needs of American travelers of all ages, including the growing number of retired Americans for whom leisure is a full-time way of life. (Photo courtesy of the National Park Service.)

more value as did the other things on which people spend their money, a fact that will take on added significance in the next section of this chapter. Only a third of the respondents thought that an RV offered less-than-average value, and 25 percent thought that RVs actually offered *better* value.

Two-thirds of all families in the survey group had camped sometime in their lives, and a surprising 57 percent had taken at least one trip within the previous three years. Camping seems to be an activity that starts young. Eighty-eight percent of the household heads who had gone camping did so before the age of 30, and 60 percent began before they were 15.

People who have camped indicate that they plan to camp more often in the future. When past camping and future intentions are combined, one-third of all respondents had camped recently *and* intended to do so in the future. As the director of the Survey Research Center remarked, "There are not too many other recreational activities, if any at all, that can boast of having the participation of one-third of the entire population."[5]

[5] Richard T. Curtin, "American Families Esteem the Camping Experience," *RV Dealer*, April 1982, p. 30.

Commercial campgrounds such as KOA are an important element in the growing recreation industry. (Photo courtesy of KOA.)

A survey of KOA campers in the province of Ontario during 1985 supports the Survey Research Center's conclusions. It reveals a loyal and prosperous customer group, that is, a market of frequent users. Ninety percent of those completing the survey planned to camp during 1986. Only 5 percent of the respondents had been campers for 1 year or less, and a surprising 64 percent had been camping for 11 years or more. Retirees, a large part of this market, made up of 19 percent of the respondents. Twenty-two percent of the respondents had camped 40 or more days during the past year, 17 percent for 30 to 39 days and 27 percent for 20 to 29 days. Weekend use, as opposed to vacations, formed a significant part of the market. Ninety-one percent of the weekend campers intended to camp as much or more in the future as they had in the past; only 1 percent did not plan to camp again.

Measured by spending patterns, KOA campers apparently were prosperous. First, 78 percent used some kind of RV, and 93 percent of those users owned a recreation vehicle. Average spending of less than $500 on a camping vacation was the rule for 26 percent; from $500 to $1000 for 23 percent; and over $1000 for 43 percent. This spending, of course, came on top of an already-heavy investment in a "mobile motel room."

In general, private campgrounds tend to be located along the main routes of travel rather than in specifically scenic areas. Because they are operated for profit, private campgrounds must locate near main arteries of traffic where, like hotels and motels, they are most convenient to the traveler and hence more likely to enjoy a favorable occupancy rate.[6] Campgrounds operated by parks and other public agencies, however, are generally located in a scenic area, often removed from the main thoroughfares. Because publicly operated campgrounds do not aim for a profit, these camps often experience lower occupancy rates in all but the peak season.

RECREATIONAL VEHICLES

To understand the significance of the growth of camping completely, we must trace the growth of the ubiquitous recreational vehicle (RV). Figure 12.1 shows RV sales statistics from 1971 to 1985. As the data illustrate, this type of accommodation is particularly susceptible to high gasoline prices and adverse economic conditions. Because over half of all new RVs (and over 30 percent of used RVs) are sold on credit, the unusually high interest rates prevailing between 1979 and 1981 probably also hurt sales in that period. On the other hand, it is clear that many of these vehicles are sold even in difficult times. Moreover, after falling in poor periods, sales climbed back to exceed previous records in the mid-1970s and have shown considerable resilience in the 1980s. Clearly, the "wheeled motel room" is here to stay.

[6] Of course, many private campgrounds are in scenic locations. Rather, our point here is that the major determinant of location for successful commercial campgrounds is accessibility to a large volume of traffic.

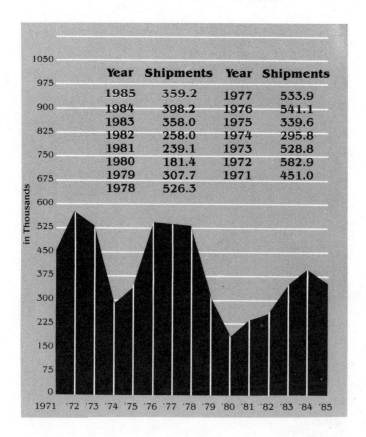

Year	Shipments	Year	Shipments
1985	359.2	1977	533.9
1984	398.2	1976	541.1
1983	358.0	1975	339.6
1982	258.0	1974	295.8
1981	239.1	1973	528.8
1980	181.4	1972	582.9
1979	307.7	1971	451.0
1978	526.3		

Figure 12.1   *Recreational vehicle shipments, 1971–1985 (thousands of units).* (Recreation Vehicle Industry Association.)

RV manufacturers have taken a number of steps to adapt their product to high gasoline costs. First of all, efforts to pare size and weight have commonly reduced overall weight by 10 percent, and in some cases by as much as 25 to 50 percent. Changing the shape of the RV to reduce wind resistance can account for as much as a 15-percent savings in fuel. In fact, Winnebago, one of the largest RV manufacturers, claims a gas mileage rating of 15 miles to the gallon for its latest models. Finally, with more small cars on the highway, new-model towable vehicles have been designed that can be pulled by subcompacts.

The Recreational Vehicle Institute of America estimated that RVs are used, on the average, for 23 days per year. Project, then, the total use of the 6 million RVs estimated by the RVIA to be in operation in 1981. At an average of 23 days of

Devil's Tower, the country's first national monument, is a popular spot for campers and recreational vehicle owners. Devil's Tower is the tallest rock formation of its kind in the United States. (Courtesy the Wyoming Travel Commission.)

RV use per year, you can see that these vehicles generated the equivalent of 138 million room-nights in competition with motels and hotels. Now compare that figure with the approximately 553 million room-nights sold by all hotels in 1981. What this analysis suggests is that RVs and camping now have a significant share of the country's total transient-rooms business.

A wide variety of recreational vehicles is available to fit various-sized families, budgets, and tastes. The camper pictured here sleeps seven. (Photo courtesy of Coleman Co., Inc.)

This RV will get 15 miles to the gallon, according to its manufacturer, because of its lighter weight and superior aerodynamics. (Photo courtesy of Winnebago Industries, Inc.)

Table 12.4   *Summary of RV sales by type, 1985*

	AVERAGE RETAIL PRICE	NUMBER SOLD (THOUSANDS)	PERCENTAGE OF TOTAL
Conventional travel trailer	$12,154	54.7	15.2%
Park trailer	16,750	7.5	2.0
Fifth-wheel travel trailer	16,034	20.7	5.8
Truck camper	6,709	6.9	1.9
Folding camping trailer	3,816	35.9	10.0
Conventional motor home (Type A)	48,809	33.6	9.4
Van camper (Type B)	23,131	6.7	1.9
Motor home (Type C)	31,281	28.4	7.9
Multiuse van conversion	18,769	164.8	45.9
Total—all RVs		359.2	100.0%

Source: Recreational Vehicle Industry Association.

A Comparison of Campers and Hotel Guests

The average rental of a commercial campsite in 1985 was probably around $10 to $12, whereas the average hotel rate was about $63. If we assume that the average camper spent $15,000 on an RV, which has an average life of 10 years, we can depreciate the RV at a rate of $1500 per year. Assuming an average use of 23 nights per year, the depreciation would come to about $65 per day of use. When we add a campground fee of $10 or $12, the cost of a night's sleep in an RV comes to around $75 or more. These are average figures, but the results suggest that many RV users spend as much or more than hotel guests do for their recreational lodging. An added economy for campers, of course, comes from preparing their own food instead of eating in restaurants. But any notion that campers are people who "can't afford" a hotel is dispelled by the rough calculation we have just made and the average retail price data in Table 12.4. Campers apparently choose camping because they find advantages in it, not because it saves them money.

Another study of the RV owner, by the Survey Research Center,[7] gives us further insights. The statistical profile of the RV owner closely resembles that of the population as a whole; that is, participation in RV use apparently is spread evenly across the country.

The peak ownership age is 35 to 44 years—the section of our population that will be growing most rapidly in the next few decades. This suggests that the growth in ownership and use of RVs in that period may increase, offering a significant market to those segments of the hospitality industry that have learned to cater to the RV community.

When ownership of RVs is examined by type of RV, some clear demographic trends emerge. The owners of motor homes and travel trailers are, on the average, older. In fact, 67 percent of motor home and travel trailer owners are over 44 years of age. Not surprisingly, the owners of the expensive motor homes (see Table 12.4) tend to have higher incomes. Owners of these two kinds of RVs are also less likely to have children at home, probably because so many of them are at the age at which their children have left home.

On the other hand, owners of vans, truck campers, and folding camping trailers tend to be younger—53 percent under 44 years of age for van owners, 56 percent of the truck campers owners, and 66 percent for the folding camping trailers owners. It may seem surprising that the least expensive RV (the folding camping trailer) attracts a significantly higher-income family until the statistics on average use shown in Figure 12.2 are examined. The pattern that emerges from this figure suggests that families who want to do a limited amount of camping purchase the relatively less expensive tent campers. Some 70 percent of these families have children at home.

On the other hand, older families who purchase an expensive motor home are able to and have made a definite life-style decision. These older, upper-income families have the vacation time—or the retirement income—to permit extended use of the RV. In fact, half of all motor home owners spend one to four months in their units.

This seems to point to a flexible set of options that makes some kind of RV affordable to nearly all North American families. We noted that the peak ownership age category (35 to 44) will be growing rapidly in the near future. All the various RV users are served by the same kinds of businesses—campgrounds, fast food, camping outfitters, and the like—and those who learn to cater to this market should therefore prosper.

---

[7] The data in the balance of this section are taken from a series of six articles that appeared in the magazine *RV Dealer* between August 1980 and January 1981.

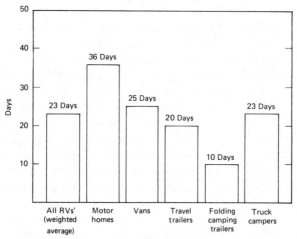

Figure 12.2   *Average number of days used per vehicle.* (*Changing Times* magazine.)

The Economics of Camping

From the standpoint of investment and operating costs, the campground is remarkably flexible. The cost per room for the construction of a budget motor hotel probably exceeds $25,000, and rooms in luxury downtown properties cost $100,000 or more. But campgrounds spend, on the average, between $1500 and $3500 per campsite. Moreover, the campground provides very little in the way of such supporting services as lobbies, restaurants, and cocktail lounges.

Although a motor hotel's staff may run as high as one employee per guest room (including all departments), a commercial campground may employ *no* full-time people other than the couple who owns or operates the camp. Rather, it probably will hire only part-time employees for seasonal peaks. In the absence of an owner, campgrounds operated by state and national parks and the like tend to employ only a small number of year-round people, but their duties—park management, maintenance, and security, for example—tend to be spread out over an entire park. In most public parks, there are no full-time, year-round employees whose duties are devoted solely to dealing with the campground. Neither private nor public campgrounds are labor intensive.

Although hotels may be said to be both capital intensive (requiring large amounts of capital for construction) and labor intensive (requiring many employees for operation), campgrounds are neither. Interestingly enough, however, *camping* itself is both labor and capital intensive.

Recall the investment necessary for an RV and you can see what has happened: the investment has been shifted from the operator (as in a hotel) to the guest. The capital investment is made by the guest, who accommodates his or her

Camping offers travelers a wide range of places to visit where a short season or limited time will not support more traditional accommodations. (Photo courtesy of KOA.)

own tastes and pocketbook at the time the RV is purchased. Like Disney World, the campground accepts all comers without regard to personal style; tent campers are accommodated right along with mobile Xanadus costing $50,000 and up.

Camping is, of course, labor intensive, and campers obviously supply their own labor. They cook the food, wash the dishes, and make the bed. Because it's all part of a "fun" outing, much of this drudgery is treated as fun, and in any case, the work usually takes the form of chores that consume only a small part of the recreational time. Of course, if we added up all the minutes spent by all campers on campground chores, we would find that more work hours are consumed in a campground than in a hotel or motor hotel. But because nobody pays for these hours, they do not appear in the money rate charged. The shift is to that most egalitarian and uniquely American institution—self-service.

From the standpoint of consumers, the new hospitality institutions offer some distinct advantages in flexibility. Most motor hotels have an occupancy percentage break-even point somewhere in the range of 60 to 70 percent. Depending on its original cost, a campground can show an acceptable profit with an annual occupancy of just above 30 percent. A seasonal campground is thus probably easier to operate profitably than is a seasonal hotel or motor hotel. Furthermore, accommodations in campgrounds can be provided in seasonal areas when a short season or limited traffic would never support a hotel. A wider range of places to visit, therefore, becomes available to travelers, and this variety encourages tourism growth.

Careers in Camping

According to KOA, the best preparation for operating a campground is actual working experience. Only a few year-round jobs exist in camping (except for ownership). Seasonal employment is widely available, and so students with an interest in campground jobs have ample opportunities to become acquainted with the working side of the business. Career opportunities in commercial camping are limited largely to campground owners. The construction cost of a typical commercial campground facility ranges between $250,000 and $1,000,000. Of this total cost, 65 to 75 percent could be borrowed from a bank.

In addition to the option of operating as an independent, both chains discussed earlier, KOA and Yogi Bear, are heavily committed to franchising, and a number of the smaller, regional chains and franchise groups are growing, too. Thus, a brand name, operating expertise, and management training are readily available to those with the necessary capital.

The Future of Tourism

We began this chapter by observing that travel and tourism are established and growing parts of the American scene. The energy crisis of the early 1970s and a recession in the early 1980s temporarily retarded the development of tourism and probably altered the kinds of services offered. Although petroleum prices have stabilized at lower levels than the peaks they reached in the early 1980s, gasoline now costs much more than it did before the energy crisis, and consumers have adjusted their behavior accordingly. Though there has been a modest annual increase in the total number of passenger miles traveled by private auto, the *proportion* of intercity travel by auto has declined. According to studies by the Hertz Corporation, the average annual number of miles that an automobile is driven has fallen from about 9500 miles in the early 1970s to roughly 8500 miles in the mid-1980s.

Among common carriers (airline, bus, and rail companies), airline sales have shown considerable growth, probably as a result of deregulation and the slower rises—and some decreases—in fares that the deregulation brought. Train and bus mileage has remained fairly stable.

Business and consumers are responsive to price fluctuations. In times of rapid travel-cost increases, according to the U.S. Travel Data Center, they will use substitutes such as the telephone or destinations closer to home.[8] Changes in the price of petroleum—a major determinant of the cost of travel—are clearly a crucial consideration in looking at the future of tourism.

[8] *National Travel Survey*, p. 26.

The Butterfield stagecoach meets the iron horse in Knott's Berry Farm's Old West Ghost Town. Knott's stagecoaches are authentic antiques that date back as far as 1847. The locomotive, #41 out of the Baldwin works in Philadelphia, was made in 1881 and operated for many years pulling narrow-gauge passenger trains in the Rocky Mountains. Today's old-time adventurers can experience what travel was like on the American frontier a hundred years ago, with their journeys interrupted by "holdups" that are staged daily by masked outlaws from the staff of Knott's funfighters. (Photo courtesy of Knott's Berry Farm.)

Because petroleum is both an economic resource and a political weapon, it is difficult to forecast its price at any point in the future. Barring a political catastrophe, however, it seems likely that although petroleum prices will fluctuate to some degree, they will not increase to anywhere near the dramatic degree they did during the energy crisis. Though many experts anticipate a rise in petroleum price levels beginning around the early 1990s, the big new factor on the tourism horizon is demographic. The move of the baby boomers into those age groups that have the highest propensity to travel suggests that tourism will continue to grow and change.

The tourism plant that is in place has largely been built to accommodate the baby boomers while they were growing up and then as young adults. But as these people enter middle age, their tastes are clearly changing. We have already seen how the hotel business is adapting itself to those tastes. A shift in the kinds of services demanded is already apparent with the all-suite hotel, for instance.

Another likely possibility is the greater significance of rail passenger traffic in some high population areas of the United States such as the Northeast and the Upper Midwest, as well as between key population centers such as Seattle and Portland, San Francisco and Los Angeles, Dallas and Houston, and Miami and

Tampa/Orlando.[9] The era of the grand North American hotels began with the expansion of railroads in the mid-1800s. A major shift to high-speed rail transportation could bring equally fundamental changes in some regions to the tourism plant of the mid- or late-1990s.

The kinds of attractions that will draw visitors in a better-educated, more affluent society are changing, too. Theme parks continue to be attractive, but educational and cultural interest are bringing North Americans back to the campus during summer sessions, and to museums and zoos. In the past, museums and classrooms were not seen as major tourist attractions, but that seems to be changing. Aspiring tourism entrepreneurs owe it to themselves to keep abreast—or, better, a little ahead—of developments on the local cultural and educational scene.

Another factor shaping tourism's offerings is the labor shortage, which suggests that the most likely attractions will be those that are not labor intensive. That is, the acceleration of a trend toward less personal service, already well established by fast food, is a distinct possibility in mass-market tourism.

In tourism, as with upscale food service, the lure of the home entertainment center as an alternative "destination" can be expected to play a competitive role in tourism. Similarly, "big ticket" purchases—computers, video and VCR systems, sports cars, and boats—all constitute competitive alternatives for the potential tourist's dollar. The industry's growth, then, will not be automatic, but we can be reasonably sure that the folks who brought us Disneyland, John Portman's grand hotels, and Ronald McDonald—in a word, the very competitive tourism business—will not rest on their laurels. Tourism will compete, and successfully, for the consumer's dollar.

Summary

We began the chapter by discussing common carriers—airlines, bus companies, and railroads—and comparing their numbers of passenger miles traveled with that of private vehicles.

Next we turned to travel agents, both travel retailers and tour operators, and how they benefit travelers as well as the hospitality industry.

We moved on to camping in national and state parks and in private campgrounds and the advantages and disadvantages of all three. We also described the campers themselves: what kinds of people are most likely to camp and why. Then we considered the various kinds of camping vehicles, paying the most attention to recreational vehicles (RVs).

[9] *Economist,* September 14, 1985, p. 28.

The business aspects of camping was our next topic. We compared campers with hotel guests and then running a campground with running a hotel. We found that camping may not always be much cheaper than staying in a hotel and that like running a hotel, camping itself may also be both capital and labor intensive.

We finished the chapter with a discussion about careers in campgrounds and about the future of tourism in general.

Franchise Systems in the Hospitality Industry

_____ THIS CHAPTER IS ABOUT _____

Franchising in the hospitality industry. Franchising of the entire business format—such as is done by Holiday Inn and Burger King—is one of the most significant developments for small businesses in the twentieth century and a really significant development in hospitality. There is a virtual certainty that you will be involved in franchising—either working for a franchisee or competing with one—if you work in the hospitality industry.

To understand franchising, you will need to see it first in terms of its economic significance. Next we will look at franchising's advantages for the franchisee and franchisor, and at its disadvantages as well. Franchising can also be regarded as a marketing system and as a management system.

Finally, we will look at some important issues and trends that will affect the future of franchising: regulation, termination and transfer of franchises, conversion, and multiple-concept franchising.

Courtesy of Kentucky Fried Chicken.

Franchising: An Overview

Probably the first firm to use franchising—at the end of the Civil War—was the Singer Sewing Machine Company. Later, near the turn of the century, the advent of the automobile and the franchised dealerships that it spawned helped franchising spread throughout the North American economy. Auto dealerships were followed closely by franchised petroleum service station networks. Then in the early 1900s, soft drink companies began to grow, by using franchised bottlers. The first franchises in the hospitality industry came in the 1920s with Howard Johnson's and A&W Root Beer.[1] The two basic types of franchise companies are those that use franchising to distribute a product or trade name and those that use franchising for a business format.

Product and trade name franchises were the earliest. Typical of these were the automobile and petroleum dealerships and soft drink-bottling organizations that gave franchising its real start. Although these kinds of franchise organizations are now declining in relative significance, they still account for nearly three-quarters of all sales by franchised companies.[2] That is, the number of product or trade name franchises is falling dramatically, but their average unit sales are more than offsetting the decline in units. Sales increases at product or trade name franchises are expected to level off at about 5 percent.[3]

Business format franchising, on the other hand, is growing by leaps and bounds. According to U.S. Department of Commerce estimates, the number of outlets using business format franchises grew by 48 percent between 1976 and 1986, and their sales more than tripled in the same period.[4]

A business format franchise, which is the kind applicable to the hospitality industry, "includes not only the product, service and trademark, but the entire business format itself—a marketing strategy and plan, operating manuals and standards, quality control, and continuing two-way communications."[5] One of the main reasons for the rapid growth of business format franchising, according to a study of the future of franchising by "futurologists" of the Naisbitt Group, is that more people have discovered that a franchise offers them the opportunity to be entrepreneurs without taking all the risks usually associated with starting a business. In addition, the shift of the economy from production to service has created an environment that encourages the growth of service franchise systems such as those found in the hospitality industry. One factor is the growth in service needs created by the greater number of working women.

[1] E. Patrick McGuire, *Franchised Distribution* (New York: The Conference Board, 1971), p. 2.

[2] Andrew Kostecka, *Franchising in the Economy, 1984-86* (Washington, D.C.: U.S. Government Printing Office, 1986), p. 1.

[3] The Naisbitt Group, *The Future of Franchising* (Washington, D.C.: International Franchise Association, 1986), p. 2.

[4] Kostecka, *Franchising in the Economy, 1984-86*, p. 4.

[5] Kostecka, *Franchising in the Economy, 1984-86*, p. 3.

Table 13.1   *Business format franchise growth areas*

	ESTIMATED 1990 SALES ($ BILLIONS)	ANNUAL GROWTH (%)
Restaurants	86.1	12.0%
Nonfood retailing	33.6	12.3
Hotels, motels, and campgrounds	22.5	9.0
Business aids and services	21.3	12.0
Convenience stores	19.4	9.5
Automotive products and services	15.9	8.5
Food retailing other than convenience stores (includes doughnut shops and ice-cream and yogurt stores)	15.9	7.0
Construction and home services	9.2	20.0
Auto and truck rental	8.9	11.0
Recreation, entertainment, and travel	6.6	29.0

Source: Adapted from Naisbitt Group, *The Future of Franchising.*

THE ECONOMIC SIGNIFICANCE OF FRANCHISING

Franchised units are generally thought of as small businesses, but *franchising* itself is big business. Franchised sales accounted for 10 percent of the gross national product (GNP) in 1983. By 1985 that proportion had doubled to 20 percent of GNP, and franchised sales accounted for one-third of all retail sales. They are projected to reach half of all retail sales by the year 2000.[6] Large companies play a major role in business format franchising, with companies with 1000 or more units accounting for over half of format franchise sales in all businesses.

In 1983 within the hospitality industry, 13 restaurant chains with over 1000 units accounted for 52 percent of all franchised restaurants and 58 percent of all franchised restaurant sales, according to the U.S. Department of Commerce. Seventy-five percent of year-round-operated hotel and motel rooms in properties of over 25 units are in franchise systems. And if seasonal and very small properties are included, the proportion is 50 percent.[7]

Hospitality leads the way in the number of business format franchises. Table 13.1 shows the 10 fastest-growing business format areas. Two of the top three, restaurants and lodging, are exclusively hospitality firms, and hospitality and tourism play a major role in four out of the remaining eight (convenience stores, food retailing, auto rental, and travel).

[6] The Naisbitt Group, *The Future of Franchising*, p. 1.
[7] The Naisbitt Group, *The Future of Franchising*, pp. 5-7.

Interested in Becoming a Franchisee?

Here Are Seven Basic Questions for a Prospective Franchisee

1. Is the company itself reasonably secure financially, or is it selling franchises to get cash to cover ongoing expenses?
   - Is the company selective in choosing franchisees?
   - Is it in too big a hurry to get your money? Is this deal too good to be true?

   Today, sweetheart deals are few and far between.

2. Does the company have a solid base of company-owned units? If it does,
   - It is in the same business as are their franchisees.
   - It is in the company's interest to concentrate on improving marketing and operating systems.

   If your primary business is operations and the company's selling franchises, the system is headed for trouble.

3. Is the system successful on a per-unit basis? To find out, you have to look at several numbers:
   - Comparable average sales of stores that have been open longer than one year (sometimes first-year sales are very high and then drop off).
   - Unit-level trends: What you really need is sales data adjusted for inflation or, better yet, customer counts at the unit level.

   A business is really only growing when it's serving more people.

4. Is the franchisor innovative across all parts of its business?
   - The company should be working on operating and equipment refinements.
   - Ask what it is doing in purchasing, recruiting, training, and labor scheduling. Is anyone working to make uniforms more attractive, durable, and comfortable?

   The best companies are consistently trying to upgrade every component of their business.

5. Does the company share sufficient support services with its franchisees?
   - In general, the company should provide guidance and strategic direction on marketing and excellent operations training. In addition, every franchisee should have contact with a company employee whose primary responsibility is a small group of franchised restaurants.
   - There are some services that a company can't provide, such as setting prices. And others are risky, such as getting involved in franchisee manager selection or outside financing.

Support services must be shared in such a way that they respect the franchisee's independence.

6. Does the company respect its franchisees?

   • In addition to formal publications, there should be regular informal forums or councils in which selected franchisees meet face to face with top management to discuss both problems and opportunities.

   • Corporate staff should collect ideas, test them, and, if they look good, involve franchisees in expanded testing.

   Franchisees should actually participate in the development of any change that will affect their units.

7. Does the franchisor provide long-term leadership for the entire system?

   • Franchisee participation is no excuse for franchisor abdication of its leadership responsibilities. Somebody has to make the formal decisions, and that must be the franchisee.

   • A primary function of the franchisor is to protect the value of each franchise by actively and aggressively monitoring operations, demanding that each unit live up to system standards.

   Perhaps a necessary long-term decision is not popular. Making tough decisions and following through may be the best real test of leadership.

Source: Adapted from Don N. Smith, Burton Shaw Lecture, Washington State University, Fall 1985.

THE FRANCHISE RELATIONSHIP

A conversation with a franchisee is likely to yield this contradiction: The franchisee clearly thinks of himself as an independent business person but is likely to refer to the franchisor as "the parent company." "Many franchisees," one report suggested, "do not really wish to be independent at all but are tempted by the opportunity to be both part of a large group, sharing in its success image and yet also maintaining an 'individual identity.'[8]

The all-too-human tendency to "have your cake and eat it too" is probably heightened by the fact that the franchisee has many of the characteristics of an independent businessperson. The franchisee has a substantial investment—ownership (of the franchise and very possibly of land, building, furniture, and fixtures or a lease on them). Beyond that, he or she has full day-to-day operating control and responsibility. For instance, the franchisee is responsible for determining the need for hiring employees, supervising the daily operation (or managing those who do that supervision), and generally representing themselves in the community as independent businesspeople. The degree of franchisee control over

[8] McGuire, *Franchised Distribution*, p. 8.

key issues varies from one franchise group to another, but many franchisees share considerable freedom of action in such significant business variables as pricing, placement of local advertising, choice of some suppliers, and additions to and renovations of physical plant. Although some aspects of the unit's budget are governed by the franchise agreement, the franchisee retains significant budgetary discretion under most agreements and, in practice, excercises even more.

On the other hand, the essence of almost all franchises in the hospitality industry is an agreement by the franchisee to follow the form of the franchisor's business system in order to gain the advantages of that business format. The franchisee *has* indeed relinquished a great deal of discretion in the management of his or her enterprise and is a system that largely defines his or her operation. The franchisee's relationship is neither that of an employee nor that of an independent customer of the franchisor.

The most common characteristics of a franchise agreement are

1. A contractual relationship setting forth the rights and responsibilities of each party.
2. The purpose of the arrangement is the efficient distribution of a product, service, or entire business concept.
3. Both parties contribute resources to establish and maintain the franchise.
4. The contract describes the contribution of each party and the specific marketing and operating procedures.
5. The franchise is a business entity that requires the full-time business activity of the franchisee or his or her representative.
6. The franchisee and franchisor participate in a common public identity.
7. There is customarily a payment of an initial franchise fee, continuing royalties, and usually a required contribution to a common advertising fund.[9]

The Franchise System

We previously used the word *system* to describe an interactive whole, in which the totality of the system is more than just the sum of the parts. "One thousand separate units plus a home office" is one way to describe a chain—the sum of the parts. But the *system* description would include factors related to the interactive way in which the system functions. The system achieves, for instance, impact and market identity through a common marketing program; economies through bulk purchasing; and operating impact in the marketplace through uniformity of menu, presentation of product, uniforms, and architecture and decor. Indeed, even the hospitality industry trade magazines' statistics generally treat the franchise group as if it were a chain that owns all the units. From the outside—and to a large degree, from the inside—the franchise group is seen as one organization.

---

[9] Adapted from McGuire, *Franchised Distribution*; and Kostecka, *Franchising in the Economy, 1984-86*

Relationships within the system are more complex than those in wholly owned, multiple-unit systems. The franchisee is an independent businessperson, yet one who has given up a large measure of independence in return for access to a proven, successful format for doing business. The franchisor's representatives are not "the boss" in the same way as a district manager would be if the company owned all the units. Likewise, the franchisee is not an employee as a unit manager would be. Later we will discuss how leadership is maintained within the franchise system. For now, we should note that the franchisee is a *member of a system* and has accepted a set of obligations that he or she shares with others in the system.

The Franchisee's Deal

The franchisee has given up a good deal of autonomy, as we've just seen, in return for membership in a system. It is time now for us to look at the very real advantages that accrue to franchisees from the deal they have struck.

THE NEW FRANCHISEE

Franchising bridges the gap between an able, intelligent individual and an entrepreneurial opportunity. The business format franchise offers a proven way of doing business, including a proven product, or products, an operating system, and a complete marketing program.

The franchise minimizes the entrepreneurial risk. Small Business Administration studies indicate, for instance, that somewhere between one-fourth and one-

Many franchisors seek new franchisees through advertising.
(Courtesy of Arby's, Inc.)

third of all businesses fail during their first year, and 65 percent fail within their first five years. On the other hand, the failure rate for *all* franchised businesses is well under 5 percent, and the failed businesses amount to less than a half-percent of total franchise sales.

In addition to a successful business format, the franchisor provides a number of services that are especially important to the new franchisee. These include screening, site selection, preopening training, and opening assistance.

Screening

Being screened to see whether you are the right person to be sold a franchise may not seem like a service. A moment's reflection, however, will show that careful franchisee selection is in the best interests not only of the company and other, existing franchisees but of the new franchisee as well.

The initial contact may be in the form of a franchise marketing brochure, and more intensive screening begins after a prequalifying phase. The potential franchisee's background and record of success—as well as financial position—are carefully reviewed. In preliminary interviews his or her personal commitment will be probed; some franchisors even interview spouses to assure themselves of the family's commitment to the project if the prospective franchisee is expected to operate the new business. Some fast-food companies also ask the prospect to spend time in an operation—as much as a week—to ensure that they fully realize the nature of the business they are entering. The ways that contacts are made during the recruitment phase of the franchise relationship are summarized in Table 13.2. Curiously, in an International Franchise Association Survey, franchisors ranked the least-used medium, a classroom session as the most effective.

Site Selection and Planning

Franchisors maintain a real estate department staffed with site selection experts. The franchise company also has its pooled experience to guide it. Given the importance of location to most hospitality operations, the availability of expert

Table 13.2 *Methods of communication in franchisee recruitment*

COMMUNICATION MEDIA	PERCENTAGE OF FRANCHISORS USING THIS MEDIUM
Marketing brochure	92%
Telephone qualifying	87
Formal presentation	80
Meeting with existing franchisees	75
On-the-job training	37
Classroom session	31
Other	17

Source: International Franchise Association.

advice is important. Many companies actually select the site for the franchisee, and virtually all reputable franchisors insist on the right to approve a site. The physical layout of the operation, from the site plan to the building, equipment, and furnishing, and even a list of small wares and opening inventory, will be spelled out in detail.

Preopening Training

Virtually all franchise organizations have some means of training the franchisee and his or her key personnel. This service ranges from McDonald's Hamburger University and Holiday Corporation's Holiday Inn University, which are extensive management training units, to simpler programs based on experience in an existing store. Table 13.3 summarizes the methods used during training and start-up. Many franchisors also provide an opening crew of lead people drawn from other units to help train the crew for the opening of a new unit.

Operations Manuals

The backbone of the operating system is a set of comprehensive operations manuals that cover operating procedures from opening to closing and nearly everything in between. All major equipment operations and routine maintenance are described in the operations manual or in a separate equipment manual.

DRAWBACKS FOR THE FRANCHISEE

Some of the more obvious drawbacks of obtaining a franchise have been implicit in our discussion: loss of independence and payment of substantial advertising assessments and franchise fees. If the franchisee has picked a weak franchising organization, field support and other management services may be inadequate.

Franchising is *not* risk free. The franchisee is generally completely dependent on the franchisor not only for marketing but often for purchasing and other operations-oriented assistance. If a franchise concept is not kept up-to-date—as many argue has been the case for Howard Johnson's Restaurants—or loses its

Table 13.3   *Methods of communication during training and start-up*

COMMUNICATIONS MEDIA	PERCENTAGE OF FRANCHISORS USING THIS MEDIUM
On-the-job training	92.5%
Formal classroom training	91.0
Meetings with company management	91.0
Preopening checklist	83.0
Meetings with existing franchisees	61.0
Other	13.0

Source: International Franchise Association.

focus—as, for instance, Kentucky Fried Chicken seemed to do for a time in the late 1970s—it is difficult for the franchisee to do much about it.

What happens when things *really* go bad is illustrated by the case of Arthur Treacher's Fish and Chips.[10] A successful and growing franchise of the mid-1970s, Treacher's then had serious difficulties ending in bankruptcy. Its national marketing efforts virtually ceased. Its product quality control system broke down, and yet the franchisees were contractually obligated to purchase only from approved suppliers. The franchisees also were required to pay both advertising fees and royalties but claimed they received little or no services in return. Many franchisees withheld payment of fees and royalties and then became involved in lengthy lawsuits which were expensive in both executive time and attorney's fees. While some Treacher franchisees weathered the series of setbacks, virtually all suffered serious losses, and many left the field.

The Franchisor's Deal

Just as the franchisee seeks benefits from the franchise arrangement, the franchisor stands to gain a number of advantages. These can be grouped under the heading of marketing, finance, and operations.

---

[10] The difficulties of a franchise system in trouble are told from the point of view of a successful multiunit franchisee in case-history form in Thomas F. Powers, "MIE Hospitality" (Guelph, Ont.: Advanced Management Program for the Hospitality Industry, 1983).

Central training facilities emphasize management training while crew training utilizes video cassettes to explain necessary unit level skills and operating procedures. (Photos courtesy of Holiday Inns, Inc. and McDonald's Corp.)

MARKETING

Franchising represents a solution to a company's marketing problem when "place" or representation in a geographically defined market is crucial. Clearly this is the case in the hospitality industry. If your restaurant company has no units in Iowa, you'll have no sales in Iowa, and so being "in place" is crucial to the marketing mix of the restaurant company with national or regional ambitions.

There is a level of distribution to be achieved in the market that causes sales to go up. First, the more units a company has in a market, the more advertising media

OGILVY & MATHER

2 EAST 48 STREET, NEW YORK 10017
907-3400

Client: HARDEE'S
Product: BURGERS
Title: "BURGER WARS" NON-NEW
Commercial No.: ISBF 7506

1. CLOWN ADJUTANT: Hey, hey General. The troops are ready.

2. CLOWN GENERAL: Cannons primed? CLOWN ADJUTANT: Check. CLOWN GENERAL: Motors checked? CLOWN ADJUTANT: Check.

3. CLOWN GENERAL: I don't like it! It's too quiet out there.

4. (MUSIC UP AND UNDER)

5. OLD LADY: There they are, girls! Let's get 'em.

6. (MUSIC AND SFX: EXPLOSIONS)

7. CLOWN GENERAL: Over the top, men.

8. (MUSIC AND SFX: AIRPLANE ENGINES AND EXPLOSION)

9. ANNCR: (VO) They called it the burger wars.

10. But now that the smoke's starting to clear,

11. one thing's pretty obvious.

12. The big boys, for all their noise... (SFX: EXPLOSION)

13. ...didn't really have anything new to say, did they?

14. Well now, someone does. (SFX: BLAST)

15. Someone who's taken the burger, rethought it, made it thicker,

16. succulent, full of natural juices;

17. taken it off the battlefield and brought it closer to where it should've been all along... home.

18. CLOWN ADJUTANT: Cheer up, General, this'll really get 'em.

19. (SFX: BOINGGG!!!)

20. ANNCR: (VO) The quarter pound burgers from Hardee's. We're out to win you over.

Few individual restaurants can afford the production cost of a television commercial. The franchisor, or the national advertising co-op, provides first-call TV commercials to franchisees for use in their local market. (Courtesy of Hardee's and Ogilvy & Mather.)

it can buy and the easier it will be for people to visit often; the restaurants are simply closer. Finally, continuous exposure of all kinds—seeing television commercials, driving past the sign and building, as well as actually visiting the restaurant—contribute to "top-of-mind awareness"; that is, being the first place that comes into people's minds when they think of a restaurant. Clearly, then, being in place in a market is a crucial advantage and one more readily secured quickly through franchising.

In the lodging industry, representation in major markets is important not only to get a share of the business in those markets but also to gain access to the business *generated* by those cities or areas for other markets. For example, travelers are more likely to stay in a hotel with which they are familiar at home, and one that can offer convenient reservation service near the trip's point of origination. Moreover, the lodging firm has a higher chance of retaining travelers as guests for the balance of the trip once they stay in one of their properties. Making forward reservations is easy and encouraged. This *system effect* reinforces the importance of representation in every major market.

This ad is provided by the franchisor to franchisees to run in their local newspapers. (Courtesy of Country Kitchen International, Inc.)

FINANCE

Any company with a proven, successful format for doing business is likely to want to expand rapidly, preferably before its approach is copied. The first franchise in the North American hospitality industry was the result of Howard Johnson's financial inability to expand with his good idea during difficult economic times. The expansion that he and his company did undertake was financed largely by the capital provided by his frachisees.

When a franchise system begins to expand, one of its major advantages is that its need to expand its fixed asset base is much less than if the expansion were made up of owned units. In most companies, the franchisee acquires the fixed assets or a lease commitment to cover those assets. Although a company earns a higher total dollar profit on sales from owned units, the franchisor's return on investment is much higher for franchised units, just because its investment is so much lower.

Not only do franchisees pay royalties on sales, they also commonly pay a franchise initiation fee. In a relatively younger franchise company, these initiation fees may help provide working capital during expansion. The major factor, however, in financing the expansion of the franchise system is the franchisee's assumption of the responsibility, through lease or ownership, of the fixed assets.

OPERATIONS

The franchisee is the owner of a business. As such, he or she can be expected to have a lively interest in how that business is run. The responsibility for the franchised operation's success is principally that of the franchisee. The franchisee's interest in his or her own operation also has important implications for the franchise company's organization. A district manager (DM) is likely to supervise somewhere between 4 and 8 company-owned units. A franchise district manager (FDM) is responsible for assisting franchisees with their operating problems and usually ensuring conformance with standards. The FDM's span of responsibility, in practice, ranges from 15 to 70 units, with 30 the maximum number of units an FDM can reasonably handle.[11]

Don Smith, the 1985 Burton Shaw Lecturer at Washington State University, has pointed out that the franchisees are also a good resource for know-how. Input from the grass roots level "creates a check and balance that enables the corporate functional support groups to keep a proper perspective on the business."[12]

> *A simple example is the sour cream gun at Taco Bell. Everyone in the Taco Bell system knew it was needed for better portion control and faster speed of service. After spending*

---

[11] Don N. Smith, Burton Shaw Lecture, Washington State University, Fall 1985. He calls what we have referred to as the FDM a Franchise Consultant, which may be a better way of thinking of the role. Field practice, however, tends toward titles like FDM.

[12] Smith, Burton Shaw Lecture.

several years and several hundred thousand dollars with no practical solution in sight, the company gave up. Finally, a franchisee showed them how it should be done. On a much larger scale, breakfast at McDonald's had been tried without success until a franchisee came up with Egg McMuffin."[13]

FRANCHISING DISADVANTAGES

The bargain struck with franchisees has its costs to franchisors. Many franchise companies find that their owned stores yield higher sales and profit margins. And if the company owned all its units—if it could overcome the organizational difficulties of a much larger, more complex organization—the profits earned from the same stores would be higher than the royalties received from a franchised store.

We should note, too, that not all franchise income is profit. Usually 2 percent of sales is needed to service a franchise system. And because of start-up costs for a new franchised unit *for the franchisor*, it may be three years before the royalties begin to contribute to the franchisor's profit.[14] In addition, the franchisor will already have made a considerable investment. The expenditures to establish a franchise system, including legal and accounting costs,[15] executives' time, and consultants' and managerial time, have been estimated at over $200,000.[16]

Perhaps the greatest drawback, however, is the loss of control. The managment of an owned operation is much more straightforward. As Rick Duffy, former vice-president of Kentucky Fried Chicken, and now one of their multiunit franchisees, put it in an interview, "When you own them, you run them. With a franchisee, you have to convince him to run them."[17]

Difficulties with franchising do lead some companies to withdraw. When Stouffer's terminated its franchise contracts, it did so because it felt that it did not have adequate quality control in its franchised operations.[18]

Functioning of the Franchise System

We have seen that the franchise relationship is one of mutual interdependence. We have looked at how franchising affects operations and marketing. In the next section we will draw together some of those observations in order to see franchising as a marketing system.

[13] Smith, Burton Shaw Lecture.
[14] Smith, Burton Shaw Lecture.
[15] Robert E. Kushell and Carl E. Zwisler III, *How to Be a Franchisor* (Washington, D.C.: International Franchise Association, 1984), p. 14.
[16] Smith, Burton Shaw Lecture.
[17] Richard L. Duffy, personal communication.
[18] *Restaurant Business*, July 20, 1986, p. 142.

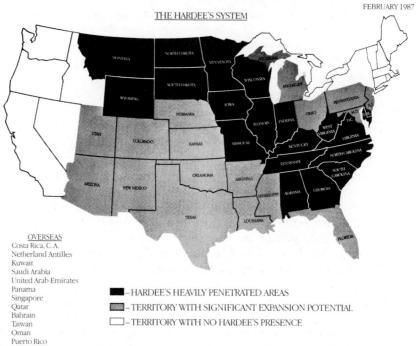

FEBRUARY 1987

THE HARDEE'S SYSTEM

OVERSEAS
Costa Rica, C. A.
Netherland Antilles
Kuwait
Saudi Arabia
United Arab Emirates
Panama
Singapore
Qatar
Bahrain
Taiwan
Oman
Puerto Rico

◼ – HARDEE'S HEAVILY PENETRATED AREAS
▨ – TERRITORY WITH SIGNIFICANT EXPANSION POTENTIAL
☐ – TERRITORY WITH NO HARDEE'S PRESENCE

Hardees's system uses franchisees as an important means to expand into new territories, as well as to penetrate established territories. (Courtesy of Hardee's.)

FRANCHISING AS A MARKETING SYSTEM

In marketing, the franchisor takes the lead, but both the company and its franchisees are essential to make the system work. We will arrange our discussion here in order of the importance of each element to the franchise system: place, product and service, promotion, and price.

Place

Building exteriors are often identical. If not, the sign will use a known corporate logo to ensure recognition. Interiors are commonly much the same in food service. Ambience and decor—all of these things we referred to as the presentation mix in the last chapter—are manipulated to secure the establishment's identity. Uniformity is more pronounced in food service than in lodging. Even there, though, the guests are given numerous cues to remind them where they are: corporate logo, signs and uniforms, for instance.

Product and Service

"No surprises" is one of the famous tag lines of Holiday Inns' advertising, and it might be used by most franchise systems to sum up their product line. In most restaurant systems, the menu offerings are identical, with minor variations. In lodging, there is more variety in individual menu offerings, and the details of decor differ, but the core product is essentially the same.

Franchisees are intelligent, independent businesspeople, and they often come up with new product ideas. Some, like Egg McMuffin, are highly successful and support the system's battle for market share. Moreover, the franchise system is a network for marketing intelligence on competitive products. Franchisees are concerned about new products in their local markets. It is the franchise company's function to meet those market trends with appropriate product innovations, but the information network is important to identifying and tracking trends, developing product ideas, and in testing and refining those ideas and product.

Promotion

At least two promotion advantages are available to franchise systems. First and most obvious is the pooling of financial resources that gives the system a large promotional war chest not only to mount a national advertising campaign (or a regional one for smaller systems) but also to develop first-rate media for local advertising efforts.

Less obvious but also important is the presence of decision makers in local markets who can respond to local trends. For instance, if couponing is used in a market, the local decision maker can assess the need to respond. For many decisions, then, the franchise organization is characterized by a very high degree of decentralization.

The local franchisees probably also becomes an affluent and influential citizen, likely to take part in local affairs in a way that benefits the company's image in that market. In a society as highly mobile as that in North America, this too is a significant advantage, because strength in many local markets adds up to significant advantages in the transient market.

Price

Although price regulation is not legal, system prices tend to be uniform, perhaps because of similar operating costs and common pricing rules of thumb. The general uniformity gives consumers an important piece of information when they are choosing where to eat or sleep. On the other hand, as with promotional practice, local decision makers can match local price trends and special conditions. In lodging, system directories provide information about price ranges, and reservation systems permit guests to secure a definite price in advance of their stay.

System Marketing

The uniformity of product and presentation and the aggregation of advertising funds are advantages of the system's centralization. Representation in many locations and flexibility in promotion and pricing decisions are advantages of the system's decentralization. As in any system, the whole is greater than the sum of the parts.

Regulation

No one should think that all is rosy. When several parties' interests are at stake, there are bound to be different views. Many franchisees feel that the franchisors don't respect their independence. Even more importantly, there have been a number of cases of questionable and downright dishonest behavior by franchisors. For these reasons, franchisee lobbying has focused on the franchisees' rights and prevention of abuse and dishonesty by franchisors. As well, the growing economic significance of franchising and franchisee investing has drawn the lawmakers' attention to franchising. As a result, a considerable body of legislation has been passed regulating franchising at both the federal and the state levels.

A major focus of regulation has been on full disclosure and fair reporting of information to prospective franchisees. In 1971 the state of California adopted a law requiring, in effect, the franchisors to file a prospectus providing information on both the franchisor and the details of the franchise contract. Several other states have passed similar legislation. In 1979 the U.S. Fair Trade Commission (FTC) published its national disclosure requirements. The FTC also forbids publication of income forecasts unless they can be reasonably substantiated. Currently, over 36 states have disclosure rules, some of which are more stringent on some points than are those of the FTC.

Failure to follow FTC regulations can be expensive. One company, Philly Mignon, was fined $80,000 plus 5 percent of franchisee sales for five years for failing to provide complete and accurate information, misrepresenting key facts about the company's record, and failing to secure suitable sites for its franchisees. The penalties were deliberately stated to be "modest" because a stiffer fine would have threatened the firm's future business, and thus its franchisees' livelihood.[19]

TERMINATING A FRANCHISE

A franchisor's failure to renew its agreement is naturally a matter of concern to its franchisees. In fact, however, over 90 percent of franchise agreements are renewed, and typically, less than 5 percent are refused renewal by the franchisor. Most of these are for failure to pay royalties or to comply with other financial obligations or quality control standards.[20] But this problem, despite its currently modest dimension, has attracted the attention of state lawmakers. In Wisconsin, for instance, the franchisor's power to terminate unilaterally or to refuse to renew without cause is sharply restricted. A number of other states are considering similar restrictions.[21]

In court, it seems, the franchisor is the "big guy" and the franchisee the "little guy." The International Franchise Association indicated, for instance, that "almost all ambiguities in the franchise contract will be construed against the fran-

---

[19] *Nation's Restaurant News*, February 13, 1984, p. 6.
[20] Kostecka, *Franchising in the Economy, 1984–86*, p. 13.
[21] *Nation's Restaurant News*, May 21, 1984, p. 6.

chisor in litigation."[22] A decision in a case between Dunkin Donuts and a franchisee is illustrative. The franchisee had intentionally and fraudulently under-reported revenue on which his royalties were computed. While upholding the company's right to terminate under these circumstances, the court actually awarded a judgment of $115,000 *to the franchisee*, to offset his original investment and give him a decent sum to start a new enterprise.

Recent Trends

As franchise chains grow and franchisees' organizations mature, conditions change, and new problems emerge. Some of these are a shortage of locations for franchisors, expensive franchising renewal provisions for established franchisees, and a lack of opportunity for expanding established franchisees. We will close this chapter by considering how both parties are moving to meet these problems.

CONVERSION FRANCHISING

There are only so many desirable locations. Large franchisors have begun to acquire other smaller chains to secure their locations and to convert their properties into those of the acquiring chains in what is sometimes called *conversion franchising*. Another occasion for conversion that is particularly prominent in the lodging industry is presented by older properties whose owners determine that it is not economically feasible to meet expensive refranchising requirements. Franchise groups, as we noted in Chapter 9, have begun to spring up to offer conversion opportunities to other franchises.

MULTIPLE-CONCEPT FRANCHISING

Once an energetic and able franchisee is successfully established in his or her franchise, that person is likely to seek opportunities for further growth. This can—and often does—mean using the successful franchise operation for expanding his or her business interests. This in turn can mean a division of interests and sometimes even a conflict of interests. To try to meet this problem by offering franchisees an opportunity within the system for further growth, some franchisors have turned to multiple-concept franchising. Pepsico, for instance, developed its rapidly growing chain of retail bakeries, La Petite Boulangerie, to offer additional opportunities to the company's successful Taco Bell franchisees.[23] Shoney's, another highly successful restaurant company, offers franchises for Shoney's, Captain D's, Fifth Quarter, and Famous Recipe.[24]

---

[22] Kushell and Zwisler, *How to Be a Franchisor*, p. 11.
[23] *Nation's Restaurant News*, December 5, 1984, p. 74, and March 11, 1985, p. 56.
[24] John J. Rohs, *The Restaurant Industry* (New York, Wertheim & Co., 1985), p. 29.

Multiple-concept franchising appears to be an effort by franchisors to keep alive the spirit of franchise systems—mutual interest—by offering to successful franchisees opportunities for continued growth.

Summary

In this chapter we examined more closely the subject of franchising as it applies to the hospitality industry. Business format franchising, as that is the kind found in restaurants and hotels, was our focus.

We looked first at the economic significance of franchising, as seen in the franchise relationship. The next section was devoted to franchising from the franchisee's point of view. Then we outlined some of the drawbacks of being a franchisee. We shifted next to the franchisor's viewpoint and the disadvantages of being a franchisor.

The following section was on the franchisor's functions, as a marketing system. Regulation was discussed, as well as terminating a franchise.

The final section was a quick look at recent trends in franchising: conversion franchising and multiple-concept franchising.

Views of the Future

———————————— THIS CHAPTER IS ABOUT ————————————

Hospitality's bright future. We will be looking at how basic forces—demand, supply, and technology—may interact to create opportunities in hospitality. You will not be surprised, however, to find that where there are opportunities, there are also plenty of problems and risks.

Some trends in hospitality seem fairly clear: fragmentation of the industry into quite distinct segments; the significance of the home as a competitor; opportunities—and challenges—for independents. At the other extreme, though, we will look at the entry and growth of conglomerates in our field.

We have noted at several points in this text that you are really in business for yourself, whether you are self-employed or work for the largest company in town. Your career *is* your business, and we will conclude with consideration of where you may want to fit in the industry's future and how you should prepare for it.

Courtesy of the New York Convention and Visitors Center.

We study the future, to paraphrase the historian, to understand the present. Trying to look ahead forces us to think in an orderly way about the forces at work today that are likely to affect tomorrow. Thus, we are really *not* trying to prophesy in this chapter but, rather, to identify the forces visibly at work today that are important to our industry. Even if the pictures of the future that this chapter envisions may be off the mark here and there, the identification of significant trends will still be important to you. As you shape your own career plans, the forces we examine in this chapter will continue to command your attention in the years to come, when you will be making your own estimates of their likely effects.

The Forces That Will Shape the Future

The most basic economic forces are, as always, supply and demand. But supply and demand operate in a changing social and technological environment. With so many variables at play, we can make no precise forecasts, but some general directions seem clear.

The Demand for Hospitality Services

Ultimately, the hospitality industry is shaped by its consumers and the products and services they need and want. Demand is affected by factors such as consumer demographics and population trends, including age, sex, and marital status. Income and employment trends are also important shapers of consumer preferences. The education of the population and the changing culture we live in influence consumer tastes and interests. In the following sections we will look at both the quantitative and the qualitative aspects of demand from the point of view of demographics, employment and income, and education.

CONSUMER DEMOGRAPHICS

In Chapter 1 we looked at the trends in the population's ages. One conclusion we reached was that the middle-aged segment of our population is growing in significance. We noted that as people move into middle age, their incomes rise. By early middle age—say around 40—the expenses of starting a family such as furnishing a house and the adjustments and expenses that come with the birth of children are behind them. This is the age when guests are most likely to travel and when their spending on eating out reaches its highest point. The increase in the affluent middle-aged population, then, represents a major opportunity for the hospitality industry. The late middle years provide an even wealthier consumer. Dubbed the "Ultras," consumers aged 50 to 64 spend over 20 percent more of their income on nonessentials than does the average consumer.[1] Because the number of people choosing early retirement has been increasing, many in this age group are likely to have more leisure.

The senior citizen population segment, however, is where leisure really reigns. Although not as prosperous as middle-aged people, seniors on the average tend to be in comfortable economic circumstances and have lots of time to spend on eating out, travel, and recreation. In recent years, there has been a trend toward more part-time employment to supplement retirement income which increases the affluence of many in this group. In addition, the mandatory retirement age has been moved up, which means that a significant percentage of people in this age bracket are still employed, usually at the highest income they have had in their lifetimes.

EMPLOYMENT, INCOME, AND DEMAND FOR HOSPITALITY

Probably the most significant social development in the last generation has been the increasing number of working women and of two-income families. In Chapter 5 we saw that many of the "service functions" of the family, such as feeding children lunch (and sometimes breakfast) as well as caring for the elderly, have been moved to social agencies such as schools and congregate meal programs. The next decade will likely see the continuing expansion of day-care services as more mothers of young children move into the work force. Whenever another meal is eaten away from home, the hospitality industry grows.

Paralleling these developments, commercial food service has benefited as women and families are more inclined—and financially able—to eat out. The growth *rate* for working women is slowing somewhat, but female employment continues to rise. With more than half of North America's mothers already in the work force, food away from home has become a *necessity rather than a luxury.* This fact suggests that food service sales are likely to continue to grow slowly from their present stable base.

Lack of time is a fact of life for families with both parents working, which results in a great tendency to eat out and in a demand for relatively fast service. Fast food, we can expect, is here to stay, but it has continually redefined itself and is likely to continue to evolve to serve the needs of a "middle-aging" population.

The two-income family has also meant growth in the number of those who can afford to travel. Although the number of hotel rooms sold has not grown appreciably in the last 40 years, there is a real possibility of an increase in some geographic markets as middle-aged prosperity and the senior "leisure class" hit the road. On the other hand, the campground and RV have been effective and growing competitors for the last generation and are likely to continue to be a strong market factor.

[1] *Restaurants & Institutions*, January 7, 1987, p. 20.

EDUCATION'S IMPACT ON HOSPITALITY

The North American population is the most highly educated in history in terms of its years of formal schooling. The average educational achievement is about 12 years, implying that at least half the population has somewhat more than a high school education.

But formal education is far from the only educational influence. If we include the pervasive effect of television and the increase in travel as educational, we can see why today's hospitality consumer is a sophisticate.

Attractions like Walt Disney World and other theme parks have done a great deal to raise consumers' entertainment expectations. A joint venture between George Lucas, the creator of *Star Wars*, and the Disney organization wed an aircraft simulator to movie projectors (outside the "windows") to create an impression of space flight. Indeed, the Disney organization has a whole division devoted to this kind of creative effort which it calls *imagineering*.[2]

In the business travel market, techniques such as videoconferencing are likely to become more widely accepted as a generation of businesspeople who take technology for granted come on the scene.

The educated consumer is, we argued in Chapter 3, a health- and nutrition-conscious consumer. Although younger consumers have shown a modest decline in nutrition concerns, over 65 percent of the "Ultras" (i.e., people aged 50 to 65) indicate that they are very concerned about their nutrition. Though consumers do appear less concerned about the whole question of processed foods than they did a few years ago, between 1983 and 1986 their concern about the fat content and cholesterol in food roughly doubled.[3] Nutrition concerns, it seems, are a permanent part of the food service landscape.

Consumerism is a movement that educates the public. Consumerists want the guest to have a part in setting businesses' agendas, not just in deciding whether or not to patronize a business. Concern, for instance, about "passive smoking," that is, the smoke that nonsmokers inhale when there is smoking around them, continues to heat up as more data come in and the U.S. Surgeon General indicates a goal of a smoke-free society by 2000. Under the circumstances, no-smoking sections in restaurants will continue to grow in number, whether voluntarily or by law. Indeed, the greater demand for smoke-free guest rooms in hotels also suggests a trend that will continue to grow in importance in lodging.

Similarly, concerns over truth in menu will continue, and voluntary nutritional labeling to avoid legally mandated labeling may well spread.

Educated consumers are people who demand value in terms of quality of product, service, and entertainment. They value themselves, want to protect their health, and are responsive to consumer groups who seek to represent those kinds of interests. Educated consumers are in the driver's seat in our marketing oriented civilization.

[2] *Wall Street Journal*, January 6, 1987, pp. 1, 16.
[3] *Wall Street Journal*, November 3, 1986, p. 29.

Supply Conditions

Food and labor are the major factors of production that we will examine in this chapter. Though the cost outlook is reasonably favorable for food itself, food service workers are likely to grow scarcer and more costly.

FOOD

The Reverend Thomas Malthus—an early nineteenth-century English economist and probably the man most responsible for earning for economics the title of "the dismal science"—offered some pessimistic conclusions about population growth and the food supply. He predicted that as the population grew faster than the food supply did, worldwide famine would result. As it turned out, the crisis that Malthus foresaw did not materialize, but his argument has been repeated ever since. Each time, however, the prophets of doom have been disproved by advances in agricultural technology.

Barring a natural catastrophe, it appears likely that food supplies will continue in abundance to the point of posing a problem of surpluses. This should mean that raw foodstuffs such as grains will continue to be relatively inexpensive. (Of course, government intervention in the marketplace, which has been fairly common, could change the outlook. Intervention could take the form of restricting growing, artificially propping up prices, or both.)

Raw food prices have exhibited a long-term decline, but the price of meat has varied because of several factors that are beyond the scope of this text. We can say, however, that there is at least a reasonable possibility that the price of meat will fall somewhat by the early 1990s, after a significant lag, reflecting lower feed costs.

More expensive beef has been only one cause in the decline of beef sales. Perhaps more fundamentally, consumers' nutrition concerns have been a big factor in the marketplace. Concerns about fat and cholesterol have led to a greater consumption of chicken and, though to lesser degree, of pork. (Pork has less saturated fat than beef does.)

Despite the falling price of some foodstuffs—and the price of meat may join that trend—when significant labor is added, as is required for convenience foods, the price of labor is more likely to dominate, and prices may rise. These processed foods—and the grocer's freezer case, generally—are directly competitive with food service. Thus, any upward price trend in convenience foods is a help to the industry in maintaining its competitiveness.

LABOR

You will recall that the number of younger workers, on whom the hospitality industry normally draws, has been declining since the late 1970s. That decline will continue into the 1990s, and we can expect that even when the trend is reversed, the shortage of people that age is likely to continue through most of the decade. Under

As soon as you drive into Hershey you know you're supposed to enjoy yourself! After all, any place that has (Hershey) candy kisses for street lights, such as those on Chocolate Avenue shown at left, must be meant for fun. The Hershey Hotel dining room is famous for fine food and the service of a classic luxury hotel.

DESTINATION CITY—HERSHEY

The emergence of "destination cities"—towns that present themselves as major tourist attractions—is already a fact of life in American tourism. In the future other towns are likely to emulate cities such as Hershey, Pennsylvania, where the local manufacturing plant (Hershey Chocolate) has been made into a tourist attraction and where even the city's street lights follow the theme. Hershey boasts a large theme

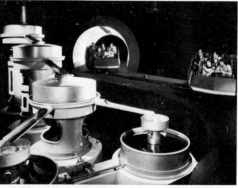

The local manufacturing plant tours became so popular that a special visitors' complex was developed to replace the former chocolate plant tour. The center includes a ride through a simulated world of chocolate, which realistically depicts the basic steps in the manufacture of chocolate.

Hersheypark, a large regional park that has themed areas such as Rhine Land (shown at right) and a variety of rides (such as "The Comet," shown above), offers an exciting day's entertainment to the whole family.

park, one of the country's finest luxury hotels, a sports complex offering a variety of indoor and outdoor sports, and a sizable convention center. The country's increasing affluence supports the growth of destination cities. (Photos courtesy of Hershey Foods Corp. and Hersheypark.)

Sports, indoor and outdoor, are a major attraction in Hershey. Spectator sports include basketball, hockey, and football. For those who want to be active themselves, Hershey's golf links beckon.

these circumstances, even as older workers are sought to fill the gaps, in many markets wage rates will continue to rise, and some companies may base their expansion plans on whether they can find the staff they need to operate. Most probably, labor costs will continue to rise; the use of part-time workers will grow; and the skills needed to motivate workers will become more important. So, too, will skills in scheduling, work simplification, and other measures aimed at alleviating labor costs.

We earlier noted the high average educational attainment of today's population. But we should also be aware that that poses some problems regarding the labor supply. Many people regard work in hospitality as too demanding, too dull, or beneath them. Although students in hospitality programs are aware of the challenge and excitement of hospitality industry careers, many people do not share those values.

Two possible solutions to the labor supply problem should be noted briefly. Immigration, both legal and illegal, is projected to provide as much as 20 to 25 percent of the work force in the 1990s. Another source of labor for the hospitality industry may well be the continuing decline in manufacturing employment.

COMPETITION

The number of restaurants is expanding at the rate of 10 percent per year, whereas the population is growing by only 2 percent.[4] Beyond that, competition in the industry has changed in kind. In the 1960s and 1970s the competition that the new concepts faced was with outmoded smaller operators. Now, however, the competition is among large established companies. Though there will always be room for new concepts to grow, the presence of established dominant brand names in many markets makes it much more difficult to get started even when the concept is really new.

As the competition has heated up, advertising expenditures have risen as well. In 1985, food service spent over a billion dollars on television advertising alone. McDonald's spent $686 million on marketing and had "top-of-mind awareness" (the name that comes to mind first is top of mind), with 41 percent of consumers queried in 1986, compared with 15 percent for second-place Burger King.[5] The massive marketing expenditures of the market leaders present another set of difficulties to a new operation seeking a toehold in a crowded marketplace.

We noted in Chapter 4 the competition of restaurants with grocery stores and especially convenience stores. In 1986, convenience stores' fast-food volume was in the range of 8 to 10 percent of their sales, and the market leaders expect to increase their food service performance to the point that the proportion is doubled. As fast food upgrades and expands its menu, the cost advantages of low-labor convenience store operations will multiply. Convenience stores obviously offer quick service and many locations, and so interindustry competition is likely to remain fierce.

[4] *Restaurants & Institutions*, October 29, 1986, p. 127.
[5] *Restaurants & Institutions*, July 23, 1986, p. 202.

TECHNOLOGY

The most revolutionary technology in all segments of the hospitality industry is the computer. With the greater pressure on cost control, information systems will continue to be essential. Perhaps even more important, however, are the managers who have learned how to interpret and use the output of those systems.

In lodging, the kinds of technology that make up the "smart hotel room" discussed in Chapter 8—technologies that improve guest services as well as control costs—can be expected to grow. Because of the competitive nature of lodging, an innovation such as using the guest-room television set as a terminal to check out guests is likely to be quickly matched by competing properties. Thus, technological advances, once successfully introduced, will spread rapidly through the appropriate segment or segments of the industry.

Emerging Trends

The only thing certain about the future is that it hasn't happened yet. Still, we can hazard a look at trends that appear well established and speculate about some that seem reasonably likely to emerge from other established trends.

A FRAGMENTING INDUSTRY

Over the past generation, there have emerged pronounced specialized divisions in the industry. In food service we've seen a division along the lines of the eating and dining markets. In lodging, the economy chains have carved a kind of niche, whereas the luxury property at the other end has sought a quite different place. In between are a number of specialized products aimed at specific target markets: superfloors, all-suites, mid-range properties, and upscale properties, for instance.

This specialization is not a coincidence. Rather, it is part of a pattern of an increasingly sophisticated, marketing-oriented industry seeking to shape its products and services to fit specific consumer segments. As competition continues and marketing skills improve, we can expect to see an even greater degree of specialization in lodging resulting from tighter market segmentation.

COMPETING WITH THE HOME

As consumers invest more in home entertainment centers—VCRs, cable and satellite television, home computers, hot tubs, and the like—they become more difficult customers to reach in the away-from-home market. One tactic we examined in Chapter 4 is to offer foods for takeout and home delivery, a development occurring across all food segments from haute cuisine to fast food. And this trend is likely to accelerate as consumers become more and more accustomed to shopping from home or via interactive cable television.

For those operations committed to serving the guest away from home—and particularly those who specialize in the dinner market, which is not as convenience bound as lunch is—we can see opportunities for those who are able to develop an ambience and operating format that combines food with entertainment. Entertainment formats—such as talking, singing, and dancing robots in combination with video games—that proved so successful in the early 1980s can be copied quickly. Moreover, their concept life is often limited because they come into fashion but then quickly become yesterday's fad. Perhaps the concept of restaurants as stages—building a flexible shell that can be restyled every couple of years—will be one solution. Another possibility is suggested by the discussion in the previous section on fragmentation. Operators have successfully identified the preferences of specific segments of the market, often by developing a product-service mix that includes an entertainment component that tempts a particular segment of people out of their home. The strategy of segmentation is likely to continue to do well, but with continuing pressure on operators to keep up with a changing, fashion- and fad-conscious consumer.

THE AGE OF THE INDEPENDENT?

In this and the next section we will explore two seemingly contradictory trends related to organization and affiliation. Certainly, the continuing growth of franchise organizations seems likely. That trend offers opportunities to those who want the advantages of owning their own business and are prepared to give up a measure of independence. The decision to seek a franchise, if it is carried out with the caution that a major investment warrants, offers a relatively low risk entrepreneurial opportunity.

There also are opportunities for those who don't want to give up planning their own operation and having full control of it. This opportunity is presented by the surge in the upscale market that comes with the growing middle-aged population segment. These are, by and large, sophisticated, demanding customers who are accustomed to travel and eating out. The mass-market, "cookie cutter" operations that most chains offer are likely to pall for many in this age group. They will dine out less or they will patronize the unique and new restaurants that catch their fancy.

One way that some entrepreneurs have taken advantage of the increasing primacy of the home is to enter the home-catering field. One of the main bars to owning one's own business is the large amount of capital needed to open the first operation. The catering business—a field that some students have entered while still in college—has minimum capital requirements and offers an opportunity to start on a small scale and grow.

CONGLOMERATES IN HOSPITALITY

Even though there are opportunities for franchisees and independents, the growth in mass-market tourism and hospitality continues to attract large companies like

Marriott, with its airline and institutional food service division as well as restaurants and hotels. Such companies could be called "hospitality conglomerates." In recent years, however, conglomerates from outside the hospitality industry, seeing our growth, have been attracted to our field because of a particular fit with what they see as their main business.

In today's world, companies buy and sell business units and are themselves bought and sold. It is like a dance in which everyone keeps changing partners. The following portrait of four conglomerates illustrates how a major business interest outside what we think of as hospitality can see organizational advantages in entering the hospitality field to capitalize on its related knowledge, systems, or marketing clout.

Allegis

Allegis includes one of North America's largest airlines, United Air Lines. It also owns the largest car rental agency in the United States, Hertz. In addition, the company has a travel wholesale operation, United Vacations, and owns the Apollo Reservation network.

What more logical development, then, than for Allegis to enter the hotel business, as it did some years ago with the purchase of Western International Hotels, now Westin Hotels. More recently, to strengthen its presence in the international market, Allegis purchased Hilton International.

We should probably note that the integration of these businesses is, to date, more limited than at first we might expect from their common ownership. Hertz reserves only cars and Westin only hotel rooms, and making a reservation at United won't lead to your being asked if you need a car or hotel room, nor does Hertz sell airline tickets or hotel rooms.

With a moment's reflection we are less surprised. These, really, are separate businesses each requiring a great deal of expertise and know-how. It just doesn't make sense to integrate them at the operating level because it would introduce mind-boggling complications. It is hard enough, for instance, to train a reservationist to the necessary level of competence in any one of those fields. Trying to develop that competence in all fields, then, would lead to very heavy training expense and reservation costs and raise the likelihood of error. Nevertheless, top management must feel that the joint expertise of the related travel and tourism enterprises gives it an edge in each market.

Bally

The Bally Manufacturing Corporation sees itself as a major factor in the leisure-time industry. The company's original business was coin-operated gaming (slot machines) and entertainment (pinball games) machine manufacturing. Bally continues to be one of the leading manufacturers of those products and, as well, has three of the most popular video games—Pac Man, Mrs. Pac Man, and Space Invaders. In addition, Bally's Operations Division is the largest operator of what it calls "family amusement centers," with over 400 locations in the United States, offering between 50 and 60 amusement games.

Bally is also the largest operator of health and fitness centers. Their units use the names of Holiday Spa, Vic Tanny, and, in New York, Jack La Lanne. As well, another subsidiary, Bally Fitness Products, manufactures exercise equipment.

Bally is also the second largest operator of theme parks in the world, operating Six Flags parks in New Jersey, Chicago, Dallas, Los Angeles, Atlanta, St. Louis, and Hollywood, Florida. Bally also operates Astroworld and Waterworld in Houston.

Bally has become a major factor in casino gaming and the hotel business, first with Bally's Park Place in Atlantic City and more recently with the purchase of the MGM Grand hotels in Las Vegas and Reno, Nevada. Annual casino revenues were over $600 million in 1986. Bally is also involved in public lotteries through its subsidiary, Scientific Games, Inc. In its advertisements, Bally says "America's Fun is Our Business." As with Allegis, the detailed logic of Bally's business definition isn't completely clear to an outsider. The link between its manufacturing arm and those using Bally's machines is clear. More generally, the company's ability to understand the leisure-time needs of Americans is probably heightened by the interaction of the units and the sharing of market research.

Pepsico

Pepsico began, of course, as a soft drink manufacturer. Pepsico is also a major factor in the snack business through its Frito-Lay subsidiary. By purchasing several food service companies, it has clearly secured a large number of outlets for its soft drinks, but that is hardly the full or even the main reason for those acquisitions. Food service is a highly profitable business for Pepsico. Its operations are well known under their own names: Pizza Hut and Taco Bell are leaders in their respective segments, and La Petite Boulangerie is a rapidly growing chain of restaurants using a French bake-shop theme as an organizing concept.

Pillsbury

The Pillsbury Company is an old-line food manufacturing company with its earliest roots in flour and baking products. Its food service companies, however, have come to represent 45 percent of its sales and over half of its operating profit. These companies include the number-two fast-food company, Burger King, as well as the S & A Restaurant Corp., operators of Steak and Ale, and Bennigans. Pillsbury also owns Quick Wok, a Chinese fast-food chain, Haägen-Dazs Ice Cream Shoppes, and Godfather's Pizza. The company, at any time, has several new concepts in various stages of testing.

Pillsbury sees itself as "a diversified, international food company uniquely positioned to serve existing and emerging needs in the food at home and food away from home markets." It describes its restaurant group as "the largest multi concept restaurant organization in the world, and a quality leader in the fast food, casual dining and full service areas."[6]

6 *Pillsbury 1986 Annual Report*, pp. 1, 14.

What is the future of fun?

In this institutional ad, aimed at investors, Bally stakes out their claim as the company that "makes America's fun their business." (Courtesy of Bally Manufacturing Corporation)

Conglomerates in Review

Companies like Allegis, Bally, Pepsico, and Pillsbury bring enormous financial and marketing resources to the hospitality industry. In many cases, companies such as these first purchase a young company with a promising operating format and give it the financial depth and organizational muscle to expand as a major national chain. From the consumer's point of view, then, they bring successful innovations to the mass market. From the point of view of the hospitality industry, they are one of the factors leading to heightened competition. Given the prospects for growth in the hospitality, leisure, and tourism businesses, we can probably expect to see more such companies entering our industry and contributing to its fast pace of change, development, and growth.

THREATS

War, pestilence, and famine have been a threat to every civilization, and that continues to be true today. On the other hand, we have passed through one of the longest periods in modern history without a major war—over 40 years. Pestilence, epidemic disease, becomes less of a problem with every advance in modern medicine. Famine is the unhappy lot of some, particularly in Africa, but it, too, seems unlikely as a major problem in North America.

On the other hand, there are problems we have been living with for some years that can't be dismissed readily. One of these is a possible resurgence of the energy crisis. Although the stocks of petroleum have been adequate in recent years, oil is not just a commodity but also a political weapon and hence unpredictable. Since the energy crisis has abated, the United States' consumption of foreign oil has increased substantially, and as prices have fallen, U.S. oil production and exploration have fallen as well.[7] Thus, the United States is vulnerable to another energy crisis.

Should a new crisis develop, we know from experience that in the short run, the hospitality industry would be badly disrupted. In the longer run, higher fuel prices seem to have resulted in a rearrangement of travel destinations that favors regional centers closer to home. But people still travel. We might expect another energy crunch to give further impetus to plans already under way to improve rail transportation which, to date, have been brought on largely by highway congestion.[8] As we noted in Chapter 12, any significant shift from highway to rail transportation would have major implications for restaurants serving travelers and especially for hotels.

Another threat whose outcome is less predictable is that of a major international or domestic monetary crisis. The economics of that danger—related to international debts in the Third World and to the trade deficit in the United States—is well beyond our concern here. We will just say that such an event could create a panic that would be terribly disruptive for businesses and individuals alike. The possibility of such a crisis has loomed for several years, however, and money managers have managed to lead us through successfully so far. We can only hope their luck—and ours—will hold.

Perhaps these two possibilities are most useful to us, though, in raising *the issue of uncertainty* in any look at the future. In this chapter we have looked at what is called a "surprise-free projection." That is, we have assumed that there will be no major unforeseen developments, either good or bad. We've said that the future will probably be a continuation of trends already in place, and usually, it is. When presenting this kind of reasoning, however, it is incumbent on the writer to note that if there *is* a surprise, some bets may be off.

The Future and You

We began this volume with an exploration of your interests in the industry and some consideration of how you might make a place for yourself in it. This is also an appropriate note on which to end. Three points particularly deserve summary consideration: an industrywide view, the notion of retained earnings, and the need to develop a personal strategy.

[7] *Wall Street Journal*, November 3, 1986, p. 6.
[8] *Meeting News*, February 15, 1986, p. 30.

THE HOSPITALITY INDUSTRY

Your interest may lie today in a particular area of the industry. They will necessarily become specialized as you take your first job after completing your schooling. Although you certainly must specialize to do an excellent job at whatever you are doing then and concentrate your energies there, it will also help you keep a view of the whole industry in mind. As the industry changes and evolves, you may encounter opportunities that suit your goals better in, say, club work or institutions. The reverse might just as easily be true. The hospitality industry is, and will continue to be, characterized by a good deal of movement from one segment to another.

In charting a career, you should keep your goals clearly in view. Your early jobs should probably be in areas that prepare you for the variety of opportunities in the hospitality industry now and in the future. Thus, experience in food service offers a background useful and often essential to practically all of the industry's components. Although front-office work (for example) is extremely rewarding, it offers limited opportunities for growth and little basis for a move to other sectors of the industry.

RETAINED EARNINGS

The notion that what you have learned is something no one can take from you is central to this text. The idea that you can learn a great deal more from every job than just the job itself is equally important. As anyone moves through a career, he or she occasionally finds a job that does not make the fullest use of his or her abilities. For these jobs to be profitable in the fullest sense, they must be explored from the perspective of what you can learn to make them really productive *for you.*

Consider the many changes that appear to be in store for the industry and the possibility of opportunities presenting themselves from unexpected quarters. Thus, what you learn through *study and experience* are the most important assets you can develop early in your career.

STRATEGIES AND GOALS

Career goals differ from person to person. Not everybody needs or wants to be a Henry Ford. Some people seek fame and fortune in a career; others want enjoyable work and an adequate income. To some, income is most important; to others helping other people is the key. The main thing to realize is that whatever your objectives are, you are more likely to attain them with consciously developed plans that move you toward definite goals.

Of course, setting goals is never easy and is always harder for some than others, so you must be patient. You may decide that, for now, your goal will be to form goals as soon as you can! If you cannot realistically set lifetime goals at the moment, you can adopt a policy of exploration and set intermediate goals that support that policy.

Although long-range goals are important, so are medium-range and short-range planning. These may even be more important for young people, because long-range goals have a way of evolving with experience and opportunity. Thus, it is important to ask yourself what you want to get done this week! What can you *learn* from your new job besides the job itself? How much should you be earning a year from now? What is the next job you want to seek with your current employer?

It is important to have goals, but it is equally important to develop the strategies and tactics for moving toward your goals. This notion invites you to see yourself as an active element in your career; not as someone who waits for things to happen but as someone who makes his or her own place in the world. Remember, no matter who your employer is, you are in business for yourself. It is your life!

Summary

In our final chapter we looked at the principal forces shaping the future of the hospitality industry. The basic economic forces are demand and supply. Demand encompasses consumer demographics; employment, income, and demand for hospitality; and education's impact on hospitality. Supply includes the supply of food and labor, and competition. We also considered technology as a major force.

Then we looked at the emerging trends: the fragmentation of the hospitality industry, competition with the home, and whether the independent or the conglomerate will reign. We illustrated the hospitality conglomerate with four examples, Allegis, Bally, Pepsico, and Pillsbury.

We examined the possible threats to the future hospitality industry.

And finally, we considered the hospitality industry in the future—and you.

Index

1

The Hospitality Industry and You

Commentary

While many of you know exactly what you want to do with your life and have your career mapped out, most are "shopping" for a career. If you are one of the latter, you may be considering several majors and a variety of career options. Even for those of you who have chosen hospitality as a career, the question of which segment of the industry you want to work in may not be settled yet. Moreover, even if you're pretty sure of what you want to do, opportunities for more advancement or more pay may come your way in the future from a different segment than the one you begun in so it's best to have an overall view. This chapter will help you address the very serious issues of career choice in a positive way.

The chapter deliberately asks you to tie the classroom to work experiences. It offers you the chance to see the start of this course as a first step in a career. You will be able to identify with both your current interests and your long-term goals. The chapter concludes by emphasizing the favorable outlook for hospitality careers.

Chapter Outline

What Is the Hospitality Industry?
    The Employee's Role in the Hospitality Industry
Why Study in a Hospitality Program?
Planning a Career
    Why Do We Work?
Employment an Important Part of Your Education
    Profiting from Work Experience
        Learning Strategies for Work Experience
        Learning from the Back of the House
        Learning from the Front of the House
    Getting a Job
        Getting in the Door
        Learning from a Job
        Other Ways of Profiting from a Job
Employment at Graduation
    The Strategy of Job Placement

The Outlook for the Hospitality Industry
  Demand for Hospitality Services
  Labor Supply
      Industry Conditions
Summary

Review of Chapter Objectives

Name five businesses in the hospitality industry:

1. _____

2. _____

3. _____

4. _____

5. _____

At this point in time, what is your career goal? _____

_____

_____

_____

Ideally, the jobs you would like to have in obtaining your career goal are:

1. _____

2. _____

3. _____

4. _____

5. _____

List the hospitality jobs that summer work experience and/or the part-time work experience would help you obtain your career goal:

1. _____

2. _____

3. _____

4. _____

5. _____

Which courses in your curriculum and elective courses will help you obtain your career goal?

1. _____

2. _____

3. _____

4. _____

5. _____

(use an additional sheet of lined paper if necessary)

In your opinion, where do you think the best opportunities will be for you when you finish your education?

_____

_____

_____

KEY WORDS AND PHRASES

In the space provided define the key word or phrase.

Hospitality (definition): _____

_____

_____

The job benefit mix from work experience is: _____

_____

_____

The "total income" from work experience such as a dishwasher, is more valuable

because: _____

_____

_____

In restaurants the "back of the house" is: _____

_____

_____

In restaurants the "front of the house" is: _____

_____

REVIEW QUESTIONS

True/False

Answer the following questions by circling T for true or F for false.

T   F   **1.** The concept of retained earnings as applied to work experience means that you should accept only a well-paid job that will compensate you for your education.

T   F   **2.** The notion of "liberality and good will" applies principally to commercial hospitality operations and not to the institutional sector.

T   F   **3.** You should choose your career path carefully in the hospitality industry because it is difficult to shift from one phase of the industry to another—say from hotels to restaurants or vice versa.

T   F   **4.** Work contributes to our self-esteem in three ways: income, self-worth, and happiness.

T   F   **5.** The "total income" derived from work experience is not only income but the learning or "retained earnings."

T   F   **6.** Important areas for observation in a field experience are formal organization and physical plant.

T   F   **7.** Charting activities in the front of the house will help you understand the flow of service through the organization.

T   F   **8.** Who reports to who in the organization is called the social organization.

T   F   **9.** In choosing your first job, starting salary should be your primary concern.

T   F   **10.** According to industry studies, those who spend the most on dining and traveling are between 35 to 54 years of age.

Multiple Choice

Choose the *one best* answer.

1. The hospitality industry today
   a. is defined as a "hospice" or house of rest
   b. includes only hotels and food service establishments
   c. traces its roots to medieval hospitals
   d. requires broadly gauged generalists

2. "Retained earnings" as applied to work experience means
   a. saving a portion of your earnings for the interest it will earn.
   b. joining a stock purchase plan with the company you work for.

    c. accepting only a well-paid job that compensates you for your education.

    d. seeking learning as well as income from a job.

3. One of the fastest growing segments of food service is

    a. fast food

    b. country inns

    c. franchising

    d. catering

4. In a social context work

    a. is a means of survival

    b. is a job with improved working conditions

    c. is a vocation

    d. produces something of value for other people

5. The formal organization of business deals with

    a. who the leaders in the department are

    b. who the influential workers are

    c. who reports to who

    d. who the owners or stockholders and managers are

6. A "vacation relief" is

    a. what you feel when you return to school in the fall

    b. the name the hospitality industry coined for resorts

    c. a worker who fills in for another on vacation

    d. a manager who pitches in when employees get overworked

7. The "benefit mix" of an entry-level job means

    a. looking at all aspects of a job in relation to what you will get from that job

    b. the professional certification of a job

    c. the combination of wages and fringe benefits such as health insurance, vacation, and pensions

    d. taking a low-pay job in a restaurant that serves good food

8. The age group *least* likely to spend money on travel and restaurants is

    a. 30 to 35

    b. 35 to 40

    c. 40 to 45

    d. 45 to 50

9. A statement that is *not* expected to be true about the hospitality industry's future is

    a. food service will continue to provide meals for families in which both spouses work

    b. that retailers like convenience stores will expand into the food service market

    c. there will be an over-supply of entry-level workers throughout this decade

    d. middle-aged persons will tend to spend more in restaurants.

Fill in the Blank

Fill in the blanks with the best answer.

1. When you gain work experience that provides you with learning experience as well as some income, the knowledge received can be viewed as

    _____ _____

2. The *benefit mix* of work experience includes _____ and

    _____.

3. The dining room manager and the service staff work in the _____ _____

    _____ _____ while the chef and kitchen crew work in the

    _____ _____ _____ _____.

4. The three reasons students select hospitality programs are: _____,

    _____, and _____.

5. In the 1990s, because of the baby boomers, competition will be stiff in the

    _____ ranks.

DISCUSSION QUESTIONS

Answer the following essay questions.

1. Name as many businesses as you can that can be considered part of the hospitality industry. Discuss the common elements that these businesses have.

2. Using the demographic charts, discuss competition for jobs in your age group 10 years from now. Discuss the outlook in the hospitality industry.

PROJECT

1. Draw a rough diagram of the kitchen and service area of the restaurant or hospitality operation where you work or have worked. Use arrows to indicate the flow of product from receiving to customer. Identify bottlenecks where service is consistently slowed.

2

The Restaurant Business

Commentary

This chapter has three basic goals. First, it helps you explore hospitality careers by discussing various kinds of restaurants. Second, it will help you adopt an organized way of thinking about the various kinds of restaurants in terms of menu, style of preparation and service, and guest needs and wants.

We can divide restaurants, for instance, into operational categories such as full-service or specialty restaurants. Specialty restaurants can be further broken down into service categories such as fast food or family restaurants. We can also look at operations in terms of their specialty items such as steak or pizza. Another way of dividing up the operations is in terms of what guests want from them. Some operations exist principally to feed hungry people—while others offer social prestige or "experience" dining. For this reason, we can speak of the "eating" and the "dining" market. The typologies developed here build toward concepts which open Chapter 3.

Finally, the chapter introduces you to the "bare bones" vocabulary needed to talk about restaurant operations. Such terms as food cost, guest count, check average, and others are defined.

Chapter Outline

The Varied Field of Food Service
The Restaurant Business
    Full-Service Restaurants
    Speciality Restaurants
        Fast Food
        Other Speciality Restaurants
The Dining Market and the Eating Market
    Dining Well
        Haute Cuisine Restaurants
        Casual Dinner Houses
        Theme Restaurants
        Ethnic Restaurants

Significant Entries into the Eating Market
  Cafeterias
  Country Cooking
  "Gourmet" Hamburgers
  Take Out and Delivery
Restaurants as a Part of a Larger Business
  Restaurants in Retailing
Operating Ratios
  Cost of Sales
  Controllable Expenses
  Capital Costs
Summary

Review of Chapter Objectives

List the major components within each restaurant category and their relative size in today's food service market. Include a short description so that you are able to contrast the different types of restaurants.

Full-Service Restaurants

1. _____

2. _____

3. _____

4. _____

Specialty Restaurants

1. _____

2. _____

3. _____

4. _____

Restaurants in the Dining Market

1. _____

2. _____

3. _____

4. _____

5. _____

6. _____

7. _____

8. _____

9. _____

Name the key operating costs for restaurants. Describe how they are used as a measure of performance.

_____

_____

_____

_____

_____

_____

_____

_____

_____

_____

_____

_____

_____

_____

_____

_____

Key Words and Phrases

In the space provided define the Key Word or phrase.

A haute cuisine restaurant can be defined as: _____

_____

A neighborhood restaurant is: _____

_____

A fast food restaurant differs from full service restaurants as follows: _____

_____

_____

The dining market serves our _____ needs while the eating market serves our _____ needs.

Theme restaurants are: _____

They are classified as _____ restaurants.

A theme restaurant's menu is _____.

Food cost is (definition): _____

Beverage cost is (definition): _____

Direct operating expenses are: _____

_____

A check average is: _____

Using the price/service chart, place names of restaurants in their approximate location on the chart. If possible list at least one restaurant in each category.

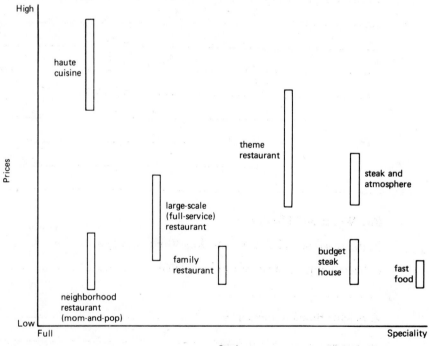

Figure 2.1   *The range of restaurants compared on the basis of service type and relative price.*

An average cover is: _____

_____

REVIEW QUESTIONS

True/False

Answer the following questions by circling T for true or F for false.

T F **1.** Hotel restaurants account for higher sales than any other food service category.

T F **2.** Sales in the restaurant industry during the last decade grew at the same rate as other industries.

T F **3.** Full-service restaurants tend to be more labor intensive than specialty restaurants.

T F **4.** Neighborhood restaurants have been replaced for the most part by franchises, fast food, and other specialty restaurants.

T F **5.** Luxury restaurants typically are not profitable because of the labor cost of classic service.

T F **6.** Introducing a new product in a fast food restaurant is easier than in a traditional restaurant because preparation of the food item is typically simpler.

T F **7.** The product that a fast food organization sells to potential purchasers of its franchise is their total operating system.

T F **8.** Although the baby boomers have grown older, they still frequent fast food restaurants although many frequent upscale fast food operations.

T F **9.** A restaurant would determine its bar cost percent by dividing bar sales by bar product costs.

T F **10.** An haute cuisine restaurant would be expected to have a lower prime cost than a fast food restaurant.

Multiple Choice

Choose the *one best* answer.

1. A donut shop is usually classified as a
   a. specialty restaurant
   b. budget restaurant
   c. full-service restaurant
   d. take-out shop

2. The largest sector in food service is
   a. institutional food service
   b. hotels, motels, and motor inns
   c. restaurants, cafeterias, and taverns
   d. commercial food service

3. Technology in fast food restaurants has
   a. developed new automated kitchen equipment
   b. automated the worker with highly repetitive tasks
   c. automated production procedures
   d. automated the customers behavior

4. Before a new menu item can be added to a fast food menu,
   a. it goes through product development, test marketing, and a major advertising campaign
   b. it is tested in a specified number of units for customer acceptance
   c. it must be modified to fit the existing packaging and equipment in the restaurants
   d. a national television, radio, and other media campaign must be developed by the chain

5. The growth of fast food units in the early 1980s
   a. decreased with the recessionary periods of the early 1980s
   b. was about level with population growth
   c. was much greater than the rate of population growth
   d. was about the same as other types of restaurants

6. Pizza restaurants have experienced growth in
   a. home delivery
   b. additional units
   c. expanded menu offerings
   d. adding breakfast as a day part

7. Restaurants such as "Steak and Ale," "Chi-Chi's," "TGI Friday's" are
   a. noted for informality and fun
   b. moderately priced, and appeal to middle-aged consumers
   c. focus on quality service at a low price
   d. serve only food prepared from scratch

8. A food service operation that can be considered a service to another organization is
   a. a restaurant in a hotel
   b. a food fair restaurant in a shopping center
   c. a fast food restaurant on an army base
   d. an ethnic restaurant

9. Cost of sales is generally divided into
   a. food cost and bar costs
   b. restaurant costs and room costs
   c. meat, dairy, and groceries cost
   d. controllable and uncontrollable costs

10. Payroll cost is
    a. a capital cost
    b. a controllable expense
    c. a cost of sales
    d. a mixed cost

MATH REVIEW

Dealing with Operating Ratios You Will Use in Restaurant Operations

Cost of Sales

Food Cost—the formula for determining food cost is:

Cost of Food Sold divided by Food Sales

$$\frac{\text{Cost of food sold}}{\text{Food sales}} \quad \frac{\$1,000}{\$3,000} = .333$$

Since *Food cost* is expressed as a percent we multiply .333 by 100 = 33.3% and we say that our food cost is 33.3 percent.

Now practice determining food cost percent:

$$\text{Cost of food sold} = 14,000$$
$$\text{Food sales} = 50,000$$

Therefore

Food cost percent = _____ divided by _____ × 100 = _____.

Now work these problems:

Cost of Food Sold	Food Sales	Food Cost (%)
$8,400	$30,000	_____
$22,050	$63,000	_____
$32,528	$85,600	_____

Beverage Cost is determined in the same way. Note: we use *Beverage Sales* only:

Beverage Cost Percent

$$\frac{\text{Cost of beverages sold}}{\text{Beverage sales}} = \times 100 = _____$$

Using this formula, which is the same formula as food cost percent, determine the beverage cost percent, or, as we say in industry, "our beverage cost" or "our bar cost."

Cost of Beverages Sold	Beverage Sales	Beverage Cost (%)
$4,500	$15,000	_____
$856	$4,280	_____
$17,550	$50,895	_____

Check Average and Average Cover

Check average is determined as follows:

$$\text{Sales divided by number of guest checks} = \text{check average}$$

$$\frac{\text{Food sales}}{\text{Number of checks}} = \frac{\$1,000}{10} = \$100$$

Now determine the check average for this day in a restaurant:

There were food sales of $1,740 and 30 guest checks were collected from the wait staff at the end of the day. The check average was _____.

However, in the above two examples, each guest check may have more than one person in the party, and most restaurants use an *average cover* which is determined as follows:

$$\text{Sales divided by total number of guests} = \text{average cover}$$

$$\frac{\text{Food sales}}{\text{Total number of guests}} = \frac{\$1,000}{40} = \$25$$

Now determine the "average cover" for the restaurant above.

The 30 guest checks were collected from the wait staff and the number of guests on each check was counted and the total was 132 guests. The average cover was _____.

Note: Most restauranteurs use the term "check average" when they really mean average cover.

DISCUSSION QUESTIONS

Answer the following essay questions.

1. Discuss the process that is used by fast food organizations to put a new food product on their menu.

2. Today some say there are major innovations or changes in restaurant concepts every three years. What changes have you noticed in the food service industry in your lifetime?

PROJECT

1. Determine how much of your food dollars you spend eating out. In a small notebook, write down the amount you spend for groceries for two weeks. Also record how much you spend eating out. Determine the percent of your food dollars you spend eating out (add up how much you spent eating out and divide by your total food expenditures—groceries plus money spent eating out—and then multiply by 100 to obtain a percentage).

3

Issues Facing Food Service

Commentary

This chapter continues the career exploration theme of Chapter 2 emphasizing, however, the dynamics of the restaurant business. After putting Chapter 2's discussion of typologies into a future-oriented model emphasizing the direction of change, the chapter turns to two important subjects. First, it explores the independent versus chain or franchise question, emphasizing the differing relative advantages of each. Then the question of changing restaurant size is explored.

The chapter next turns to a topic that has a vital impact on operating practices and trends: consumers. First, you will look at consumers as people—who they are, what kind of customers they are, and what their concerns are. Then the focus shifts to organized, collective action led by consumerists. Finally, we consider the consumer's and the industry's interest in convenience.

Chapter Outline

Organizational Form: Chain, Independent, or Franchise?
Chain Specialty Restaurants
Brand Recognition
Site Selection Expertise
Access to Capital
Purchasing Economies
Control and Information Systems
Personnel Program Development
Performance of the Top 100 Restaurant Companies
Operating Advantages of the Independent
Brand Recognition
Site Selection
Access to Capital
Purchasing Economies
Control and Information Systems
Personnel

Review of Chapter Objectives

List the advantages and disadvantages for chains and independents.

Brand Recognition

Chains _____

Independents _____

Site Selection

Chains _____

Independents _____

Access to Capital

Chains _____

Independents _____

Purchasing Economies

Chains _____

Independents _____

Control and Information Systems

Chains _____

Independents _____

Purchasing Economies

Chains _____

Independents _____

Flexibility

Chains _____

Independents _____

Describe How Consumer Demand in the Restaurant Industry Is Affected by

Age _____

Income _____

Family size _____

Two-income households _____

Name some key consumer problems and concerns about dining in restaurants. How has the restaurant industry responded to these demands?

	Concern	*Industry Response*
1.	_____	_____
2.	_____	_____
3.	_____	_____
4.	_____	_____
5.	_____	_____
6.	_____	_____

KEY WORDS AND PHRASES

Fill in the following blanks with the best word or phrase.

In this chapter restaurants are classed as a unit of a C _____, a F _____, or an I _____.

The major competitive differences between chain and independent restaurants are in the areas of:

1. _____

2. _____

3. _____

4. _____

5. _____

6. _____

The difference between a chain and a franchise is: _____

_____

Consumer demand is affected by:

1. _____

2. _____

3. _____

4. _____

Major consumer concerns are:

1. _____

2. _____

3. _____

Consumerism has as its objective: _____

_____

REVIEW QUESTIONS

True/False

Answer the following questions by circling T for true or F for false.

T   F   1. An example of economy of scale is that savings are made by dividing costs among a number of units.

T   F   2. An independent restaurant has better site selection than a chain because they know their local real estate people.

T   F   3. While an independent operator may not be able to obtain significant price breaks from a purveyor, he or she can demand consistent top of the line quality that will help compete with chains.

T   F   **4.**   The cost of training is usually higher for an independent unit than for a chain-run operation.

T   F   **5.**   A franchisee is typically an independent owner-operator.

T   F   **6.**   In a rapidly changing society, fast food chains are able to remain the same if they constantly tell their customer what their purpose is.

T   F   **7.**   The fast track "yuppies" who earn $30,000 or more a year, contrary to what you hear, actually spend *less* on food away from home.

T   F   **8.**   While consumers talk about reducing sugar, fat, and cholesterol in their diets, few have changed their eating habits.

T   F   **9.**   Nutritional labeling would negatively affect the consumers view of fast food.

T   F   **10.**   For many consumers, convenience is more important than food quality and price when making dining-out decisions.

Multiple Choice

Choose the *one best* answer.

1.   To promote brand recognition, most chains
   a.   simplify their ads
   b.   use word-of-mouth
   c.   depend on consistency in each unit
   d.   spend around 3 percent of sales on advertising

2.   The "additive effect" means that
   a.   total advertising is equal to the sum of the budgets of all units
   b.   television commercials are added as units are added
   c.   total sales are increased through additional franchisees
   d.   consumers concern has led to the use of fewer additives in food

3.   One operating advantage that an independent *usually* has over a chain or franchise is
   a.   rapid adaptation to changing situations
   b.   ability to choose a local site for the restaurant
   c.   friendly bankers willing to loan money
   d.   negotiating with suppliers

4.   An independent operator usually does *not* have as much expertise as a chain with
   a.   control systems
   b.   flexibility of decision making
   c.   motivation to succeed
   d.   operational supervision

5. If your best friend decided to go into the restaurant business today, the advice you would *not* give him or her would be:
   a. the operation must define itself in terms of the customers' needs
   b. the operation must be aware of changing consumer needs
   c. the operation must be willing to accede to the preferences of its customers
   d. the operation must reflect the personality of the owner

6. The reason many fast food chains sell hamburgers, French fries and milk shakes rather than "healthier" food is
   a. because these foods are easy to prepare
   b. their customers prefer this menu
   c. because these foods fit the fast food restaurant image
   d. because it's a subversive plot to undermine the health of Americans

7. Younger consumers, compared to middle-aged consumers,
   a. spend a higher percentage of their income on food away from home
   b. spend more each time they dine away from home
   c. have about the same spending pattern on food away from home
   d. are not good food service customers because they cannot afford to dine out

8. Consumer preferences today tend to
   a. desire both healthy foods like salads and high fat foods like ice cream
   b. be going toward healthier food with a decline in high fat junk foods
   c. demand more rich, high fat food such as French fries and milk shakes
   d. be changing little

9. Current consumer issues in food service include
   a. cleanliness of premises, food preservatives, health foods
   b. food prices, truth in menu, nutrition
   c. nutritional health, food additives, alcohol consumption
   d. insurance liability, food and exercise, sulfites in food

10. The additive that has caused health problems in recent years is
   a. phosphates
   b. propionates
   c. monoglycerides
   d. sulfites

Fill in the Blanks

Fill in the blanks with the best answer.

1. Spreading a centralized activity over a large number of units represents

_____ of _____.

2. Standardized procedures that lower the cost of _____ are important in _____ and _____ jobs.

3. An independent operator can either own and operate their own restaurant or buy a _____.

4. Dealing with consumers with full candor rather than being evasive about food served in restaurants is called _____ in _____.

5. A new term for nibbling rather than dining in restaurants is called _____.

DISCUSSION QUESTIONS

Answer the following essay questions.

1. Identify an independent restaurant in your area. Compare this restaurant with a chain restaurant that is similar in size and menu. What advantages and disadvantages does each restaurant have?

2. Discuss one consumer issue related to restaurants that concerns you. If you operated a restaurant, how would you deal with this issue?

3. Which restaurants are you familiar with that have dealt with consumer issues? Discuss how they have made a consumer demand profitable for their operation.

PROJECTS

1. Collect menus from a chain operation, a franchise operation, and an independent restaurant. Compare these menus for flexibility.

2. Visit three restaurants that you think may be successfully dealing with nutrition problems. Talk with their managers and find out, if possible, if consumers appreciate attention to their concerns, and if this has affected their business positively.

4

The Future of the Restaurant Business

Commentary

Everyone likes to imagine the future! In this chapter you will look at the future of food service, not at a distant, far away future (this is almost impossible to predict), but at the next 10 or 15 years. In our society change has become an everyday occurrence, and you can adjust more easily to changes than your parents can because you have grown up with it. Some have said that concepts need to change as rapidly as every three years! The predictions we make in the chapter are based on trends that seem clear in the 1980s and that experts predict will continue for some years.

You will focus your attention on equipment and technology, energy costs, and competition, with an emphasis on how the food service industry may respond in the near future. The restaurant industry is a highly competitive one—and the industry has lots of competition from "outsiders," as well. This chapter will help you develop your skills in analyzing competitive trends. Finally, most important to you, employment opportunities in the future will be explored.

Chapter Outline

The Restaurant Industry: A View of Where We're Going
The Food Service Equipment of the Future
    Scaled-Down and Mobile Units
Energy Costs and Food Service
    Energy and the Transportation System
    Energy and Food Processing
    Energy and Disposables
    Energy and the General Hospitality Environment
Competition
    Competition within the Food Service Industry
        Advertising and Promotion
        Development of New Products
        Expansion of Day Parts

Review of Chapter Objectives

In Chapter 2 you looked at various restaurants in terms of price and service. Now we will look at restaurants and compare their complexity of delivery and how recently they entered the restaurant scene. Chose an actual restaurant for each category below and describe the complexity of service. Include food quality, menu complexity, service, prices, and ambience.

Name of restaurant   *Description of Delivery*

Traditional/high
priced restaurant   _____

_____

_____

Traditional/low
priced restaurant   _____

_____

_____

Innovative/high
priced restaurant   _____

_____

_____

Innovative/low
priced restaurant   _____

_____

_____

What are computers used in food service for? _____

_____

_____

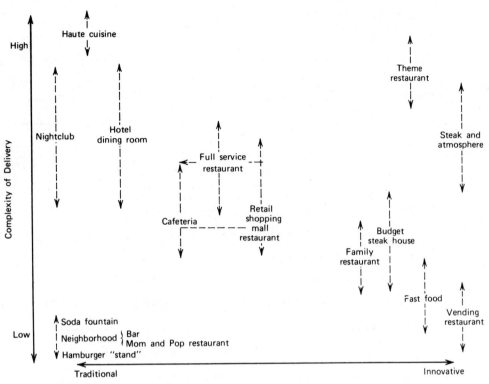

Figure 4.1.   *A Restaurant Typology*

The cost of energy will or will not impact food service. Briefly describe the impact of energy costs of the following:

Transportation _____

_____

Food processing _____

_____

_____

Disposables _____

_____

Food service meets competition in different ways. Describe how competition is met in the following areas:

Advertising and
promotion _____

_____

New Product
Development _____

_____

Day Part
Expansion _____

_____

Service
Expansion _____

_____

Prices _____

_____

Location _____

_____

In recent years restaurants have taken sales from grocery stores. How have they
responded? _____

_____

_____

KEY WORDS AND PHRASES

Fill in the following blanks with the best word or phrase.

Characteristics of a complex delivery system are: _____

_____

The feasibility of automation with regard to cost and guest acceptance in the
future: _____

_____

_____

The impact of computers will be: _____

_____

"Scaled" down units are usually feasible: _____

_____

Mobile restaurant units are used: _____

_____

Restaurant expansion is expected to: _____

_____

Define defensive and offensive new product expansion: _____

_____

_____

A "day-part" is: _____

Co-locating is: _____

In-home entertainment centers compete with restaurants because: ____

_____

The "baby bust" will contribute to: _____

Employment and entreprenurial opportunities will be: _____

_____

REVIEW QUESTIONS

True/False

Answer the following questions by circling T for true or F for false.

T   F   **1.**   In the next 10 years, automation and computerization of food service facilities will be commonplace.

T   F   **2.**   The problems of automation in restaurants are those of acceptance and cost rather than technical know-how.

T   F   **3.**   Mobile fast food restaurants have been designed and operated where there is a short-term demand for a restaurant.

T   F   **4.**   Although energy costs may increase in the future it is unlikely that in the next 10 years (barring a catastrophe) fast food operations will need to "dispose" of their plastic "disposables."

T   F   **5.**   New products are sometimes developed and added to menus to gain or just maintain market share.

T   F   **6.**   "Day part" expansion means that restaurants try to increase their overall sales volume by opening earlier or later, or by adding or enhancing a meal or snack period.

T   F   **7.**   The typical customer who buys sandwiches at the corner "C" store is a young man.

T   F   8.   Supermarkets compete effectively with restaurants because of price.

T   F   9.   Grocery store food prices have been growing at a slower rate than restaurant menu prices.

T   F   10. To be successful, existing fine dining restaurants have found it necessary to adapt to the aging baby boomers who prefer a more casual dining experience.

Multiple Choice

Choose the *one* best answer.

1. In the next 10 or 15 years, the restaurant industry will
   a. become much more automated
   b. be the same as it is today
   c. experience continued growth in specialty restaurants
   d. have an oversupply of unskilled workers

2. An innovative restaurant will typically
   a. have a limited menu
   b. tend to have a formal atmosphere
   c. try to get away from fast food because of the aging baby boomers
   d. have a complex delivery system

3. Computerization in food service
   a. will be able to replace workers
   b. will provide management with a cost control tool
   c. will be too expensive for all but large restaurants
   d. will not be applicable to many food service operations

4. Automation in the restaurant industry will probably occur in
   a. automated equipment
   b. robot servers
   c. information processing systems
   d. employee-free cooking stations

5. Successful centralized production facilities
   a. require a change from traditional restaurant thinking to factory thinking
   b. require traditional restaurant theory to maintain quality
   c. depend on a computerized distribution network
   d. operate independently of the restaurant

6. country-western festival is being held for three weeks this summer. They ld make use of the following innovative restaurant:
   a. scaled down restaurant
   b. permanent fast food restaurant

    c. commissary
    d. mobile unit

7. Energy intensive frozen food will continue to be used by food service because
    a. the cost of petroleum is expected to decrease
    b. of labor savings
    c. of new freezing processes
    d. of innovative cooking equipment

8. In the 1990s, restaurants will be impacted most by
    a. competition
    b. high labor costs
    c. computerization
    d. energy conservation

9. "Day part" expansions means that restaurants will
    a. have higher payrolls
    b. make better use of their capital investment
    c. have 24-hour operations
    d. be open for breakfast

10. A restaurant that has an agreement with a 24-hour grocery store to operate their stores on the same sites is an example of
    a. down-scaling
    b. locating strategy
    c. service expansion
    d. co-locating

Fill in the Blanks

Fill in the blanks with the best answer.

1. _____ _____ sales have grown approximately one and one-half times the rate of all restaurant sales.

2. Energy costs in 1985 accounted for _____ percent of operating costs in food service.

3. Restaurant expansion has slowed because of a slower growth of _____ _____ and _____ for consumer dollars.

4. When a fast food restaurant begins to lose market share, that is, when other restaurants take their business, they can meet this competition by introducing _____ _____.

5. Nearly three-quarters of the people working in fast food are between the ages of _____ and _____.

DISCUSSION QUESTIONS

Answer the following essay questions.

1. Describe the differences between what is technically possible in the restaurant industry and what is actually happening.

2. In general, comment on the age groups in our society and the effect these groups have on competition between restaurants.

3. Discuss the labor outlook in the industry and how it will affect your career.

PROJECTS

1. Using Figure 4.1 in your text, pick out three restaurants (traditional, middle of the road and highly innovative). Visit these restaurants and observe who their customers are. How are they dressed? What is their age? In other words, note everything you can about the customers that visit each restaurant (even things like the kind of cars/motorcycles that you see in the parking lot). Write a report describing the differences (you may wish to make a table) and make general statements about these differences.

2. Write a description of a restaurant you would like to design. Choose a definite age group and describe their interests as a starting point. Then describe the ambience, the service, and the menu. Finally, where would you locate your restaurant?

5

Institutional Food Service

Commentary

This chapter revolves around contrasts. First, there is the contrast between the institutional market and restaurant food service. Second, and even more important is the contrast between the institution that chooses to operate their own food service and those that choose contract companies.

The four principal institutional markets are identified and discussed in some detail. *Business and industry (B&I)* serves factory and office; *college and university* probably serves you—and hundreds of thousands of other students, a huge market but one that is changing rapidly. Before considering *school and community food service*, the chapter pauses to look at the impact of social change—particularly the way the family functions—on demand for institutional food service. This lays the ground work you need to understand the growth in school food service and the likely trends toward growth in community food service systems for the aging. Finally, we turn our attention to *health care food service*, discussing briefly the profession of dietetics and its allied paraprofessionals.

We consider some food preparation and delivery systems that are common to all segments of the industry ranging from preparation from scratch to the use of frozen chilled foods. At this point, too, we look at vending as a convenient and cost effective way of delivering food service.

The question of an institution's contracting for food service or operating its own is an interesting one and a look at the different operating styles and the risks and rewards they entail may help you think about which kind of operation you would like to work for.

Also considered in this chapter—very briefly—are two highly specialized institutional food service operations: military food service and in-flight food service.

Unfortunately many HRI students overlook the many opportunities in the growing institutional food service field. We hope that this exploration will open your mind to the very real challenges in institutional food service.

Chapter Outline

Comparing Institutional and Commercial Food Services
Contract Companies and Institutional Operations
Institutional Food Service Operations
    Business and Industry Food Service
    College and University Food Service
    Health-Care Food Service
        The Dietetic Professional
        The Dietetic Technician
        The Dietary Manager
        Dietary Department Organization
        Trends in Health-Care Food Service
        Entreprenurial Opportunities
    School and Community Food Service
        The National School Lunch Program (NSLP)
        The School Food Service Model
    Food Service Programs for the Aging
Preparation and Delivery Systems
    Vending
Who Operates an Institution's Food Service?
    Responsibilty for Institutional Operations
        Institutional Operators
        Contract Companies
Other Institutional Food Service Segments
    Military Food Service
    In-Flight Food Service
The Future of Institutional Food Service
Summary

Review of Chapter Objectives

Describe the principal differences between *institutional* and *commercial* food service:

Customer _____

Client _____

Budget target _____

Sales predictability _____

Type of menu _____

Describe the principal differences between *institutional operators* and *contract companies* (both of whom provide institutional food services):

	Institutional	Contract
Who do they work for	_____	_____
Areas of heavy market share	_____	_____
	_____	_____
	_____	_____
	_____	_____
Economies of scale	_____	_____
Control of operations	_____	_____
Management expertise	_____	_____
Contrast in benefits	_____	_____

Name the *four* major segments of institutional food service and characteristics of each:

Segments	Characteristics
1. _____	_____
	_____
	_____
2. _____	_____
	_____
	_____
3. _____	_____
	_____
	_____
4. _____	_____
	_____

Describe the rapidly growing elderly institutional food service market in terms of:

1. Demographics _____

_____

2. Changing family roles _____

_____

3. Income levels of elderly _____

_____

4. Nutritional and social goals of food service programs _____

_____

KEY WORDS AND PHRASES

Fill in the following blanks with the best word or phrase.

Today, the institutional "captive" market is _____

_____

The client for an institutional food service is _____

_____

The sales in business and industry institutional food services are directly related to

_____ and _____

Describe the following board plans:

Full _____

Flexible _____

Credit card _____

Package price advantages _____

The female labor force participation rate can be defined as: _____

_____

NSLP stands for: _____ _____ _____ _____

The four elements of the NSLP model are:

1. _____

2. _____

3. _____

4. _____

The social needs provided by the NSLP are: _____ and _____

By pooling subsidies, school lunches are paid for by: _____

_____

Population trends for the elderly until the end of the century: _____

_____

Congregate meals can be defined as: _____

_____

_____

Deinstitutionalization of social services for the elderly can affect food services by:

_____

Describe the differences among these occupations:

Therapeutic dietitian _____

Administrative dietitian _____

Registered dietitian _____

Dietetic technician _____

Dietary manager _____

DRGs are _____ _____ _____ and can be defined as

_____

Nutritional support companies perform the function of _____

_____

Briefly describe the food service systems below:

Conventional food service system _____

_____

Ready foods system _____

_____

Convenience food system _____

_____

The "delivery system" in institutional food service means: _____

_____

The leading product sold from vending machines is: _____

Manual vending is: _____

"The 400" are: _____

The four categories of military food service groups are:

1. _____

2. _____

3. _____

4. _____

REVIEW QUESTIONS

True/False

Answer the following questions by circling T for true or F for false.

T   F   **1.** People who eat in institutional food service operations today usually have no other choice of places to eat.

T   F   **2.** The food service operation in an institutional setting is almost always a small part of a larger organization whose purpose is usually something entirely different.

T   F   **3.** Institutional food service is usually not in competition with nearby restaurants and fast food operations.

T   F   **4.** A problem with a board plan is that sales volume is difficult to predict in advance.

T   F   **5.** College enrollments are expected to decline until the mid-1990s.

T   F   **6.** The greatest impact of the increase in working women has been in luncheon food service sales.

T   F   **7.** The federal government has continually increased funding for school lunch programs because of the needs of working mothers.

T   F   **8.** School lunches are a bargain because usually federal, state, and local governments subsidize the cost.

T   F   **9.** A registered administrative dietitian is trained in nutrition, but is involved with managing the dietary department rather than with day-to-day dietary education for patients and planning special diets.

T   F   **10.** The effect of government programs like DRG and RUG has been to extend patient stay in hospitals and thus increase the total number of meals served.

Multiple Choice

Choose the *one best* answer.

1. Commercial and institutional food services are distinctly different in terms of
    a.   the firms that operate in these sectors
    b.   competition
    c.   the purpose of the organization
    d.   meeting cost goals

2. The largest segment of the total institutional market (in terms of sales) is
    a.   business and industry
    b.   colleges and universities
    c.   health care
    d.   schools

3. Business and industry food service
    a.   provides food for workers in factories, offices, and commercial establishments
    b.   is a vending food service operation
    c.   pertains to operations managed by contract food service companies
    d.   is a company that operates in both the commercial and institutional setting

4. The female labor-force participation rate is
    a.   the number of women in factory jobs
    b.   the proportion of women employed in the food service industry
    c.   women working in the labor force compared to women working at home
    d.   the proportion of working women and women seeking employment in the population

5. The school lunch program as it exists today in the United States
    a.   attempts to meet today's social problems
    b.   is subsidized by federal funds which benefit primarily middle- and high-income families
    c.   is a vehicle for using surplus food commodities
    d.   is dominated by contract food service feeders

6. The segment of the U.S. population that has the highest growth *rate* is
    a.   babies
    b.   teenagers
    c.   middle aged
    d.   seniors

7. The dietary department is usually organized under
    a.   the administrative services division of the hospital
    b.   the professional services division of the hospital
    c.   the fiscal services division of the hospital
    d.   the general services division of the hospital

8. The food service system most commonly chosen for school lunches in a large city school district with many sites is a
   a. ready food system
   b. convenience food system
   c. centralized commissary
   d. frozen food system

9. Vended meals are most common in
   a. government locations
   b. factories
   c. offices
   d. grade and high schools

10. In a *small* institution, a contract food service company can operate more efficiently in the area of
    a. quality control
    b. personnel scheduling
    c. purchasing
    d. menu change

Fill in the Blanks

Fill in the blanks with the best answer.

1. The major growth in business and industry has been in _____ and _____ while less growth has occurred in _____.

2. The impact of working women/working mothers has particularly impacted institutional food service for _____ and _____.

3. The four elements of the daily nutritional requirements are:
   1. _____ 2. _____ 3. _____ 4. _____

4. Higher participation rates in school lunch programs results in higher _____ and _____.

5. The criteria for congregate meals are to provide food for the _____ which is _____ cost, _____ sound, and in _____ settings. The program provides at least _____ meal per day, _____ days a week.

6. The three categories of health care food service facilities are:
   1. _____ 2. _____ 3. _____

7. A RUG is a _____ _____ _____ and is the nursing home equivalent of a _____ _____ _____.

DISCUSSION QUESTIONS

Answer the following essay questions.

1. Discuss the importance of the client to the contract food service company and how the client's needs can be accommodated. Does the institutional operator have the same problem?

2. If you had to choose between an institutional or a contract food service company for university food service, which would you choose? Support your choice.

3. Describe how you might go about increasing the participation rate in a high school lunch room.

PROJECT

1. Visit a hospital and diagram the product flow from receiving the food to patient. Identify the type of system, describe the delivery system in use, and assess potential problems (either for the hospital or for the patient). Find out who operates the food service: the hospital or a contract food service company. Finally, what are the opportunities for *you* in health care food service?

2. You have been asked to replace a cafeteria in a factory running three 8 hour shifts, 5 days a week, with vending machines. Devise a menu with all vended products. Decide whether you would have manual vending, how often you would refill the machines, how to ensure the safety of the food, reconstitution, and how to control the collection of money.

6

The Hotel and Motel Business

Commentary

This chapter will help you to think of the hotel business as responding to the guest and the needs of a community, as well as changes in transportation patterns. Hotels are, therefore, related to their function and location.

The basic locations of hotels tell you a lot about their function for the guest and so we consider those in some detail. Another way of considering function is in terms of guest type, thus we look at hotels serving business travellers, conventioneers, and tourists.

Lodging is not always profitable—because sometimes a hotel is built largely to fill community needs even if the number of guests is not at a level that will be profitable.

The word "chain" suggests common ownership but most hotel "chains" are really franchise groups. The franchise system provides benefits to hotel operators and guests alike in terms of a hotel's identity and service level, its referral and reservation services and its assurance of quality operations. This makes franchising an integral part of any discussion of lodging.

Chapter Outline

Referral Systems
Inspection Systems: Quality Assurance
Determining Hotels' Value and Function
Summary

Review of Chapter Objectives

Trace the growth of hotels during this century, focusing on transportation patterns: _____

_____

_____

_____

In terms of economic *factors* and cost factors, describe the evolution of the *hotel* to

motel to *motor-hotel*: _____

_____

_____

_____

Categorize hotel—motels by: (1) location, (2) function, and (3) market.

	Location	*Characteristics of Location*
1.	_____	_____
2.	_____	_____
3.	_____	_____
4.	_____	_____
5.	_____	_____
6.	_____	_____
7.	_____	_____

	Function	*Description of Services*
1.	_____	_____
2.	_____	_____
3.	_____	_____

Market	*Guest Needs*
1. _____	_____
	_____
2. _____	_____
	_____
3. _____	_____
	_____

Hotels are important, even necessary in many communities. Discuss their effect on a community as follows:

Economic impact on a community   _____

_____

Hotels fulfill social needs of a community   _____

_____

The profitability of hotels in some real estate developments   _____

_____

_____

What is the advantage of franchise and referral systems?   _____

_____

_____

_____

KEY WORDS AND PHRASES

Fill in the following blanks with the best word or phrase.

The largest cost in building hotels and motor hotels is   _____

_____

The advantages of downtown hotels are   _____

_____

Convention hotels attract two markets:
(1) _____

(2) _____

A *transient* property is one which _____

_____

A *destination* property is _____

_____

Hotel *externalities* can be defined as _____

_____

A franchise system is _____

A referral system is _____

Franchise and referral groups generally require the following services and physical plant: _____

_____

A quality assurance inspection system for franchise and referral groups does the following: _____

_____

REVIEW QUESTIONS

True/False

Answer the following questions by circling T for true or F for false.

T   F   **1.** Early motels, compared with hotels, had lower land costs and construction costs.

T   F   **2.** Motor hotels resemble motels in number of guest rooms and services more than they do hotels.

T   F   **3.** Today, nearly all successful downtown hotels have converted to a motor hotel format.

T   F   **4.** Convention hotels typically are built with multimeeting rooms and spacious and luxurious guest suites.

T   F   **5.** The typical stay in a resort hotel is one-to-two days.

T   F   **6.** Many small town community hotels have been built without great profit expectations.

T   F   **7.** Referral systems no longer exist that allow owner/operators the privilege of using their own name and rate structure.

T   F   **8.** A computerized reservation system will not work well if each hotel does not update their reservations daily.

T   F   9. With computerized reservations systems reservations are usually made at the local hotel and fed into the central reservation bank.

T   F   10. Computerized reservation systems are sometimes combined with WATS systems.

Multiple choice

Choose the *one* best answer.

1. The building of hotels has traditionally followed
   a. economic patterns
   b. the building of motels
   c. transportation patterns
   d. demographic patterns

2. The boom years for small motel building were in the
   a. 1910–1920s
   b. 1930–1940s
   c. 1950–1960s
   d. 1970–1980s

3. The *greatest* appeal of early motels was
   a. informality
   b. no tipping of bellmen
   c. their restaurants
   d. location on or near highways

4. A motor hotel is distinctly different from a motel in
   a. size and services
   b. location
   c. informality
   d. guest room size

5. A resort hotel is *not* a
   a. recreational destination
   b. entertainment destination
   c. leisure destination
   d. en route destination

6. A standard motor hotel
   a. depends mainly on rooms business
   b. would have 1 dining room less than 100 seats
   c. would have 1 dining room with more than 100 seats
   d. would have accommodations for large meetings (500 or more)

7. The most important guest in most hotels is the
   a. tourist
   b. family
   c. convention goer
   d. business traveler

8. Benefits to others rather than a hotel are called
   a. franchises
   b. feasibility studies
   c. referral services
   d. externalities

9. Usually the following is *not* the function of a franchising agency for hotels
   a. use of franchise name
   b. pooled advertising
   c. referral service
   d. allowing individuality of properties

10. Quality assurance
    a. is the day-to-day responsibility of the franchisee
    b. is based on enforcement by the chain inspection
    c. is an inspection based on a WATS system
    d. assures the guest that there will be a restaurant, swimming pool, room service, and a 24-hour front desk

Fill in the Blanks

Fill in the blanks with the best answer.

1. The location of hotels is determined by _____ and

   _____.

2. After World War II the new market for motels was _____.

3. The largest single costs of most lodging facilities are _____ and

   _____. These are called _____ costs.

4. A resort hotel is defined as one which is a _____ destination.

5. The kind, degree, and probable cost of services is suggested to travelers when

   they see a _____ name or _____ identity.

DISCUSSION QUESTIONS

Answer the following essay questions.

1. Discuss the differences between an independent hotel, a chain hotel, a franchise hotel, and a hotel that is part of a referral group. What combinations of these might exist (e.g., an independent hotel that belongs to referral system)?

2. In your opinion, how might future changes in transportation affect the lodging business?

3. Describe a real-estate development package that you think would be important in revitalizing a decaying downtown area.

PROJECTS

1. Visit a local hotel and find out how they make reservations in another city. Are they computerized or use a WATS line, a teletype, or telephone?

2. Obtain a national directory for a major hotel chain (or more than one if possible). Is there any correlation between size of city and location of hotel? What services are standard in each hotel? What is the range of their rates? Discuss other factors you see that tell you things about these hotels. For example, are there services that will attract a particular hotel market?

7

Hotel and Motel Operations

Commentary

This chapter has two goals. One is to facilitate the career exploration question of "What's it like to work in a hotel?" The other is to provide operations-oriented students with materials that speak to their interests.

Here we provide you with the bare minimum trade vocabulary that hotels use when they discuss their key operating ratios. In hotels, food and beverage operations are important, *but*, subordinate to the hotel's overall goals, and this chapter acquaints you with the unique qualities of hotel restaurants.

Chapter Outline

Major Functional Departments
    The Rooms Side of the House
    The Front Office
        Telephone
        Housekeeping
        The Bell Staff
    Food and Beverage Department
        Restaurants
        Banquets
        Food Production
        Sanitation and Utility
    Staff and Support Departments
        Sales and Marketing
        Engineering
        Accounting
Income and Expense Patterns and Control
    The Uniform System of Accounts
    Key Operating Ratios and Terms
    Capital Structure
Entry Ports and Careers
    Front Office
    Accounting

       Sales and Marketing
       Food and Beverage
Summary

Review of Chapter Objectives

List the major functional departments in large hotels:

Departments on the Rooms Side

_____

_____

_____

_____

Food and Beverage Departments

_____

_____

_____

_____

_____

Staff and Support Departments

_____

_____

_____

Describe, in general, the check-in, check-out procedure in a hotel. Include interactions with other departments.

_____

_____

_____

_____

Explain the biggest source of profit in a hotel and the food and beverage depart-ment's importance to the hotel's success.

_____

_____

_____

Explain how Statements of Income and Expense are used to measure the perform-

ance of a hotel. _____

_____

_____

_____

The formulas for the key operating ratios are:

   Occupancy percentage = _____

   Average rate = _____

   Number of guests per occupied room = _____

   Average rooms cleaned per maid day = _____

Explain the effect of good and bad times on capital-intensive hotels _____

_____

_____

_____

KEY WORDS AND PHRASES

Fill in the following blanks with the best word or phrase.

The difference between *departments* and *functional areas* is _____

_____

In small properties _____ employees are given supervisory rules.

The departmental income is _____

_____

An "on change" room is one which _____

_____

A "ready to rent" room is one which _____

_____

If reservations are "closed" it means that _____

_____

Overbooking means that _____

_____

A "no show" is _____

_____

A guaranteed reservation is _____

_____

The night auditor determines the days's closing balance by _____

_____

_____

The job of the concierge includes _____

_____

_____

A *typical* hotel's food and beverage sales and profitability compared to room sales

are _____

_____

A full-service hotel restaurant's hours of operation are related to _____

_____

The responsibilities of the chef in a hotel are: _____

_____

_____

Dishwashers are important in three ways: (1) _____,

(2) _____ (3) _____

The steward in many hotels is _____

_____

The HSMA _____ _____ _____ _____

is an organization that _____

_____

_____

The engineering staff is responsible for _____

_____

_____

Define these terms related to the hotel accounting department:

Back office _____

House ledger _____

City ledger _____

Guest folio _____

The Uniform System of Accounts for Hotels is _____

_____

A revenue department is _____

Departmental Income is defined as _____

_____

Undistributed operating expenses are _____

_____

Total income before fixed charges is _____

_____

Capital costs include _____, _____, _____,

_____ and _____

Depreciation is _____

_____

Capital intensive means that _____

_____

A leveraged hotel is one which _____

_____

REVIEW QUESTIONS

True/False

Answer the following questions by circling T for true or F for false.

T   F   **1.** Although two properties vary dramatically in size, the executive staff of each are responsible for the same functional areas.

T   F   **2.** A "room block" means that a hotel room is not yet ready to rent because housekeeping is cleaning it.

T   F   **3.** To avoid overbooking it is necessary to watch only guest reservations.

T   F   **4.** Most guests arrive at hotels after 6:00 P.M.

T   F   **5.** The "closing" balance of accounts received equals the previous day's balance of accounts owed minus payments plus charges.

T   F   **6.** If a hotel serves transient guests, its restaurant would serve the greatest number of guests at breakfast and dinner.

T   F   **7.** Sales and marketing mean the same in hotels.

T   F   **8.** In a hotel property, regardless of its size, management should determine a periodic equipment maintenance schedule and see that it is carried out.

T   F   **9.** Departmental income usually does not show administrative costs.

T   F   **10.** A "leveraged" hotel is one in which the investor has typically made a modest initial investment, advantageous in good economic times or bad.

Multiple Choice

Choose the *one* best answer.

1. Major elements in hotel front offices usually do *not* include
   a. reservation files
   b. front desk job descriptions
   c. house ledger
   d. accounting machine

2. A computerized front office system is a
   a. PMS system
   b. POS system
   c. ECR system
   d. PDQ system

3. Communication is absolutely critical for smooth room rental between the front desk and
    a. the restaurant
    b. the manager
    c. housekeeping
    d. the bell staff

4. An important part of checking-in hotel guests is
    a. receiving payment
    b. verifying the guest's departure date
    c. notifying housekeeping
    d. putting the room "on change"

5. Full-service hotel dining rooms choose their hours of operation to coincide with the time
    a. a few guests may need food service
    b. of check in and check out
    c. most guests will be in the dining room
    d. nearby restaurants are open

6. Which function does *not* describe hotel marketing?
    a. designing and building a hotel to suit the needs and tastes of guests
    b. selling your property to guests vis-à-vis your services
    c. selling your property to groups of guests
    d. selling your property to everyone

7. The two duties of the accounting office are
    a. accounts receivable and accounts payable
    b. accounts receivable and financial reporting
    c. bookkeeping and comptrolling
    d. accounts and profit and loss statements

8. What a guest owes a hotel is usually kept track of at the front desk in the
    a. house ledger
    b. guest ledger
    c. city ledger
    d. bookkeeping ledger

9. Costs that are divided among all departments are called
    a. undistributed operating expenses
    b. schedule of expenses
    c. departmental expenses
    d. direct expenses

10. Writing off the cost of building a hotel over a period of years is called
    a. interest   c. depreciation
    b. capital cost   d. leverage

Fill in the Blanks

Fill in the blanks with the best answer.

1. The major source of hotel profit is _____ _____.

2. The employee who usually handles guest complaints at check out and often is the person responsible for guest returning to the hotel is the _____ _____.

3. A method of keeping track of vacant rooms is called _____ of vacant rooms. There is often a _____ card for each room and these are kept in the _____.

4. If a guest cancels their reservation, the hotel generally gives them a _____ _____ for their records in case they are inadvertently charged for the room later.

5. The front desk clerk with accounting responsibilities is called the _____ _____.

MATH REVIEW

Problems using operating ratios. (Review formulas for operating ratios.)

Occupancy rate problems

Determine occupancy percentage in a 100 room hotel in which 75 rooms were rented.

The formula for occupancy percentage is

$$\frac{O \qquad P}{\qquad} = \frac{R \qquad S}{T \quad R \quad A} \times 100$$

The occupancy percentage was _____%

Now determine the following occupancy rates for a hotel with 1000 rooms.

1. For one night when 857 rooms were occupied. The occupancy rate was _____%

2. For the month of June (30 days) when 19,500 rooms were rented. The occupancy rate was _____%

3.   For a week

Rooms Rented

Sun	Mon	Tue	Weds	Thur	Fri	Sat
460	950	980	1000	1000	350	245

The occupancy rate was _____%

On average, how many rooms were rented a night in a 250 room hotel with an average occupancy rate of 83%? The average number of rooms rented per night

was _____.

Average rate problems

Determine the average rate in a 100 room hotel that rented 90 rooms with $4600 revenue.

The formula to determine average rate is

$$\frac{A \qquad R}{} = \frac{D \qquad S}{N \qquad of\ R \qquad S}$$

The average rate was $ _____

In a 100 room hotel that rents single rooms for $35, doubles for $40, and suites for $60, determine the average rate and occupancy percentage for this night:

Singles: 64 rented
Doubles: 15 rented
Suites: 4 rented

The average rate was $ _____

The occupancy percentage was _____%

Number of Guests per Occupied Room

Determine the number of guests per occupied room in a 100 room hotel. A total of 75 rooms were rented; 30 of these were double occupancy and the remainder single occupancy.

The formula to determine the number of guests per occupied room is:

$$N\text{\_\_\_} of\ G\text{\_\_\_} per\ O\text{\_\_\_} R\text{\_\_\_} = \frac{N \qquad of\ G}{N \qquad of\ O \qquad R}$$

The number of guests per occupied room was _____.

In a 200 room resort hotel, determine the number of guests per occupied room for this week:

	Sun	Mon	Tues	Wed	Thur	Fri	Sat
Singles	24	34	29	38	32	28	20
Doubles	145	121	134	142	148	130	97
3/room	18	10	9	14	12	20	5
4/room	6	8	9	5	6	8	1

The number of guests per occupied room was _____.

Average rooms cleaned per maid day

Determine the average rooms cleaned per maid day in a 100 room hotel. The hotel rented 60 rooms and 5 maids working 8-hour shifts each were on duty the next day to clean them.

The formula to determine the average rooms cleanred per maid day is:

$$A\_\_\_\_ R\_\_\_\_ C\_\_\_\_ \text{ per } M\_\_\_\_ Day = \frac{N \qquad R \qquad O}{N \qquad S}$$

The average rooms cleaned per maid day was _____.

Determine all of the ratios for this 250 room hotel:

	Number of Rooms Rented	Rate per Night
Singles	205	$65
Doubles	35	$75
Suites (all	8	$120
double occupancy)		

Total number of maid hours required to clean was 12 maids working 8-hour shifts, and 6 maids working 6-hour shifts.

Occupancy percentage = _____%

Average rate = $_____

Number of guests per occupied room = _____

Average rooms cleaned per maid day = _____

DISCUSSION QUESTIONS

1. Discuss why the clerks working on the front desk are important to the success of the hotel.

2. Explain how and why overbooking occurs in a hotel.

3. Discuss why a concierge would need to know the town the hotel is located in.

4. What are the main career paths for entry into the hotel business? Discuss the one path that looks best to you, citing the needed experience it will give you (or the needed experience it will not give you).

PROJECTS

1. Visit a hotel that has a concierge and find out what his or her job is and how guests are handled.
2. Review the leading trade journals for the lodging field (*Lodging, Hotel-Motel Management,* or others that your library may have) and report on an article relating to this chapter.

8

Automating Operations and Services in Hotels

Commentary

As most of you are familiar with computers if only to play computer games (which, of course, are software packages) you will become involved with this chapter immediately. Most of the tasks that the computer has taken over are the dull routine jobs that nobody likes to do, however, computers also make an important contribution in improving guest services and providing instant communication within lodging chains and referral systems such as those of a computerized reservation service.

The hotel industry is a late arrival in computerization but is moving to catch up rapidly. The understanding of how computers improve operational control and guest service is essential today. In future years it will become even more important.

Chapter Outline

Computers: The Heart of Lodging Technology
Interfaces
> Hardware and Software

Common Uses of Technology in Hotels
> Technology and Operations
>> Property Management Systems (PMS)
>> Call Accounting
>> Security
>> Word Processing
> Videoconferencing
> Energy Management
>> Demand
>> Usage
>> Control Systems
> The Smart Guest Room

Summary

Review of Chapter Objectives

The three components of a computer system are (1) _____, (2) _____, and (3) _____

The input device of a computer is usually called a _____

The central processing unit of a computer contains three units: (1) _____, (2) _____, and (3) _____

The output unit of a computer is usually a (1) _____ or a (2) _____

Name three common interfaces in a hotel computer system, for example, house-keeping with front desk: room status

1. _____

2. _____

3. _____

The Property Management System (__ __ __) automates the _____ office and the _____ office.

Call accounting is _____

An electronic key system is _____

_____

Videoconferencing is _____

_____

Energy costs in hotels are determined by both _____ and

_____.

Four examples of new technology in "The Smart Guest Room" (e.g., thumb print or retina scan in lieu of keys) are:

1. _____

2. _____

3. _____

4. _____

KEY WORDS AND PHRASES

Fill in the blank with the number representing the corresponding definition.

1.	Microprocessor	_____	a.	One computer orders another computer to transfer data
2.	System	_____	b.	Computer programs
3.	Input device	_____	c.	CRT
4.	CPU	_____	d.	Microchip
5.	Output device	_____	e.	Made up of control unit, arithmetic logic unit, and memory unit
6.	Binary numbers	_____	f.	Computer screen displays a set of choices or options for the user
7.	Software	_____	g.	Can be programmed to have computational capacity
8.	Interface	_____	h.	Zero and one; compared to on/off switch
9.	Smart terminal	_____	i.	An interactive whole
10.	POS	_____	j.	Keyboard
11.	On line	_____	k.	Satellite-transmitting antenna
12.	Poll	_____	l.	Point-of-sale terminal
13.	Machine-readable	_____	m.	A communications, videoconferencing system used by many hotel properties
14.	Down-load	_____	n.	Used for correspondence, direct mail, reports, and other printed materials
15.	Menu driven	_____	o.	Data that can be read by a computer
16.	Word processing	_____	p.	To send reports to units from chain headquarters
17.	Mail merge	_____	q.	Individually typed letters for a mailing list
18.	Uplink	_____	r.	Interaction between two components in a computer system
19.	HI-NET	_____	s.	Directly connected to the computer

20. Peak load control   _____   t.   Can turn off equipment as upper de-
    system   mand level is reached

REVIEW QUESTIONS

True/False

Answer the following questions by circling T for true or F for false.

T   F   **1.** The memory of the computer is contained in the CPU.

T   F   **2.** A 256K computer's memory holds 256,000 bits of informa-
                tion.

T   F   **3.** When the front desk and the restaurant of a hotel are inter-
                faced with a computer it is possible for restaurant charges to be
                posted directly to a guest folio.

T   F   **4.** A mainframe computer would be the most economical com-
                puter for a front desk.

T   F   **5.** The PMS automates the front and the back of the house
                activities in a hotel.

T   F   **6.** A PMS can improve guest service by more accurate and faster
                communications while reducing payroll at the same time.

T   F   **7.** A guest walk-in menu is designed for a quick service restau-
                rant.

T   F   **8.** A problem with a computerized reservation system is that it is
                unable to provide accurate information about future reserva-
                tions.

T   F   **9.** At present, most companies have eagerly accepted videocon-
                ferences as cost effective (compared to renting hotel rooms).

T   F   **10.** In-room video check-out allows the guest to inspect and pay
                their bill via an in-room TV screen.

Multiple Choice

Choose the *one* best answer.

1. The CPU is made up of three units
   a. keyboard, CRT, and printer
   b. control, arithmetic, and memory
   c. input, processing, and output devices
   d. program storage, keyboard, and printer

2. The part of the computer that would calculate the profit and loss statement
   for a hotel would be the
   a. arithmetic/logic unity   c. memory
   b. control unit   d. CRT

3. Data such as guest records would be stored in
   a.   arithmetic/logic unit
   b.   control unit
   c.   memory
   d.   CRT

4. A hotel chain with computers interconnected between the head office and the hotels are
   a.   on-call accounting systems
   b.   machine-readable
   c.   POS terminals
   d.   on-line

5. A national reservation system would require a
   a.   PC
   b.   minicomputer
   c.   microcomputer
   d.   mainframe

6. For the most rapid and automated call back system, a hotel would choose
   a.   long-distance operator call back
   b.   interface with PMS
   c.   teleprinter
   d.   voucher system

7. At present, computerized hotel key systems
   a.   involve a guest finger print code at the door
   b.   consist of a plastic card encoded by a microcomputer
   c.   are menu driven key systems
   d.   do allow thieves to enter rooms if a previous guest takes his or her key and the thief finds it

8. "Mail merge," useful for direct mail
   a.   is part of the word processing package
   b.   increases typists' time
   c.   requires individually written letters to a number of people
   d.   automatically weighs outgoing mail and affixes postage

9. Videoconferencing
   a.   is based on a receiving desk called an "uplink"
   b.   competes particularly with the large meeting market
   c.   has the ability to bring people together on a TV screen in meeting rooms and every guest room
   d.   has canceled a number of hotel conventions

10. Peak load control systems are used to control
    a.   demand charges for energy
    b.   total electric usage
    c.   thermostats
    d.   optimized start and stop equipment

Fill in the Blanks

Fills in the blanks with the best answer.

1. A computer *system* must contain a _____, _____, and
   _____.

2. To have computerized room status, the front desk would need to interface with
   the _____ department.

3. Data stored outside the computer are commonly stored on _____.

4. The core features of a PMS in the back house are _____,
   _____, _____, and _____.

5. A hotel computer continuously interconnected with the home office computer
   is said to be _____ _____.

DISCUSSION QUESTIONS

1. Compare tasks that can be performed manually or by computer in the front of
   the house. Choose one of the following: check in/check out, folio accounting,
   telephone accounting, guest reservations, night audit, group registration,
   housekeeping, room status.

2. Of the computerized features of the smart guest room, which will the guest like
   most? Least? Can you envision problems occurring with any of these new
   services?

PROJECT

1. Visit a hotel with a computerized front desk or PMS to gain an understanding
   of how it works. (Be sure to contact the hotel ahead of time and make an
   appointment when the front desk is not busy.) Be aware of such features as
   interfacing, menu-driven software, and so forth.

9

Forces Shaping the Hotel Business

Commentary

The "economics" of hotels—what makes them work as money making enterprises—is a complicated subject. We tackle it in this chapter by seeing why overbuilding is such a common feature of the business. What we find is that hotels are built not just to serve the needs of rooms customers but also those of developers, franchisors and chain operators, and the community. When a hotel is needed in an area, rather than one, a cluster of hotels is usually built. Factors we will consider in our review of hotels' economics include cycles of building, capital intensity and degree of competition. These will help us understand the differing merits of the decision to invest in hotels.

The result of fierce competition has been exciting in recent years. It has been characterized by the emergence of new types of hotels such as the "all suite" and the development of a segmentation strategy in the business. The offering of generous amenities and new guest services are also part of this competitive pattern. Food service is a highly individualized competitive strategy in any hotel and the young person with food service experience is of particular value in the hotel industry.

Chapter Outline

The Economics of the Hotel Business
    A Capital-Intensive Business
    A Competitive Business
    A Growth Business?
Considerations in the Hotel Investment Decision
    Financial
    Real Estate
    Operation
        Risks and Rewards

Review of Chapter Objectives

After you have read this chapter you should have a good understanding of the economics of the hotel business. To aid you we direct your review to these questions.

Why are hotels built in cycles? _____

_____

_____

Describe the capital intensity of the hotel business. _____

_____

_____

Is the hotel business a growth industry compared with others? Why? _____

_____

_____

Why do individuals and companies invest in hotels? _____

_____

_____

What type of hotel owner is usually interested in a management company and what are the advantages to this owner? _____

_____

_____

Briefly describe the following segments of the lodging industry. Include the type of accommodation, their customers, and any unique characteristics:

First class hotels _____

_____

Business and tourist hotels (midscale) _____

_____

Economy properties _____

_____

Courtyard properties _____

_____

Hotels with executive floors _____

_____

Upscale properties _____

_____

All-suite hotels _____

_____

Luxury hotels _____

_____

Conference centers _____

_____

Condominiums _____

_____

Discuss the reasons why hotels have become specialized. _____

_____

What are some ways hotels have survived the fierce competition? What single
service is the most difficult to copy? _____

_____

_____

_____

KEYS WORDS AND PHRASES

Fill in the blanks with the best words or phrase.

Capital costs for hotels are _____.

"The equity holders' stake" is _____

_____

A recapitalized property is one which _____

_____

A management company is _____

_____

A management contract is _____

_____

Segmentation of hotels refers to _____

_____

An "executive floor" is _____

_____

Refranchising a property means that _____

_____

Converting a property means that _____

_____

A time-share is _____

_____

Time-share swapping means _____

_____

The distinguishing characteristics of hotel restaurants are

    Operated by hotel _____

    Leased _____

    On-site franchised _____

A superfloor is _____

Personal amenities are _____

_____

Upgrading and the hotel industry refers to _____

_____

REVIEW QUESTIONS

True/False

Answer the following questions by circling T for true or F for false.

T   F   **1.** The hotel business in a particular market is dependent on the demand for rooms rather than the supply.

T   F   **2.** Overbuilding hotel rooms in a local market is often a problem when a sudden need arises and a number of chains decide to build.

T   F   **3.** Most mortgage holders who take over bankrupt hotels are forced to operate them.

T	F	4.	The lodging industry, if one looks at numbers of rooms sold, is a solid growth industry.
T	F	5.	Chain hotels cannot operate as management companies.
T	F	6.	Hotels today can be divided into three classes of properties: (1) first class, (2) business and tourist, and (3) rate sensitive properties.
T	F	7.	The size of the economy hotel market is estimated to be at least 50 percent of hotel rooms business.
T	F	8.	Executive floors are rented only to business executives.
T	F	9.	Specialized conference centers catering to corporate education have not proven successful.
T	F	10.	Fitness facilities in hotels are expensive capital investments.

Multiple Choice

Choose the *one* best answer.

1. In general, the hotel business is dependent on
   a. the business cycle
   b. the restaurant business
   c. the season of the year
   d. construction costs

2. In the lodging business
   a. variable costs dominate over capital costs
   b. fixed costs dominate over capital costs
   c. payroll costs dominate over variable costs
   d. capital costs dominate over variable costs

3. In recent years, hotel
   a. room rates have risen relative to the consumer price index
   b. restaurant prices have remained about the same
   c. costs to the traveler have stayed in pace with inflation
   d. restaurant and room rates have both dropped

4. In the United States, the 1981 tax law stimulated hotel building by
   a. providing government loans at low interest
   b. allowing higher depreciation deductions
   c. allowing liberal expense account deductions
   d. allowing consumers to deduct hotel stays from their taxes

5. A hotel management company that operates hotels for hotel owners
   a. does so without a written contract
   b. does not assume complete operational responsibility for the property
   c. provides furniture, fixtures, and working capital
   d. pays operating expenses from the cash flow

6. The Marriott courtyard concept is characterized by
   a. luxurious outdoor restaurants
   b. two room suites
   c. minimal food and beverage facilities
   d. additional meeting room facilities

7. A hotel that faces refranchising
   a. must reinvest in the property
   b. can choose to change its affiliation
   c. is not wise to try to serve another market
   d. can easily convert to an all-suite property

8. Which of the following statements is *not* correct? All suite hotels
   a. are located near corporate clients
   b. are built on less expensive land than conventional hotels
   c. are represented at every level of the market but tend to be in the mid-scale market
   d. have full service food and beverage facilities

9. Most long-stay guests in all-suite hotels are
   a. professional people
   b. mobile construction workers
   c. salespeople
   d. retirees

10. Hotel segmentation
    a. has been a solution to the oversupply of hotel rooms
    b. has just kept up with the demand for rooms and new services
    c. has been limited to consumer demand
    d. has led to specialized hotel building in saturated markets creating oversupply

Fill in the Blanks

Fill in the blanks with the best answer.

1. Before a hotel is built, the hotel company generally spends a great deal of money on _____, _____, and _____.

2. _____ costs in hotels will continue regardless of the volume of business the property does.

3. The three parts to hotel investment are: 1. _____, 2. _____, and 3. _____.

4. The two kinds of management companies are _____ and _____.

5. "Executive floors" in a midscale hotel are an attempt to gain a share of the _____ market.

DISCUSSION QUESTIONS

1. Discuss why restaurants might have a better chance than hotels of surviving an economic downturn. Relate your discussion to costs.

2. Discuss the differences in the facilities and hours of operation required in a traditional hotel restaurant and those required in an all suite or courtyard restaurant. How do the facilities and hours of operation affect building and operating costs?

3. Discuss the reasons why advice was given to young people to gain food service experience if they wish to go into the hotel business.

PROECTS

1. Place the hotels in your community into market categories (i.e., economy, midscale, all-suite, etc.). Visit two or more in different categories and list the differences in rates, facilities and services.

2. Obtain advertising materials for several local hotels. Assess their market from this material. What services or facilities are they offering as a competitive strategy?

10

Tourism: Front and Center

Commentary

Our major goal in this chapter is to alert you to the scope and size of tourism and its impact on the nation's economy and on the local community. Tourism as an industry is fragmented into many businesses that serve the "fun seeker" or traveler. Note that the one industry that is present in every setting is *food service* and we stress again, the transferability of food service skills.

You will want to take a close look at *who* spends travel dollars, and in our next chapter we will look at *where* they go. Finally, it will probably not surprise you to learn that Americans travel abroad more frequently than foreigners visit us. You should know how this affects our economy.

Chapter Outline

Travel and Tourism
    Growing Leisure
    Income Trends
    Demographics
Travel Trends
    Mode of Travel
    Price Sensitivity
    Travel and Lodging
    Women and Travel
The Economic Significance of Tourism
    Travel Industry Receipts
    Tourism and Employment
    Publicity As an Economic Benefit
The United States As an International Tourist Attraction
Is Tourism an Industry?
Noneconomic Effects of Tourism
    Crowding
    Favorable Noneconomic Effects
Summary

Review of Chapter Objectives

Briefly describe the size of the tourist industry. _____

_____

_____

State how the following factors support the growth of travel and tourism.

Leisure _____

Income _____

Demographics _____

Business traveling _____

What are the most significant reasons why people travel? _____

_____

_____

How far does the average person travel and how does he or she get to his or her

destination? _____

_____

Compare the growth of the travel industry to the growth of the economy.

_____

Describe how tourism affects employment. _____

_____

_____

Discuss the significance of the international tourist market to the United States.

_____

_____

_____

Discuss the international tourist market with respect to the U.S.'s balance of pay-

ments. _____

_____

Describe how the rise and fall of the U.S. dollar affects tourism. _____

_____

_____

How can tourism be considered a major export? _____

_____

_____

Why is tourism an industry difficult to study as a field? _____

_____

_____

Assess the noneconomic impacts of tourism.

Favorable _____

_____

Unfavorable _____

_____

KEY WORDS AND PHRASES

Fill in the blanks with the best word or phrase.

Describe the difference between a "smokestack" industry and the tourism industry.

_____

Define tourism. _____

_____

_____

Tourist organizations include the following from the:

Hospitality industry _____

Transportation industry _____

Recreation industry _____

Support industries _____

Describe what is meant by "quality time" for tourists. _____

_____

The unique characteristics of the following travelers are:

Two-income-family travelers _____

_____

Middle-aged travelers _____

_____

Senior travelers _____

_____

Define the meaning of a trip. _____

_____

Define a "person trip." _____

Describe the effect of gasoline prices on travel. _____

_____

Who are the majority of hotel–motel users? _____

A short profile of a business traveler: _____

_____

What are the travel multiplier and "a chain of expenditures"? _____

_____

What is the rank of tourism among other industries in business receipts and jobs?

_____

What is the difference between total tourist receipts and total tourist arrivals in the

international market? _____

_____

_____

Define the U.S. travel deficit. _____

_____

What is the effect of crowding on tourist attractions? _____

_____

Define crowding out. _____

What is the carrying capacity of a destination? _____

_____

REVIEW QUESTIONS

True/False

Answer the following questions by circling T for true or F for false

T   F   **1.** For tourism purposes, a trip is defined as 50 miles or more away from home.

T   F   **2.** Deregulation of airlines led to higher air fares.

T   F   **3.** Auto costs have resulted in consumers buying smaller cars, keeping them longer, and shorter trips.

T   F   **4.** Business travelers can be characterized as representing all phases of society.

T   F   **5.** Not only does tourism generate billions of dollars in direct sales, but it creates a chain of related expenditures that boost other businesses in the community.

T   F   **6.** During economic downturn, tourism sales take a significant nosedive.

T   F   **7.** On a worldwide scale, Americans spend more money in other countries than persons from abroad spend in the United States.

T   F   **8.** Total tourism receipts often do not show a direct relationship to tourist arrivals.

T   F   **9.** The relationships among the industries that serve tourists generally do not extend into inter-industry career ladders.

T   F   **10.** Dollar sales are the only positive effects of tourism on a community.

Multiple Choice

Choose the *one* best answer.

1. The statement that is *not* true about two income families is: Two income families
   a.   seek low-cost leisure activities
   b.   have leisure time but use much of it for family maintenance and household chores
   c.   seek good value for their leisure dollar
   d.   have more time away from work than their parents had at their age

2. Elderly travelers in general
   a.   are not price conscious if security is assured
   b.   often travel during off seasons

    c.   have not responded to group rates

    d.   have not been a lucrative travel market

3.   The first reason for traveling (1985 survey) was

    a.   to visit friends and relatives

    b.   for pleasure

    c.   for business

    d.   for convention travel

4.   Business travelers

    a.   comprise 50 percent of the travel market

    b.   are an affluent, well-educated, upscale market

    c.   are usually salespeople

    d.   do not include convention goers

5.   In North America, tourism

    a.   is the number one business in terms of sales

    b.   provides more jobs than any other single business except health care

    c.   generates about $250 million in receipts

    d.   as an industry is not significant to the overall economy

6.   In general, tourism receipts have

    a.   grown more slowly than the economy

    b.   grown at the same pace as the economy

    c.   grown faster than the economy

    d.   shown no growth

7.   The travel industry

    a.   has outperformed other industries in contributing to job growth

    b.   has not significantly contributed new jobs because of automation

    c.   has created some new jobs but only in the food service and hotel–motel sector

    d.   has created roughly 5 million new jobs

8.   The single industry that employs the most people to serve travelers is

    a.   air transportation

    b.   hotels and motels

    c.   food service

    d.   amusement and recreation services

9.   The statement that is *not* true is

    a.   the U.S. share of arrivals was lower than its share of dollar receipts

    b.   travel to the United States is more expensive than travel to other countries

    c.   most of the travelers to the United States come from Canada and Mexico

    d.   the rise of the value of the U.S. dollar is accompanied by a rise in tourism receipts

10. The most serious negative effect of tourism is
   a.   pollution
   b.   hostility of local residents
   c.   traffic jams
   d.   crowding

Fill in the Blanks

Fill in the blanks with the best answer.

1. Of the people who take a trip (as defined in the text) _____ percent will stay overnight in a hotel or motel.

2. The chain of expenditures felt throughout a community, initiated by tourist dollars is called the _____.

3. The travel industry employs about _____ persons; _____ percent of all food service employment is tourism; and travel related businesses have increased overall employment _____ times the overall economy.

4. The two measures of the success of tourism are _____ and _____.

5. The federal agency established to promote tourism is the _____.

DISCUSSION QUESTIONS

1. Discuss the effect gasoline prices have on tourist destinations.
2. Discuss the differences in job mobility between the hospitality and the tourism industry.
3. Discuss the travel multiplier effect a theme park like Disney World has had on its surrounding community.

PROJECTS

1. Identify an event in your community or nearby that was designed specifically to attract tourists. What are the resulting benefits to the community?
2. Contact your local chamber of commerce and obtain local tourism information. Find out how your community supports tourism activities. Their officials may be able to tell you the impact of tourism on your community.

11

Destination: Tourism Generators

Commentary

In this chapter we look at the "fun" side of tourism, and many a student's dream to travel has come true when he or she puts on a backpack and heads for either a theme park or the scenic wonder of a national or state park. These places offer lots of opportunity for summer work as well as the fun of meeting new friends, many also studying in hospitality programs. But underlying the fun of tourist attractions for you is always the business side, and in this chapter we would like you to take note of the vast numbers traveling with the resulting economic impact on the communities that serve as travel destinations—as well as cities and towns that serve them along the way.

Travelers are going places—that is, to specific places, to destinations. Their reasons for travel are important. Understanding what makes destinations successful will help you to understand what makes mass market tourism tick.

Chapter Outline

Motives and Destinations
Mass-Market Tourism
Planned Play Environments
Artificial Environments
    Theme Parks
        Themes
        Scale
    Regional Theme Parks
        Employment and Training Opportunities
    Casinos and Gaming
        Las Vegas
        Atlantic City
        Casino Markets and the Business of Casinos
Urban Entertainment Centers
Temporary Attractions: Fairs and Festivals
Natural Environments
Summary

Review of Chapter Objectives

Why is recreation for most Americans more than just play? _____

_____

_____

_____

Travel destinations include manmade and natural attractions. Give examples of these:

Manmade _____

_____

Natural _____

_____

Compare the traveler today and the traveler just a few decades ago and the impact of this "new" traveler on the hospitality industry. _____

_____

_____

_____

Describe some of the activities theme parks offer to attract visitors. _____

_____

_____

_____

_____

Describe the difference between the tourist market for national and regional theme parks. _____

Describe the work experiences offered to students by theme parks. _____

_____

_____

Describe the economic impact of casinos on a community. _____

_____

_____

_____

_____

Discuss the moral and social issues of gambling. _____

_____

_____

_____

_____

Describe ways in which cities and towns have developed tourism. _____

_____

_____

_____

_____

Name some of the advantages and problems associated with natural tourist attractions. _____

_____

_____

_____

_____

KEY WORDS AND PHRASES

Fill in the blanks with the best word or phrase.

What is the difference between *primary* and *secondary* attractions? _____

_____

_____

What is the mass institution of tourism? _____

_____

What is a "play" environment? _____

_____

Give some examples of planned play environments. _____

_____

What is a *theme* park? _____

_____

Describe the *scale* of activities in a typical theme park. _____

_____

_____

The four general Casino markets are:

1. _____

2. _____

3. _____

4. _____

What is the measure of a player's theoretical loss based on and what is it used for?

_____

_____

_____

What does the volume of play affect? _____

_____

Who are casino "comps" given to? _____

_____

Why are "temporary" attractions important to a community? _____

_____

_____

What are staging areas? _____

REVIEW QUESTIONS

True/False

Answer the following questions by circling T for true or F for false.

T   F   1. Secondary travel destinations are places of interest that tourists stop to see on their way to a major attraction.

T   F   **2.** A recent development in recreation are destinations designed almost exclusively for play.

T   F   **3.** Customers for regional theme parks come from all over the country.

T   F   **4.** Gambling in the United States is limited to Nevada and New Jersey.

T   F   **5.** Gambling hotels favor high roller losers with "comps" more than a heavy gambler who wins.

T   F   **6.** Often, regional amusements serve to encourage local residents to spend their money at home, boosting their own economy, rather than spending travel money away from home.

T   F   **7.** Usually local festivals and fairs are staffed by unpaid volunteers.

T   F   **8.** National parks are a unique U.S. contribution to recreation.

T   F   **9.** The recreation activity that is the most recent innovation is fairs and festivals.

T   F   **10.** A staging area is a nearby community providing lodging and other services for tourists visiting parks.

Multiple Choice

Choose the *one* best answer.

1. The statement that characterizes theme parks is
   a. theme parks attempt to set standards of dress and behavior for their guests
   b. theme parks are similar to traditional amusement parks in size
   c. educational theme parks dominate over parks with rides
   d. today's traveler expects a theme park environment that in addition to rides will stimulate and entertain him or her

2. National theme parks
   a. focus their advertising on the national market
   b. have not generally been financially successful
   c. are based on local fairs and festivals
   d. gained importance with increasing travel costs and inflation

3. Important differences between Las Vegas and Atlantic City in terms of tourism are
   a. Las Vegas draws from a larger nearby population base than Atlantic City
   b. most visitors arrive in Las Vegas by car and by rail in Atlantic City
   c. Atlantic City has much more convention business than Las Vegas
   d. Las Vegas has many more hotel rooms than Atlantic City

4. The four casino market groups include
    a. high rollers, low rollers, day trippers, bus trade
    b. high rollers, bus trade, car trade, airplane trade
    c. roulette, blackjack, poker and slots
    d. high table rollers, high slot rollers, tourists, bus trade

5. A "marker" is a casino term for
    a. a high roller
    b. an extension of credit
    c. a person who will undoubtedly lose his shirt
    d. a gambler who tries to use a marked deck

6. Fairs and festivals are *not*
    a. staffed heavily with volunteer workers
    b. social and culturally important to the community
    c. designed solely for bringing in tourists
    d. used as community revitalization

7. The first national park created by Congress in 1864 was
    a. Yellowstone
    b. Niagara Falls
    c. Grand Canyon
    d. Yosemite

8. The major hospitality accommodation in national parks is
    a. camping sites
    b. tourist courts
    c. lodges
    d. motor hotels

9. The congressional act which established the National Park System was the
    a. National Park Service Act
    b. National Park System Act
    c. Travel and Recreation Park Act
    d. National Parks and Conservation Act

10. The reason for limiting automobiles in national parks is
    a. to prevent traffic jams
    b. inadequate parking facilities
    c. to reduce crowding and destruction of the park
    d. to provide strictly wilderness areas

Fill in the Blanks

Fill in the blanks with the best answers.

1. As society become affluent, travel and tourism have become a _____
institution.

2.   A theme park is a _____ environment.

3.   Casino gambling in the United States is limited to _____ and _____.

4.   The two purposes for establishing the National Park System were for _____ and _____

5.   The _____ of _____ established the National Park System.

DISCUSSION QUESTIONS

1.   Discuss the reasons why theme parks offer a variety of entertainments.

2.   Discuss the differences gambling has created in Las Vegas and Atlantic City. Include the population each draws on, the mode of transportation, the growth of each city, and the number of hotel rooms.

3.   Discuss the impact play and business tourism centers have on their community. Include the positive and negative impact. You may wish to use a specific example such as a superdome or convention center.

PROJECTS

1.   Visit an urban recreation or conference center. Describe the facilities provided for travelers, tourists, and local residents. Which are specifically hospitality operations and what markets do they draw on?

2.   Visit a nearby park (national park if possible). Analyze facilities in the park in terms of preserving the park's natural beauty. Outline a planned staging area for the park, listing the necessary facilities and how these could be controlled to preserve the surrounding beauty of the area.

12

Businesses Serving the Tourist

Commentary

The wide range of job opportunities in the hospitality industry is further illustrated in this chapter as we describe travel agencies and campground activities. However, even if you choose a more typical career in a restaurant or hotel, you should know how a travel agency can help your business—and the competition that campgrounds and RVs are to the hotel business in particular.

It is always fun to speculate on the future and the future of tourism is no exception. A key determinant to how people will travel seems to be oil prices, but high oil prices do not stop Americans from traveling—when prices go up they just stay closer to home. Also, the middle aging of the baby boomers will probably lead to some very exciting developments as these middle-aged and prosperous "boomers" can afford to travel. All of this leads us to believe that tourism will continue to be a major part of the hospitality industry.

Chapter Outline

Passenger Transportation
Channels of Distribution: Travel Agents
Camping
    Private Campgrounds
    Campers
    Recreational Vehicles
A Comparison of Campers and Hotel Guests
The Economics of Camping
Careers in Camping
The Future of Tourism
Summary

Review of Chapter Objectives

How does the travel agent service the hospitality industry in particular hotels?

_____

_____

_____

How does the travel agent act as a middleman?   _____

_____

_____

What is the size of today's campground industry?   _____

_____

_____

Describe the "typical" campground customer.   _____

_____

_____

Describe why people camp and how much they spend on camping.   _____

_____

_____

_____

_____

Contrast campgrounds and hotels:

    Total room nights   _____

    Total room nights   _____

    Cost per room   _____

    Capital cost   _____

    Labor cost   _____

    Income level of campers   _____

    Location   _____

What are the major trends in the travel business?   _____

_____

_____

Describe possible future developments in the travel industry. _____

_____

_____

_____

KEY WORDS AND PHRASES

Fill in the blanks with the best word or phrase.

Describe common carriers engaged in intercity traffic. _____

_____

What is a passenger mile? _____

_____

What is the difference between a travel operator and a travel retailer? _____

_____

_____

_____

What is camping day use? _____

_____

Describe the growth of camping in national and state parks. _____

_____

What do campground services include? _____

_____

What are today's campground chains? _____

_____

What are the sources of campground income? _____

_____

What is the size of the camping market? _____

_____

What are some differences between private and public campgrounds? _____

_____

_____

What is an "RV"? _____

What is the *age* and *income* of RV owners (differentiate according to type of RV)?

_____

_____

What does seasonal flexibility of campgrounds mean? _____

_____

How would energy costs and demographics most likely affect future tourism?

_____

_____

REVIEW QUESTIONS

True/False

Answer the following questions by circling T for true or F for false.

T   F   1. Intercity travel has remained stable over the past 10 years.

T   F   2. Most international air travel is booked through travel agents.

T   F   3. Overnight stays in both national and state parks have increased in recent years.

T   F   4. The majority of KOA campers "camp" in recreational vehicles.

T   F   5. Private campgrounds are usually located in scenic areas.

T   F   6. One can say that while hotel rates are higher than campground fees, the cost for the average RV camper is as much or more for a night's sleep.

T   F   7. For RVs in total, ownership or use includes all segments of the North American population, but specific types of RVs address specific markets by age and income.

T   F   8. An RV of one form or another is affordable by most North Americans.

T   F   9. Campers have, in effect, switched the capital and labor costs to themselves, when compared to hotels.

T   F   10. Mass market tourism in the future will probably be even *less* labor intensive.

Multiple Choice

Choose the *one* best answer.

1. Public intercity travel sales are mostly from
   a. commuters
   b. tourists
   c. businesspeople
   d. working people

2. The meaning of 10,000 passenger miles is
   a. 100 people each traveling 200 miles
   b. 10,000 people traveling 10,000 miles each
   c. a common carrier traveling 10,000 miles
   d. one auto traveling 10,000 miles

3. The means of public transportation that has consistently grown in the last 10 years is
   a. air
   b. helicopter
   c. bus
   d. rail

4. Travel wholesalers specialize in
   a. selling package tours and making travel arrangements
   b. operating travel tours
   c. booking transportation on all kinds of carriers
   d. making travel arrangements for clients

5. The amount of domestic hotel reservations made by travel agents is about
   a. 10 percent
   b. 25 percent
   c. 50 percent
   d. 75 percent

6. Hotels that find relationships with travel agents especially profitable are
   a. convention hotels
   b. budget hotels
   c. resort hotels
   d. midscale hotels

7. Private campgrounds today
   a. offer few amenities
   b. average about 20 campsites and occupy 10 to 25 acres
   c. do not have chain affiliations
   d. must continually upgrade and offer more services

8. The primary reason most Americans choose a camping vacation is
   a. because camping is inexpensive
   b. because Americans prefer the out-of-doors

c. because campsites are located near major tourist attractions

d. because Americans like to travel by auto

9. Publicly operated campgrounds
    a. locate convenient to travelers
    b. operate for profit
    c. are frequently leased or franchised
    d. usually have lower occupancy rates than private campgrounds

10. The RV that receives the *least* use is the
    a. motor home
    b. van camper
    c. truck camper
    d. folding camper trailer

Fill in the Blanks

Fill in the blanks with the best answer.

1. Common carriers include _____, _____, and _____. The common carrier which accounts for most passenger miles is _____.

2. Travel agents charge on average about _____ percent on domestic air fares and _____ percent on international travel.

3. Overnight stays in campgrounds are usually in _____.

4. The average campground contains around _____ campsites and covers _____ acres. About _____ of all campgrounds are open year round.

5. Private campgrounds are located _____ while public campgrounds are located in _____.

DISCUSSION QUESTIONS

1. Discuss why campgrounds open year round tend to be more profitable than seasonal operations.

2. Discuss changes you think will occur in tourism before the end of the century. Justify your predictions by using current trends.

PROJECTS

1. Visit with your local travel agency and find out where their customers usually travel and how often they travel. Find out if the agency has made arrangements with hotels or resorts.

2. Locate a private and a public campground. Visit each and compare their location, size, services, rates, and facilities. Determine how many people are required to provide each campground service.

13

Franchise Systems in the Hospitality Industry

Commentary

It is surprising to many students that a "chain" of restaurants or hotels may be composed of many independent owners and operators. Buying a franchise is a way that the "little" guy can become part of a large chain, but still own his or her own business. In this chapter you will find out how a franchise business works—who usually does what under the contract agreement. You will find that both the franchisor and the franchisee assume contractual responsibilities and that both sides must carry out these obligations to achieve a profitable operation. There are advantages and disadvantages for both parties to the franchise agreement and these are reviewed in some depth in this chapter.

Because, as you may suspect, there have been problems with dishonest franchising companies (and with dishonest franchisees although less frequently), legislation has been passed in many states that requires franchising companies to publish accurate and full pictures of their finances and the success of their units. You will also learn how to evaluate a franchise should you ever wish to become an independent franchisee.

Chapter Outline

Franchising: An Overview
    The Economic Significance of Franchising
    The Franchise Relationship
    The Franchise System
The Franchisee's Deal
    The New Franchisee
        Screening
        Site Selection and Planning
        Preopening Training
        Operations Manuals
    Drawbacks for the Franchisee

The Franchisor's Deal
    Marketing
    Finance
    Operations
    Franchising Disadvantages
Functioning of the Franchise System
    Franchising as a Marketing System
        Place
        Product and Service
        Promotion
        Price
        System Marketing
Regulation
    Terminating a Franchise
Recent Trends
    Conversion Franchising
    Multiple-Concept Franchising
Summary

Review of Chapter Objectives

What is the size of franchising in the hospitality industry? _____

_____

In a franchising contract, what is the franchisee responsible for? _____

_____

_____

_____

What does the franchisor agree to furnish in a franchising contract? _____

_____

_____

_____

Briefly state in your own words the characteristics of a franchise agreement.

1. _____

2. _____

3. _____

4. _____

5. _____

6. _____

7. _____

Characterize the advantages and disadvantages of a franchise for both franchisee and franchisor.

	Advantages	*Disadvantages*
Franchisee	_____	_____
	_____	_____
	_____	_____
	_____	_____
Franchisor	_____	_____
	_____	_____
	_____	_____
	_____	_____

Describe the services franchisors provide franchisees. _____

_____

_____

_____

_____

What are the three factors in achieving higher sales in a market?

1. _____

2. _____

3. _____

Describe how franchising functions as a marketing system and as a management system.

Marketing System	*Management System*
_____	_____
_____	_____
_____	_____
_____	_____
_____	_____

Identify common problems between franchisor and franchisee. How are these problems settled?

Problem	Resolution
_____	_____
_____	_____
_____	_____
_____	_____
_____	_____

Describe how franchisors deal with saturated markets. _____

_____

_____

_____

_____

KEY WORDS AND PHRASES

Fill in the blanks with the best word or phrase.

What is product or trade name franchising. _____

_____

What is business format franchising? _____

_____

What does the franchise system identify the franchisee and franchisor as?

_____

_____

_____

What is a franchisee? _____

What is a franchisor? _____

What are the four elements of the marketing system? _____

_____

Why is the franchise system marketing advantageous? _____

_____

What does decentralization of franchise marketing use? _____

_____

What does regulation with respect to franchisors focus on? _____

_____

What is conversion franchising? _____

What is multiple-concept franchising? _____

REVIEW QUESTIONS

True/False

Answer the following questions by circling T for true or F for false.

T   F   **1.** Product and trade name franchises have to a large extent saturated the market, but sales continue to grow at about 5 percent.

T   F   **2.** A franchised unit is considered a small business.

T   F   **3.** Overall the hospitality industry can be considered highly active in business format franchising.

T   F   **4.** Generally the franchisee has the capital while the franchisor has the expertise.

T   F   **5.** Most franchisors insist on approving sites for units.

T   F   **6.** If a parent company goes bankrupt the franchisee may still have contractual obligations.

T   F   **7.** Usually the franchisor is completely dependent on the franchisee for marketing.

T   F   **8.** Under a franchise agreement the franchisor is the owner of the business.

T   F   **9.** Franchisors often learn that profits from company-owned stores earn more than royalties received from a franchised store.

T   F   **10.** Franchise legislation generally favors the franchisee.

Multiple Choice

Choose the *one* best answer.

1. Business format franchising is
   a. an insignificant part of the gross national product
   b. an industry experiencing slow growth

    c.   an industry encouraged by the growth of manufacturing

    d.   an industry providing product, service, trademark in addition to an entire business format

2. If you wished to buy a franchise, which of the following would you *not* expect of a successful franchising company?

    a.   financial security

    b.   large number of company-owned units

    c.   providing experienced managers and employees for your unit

    d.   access to sales and customer counts of their stores

3. The franchisee

    a.   has a substantial capital investment in the franchise

    b.   is not responsible for buying or leasing building, furniture, and fixtures

    c.   relies on the parent company to train employees

    d.   expects the franchising company to be responsible for generating sales in the community

4. The franchising company

    a.   has full day-to-day operating control

    b.   has investment in building or a lease

    c.   exercises budgetary discretion in the unit

    d.   enforces quality control at the unit

5. A franchising group

    a.   is a chain that owns all the units

    b.   is a multiple unit system owned by the franchisor

    c.   generally consists of independent businesspeople who own one or more units

    d.   consists of a group of businesspeople who jointly own the unit with the parent company

6. Franchisors offer a service called "screening" that means that

    a.   new unit managers are interviewed by the parent company

    b.   the potential franchise buyer is evaluated

    c.   suppliers are evaluated in the new area

    d.   potential customers are interviewed in a market area

7. Franchisors do *not* provide franchisees with

    a.   operating manuals

    b.   site selection expertise

    c.   financial support

    d.   training for start-ups

8. When a franchising system begins to expand

    a.   it requires large inputs of capital by the parent company

    b.   the return on investment is lower for franchised units than on owned units

      c. the franchisor acquires fixed assets or leases

      d. financing is provided by franchisees

9. The greatest problem that successful franchisors have is

      a. maintaining consistency and quality control

      b. collecting royalties and fees

      c. recruiting franchise buyers

      d. selling company products to units

10. Disclosure rules require publication of

      a. income forecasts

      b. partial company records

      c. selected unit sales

      d. complete company records

Fill in the Blanks

Fill in the blanks with the best answer.

1. The parent company is called the _____ while the individual or company buying the franchise is called the _____.

2. The two promotion advantages that franchise companies have is _____ and _____.

3. The number of units a district manager for a chain can supervise is from _____ to _____ units while a franchise district manager can supervise from _____ to _____ with _____ the maximum number he or she can reasonably handle.

4. A small chain acquired by a large franchisor who then converts the small chain to their units is called _____.

5. A franchisor that offers more than one franchise to franchisees is called _____.

DISCUSSION QUESTIONS

1. Discuss the advantages a franchisee has and those that the franchisor has when they make a deal.

2. Discuss how a parent company helps a franchisee with their market. Include the amount of freedom that the franchisee has in this area.

3. What protection is afforded franchisees when they buy franchises?

PROJECTS

1. Write to a franchising company and ask for the brochure that they give to prospective franchisees. Evaluate the information they send you against the "Seven Basic Questions".

2. Make a list using the yellow pages and trade journals of franchise groups in the hospitality industry. Identify multiple concept franchises.

14

Views of the Future

Commentary

It is appropriate to conclude this text with consideration of the future. This chapter makes it clear that this is not an attempt at prophecy. The way we approach the topic is to try to see rational cause and effect relationships rather than "guess the future." We concentrate on trying to isolate the *forces* at work in the industry. To this end, we look at the factors shaping consumer demand as well as those affecting the supply of resources used in hospitality, principally food and labor. Naturally, we are also concerned with the framework within which supply and demand operate that leads us to look at competition and technology. Having identified basic forces, we review emerging trends.

One of your principal concerns is to deal with your own personal future. The text has emphasized that you are in charge of your own career, and in this respect, you are in business for yourself. Has your attitude toward the hospitality industry changed since you began this course?

Chapter Outline

Views of the Future
The Forces that Will Shape the Future
The Demand for Hospitality Services
    Consumer Demographics
    Employment, Income, and Demand for Hospitality
    Education's Impact on Hospitality
Supply Conditions
    Food
    Labor
    Competition
    Technology

Emerging Trends
    A Fragmenting Industry
    Competing with the Home
    The Age of the Independent?
    Conglomerates in Hospitality
        Conglomerates in Review
    Threats
The Future and You
    The Hospitality Industry
    Retained Earnings
    Strategies and Goals
Summary

Review of Chapter Objectives

Briefly describe how the following will affect the demand for hospitality services:

Demographics _____

_____

_____

Employment _____

_____

Income _____

_____

Education _____

_____

Describe how the major factors of production will affect the hospitality industry of the future:

Food _____

_____

Labor _____

_____

In general, describe the form in which competition the hospitality industry exists. _____

_____

_____

Describe the recent emerging trends that will most likely become more pronounced in the future. _____

_____

_____

What is the outlook for the independent and the chain of the future? _____

_____

_____

_____

Outline the strategy and tactics of personal development appropriate to your vocational goals. _____

_____

_____

_____

_____

KEY WORDS

Fill in the blanks with the best word or phrase.

What are the two major forces that shape the future of the hospitality industry?

_____

What is an "ultra"? _____

Describe the difference between the dining market and the eating market.

_____

What are the two factors of production? _____

What are the specialized products for specific markets? _____

_____

How will home entertainment centers affect the future? _____

_____

What will restyling be necessary for? _____

_____

What is fragmentation? _____

_____

What are conglomerates? _____

_____

What is a "surprise free" projection? _____

_____

Why are retained earnings important? _____

_____

Why are short- and long-term goals different? _____

_____

What are career strategies and tactics? _____

_____

REVIEW QUESTIONS

True/False

Answer the following questions by circling T for true or F for false.

T   F   **1.** While the rapid growth rate of women moving into the work force has slowed, it is gradually increasing which will most likely have a positive effect on food service sales.

T   F   **2.** Because of consumer health interests, the consumption of chicken should remain high.

T   F   **3.** In general, it is difficult to find long-term employees for many hospitality jobs, especially unskilled and semiskilled positions.

T   F   **4.** Computer use in the hospitality industry has peaked and is not expected to have much future growth.

T   F   5. The successful restaurant of tomorrow will have to keep up with the current fashions and fads in food and ambience.

T   F   6. Hospitality conglomerates are usually integrated at the operating level.

T   F   7. Conglomerates of related businesses have enormous financial and marketing resources.

T   F   8. If another energy crisis occurred, people would continue to travel, but not as far from home.

T   F   9. Career movement from one segment of the hospitality industry to another is difficult.

T   F   10. If you are not ready to set a career goal, career exploration is advisable.

Multiple Choice

Choose the *one* best answer.

1. The consumers, called the "ultras," who spend more of their income on non-essentials than any other age group are
    a. teenagers
    b. young professionals
    c. late middle-aged people
    d. seniors

2. In the next 10 years, barring unforeseen events
    a. fast food formats will remain about the same
    b. food service sales due to women entering the work force will decrease
    c. campers will switch to hotel users as their income rises
    d. travel in general will increase because of the prosperity of the middle-aged population

3. Education of the population impacts the hospitality industry to the greatest degree with
    a. consumer issues
    b. political issues
    c. market issues
    d. business issues

4. Before the end of the century, barring unforeseen events,
    a. food supplies will become scarce to the point of a Third World famine
    b. food supplies will be somewhat less than today
    c. there will be barely enough food
    d. there will be problems of surpluses

5. The supply of workers in unskilled and semiskilled jobs into the 1990s looks
    a. pessimistic
    b. stable

    c. like slightly more than demand

    d. optimistic

6. Which of the following will probably *not* take place by the year 2000
   a. labor costs will increase
   b. more older workers will be recruited for hospitality jobs
   c. part-time workers will decrease
   d. workers in manufacturing will shift to hospitality work

7. The fiercest restaurant competition in the 1990s will most likely *not* be
   a. the continuing war of the burgers
   b. from "C" stores
   c. between chains
   d. between independents

8. A business that requires less capital to start up is
   a. catering
   b. franchising
   c. a fast food restaurant
   d. a diner

9. Hospitality conglomerates
   a. are known for their stability
   b. do not provide competition for independents
   c. buy and sell businesses and may also be bought or sold
   d. contain only hospitality businesses

10. The job experience offering the most flexibility in moving from one industry segment to another is
    a. hotel front desk employee
    b. housekeeper
    c. restaurant cook
    d. porter

Fill in the Blanks

Fill in the blanks with the best answer.

1. The future of the hospitality industry will be shaped by _____ and the _____ and _____ they demand.

2. Demographics include such statistics as _____, _____, and _____.

3. Three factors that affect future demand are _____, _____, and _____.

4. A highly fragmented hotel industry is termed market _____.

5. A hospitality _____ is a company that owns one or more businesses, one or more of which are part of the hospitality industry.

DISCUSSION QUESTIONS

1. Discuss how the level of education in a population affects the hospitality industry.
2. Discuss the impact a new cheap energy source would have on the future of the hospitality industry.
3. Discuss how space travel available to the mass market would affect the hospitality industry.

PROJECTS

1. Visit the company that you would like to work for in the future. Find out how they recruit employees. Write a job résumé and evaluate how your experience so far will measure up now—and when you finish your schooling.
2. Find out what you can about hospitality conglomerates. Identify the businesses within the conglomerate. Find out how large the company is and any other information that would be of interest. (You might like to follow their stock in the financial pages of your newspaper.)